THE JACOBEAN PLANTATIONS IN SEVENTEENTH-CENTURY OFFALY

The Jacobean plantations in seventeenth-century Offaly

an archaeology of a changing world

JAMES LYTTLETON

FOUR COURTS PRESS

Typeset in 11 pt on 13 pt ArnoPro by
Carrigboy Typesetting Services for
FOUR COURTS PRESS LTD
7 Malpas Street, Dublin 8, Ireland
www.fourcourtspress.ie
and in North America for
FOUR COURTS PRESS
c/o ISBS, 920 NE 58th Avenue, Suite 300, Portland, OR 97213.

A catalogue record for this title is available
from the British Library.

ISBN 978-1-84682-492-0 pbk
ISBN 978-1-84682-393-0 hbk

Printed in Spain
by Castuera, Navarra.

Contents

Abbreviations

BAR	*British Archaeological Reports*
D.	depth
diam.	diameter
dims	dimensions
EHR	*English Historical Review*
fl.	*floruit* (flourished)
H.	height
IHS	*Irish Historical Studies*
IJHA	*International Journal of Historical Archaeology*
int.	internal
JCHAS	*Journal of the Cork Historical and Archaeological Society*
JKAS	*Journal of the County Kildare Archaeological Society*
JRSAI	*Journal of the Royal Society of Antiquaries of Ireland*
n.d.	no date [given]
n.p.	no place [of publication given]
OPW	Office of Public Works (Ireland)
pers. comm.	personal communication
PRIA	*Proceedings of the Royal Irish Academy*
QUB	Queen's University Belfast
T.	thickness
TCD	Trinity College Dublin
UCC	University College Cork
UCG	University College Galway
UJA	*Ulster Journal of Archaeology*
W.	width

Preface and acknowledgments

In 1619–20 a number of Gaelic Irish lordships in Offaly, namely Éile Uí Chearbhaill, Delbhna Eathra, Fir Cheall and Muintir Thadhgáin had to contend with the arrival of British settlers during the reign of James I. These ethnic groups – native and newcomer alike – were by no means passive participants in a colonial process underpinned, as has traditionally been argued, solely by paradigms of domination and resistance. There was, instead, a negotiation of power and identity involving more subtle responses of collaboration and evasion. By re-appraising the various categories of secular and non-secular buildings such as tower houses, fortified houses, farmhouses and churches, one can go beyond morphological concerns and explore the extent to which individuals influenced their own social, economic and cultural positions in society, and how the physical and mental worlds of the Gaelic Irish and 'New English' were, indeed, challenged and transformed by encounters with the other.

This book is the culmination of a journey that I embarked upon ten years ago in exploring the archaeology and history of the Jacobean plantations in Co. Offaly. Through the course of the fieldwork and research, I enjoyed much support and generosity from individuals, to whom I would like to express my gratitude. I am hugely indebted to my supervisor, Dr Colin Rynne, in the Department of Archaeology at University College Cork. His enthusiastic support and wise guidance over the years was truly invaluable, and greatly helped my development as an archaeologist. Other scholars in this department and elsewhere who also graciously gave of their time and knowledge include Matthew Johnson, Rolf Loeber, Barra Ó Donnabháin, Tadhg O'Keeffe, Raymond Gillespie, Tomás Ó Carragáin, John Sheehan, Mick Monk, Aidan O'Sullivan, Elizabeth FitzPatrick, Kieran O'Conor, Brian Mac Cuarta, Sarah Gearty, Michael Stanley and Griffin Murray. I wish to express my gratitude to Conor McDermott and Hugh Kavanagh for drawing up the various maps that can be seen in the book. I would also like to thank Tony Roche of the Photographic Section within the National Monuments Service of the Department of Arts, Heritage and the Gaeltacht for providing some of the photographs included in the following chapters. I wish to extend sincere thanks to my aunt and uncle, Mary and Liam Jones of Ballingorraun, near Moneygall, Co. Offaly, for their generosity in providing a roof over my head in the long months that I was engaged in fieldwork. I would also like to thank the various landowners, including the earl and countess of Ross, the Serviss, Ardall and Chatsworth families as well as numerous other landowners across Co. Offaly, who gave me permission to survey the buildings that are the subject of this book. Many of these buildings remain family homes to the present day, and these individuals graciously allowed me access into their private abodes. Michael Byrne and the Offaly Historical and Archaeological Society based in Tullamore kindly allowed me access to various cartographic and photographic collections held in their research facility. It would be remiss of me not to mention Michael Potterton, editor at Four Courts Press, whose expertise and advice was of immense help in the final stages of preparing this book. It goes without saying that this book could not have been produced without the financial support of the Irish Research Council and the Department of Archaeology in UCC at both doctoral and post-doctoral level, and for this I sincerely give thanks. Finally, but certainly not least, I wish to express gratitude to my mother and father, Philomena and Gerard, for their unstinting support and interest in my work – those summer daytrips in my youth surely proved their worth.

CHAPTER 1

Introduction

The sixteenth and seventeenth centuries witnessed profound cultural, social and economic change in Ireland, which saw the native lordships that encompassed most of the island being assimilated into a more expansive centralized English (and later British) state. Periodic rebellions by the indigenous Catholic order, both Anglo-Irish and Gaelic Irish, were followed by the widespread confiscations of lands and their resettlement by English, Welsh and Scottish settlers who were largely Protestant, and whose loyalty to the crown was more assured. The plantation schemes implemented in Munster, Ulster and the eastern portions of Cos Laois and Offaly have been well documented (fig. 1.1). Less well known are a series of smaller plantations that were established in the midlands in the years 1619 and 1620 as government officials sought other opportunities to confiscate and resettle lands. Included in this further trawl of native territories were a number of lordships in the west and south of Co. Offaly that lay beyond the reach of the earlier Tudor plantation – Éile Uí Chearbhaill (O'Carroll), Delbhna Eathra (MacCoghlan), Fir Cheall (O'Molloy) and Muintir Thadhgáin (Fox) – lands within the catchment of the River Shannon in the very heart of Ireland.

Since the early sixteenth century, these midland lordships attracted the attention of English officials who were well aware of the strategic importance of the Shannon river basin (fig. 1.2). Securing the Irish midlands, including these territories, was seen as imperative by the crown administration, which was anxious to secure the civil and religious reform of the whole island of Ireland in order to preserve and enhance English hegemony. As such, successive government administrations pursued a varied approach, combining sporadic military campaigning, with more benevolent policies such as surrender and regrant in which the native elite were granted back their estates under title recognized by English law. In recognition of the status held by the leading notables, the chiefs of these native lordly families such as the O'Carrolls, the MacCoghlans and the Foxes, were granted the status of tenant-in-chiefs with knighthoods and positions as seneschals in a shire that was increasingly expanded during the course of the late sixteenth and the turn of the seventeenth century, encompassing the earlier Gaelic polities in its path. In the same period, we see a trickle of English settlers into the lordships, decades before the renewed phase of plantations in 1619–20 that were set to transform the landed elite in these western territories. Thus, well before the Jacobean schemes, the stage was set for the absorption of these native lordships into the embryonic British Empire through the process of plantation.

The plantation schemes of 1619 (Éile Uí Chearbhaill) and 1620 (Delbhna Eathra, Fir Cheall and Fox's Country) sought the complete and final subjugation of

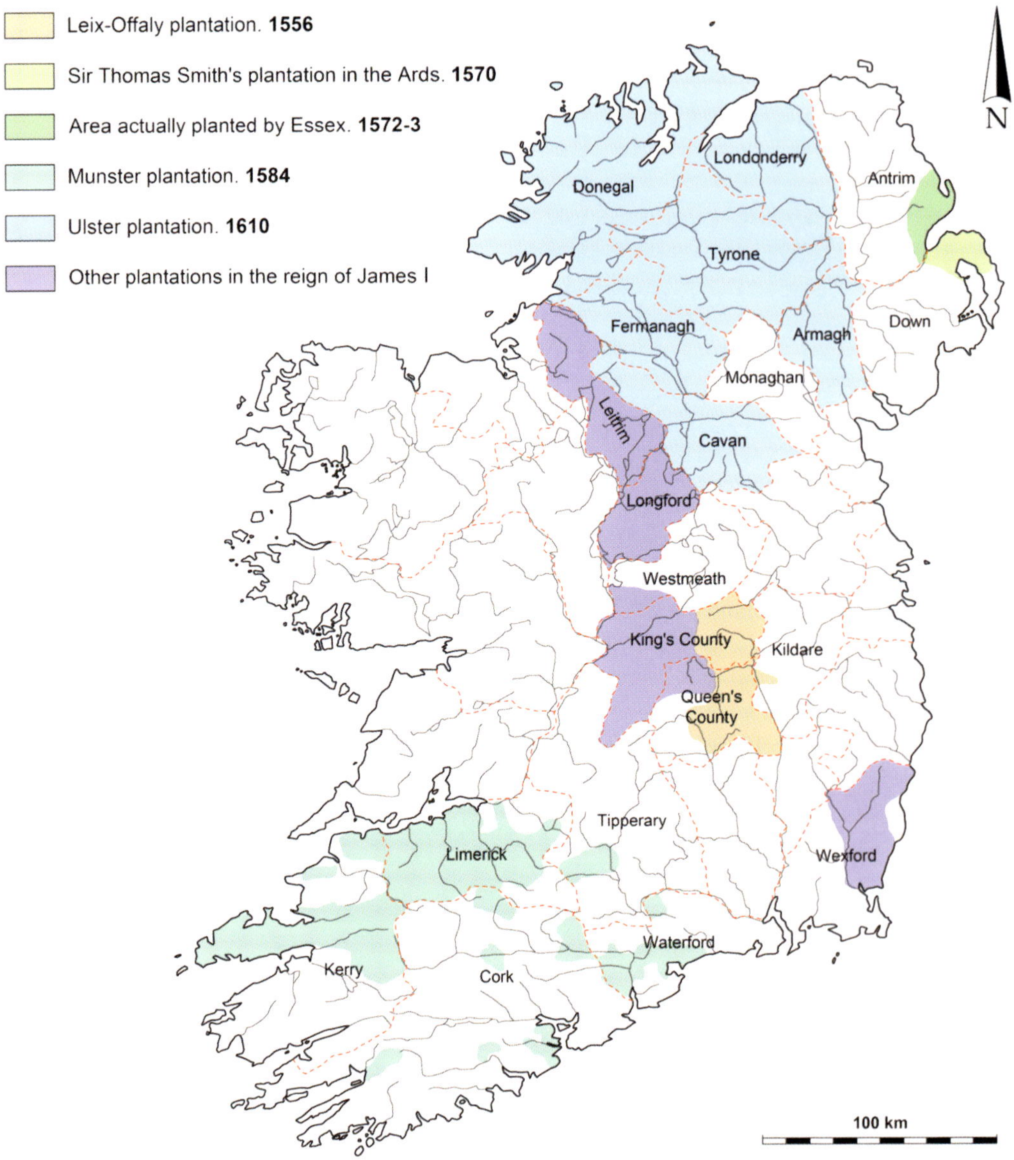

1.1 Plantations in sixteenth- and seventeenth-century Ireland (prepared by Hugh Kavanagh).

the native lordships to the process of civil and religious reform. The crown government anticipated that the partial dismemberment of native estates and the thin sprinkling of British proprietors would induce the indigenous population to conform to the benefits of civil living and to adhere to the reformed faith. Social reform was to be abetted by the introduction of English forms of tenure, estate organization,

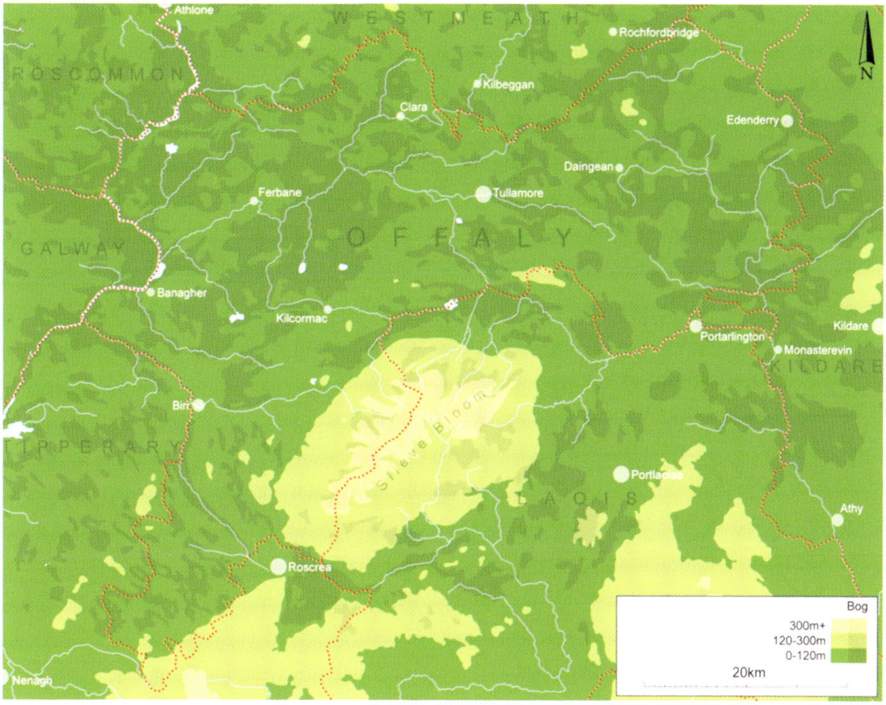

1.2 Topographical map of Offaly (prepared by Conor McDermott and Hugh Kavanagh).

settlement and education. However, the plantation schemes were undermined right from the beginning by corruption and the lack of suitable undertakers, many of whom were of insufficient means to become productive landlords. As a result, the schemes in west and south Offaly did not reach their full potential. However, while the Jacobean plantations in their own right did not really attract British settlers, the partial dismemberment of native lands opened up the region to less formal settlement in the post-plantation era. In the decades up to the 1640s, the building of new landed residences took place, as well as the restoration of older seats. The establishment of villages and towns not only encouraged the growth in population and industry, but also facilitated the development of a local market for the produce of the new country estates. Innovative agricultural practices were introduced, while the enclosure of farmland appears to have commenced. Attempts were also made to foster local industry by establishing tanneries and glassworks, though it appears that no attempt was made to introduce ironworking as in other planted areas of the country. While the Gaelic Irish lordships inevitably succumbed to the process of anglicization, the principle objective of creating a society that, in the words of Sir John Davies, the attorney-general based in Dublin Castle, 'would in tongue and heart and every way else become English', was not to be completely attained as the process of acculturation and hybridization modified native and planter culture alike.[1]

It must be borne in mind that the plantations in the Offaly lordships were taking place in the context of English global expansion. The cessation of hostilities with Spain in 1604 meant that capital once absorbed by the war effort could now be diverted into establishing colonies, whether in Virginia, Newfoundland, New England, the Caribbean or Ireland.[2] Many individuals came to be associated with colonial schemes on both sides of the North Atlantic, representing a coalition of government, gentry and mercantile interests that sought to create an empire that would rival that of the Spanish and Portuguese. Thus, the early settlements in Ireland as well as those in North America were developed against a background of feared Spanish intervention in southern Ireland and Spanish dominance in the New World.[3] The plantations in Ireland were important as they were the first large-scale enterprises engaged upon by the crown that were at least a partial success to the extent that they may have provided some kind of model for subsequent schemes overseas, which involved complex logistical problems of funding, transporting and settling a wide cross-section of society. Initial failures and successes in both Ireland and North America added to the reservoir of experience, which would ensure the continuity of such settlements.[4] The plantation of the various lordships in Co. Offaly and elsewhere in Ireland acted as a sort of laboratory or stepping stone for the development of English colonies further afield. That contemporaries recognized an Atlantic context to their endeavours is illustrated by Fynes Moryson's description of Ireland as 'this famous island set in a Virginian sea'.[5]

The planners of these settlements in Ireland and America placed great emphasis upon the development and exploitation of natural resources, with the colonies on the periphery supplying raw materials in exchange for finished goods produced by the home country.[6] It was also argued that the same colonies could absorb excess population from the homeland, increase chances of economic improvement for many in their new surroundings and lessen the burden on those who remained at home.[7] Indeed, Ireland no less than the North American colonies, was to be equally dependent on English goods.[8] Yet the potential of developing a substantial mercantile economy on both sides of the Atlantic was not always appreciated in official circles; in 1605 Arthur Chichester, the lord deputy of Ireland at the time, observed that it was 'absurd folly to run all over the world in search of colonies in Virginia or Guiana, whilst Ireland was lying desolate'.[9] Indeed, such global expansion was to stretch English mercantile resources a few years later. Through the crown's insistence that the London Companies should be involved in the Ulster Plantation, fifty-five of the fifty-six companies withdrew their support for the Jamestown venture in Virginia, contributing to the near failure of the American colony when over half of the settlers died from hunger and disease during the years 1609–11, the so-called 'Starving Time'.[10] Such disastrous experiences in North America made settlement in Ireland look all the more alluring. An anonymous commentator around 1600, writing on the possibilities of settling the St Lawrence valley, noted the following:

> The country [the St Lawrence basin] seems … to be cold and to bring forth commodities as cold countries doth, with industry. Our country people, having ever been bred with plenty in a more temperate air and naturally not very industrious at home, [are] less to seek out places where their labors are present and their hopes a little deferred. Whereof we have too good experience by Ireland which [is] near us, a temperate and fertile country, subject to our laws and half civil, the ports and many towns friendly inhabited.[11]

The scale of English and Scottish migration into Ireland in the second decade of the seventeenth century dwarfed the English settlements in North America. The fort at Jamestown could have fitted into Coleraine's walled area forty-eight times over.[12] Total population estimates of the settler population in Ireland are difficult to arrive at, given the limitations of the documentary sources though it has been estimated that the British newcomers accounted for about one tenth of the population, between 80,000 and 125,000 people by 1641, with as many as 70,000 of these residing in Leinster and Munster, and most of the balance to be found in Ulster.[13] This compares with the English population in North America, which stood at just 2,700 by the end of the 1620s.[14] It would appear that Ireland provided a more attractive proposition for would-be settlers, and that the Irish kingdom siphoned off the skilled workers who were in demand in the American colonies. However, according to Nicholas Canny, the two migratory movements complemented rather than competed with each other, with the northwest of England along with the west and southwest lowlands of Scotland supplying migrants to Ireland, whereas the south and southeast of England provided the same for America. If there was competition for settlers, it was confined to the hinterland of Bristol, where the Munster proprietors appear to have had an advantage over their rivals.[15] Charles Orser has identified four influences in the material behaviour of modern societies on both sides of the Atlantic, namely, colonialism, capitalism, Eurocentrism and modernity. The pervasive nature of these influences suggests that there is much value in comparative studies that would look at the spread of British settlement and material culture across Ireland and North America at both macro- and micro-scales of analysis.[16]

Archaeological research on the plantations in Ireland

The demise of the Gaelic lordships in west and south Offaly was taking place against a background of renewed colonialism, nascent capitalism, the Renaissance and the great religious schism rendered by the Reformation and Counter-Reformation. People were reassessing the world around them and their place in the greater cosmological order. Such processes impacted upon the way in which people interacted with each other and the physical environment, leading to changes in the consumption of goods and materials, in the management of the surrounding landscape, and in the types of buildings erected. This book looks at such changes in the realm of settlement and architecture, and offers a multi-disciplinary approach in the interpretation of archaeological remains, utilizing archaeological, historical, geographical and sociological perspectives. This can allow for a more contextualized, sensitive understanding of the lives of people that lived in these midland territories, lives that were characterized by ambiguous and shifting identities. Looking at various categories of late medieval and early modern architecture, namely tower houses, fortified houses, houses and churches, affords us the opportunity to see how the midland lordships were fundamentally transformed in the early modern period, from a society in which rule was exercised by a kinship-based elite to one in which power was exercised by a centralized state under a single crown, where economic relationships had moved from feudal interdependence to more individualistic involvement in a nascent capitalist market, and where religious doctrine was no longer the preserve of a single church.

In one of the better known schemes in Ireland, the Ulster Plantation, the relative wealth of documentary and cartographic sources on the confiscation and resettlement of lands has encouraged archaeological research on colonial settlement there, going back as far as the 1950s.[17] Research on plantation-era archaeology was taking place in Ulster at a time when little or no interest in similar sites was being shown by archaeologists south of the border. However, this reticence has certainly changed in the last two decades, with archaeological research exploring aspects of English colonial settlement, though largely in the Munster region.[18] The midland plantations, which covered Cos Leitrim and Longford, along with areas of Laois, Offaly and Westmeath, have received some attention from historians and geographers, though not from archaeologists.[19] This shortfall is clearly underlined by the remarkable comment of de Breffny and Ffolliott that 'settlers were established in Longford, Leitrim, Offaly and Wexford … Those who failed to get a sequestered tower-house built farmsteads, of which few traces survive, or else made do with simple log-houses until they could achieve something more substantial'.[20] Such an assertion creates a picture more reminiscent of frontier country in nineteenth-century North America than seventeenth-century Ireland, bearing little relation to what is known of Irish vernacular architecture in the early modern period.

The lacuna in knowledge has been filled to an extent by Caimin O'Brien and David Sweetman in their *Archaeological inventory of County Offaly* and an unpublished transcript entitled 'County Offaly, Urban Archaeological Survey' by John Bradley, Andrew Halpin and Heather King, which both identified most of the extant early modern secular and religious sites across the county, though the larger environmental and cultural context still remained to be explored.[21] Elizabeth FitzPatrick and Caimin O'Brien's *The medieval churches of Offaly* has placed the county's numerous churches and graveyards in the context of the Reformation, Counter-Reformation and plantation.[22] In his article 'Castles and fortifications of County Offaly *c.*1500–1815', Paul Kerrigan discussed the better documented tower houses and fortified houses, but without an elaboration of their architectural details, while Margaret Sheehy explored the development of architecture in the early modern period in her article 'Architecture in Offaly', but made some erroneous observations.[23] Other articles have looked at aspects of secular society in early modern Offaly such as the tower house at Coole owned by a Gaelic Irish lordly family or the glass furnace operated by Huguenot immigrants near Shinrone.[24] Some postgraduate research has also provided comparative material in relation to the study of tower houses. Niall Fennelly's work provides architectural analysis on tower houses across most of Co. Offaly, with the exception of the barony of Clonlisk, while Andrew Tierney's work on Leap Castle, a tower house and one of the chief strongholds for the O'Carrolls, combines architectural interpretation with an exploration of the nineteenth-century fascination with the gothic literary genre.[25]

Archaeology, with its emphasis on material remains, including buildings and their surroundings, can offer a provocative and insightful view on the physical environment of that time. Rolf Loeber has called for a multi-disciplinary approach, a view very much informed by his own work on the compilation of unpublished documentary surveys of sixteenth- and seventeenth-century settlement, not only across Offaly but in Éile Uí Chearbhaill in particular.[26] The latter, which takes the form of an unpublished transcript entitled 'Geographical calendar of landownership in Ely O'Carroll in the 16th and 17th centuries', includes brief descriptions on the nature of surviving remains on those documented sites, an approach that had hitherto not been adopted by historians.

The limitations of the documentary sources

Historical research, by its nature, is focused on the written record. However, the pre-eminence of the documentary record in early modern Irish studies can be questioned on three counts: the variation in survival, the partiality of original authors and the essentialist nature of modern research. The survival of documentation from the early modern period, while more extensive and better preserved than sources of late medieval date, can still be fragmentary. In tracing the various documentary and cartographic sources that could be brought to bear on studying early modern Offaly, it was found that the Civil Survey (1654) for the county was long missing and that some baronial and parish maps from the Down Survey (1655–6) were also non-extant, typifying the problems of survival. Indeed, most of the surviving documentary sources take the form of grants, deeds and leases, which typically detail properties in terms of townlands held by named individuals without any further elaboration, except maybe for a breakdown of acreage into profitable and unprofitable land.

The partiality of written sources can also be questioned. Such writings, whether they are in the form of government legislation, correspondence between officials, inventories of household goods, estate rentals, legal depositions or private correspondence between individuals, originate from literate sources that were overwhelmingly representative of the social elites. These documents were designed to serve the economic and administrative interests of the landed families. Nor were they ever compiled with a view towards answering the potential questions of future archaeologists. As sources of information relative to their times, they need subtle and careful interpretation. People in the lower orders are poorly represented in such documentary sources. This has created a top-heavy approach to the study of early modern society, which ignores the greater proportion of the population and relegates them to the role of passive participants on a stage where social, political and economic forces held perpetual sway over their lives. One solution to redress this bias in historical research towards the social elite may be found in an archaeological approach that places political and cultural change within the context of material culture and the surrounding physical environment.

Another feature of much historical writing on sixteenth- and seventeenth-century Ireland is its essentialism, that the cultural identity of the population essentially falls upon ethnic fault lines between Gaelic Irish, Anglo-Irish (or Old English) and New English. Written sources such as the state papers relating to the government of Ireland or private correspondence between prospective planters in Co. Offaly such as Matthew de Renzy and government officials reinforce a dogmatic view that the population of seventeenth-century Ireland was divided into three different, and at times antagonistic, ethnic groups. Modern historical research has very much absorbed these overarching ethnic constructs, which colours the debate on early modern society in Ireland. Archaeologists can break free from the constraints of national histories, with their cultural assignations of native Irish or New English, which still carry potency in the modern cultural consciousness of Ireland. In these names used to describe archaeological monuments are buried concepts of our present sense of belonging and place. Archaeologists can construct alternative narratives of social organization and cultural identity free from the constraints of documentary research. This does not involve ignoring the written sources but an assertion of an archaeological discourse based on its own epistemological structures and data, utilizing contemporary writings and cartographic sources as only one aspect of the evidence available, depending on its relevance to the archaeological analysis.[27]

1.3 Remains of the late medieval tower house and seventeenth-century house at Clonlyon Castlequarter. Matthew de Renzy, a German settler living in the locality in 1620, recorded that Tadhg Óg MacCoghlan held the castle of *Clun Leighean*. His kinsman, Donough Coghlan, owned the property at the time of the 1641 rebellion.

Problems of monument survival

As with documents, however, the archaeological data is subject to the vagaries of survival over time. Archaeological sites can suffer the vicissitudes of wars, rebellions, forfeiture of estates, economic dislocation and changing means of agricultural production. The first edition of the Ordnance Survey 1:10,516 series *c.*1840 offers a baseline from which to analyse the degradation of archaeological sites, the rate of which has accelerated due to more extensive and intensive agricultural activities. Analysis of this cartographic source suggests that the proportion of monuments destroyed since first recorded in the mid-nineteenth century is close to 30 per cent in most counties.[28] While most of these sites were of earthwork form, typically ringforts, many masonry structures such as tower houses and fortified houses have also fallen victim to agricultural intensification. Fieldwork in west and south Offaly looking at sites associated with the Jacobean plantations has identified twenty-nine tower houses and seventeen fortified houses that have survived to varying degrees (fig. 1.3). There are also sixty castle sites in the study area, where tower houses and fortified houses were probably located. These figures suggest that over half of the original tower houses and fortified houses in west and south Offaly, representing the homes of the early modern elite landholding classes, have been demolished.

Also problematic is a clear bias in survival and preservation towards sites associated with the literate elite of early modern Offaly. Non-elite settlement in Co. Offaly and elsewhere in Ireland is extremely difficult to study (certainly without excavation) due to poor rates of preservation and recognition. But in recent times certain scholars, including Colin Breen, Audrey Horning, Nick Brannon, Rolf Loeber, Kieran O'Conor and Eric Klingelhöfer, have sought to redress this imbalance with field survey, excavation and the interrogation of cartographic and documentary sources to elucidate the physical nature of the cabins and houses that would have housed the bulk of the population.[29]

The material culture as a medium

There is a reticence on the part of many Irish archaeologists to embrace theoretical discourse, as can be seen in the dominance of traditional empirical narratives in the interpretation of medieval and early modern society in Ireland, with most discussion and debate focused upon the typology and dating of specific settlement forms and artefact types. This may stem from a belief that historical sources already provide the most objective explanation of how past societies operated. While undoubtedly important, an over-emphasis on such empirical concerns can obfuscate a more sensitive understanding of the social and cultural conditions that gave rise to particular material expressions. Modern publications discuss aspects of particular building types, yet few have placed these buildings in their social or cultural context.

The systematic recording of historic buildings such as tower houses and fortified houses can inform the archaeologist of trends in location, layout, form and chronology. Such information is necessary to understand the trajectory of architectural development, but it is equally important to follow through with the creation of a narrative that seeks to place these buildings in their cultural and social context on the basis of the data observed. There has been criticism of a tendency in castle studies to refrain from discussing how buildings were viewed and reflected upon by audiences in the past. As a result, academic narratives mostly revolve around the construction of buildings rather than their actual use.[30] There is a danger that discussion of architecture solely focused upon typological development divorces buildings from the society and people that created and used them in the first place. Attention to historical and cultural context allows human beings an active role in creating meaning and in shaping the world around them; they are seen to interact with their environment rather than simply react to it. Material culture is thus viewed as a medium of communication and expression that can condition and at times control social action.[31]

The Gaelic lordships that occupied the present area of Co. Offaly were more than a series of lines on a map, but encapsulated the core attributes of a kinship-based society whose economic, social and political activity revolved around reciprocal relationships between the landowning elite and their followers. These human relations consequently impacted upon the environment, both natural and built, as people used space as an active agent to consolidate or transform social relations. Material remains such as buildings were not some passive reflection of a more substantial past. Many archaeologists have used the work of Pierre Bourdieu, who has created the notion of *habitus*, where people tend to create and recreate the physical environment around them according to implicit notions of cultural norms, which they have inherited since their childhood through socialization. Such notions can change, from one generation to the next, or from one class to another, according to the different material conditions that people experience. The major implication of habitus is that cultural norms tend to be installed and reproduced through use of materials and mundane practice, with such modes of behaviour being construed as common sense.[32] As David Austin and Julian Thomas observe, 'the significance of Bourdieu's account is, therefore, that it allows some active role for the human subject in history, while still being able to explain why social reality does not dissolve into formless chaos'.[33] The permanence and materiality of buildings and artefacts encourages their deployment and orchestration to create and reproduce contexts of meaning. Material culture allows for the creation of a context for discourse, defining what can and cannot be done or said.

Anthony Giddens has suggested that in pre-industrial societies, social coherence is achieved through routine face-to-face interactions between people. In line with Bourdieu's work, Giddens places an emphasis on routine and mundane practices as a manner of reproducing normative behaviour, which again leads to an interest in how the experience of space and materiality structures the consciousness of the individual.[34] However, Giddens goes beyond Bourdieu's concern with architecture to embrace the role of locales as settings for encounters in which human action is structured in time and space. How people meet, part, exchange, labour and communicate is augmented with a concern for content and meaning, in other words how space is experienced and interpreted. The act of physically moving through space is seen as the equivalent of reading and interpreting meaning according to a habituated tradition of rationale or, as Bourdieu calls it, 'habitus'.[35]

Following on from this, the archaeologist Matthew Johnson has highlighted three central ideas that should underpin a social study of buildings: performance, materiality and agency. Performance is about the way social action takes place within a house, with implicit beliefs in how gender, social status, religious beliefs and hospitality are structured, like in the daily routines of a household surrounding work and rest. Materiality suggests that material things do not simply reflect ideas, but actually embody and enforce those ideas, acting as a backdrop against which ideas on social performance are played out. There is a recursive relationship between house and social action, acting back-and-forth on each other, as houses built long before and modified by successive generations influenced present-day actions. Agency is about the way humans used performance and materiality together in an active manner, acting in subtly different ways to renegotiate or transform the social world around them. Humans, whatever their social and cultural backgrounds, are not passive entities, absorbing and replaying cultural values in an uncritical manner.[36]

Colonial past and present perspectives

Due to the character of modern Irish archaeology, which is predominantly pragmatic and non-theoretical, nationalism and the political dimensions of archaeological practice are not generally seen as relevant by archaeologists.[37] This situation is even more striking when compared with other disciplines such as history, where there has been an ongoing debate about the extent to which different perspectives on the writing of modern Irish history reflect the contemporary political and intellectual climate in which authors finds themselves.[38] The practice of archaeology is socially constituted in the present with the exploration of monuments and artefacts very much informed by contemporary cultural and political norms. Contrary to claims that archaeology is an objective science through which the analyses of material remains produce interpretations of a fragmented past, these interpretations are produced in an intellectual environment very much informed by the assumptions and ideals of present society. As such, contemporary politics has profoundly influenced schools of archaeological thought across the globe.[39]

The nineteenth century saw the elevation of Ireland's prehistoric and early medieval legacy, which, despite the involvement of Protestant intellectuals, became increasingly associated, not only with a Gaelic identity, but with a Catholic one as well. The tribulations of Catholics in the sixteenth and seventeenth centuries were expounded upon by Victorian and early twentieth-century historians such as M. O'Reilly in his *Memorials of those who suffered for the Catholic faith in Ireland* (1868) and P.F. Moran's *Historical sketch of the persecution suffered by the Catholics of Ireland under the rule of Cromwell and the Puritans* (1907). Such literature promoted a nationalistic perspective that placed an emphasis on the losses of the Irish Catholic population suffering under the yoke of English Protestant oppression.[40] The establishment of two separate jurisdictions on the island from the early 1920s saw the legitimization and assertion of distinct cultural identities, one Catholic, the other Protestant. On both sides of the border, there was the creation of historical narratives to validate the present – in Northern Ireland, Irish history was ignored in state schools, with British history that celebrated colonialism and imperialism being taught instead. In the Irish Free State, the history taught in the classroom placed an emphasis on a catalogue of wrongs suffered by the Irish population, punctuated by periodic outbreaks of nationalist uprisings. Very separate events such as the uprisings of the early modern period (1798), Robert Emmett's rising (1848), the Fenian revolt and 1916 were elided to portray continuity in the struggle against English imperialism.[41] In the spirit of the times, the name of the county that is the subject of this book was changed from King's County to Offaly by a Sinn Féin dominated county council in June 1920. The existing name was deemed to be encumbered with 'the trait of the invader', making it necessary to replace it with the 'ancient and illustrious title of Offaly'.[42] Southern Protestants, marginalized to a degree by the cultural and religious ethos of the newly independent state, were not encouraged to assert or celebrate their colonial heritage. Even as late as 1973, J.J. Horgan, president of University College Dublin, could assert that the

> main function of the National University of Ireland ... has been and will be to build the Irish nation. A large part of the task is rebuilding: the recovery of the almost obliterated spirit and traditions in which our country lived and developed up to the disasters of the seventeenth century.[43]

The cultural and political marginalization of Irish Protestant culture had consequences for the appreciation and study of plantation-period settlement with hardly any archaeologists in the independent Irish state taking an active interest in the numerous post-medieval sites found scattered across the countryside. In contrast, north of the border, H.C. Lawlor included plantation castles in his *Ulster: its archaeology and antiquities* published in 1928, while such buildings also featured prominently in the Preliminary Survey of the Ancient Monuments of Northern Ireland (1940). Since the 1950s, archaeologists such as Edward Jope and Dudley Waterman, and geographers such as Philip Robinson, published articles on early modern architecture in journals like the *Ulster Journal of Archaeology* or *Ulster Folklife*. During the 1980s, a number of plantation-period sites were excavated as a means of comparing the accuracy of known historical contexts.[44] It can be argued that Stormont administrations, dominated by Unionist and Protestant interests, were only too willing to provide support for archaeological surveys of buildings that could be used to celebrate Ulster's colonial past and assert the legitimacy of the fledgling Northern Ireland state. Of course, they were helped by the fact that the foundations for the study of the Ulster Plantation had been laid by historians in previous generations such as Revd George Hill and T.W. Moody in the late nineteenth and early twentieth centuries. In the Free State, the response to the same heritage was very much muted, with only Harold Leask publishing research on fortified and non-fortified houses of the early modern period. As early as 1913, he published an extensive survey of an H-plan house and grounds in Oldbawn, near Tallaght, Co. Dublin.[45] The depth of this study was not to be repeated. Leask, however, was to pursue his interest in early modern buildings with his *Irish castles and castellated houses*, first published in 1941, and *Early seventeenth-century houses in Ireland* (1961). Leask, while a shining light, was a lonely one, with most architectural historians and archaeologists south of the border shying away from buildings redolent of a colonial legacy. Foreign scholars commented upon such reluctance among Irish archaeologists to engage with the post-medieval period, with Eric Klingelhöfer viewing it as a result of the prevailing political atmosphere in the twentieth century, though Charles Orser saw the richness of Ireland's prehistoric legacy as diverting interest from later periods rather than any prevailing political ethos.[46]

In recent years, the archaeology of the seventeenth-century plantations has received more equitable treatment, with archaeologists now more than ready to engage in the study of their material and cultural legacy. Such a rapprochement is symptomatic of a growing interest among Irish archaeologists in the material culture and landscape of post-medieval Ireland that extends well beyond the seventeenth century. The establishment of the Irish Post-Medieval Archaeology Group in 1999 created a forum for a growing interest in Ireland's post-medieval archaeology, covering diverse topics such as nineteenth-century industrial archaeology, twentieth-century military memorials and eighteenth-century ceramics as well as seventeenth-century plantation sites. There is a strong awareness among archaeologists of the need to foster greater public and professional awareness, to develop academic and vocational training, to cultivate inter-disciplinary ties with other disciplines such as history, cultural geography, folklife studies, and to promote closer ties with historical archaeologists working on similar issues elsewhere around the globe.[47]

By examining the remains of sixteenth- and seventeenth-century buildings in west and south Offaly, this book illustrates, from a materialist perspective, the profound social, cultural, economic and political changes that brought about the demise of the Gaelic lordships there. Chapter two provides a historical background to the English plantations in the midlands and the development of a colonial ideology that underpinned the crown's efforts to assimilate Gaelic society into a centralized nation state. Chapter three looks at the process involved in the assimilating, shiring and planting of the individual lordships through the sixteenth and early seventeenth centuries – the Jacobean plantations did not mark a cultural watershed, but were the culmination of sustained English interest in the region. When looking at the archaeology of settlement in the region, it is important to recognize that changes in architecture and form could also be accompanied by fundamental changes in the appearance of the surrounding landscape. Chapter four thus details the changes wrought upon the landscape through woodland clearance, the enclosure of farmland and the intensification of agriculture, as well as providing a consideration of roads, rivers and other natural features as routes of communication. The core of the book, chapters five to eight, entail a detailed discussion of the various settlement types to be found in plantation-era Offaly – tower houses, fortified houses, manor houses, farmhouses, churches and glebe houses. Changes in architectural form and space are considered in the context of greater societal transformations such as colonization, the decline of feudalism, nascent capitalism, the Renaissance, the Reformation and the Counter-Reformation. Chapter five covers the continued construction and occupation of tower houses in early modern Offaly. These castles did not survive into the early modern era as some medieval vestige, but were an integral part of the cultural and material environment of early modern Ireland. Chapter six looks at the fortified house, an architectural genre associated with the new political and cultural order that was embraced by native and planter alike. Chapter seven also looks at other houses, though this time without the defensive features to be found in the buildings previously discussed. In an effort to remedy the book's focus on elite settlement, this chapter also includes a discussion on a number of early farmhouses that date to the seventeenth century – a rare insight into the development of vernacular architecture among the general population. Given that this period was riven by religious dissension and schism, when faith held more of a central place in society than today, chapter eight looks at churches, glebe houses and grave memorials. Despite the general delapidation of churches in early modern Offaly, a number of Catholic and Protestant churches were still maintained as places of worship with their interiors suitably furnished to create appropriate levels of solemnity. Chapter nine, the final chapter, concludes with a rounding up of issues pertinent to our understanding of the passing of the old order and the emergence of an Ireland more recognizable to modern eyes.

CHAPTER 2

The history and ideology of plantation in the Irish midlands

Introduction

An analysis of relations between native and settler populations in early modern Offaly must take into account the origins and development of English colonial endeavour in Ireland as a whole. The decline of the earlier Anglo-Norman colonies, combined with a more assertive Anglo-Irish and Gaelic Irish political culture, posed a threat to the long-term interests of a Tudor and Stuart state that was very much under threat from continental powers. From the 1530s onwards, the crown sought to regain ground in terms of people and territory that it had lost since the high medieval period. This was to be achieved by various means including the confiscation and redistribution of lands under schemes of plantation. The earlier Tudor plantation of the eastern portions of Cos Laois and Offaly played an important role in the expansion of the new colonial order in the region and a discussion of earlier efforts by the crown to enforce political conformity contextualizes subsequent efforts by the Jacobean regime in west and south Offaly. This provides an opportunity later in the chapter to explore the motivations and ideologies that propelled English colonialism at the time and how early modern commentators sought to justify the dismemberment and dispersal of populations that had occupied lands for centuries till then.

The consolidation of the Dublin Pale

In the period following the fall of the Kildares, colonization in the midlands was relatively benign compared with later periods. The confiscation of properties was limited to those belonging to the Kildares and other major absentee landowners, along with property associated with the recently dissolved monasteries. The dissolution of the monasteries resulted in large areas of land coming into the hands of the government. In the Pale, these monasteries were granted both to Old English and New English families. Those monasteries in Gaelic Irish and Old English areas not under direct government control were passed into the hands of local lords. Such sites that were in strategic locations, however, were granted to New English army officers such as the abbey of Durrow in Fir Cheall, which was granted to Nicholas

Herbert in 1561.[1] The transfer of land with the dissolution of the monasteries did not necessarily herald colonization, as such grants did not consist of the wholesale expropriation of native held property. Properties were granted to individuals for twenty-one years, normally without obligations to settle English tenants or to remove the existing native population. Indeed, seldom were there conditions to build fortified residences or establish new towns.[2] Nonetheless, despite these qualifications, the early grants of confiscated monastic lands often became the first anchors of renewed English settlement and colonization.[3]

The western border of the Dublin Pale was made more secure with the establishment of two garrison forts, Fort Protector (Co. Laois) and Fort Governor (Co. Offaly), in the neighbouring territories of the O'Moores and O'Connors respectively, while elsewhere the government established its hold over certain castles, securing important strategic areas to the southwest (Barrow corridor) and to the north of the Pale. Bridgeheads were created northwards as far as Newry, westwards to Athlone and southwards as far as Waterford city.[4] The appointment of English seneschals – army officers with powers of martial law – to operate in native territories bordering the Pale, was seen as a transitory measure, before common law could be properly enforced through the shiring of the same territories. Subsequently, new counties were created in these lands with an administrative structure including a sheriff, justices of the peace, tax collectors, and an escheator to hold inquisitions. Westmeath (1542) was the first county to be created, followed by Carlow (*c.*1550), Laois (*c.*1556) and Offaly (1556).[5] In general, however, beyond the frontier areas of the Pale, lord deputies were principally concerned with promoting stability by negotiating settlements with existing lordships in Leinster, with a military presence only required when such agreements were being negotiated or being visibly cast aside. Hence, the focus of crown policy for Ireland down to the end of the governorship of the earl of Sussex in 1564 was to consolidate its position in the Pale where it was historically most secure.[6]

Fort Protector and Fort Governor: the dawn of plantation

The establishment of Fort Governor (now Daingean) and Fort Protector (now Portlaoise) played a part in improving the defences of the Dublin Pale. As mentioned above, these garrison forts were situated in the lordships of the O'Moores and the O'Connors, bordering the western reaches of the Dublin Pale, territories in present-day east Laois and Offaly, which were up until then beyond the reach of the government due to the difficult terrain of bogs and woodland in the area. Agricultural land was granted to soldiers in the vicinity of these forts to allow a level of self-sufficiency and productivity to reduce costs for the exchequer.[7]

The territories in which these garrison forts were established saw in the early 1550s an important innovation in government policy that was to have fundamental repercussions for the political, cultural and economic development of Ireland. The areas surrounding Fort Governor and Fort Protector experienced the first widespread confiscation of native properties in the Tudor period, acting as a prelude to the introduction of new settlers. A scheme of plantation was implemented, with two thirds of the land confiscated from the natives being granted to soldiers or to prospective owners from the Pale. These grants specified that planters had to reside on their newly granted lands, arm their tenants, exclude the original owners from their possessions and pay a proportion of all cesses for the maintenance of the garrisoned forts.[8] The government sought a balance between the various ethnic groups: New English, Anglo-Irish and loyal Gaelic Irish. This scheme of plantation had commenced without the area being shired; a situation that was remedied in 1557 when a law was passed to create Queen's County (later Laois) and King's County (later Offaly). At the same time, the earlier garrison forts were renamed after the then current reigning monarchs, with Fort Governor becoming Philipstown and Fort Protector renamed as Maryborough.[9]

Seven years later, further grants of land were made, resulting in about twice as many planters though including most of the former grantees. These new planters consisted of New English, Palesmen and Gaelic Irish. The O'Connors and O'Moores were transplanted from these lands to the west, with the O'Moores forced to settle in west Offaly, in an area adjoining the Shannon.[10] Conditions of this new plantation scheme outlined the responsibilities of planters. These now obliged each planter to be prepared to defend the country with most of his servants and tenants, armed and supplied for three days. A certain number of infantry and horsemen were to be maintained, depending on the size of the estate. Furthermore, intermarriage and Brehon law were prohibited, and the use of English language, dress and manners was to be encouraged among the planters' sons and chief servants. Once every year, the head of the estate was to appear in person in front of the constable or sheriff of the county with all the men under his responsibility to answer for any alleged misdemeanours during the previous twelve months. The grantee was to keep open or closed as required all fords and passes in his estate and he was not to destroy any castle, bridge, pavement or togher, except where such passes were adjacent to Gaelic Irish territory. The planter was to reside continually on his estate, and yet these conditions failed to specify the construction of any particular buildings or the number of English tenants to be settled.[11]

In 1567, the then current lord deputy, Sir Henry Sidney, was able to report on a visit to Maryborough that

> there was such obedience showed and used as well of the soldiers and English there lately planted as of the Irishry there inhabiting, as considering the infancy of any good order in that country, was marvelled at by as many as saw it, and so was the great increase of tillage that through quiet was there seen.[12]

Small villages grew in the immediate vicinity of the forts at Maryborough and Philipstown, which were incorporated in 1569–70. The plantation of east Laois and Offaly was the first experiment by the Tudor government in establishing colonial settlements in Ireland, providing a template for future plantations, though with the significant difference that the introduction of English tenants was stipulated more explicitly in the later plantations.[13]

Bearing in mind the experience with Sir Thomas Smith's abortive schemes in east Ulster in the 1570s and the collapse of the Munster Plantation in 1598, it should come as no surprise that the new settlements established in east Laois and Offaly experienced much dislocation in the latter half of the sixteenth century. Indeed, settlers in the midlands faced eighteen separate uprisings between 1563–4 and 1603.[14] This succession of rebellions illustrated the weakness of the new settlements, but the Tudor plantation survived, with the inhabitants or their successors able to revive former settlement sites. As far as is known, few if any of the sixteenth-century settlements in Laois or Offaly were permanently deserted after 1603.[15] A visitor in 1610 noted that between Philipstown and Maryborough

> prettye castles & howses may be seene ... som that weare newly built, and som old wales repaired & in some places in the fields English people making harvest, but not so aboundantly as wold be looked for.[16]

However, further progress was made as a government commission in 1622 reported that the midland plantation was 'for the most part well built and peopled by the English'.[17]

The Jacobean plantations of the midlands

In the years following the establishment of the Ulster Plantation in 1610, there was resentment among soldiers and officials who felt that their services had not been duly rewarded with grants of land in that northern province. Favours were still owed to these and to courtiers in England, and at a time of continual financial constraints for the crown, the confiscation of more native land offered a relatively painless expedient.[18] There were concerns that classically organized plantations, like the earlier schemes in Munster or Ulster, would provide little opportunity for servitors with relatively small finances. A more informal plantation was preferable because it would have been more permissive than a classical plantation on the issue of retaining native tenants, which was an important consideration for those who had no estates in England or Scotland to draw tenants from.[19]

The personal interest of James I (1603–25) in establishing British settlements in Ireland reinvigorated the ideal that plantations were the best means of promoting civility. This encouraged official circles to renew their search for defective titles so that at least some native lands could be reserved for British settlers. It was hoped that these settlers by their example could promote and engender civil living among their native neighbours.[20] Between 1610 and 1622, informal plantations were implemented in a number of native territories, stretching from Wexford in the southeast, to Leitrim in the northwest. Several leading septs in the present-day counties of Wexford, Westmeath, Longford and Leitrim, along with the western and southern areas of Laois and Offaly (not previously covered by the Tudor plantation), were to come within the ambit of these schemes. Strategic considerations were taken into account as recalcitrant Ulster nobles during the Nine Years War had used the Shannon corridor to reach Connacht and Munster. The relative poverty, small size and political insignificance of these midland territories, also meant that native landowners there were not capable of mustering sufficient opposition to the projected schemes of confiscation and plantation.[21]

Unlike earlier plantations that focused on creating self-contained colonies of British settlers, with resident landlords and tenants set apart from the native Irish, the main emphasis now was on establishing a thin settlement of British undertakers and restructuring native landownership. These more informal plantation schemes employed a version of the older Henrician policy of 'Surrender and Regrant', with native landowners obliged to surrender their estates to the crown, in return for which they would receive under secure title typically three-quarters of the original property. The remaining quarter would be passed onto undertakers who would become promoters of civil and industrious living in their new estates. Native lords were to become part of this anglicizing process, forgoing their old dynastic titles. The politically more benign conditions in the opening decades of the seventeenth century clearly encouraged the government to promote civil and religious reform in these territories in a manner that did not involve the removal of Irish landowners or tenants from their former lands as was the case in Ulster.[22] The principle of promoting anglicization among the native population by landlords of British origin was now in vogue, rather than wholesale colonization involving the settlement of large numbers of British tenants.

These schemes in the midland territories also sought to reduce the number of small freeholders, with lesser proprietors deprived of their old order status, joining the ranks of the existing tenantry in the new dispensation. Thus a social transformation of the lower social classes of native society became a central feature of government policy.[23] In Wexford, two corporate towns were to be established, while in the midlands, three corporate towns, one each in Leitrim, Longford and Offaly, were to be created. In addition, a number of market centres as well as some fairs were to be allocated among the native grantees and undertakers. These would underpin the development of a more advanced economy that would compensate for the losses of the native freeholders in the long run. As in Ulster, allocations of land were also to be made for the maintenance of churches and schools that abided by the reformed faith.[24]

Much has been made by historians of the insufficient nature of these plantations when compared with the more formally planned schemes. The English officials who received grants of lands under these schemes did not necessarily reside on their newly gained properties. Such criticism was summarized by Aidan Clarke, who regarded these schemes as nothing more than 'a new, predatory form of surrender and regrant directed towards the enrichment of the New English'.[25] Contemporary observers were also of the same opinion, with Sir Francis Blundell commenting in 1622 that the scheme implemented in Longford and Éile Uí Chearbhaill at the time did not merit the appellation of 'a plantation, but a show of something where nothing is done', with the undertakers only willing to 'scramble for the rents' while they lived in Britain 'without making any plantation at all'. Blundell considered the schemes in Leitrim and in the smaller midland territories such as Delbhna Eathra and Fir Cheall as no better. In all these cases, however, he acknowledged that the plantations were still in their infancy and were encountering legal challenges, particularly from Sir John MacCoghlan, a local magnate in Delbhna Eathra.[26] The chief significance of these midland schemes was that it was still possible as late as 1622 for English interest groups to advocate informal, rather than formal, plantations as best suited to conditions on the ground, with such schemes being considered the best means of realizing Edmund Spenser's ambition to have the entire country subjected to plantation.[27]

The attraction of the plantations in Ireland

What inspired members of England's gentry to become involved in the subjugation and resettlement of west and south Offaly, despite the considerable obstacles encountered in establishing plantations there? The limited opportunities for younger sons in England and the recognition that there was opportunity in Ireland to establish oneself as a major landowner attracted many enterprising officials and soldiers, including men with the literary calibre of Edmund Spenser, Sir John Davies, Gerard and Arnold Boate and Sir William Petty.[28] Sir Thomas Smith, the chief organizer for a plantation in the Ards Peninsula in the 1570s, attributed the lack of opportunities in England to the closure of the monasteries; nonetheless, the absence of military service during the early years of Queen Elizabeth's reign also may have frustrated many ambitions. At the time, there was a literary genre that looked nostalgically to the reigns of Henry VIII and Edward VI, when military service was held in high regard. Those who owned some property but found it difficult to advance themselves in English society recognized the opportunities for social and economic advancement in Ireland.[29] As one lord deputy of Ireland, Thomas Wentworth, observed, these were 'private men … whose sole ends and aims have been their own enriching and such who have had no hand here in public affairs have only been prosperous for themselves and compassed much wealth'.[30]

Lower down the social scale, it was recognized that poorer sections of society in the overcrowded towns and cities of England could be transported out of the country, thus relieving the burdens of support on the parishes.[31] This was given explicit recognition in a document outlining why the London companies should invest in the Ulster Plantation. The document speculated on creating employment opportunities for the poor of London, with the objective of easing the city 'of an insupportable burthen of persons'.[32] Growing population, tenurial reorganization and rent increases had indeed motivated many of the English and Scottish tenants and leaseholders to settle in Ulster. Many of these had arrived looking for opportunities to invest what little capital they possessed so as to reverse the financial penury that they had experienced back in their homelands.[33]

The success of the various plantation schemes depended upon the dismemberment of the Gaelic Irish lordships, the dispersal of native kinship groups and the settlement of English and lowland Scottish gentlemen who would provide a new class of landowners. In turn, it was felt that this would encourage further settlement by a broader section of British society. Such an ideal could only be achieved by force, but it was argued that, once implemented, the way was paved for clergy, teachers and lawyers to engage in the reform of the Gaelic population so that, as Sir John Davies put it, 'the next generation would in tongue and heart and every way else become English so as there will be no difference or distinction but the Irish sea between us'.[34] This was the only solution if existing British settlement was not to be eventually absorbed into native society. Early modern English writers were aware of the perils of assimilation and acculturation when in the midst of any native society. A chief hazard was that whatever group of English people went to settle in Ireland, like the earlier Anglo-Norman colonizers before them, could become assimilated into a barbaric native society.[35] Indeed, one of the more important messages in Edmund Spenser's book, *A view of the present state of Ireland*, was that any group of civilized people who settled among uncivil peoples, and who sought to achieve social reform through peaceful means, would inevitably become absorbed into the corrupt ways of their host society.[36]

Many commentators sought precedents and analogies from a variety of sources to justify the dismemberment and dispersal of a population, which had occupied for centuries lands earmarked for settlement. The humanist tradition, with its value on reform through education and example, permeates much of the early modern literature on colonization. It is not coincidental that such literature on the assimilation and acculturation of Gaelic society mainly coincided with, or quickly followed, foreign conflagrations, and that the two most creative periods were 1590–1610 and 1641–52, when England was most acutely aware of Ireland's strategic importance and the scope for the utilization of confiscated lands was at its widest.[37]

Theorists and philosophers extolling the virtues of honour and patriotism had an inspirational influence on the planners of various plantation schemes, if not in shaping the actual form of the various plantations.[38] As an example, Sir John Davies drew from classical, religious and foreign precedents in his planning of the Ulster Plantation.[39]

Classical precedent and the influence of the Renaissance

In the early modern period, a new world had opened up for Englishmen, not only in a physical sense, but also in a conceptual and intellectual manner. Proponents of civil and religious reform in Ireland were educated in a humanistic tradition, which celebrated the classical tradition, especially the legacy left behind by the Romans. Sir Thomas Smith, a leading intellectual, looked back on the establishment of Fort Governor and Fort Protector in the midlands as heralding a new era of colonization in Ireland. These forts grew into towns that gradually spread their influence and their inhabitants across the surrounding countryside, very much as a Roman colony would have done, an analogy that may not have been lost on Smith.[40] Sir Thomas himself undertook a plantation scheme in the Ards Peninsula in Co. Down (1571). His study of classics aroused his interest in colonialism, and it may have been the case that he inspired one of his students, Richard Eden, to translate Peter Martyr Anglerius' *De Orbe Novo* as a means of encouraging Englishmen to emulate Spanish efforts in the Americas.[41] Smith held the view that the English were the new Romans who had come to civilize the Irish, as the old Romans had once civilized the ancient Britons. He made a surly claim that

> as I do understand by histories of thyngs by past, how this contrey of England, ones as uncivill as Ireland now is, was by colonies of the Romaynes brought to understand the lawes and orders of thanncient orders whereof there hath no nacon more streightly and truly kept the mouldes even to this day then we, yea more than thitalians and Romaynes themselves.[42]

Planters in the Munster Plantation (1585), with a literary bent, also approached the problem of assimilating and acculturating the Irish with reference to Roman models and Machiavellian warnings. Richard Beacon in *c.*1589 recommended that the crown should adopt towards the Irish an 'ancient policy used heretofore by the Romans upon any suspicion of foreign invasion, to place strong garrisons in every of their fortresses, to disarm them, and to take sufficient pledges of the great and suspected men'.[43] Beacon defended the controversial actions of Richard Bingham, one time president of Connaght, who, 'by his singular art and skill in military discipline as an other Cesar, suppressed at the last Vercingetorix and the rebelling Gaules'.[44] Sir

William Herbert, an undertaker in Castleisland, Co. Kerry, wrote a Latin tract at the same time entitled *Croftus, sive de Hibernia liber,* in which he called for extensive plantation in Munster, using the example set by the Anglo-Normans and indeed the Romans before them. Of interest in the margins of this tract are acknowledgments to Niccolò Machiavelli's *Prince.*[45] Another of these Munster planters was Edmund Spenser, the author of the *Faerie Queene* and *A view of the present state of Ireland.* He repeated the sentiments of Smith when he asserted in the latter work that 'the English were at first as stout and warlike a people as ever were the Irish, and yet you see are now brought to that civilty, that no nation in the world excelleth them in all goodly conversation'.[46] In the same work, Spenser cited Machiavelli, 'where he commendeth the manner of the Romans' government, in giving absolute power to all their consuls and governors, which, if they abused, they should afterwards clearly answer'.[47]

The great Renaissance political thinker, Machiavelli, had repeatedly advocated colonization on the basis of economic viability, political stability and strategic value, using Roman parallels to justify his position.[48] Machiavelli contrasted the barbarism of the medieval world with the civilization of the earlier Roman Empire as an argument to eradicate the last vestiges of medievalism.[49] This anti-medievalism was picked up by English scholars such as Smith and explains why the Roman allusion appeared so frequently in sixteenth-century writing on Ireland. This usage of classical analogy was to continue into the seventeenth century, with individuals like Thomas Blennerhassett in 1610 declaring that James I should comport himself as a Roman emperor on the basis of his colonial ventures in Ulster,[50] while Sir John Davies called on his contemporaries to complete the conquest of Ireland alluding to the Roman general Julius Agricola who had civilized 'our ancestors the ancient Britons' who had up until then been 'rude and dispersed, and therefore prone upon every occasion to make war'.[51] However, Quinn comments that, in most respects, Roman analogies and precedents, and the reading in Machiavelli, had only marginal and occasional practical importance in the later development of colonial planning in early seventeenth-century England.[52] This may be borne out by the later plantations under James I in Wexford and the midland territories, where, instead of self-contained colonies of English settlers, with landowners and tenants set apart from the native populace, only a thin sprinkling of English undertakers with the cooperation of native landowners and freeholders would underpin the spread of civility and reform.

Religious reform

Commentators also sought divine approbation through quotations of the Scriptures. Along with many of his contemporaries, Spenser believed that moral reform, as it was conceived by classical authors and their Renaissance successors, could not be divorced from politico-religious considerations. Religious reform was considered to be integral to the civilizing process, as contemplation of the individual's relationship with God would pave the way for the embrace of more public reforms. King James I, an enthusiastic supporter of plantations in Ireland and further afield, regarded such schemes as 'the only ordinary means to reduce the people to civility and religion'.[53] Plantation schemes included clauses for the endowment of sufficient lands to the established church so as to secure the proper maintenance of its clergy. In the midland territories such as Éile Uí Chearbhaill, church land was to be deducted before the assignation of the appropriated proportions to undertakers.[54]

Spenser believed that Christians had an obligation to use force to defend and advance the cause of the true faith, to maintain order at times of unrest and to extend the boundaries of civility into 'barbaric' regions.[55] Edward Barkley asserted 'how godly a dede it is to overthrowe so wicked a race the world may judge: for my part I thinke there canot be a greater sacryfice to God'.[56] The English promoters of the plantations in the late sixteenth century believed the Irish to be nothing more than pagans in their religious practices. Indeed, this view was to be encouraged by the Old English, where one of their number wrote an unpublished pamphlet *On the disorders of the Irishry* issued in 1572, which declared that the native Irish and their laws were 'contrary to God his lawe and also repugnant to the Queens Majesties lawes'.[57] This propensity among Protestant commentators to use divine approbation could be seen in official circles where Ralph Rokeby, Chief Justice of Connacht in 1571 declared that 'It must be fire and sword and the rod of God's vengeance that must make these stubborn and cankered hearts yield for fear'.[58] Even Sir Thomas Smith proclaimed that God 'did make apte and prepare this nation [the English] ... to inhabite and reforme so barbarous a nation [the Irish] as that is, and to bring them to the knowledge and lawe were both a goodly and commendable deede, and a sufficient worke of our age'.[59]

There was a tendency to regard the religious practices of the native Irish as completely alien and, indeed, abhorrent to the accepted norms and practices not only of the established church, but also by the standards of contemporary European Catholicism. Edmund Tremayne asserted that religion was 'totally lacking' in Munster, with churches 'onlie like stables' and declined to declare the Irish 'ether Papists nor Protestants but rather such as have nether feare nor love of God in their harts that restreyneth them from ill'.[60] Spenser even doubted their true knowledge of Catholic doctrine, writing that 'they are all Papists by their profession, but in the same so blindly and brutishly informed for the most part as that you would think them atheists or infidels'. Thus, the English adventurers of the sixteenth century had little difficulty in convincing themselves that they were bringing the benefits of true religion to misguided people no better than heathens.[61] This sense of righteousness was to continue among officials and servitors into the next generation, with Lord Deputy Mountjoy expressing the opinion that 'the poore people' of Ulster 'never had the meanes to know God' and describing one of the native lords in the same province as 'proud, valiant, miserable, tyrannous, unmeasurably covetous, without any knowledge of God, or almost any civility'.[62] In 1604, Davies wrote that

> the churches are ruined and fallen down to the ground in all parts of the kingdom. There is no divine service, no christening of children, no receiving of the sacrament, no Christian meeting or assembly, no, not once a year; in a word, no more demonstration of religion than among Tartars or cannibals.[63]

To acknowledge the Irish as Christian would have meant acknowledging them as civilized as well, something that propagandists for civil and religious reform in Ireland could never countenance. These writers would follow up their arguments with patronizing and derogatory accounts of Irish dress, habits, customs, architecture and farming practices.

Education was to play a central role, reflecting the humanist principle in the value of instruction in promoting moral behaviour, and paving the way for the furtherance of the reformed faith by 'some discreet ministers of their countrymen' who 'by their mild persuasions and instructions as also by their sober life and conversation, may draw them first to understand and afterwards to embrace the doctrine of their salvation'.[64] Conversion of the population by Irish-speaking ministers would only commence after the existing social institutions in Ireland had been obliterated and a new social order created to take its place, as

> instruction in religion needeth quiet times, and ere we seek to settle a sound discipline in the clergy, we must purchase peace unto the laity; for it is ill time to preach among swords, and most hard or rather impossible it is to settle a good opinion in the minds of men ... which have a doubtless evil opinion of ourselves: for ere a new be brought in, the old must be removed.[65]

The subjugation of Ireland in a global context

Canny has commented on how many of these new landlords were well travelled and some well read.[66] A few had travelled on the Continent, even going as far as fighting Turks in Hungary, while others would have ventured across the Atlantic to the Americas.[67] As many as five of the eight principal architects in the plantation of Munster also played significant roles in expanding English commercial and strategic interests, not only in America but in Asia as well.[68] Famous early colonists in America – Drake, Gilbert, Grenville, Frobisher, Raleigh, Lane and Harriot – had previously visited or served in Ireland.[69] All were interested in travel and adventure, and through their experiences and their reading of travel literature, they had arrived at notions of how primitive peoples would measure up to acceptable standards of civilized behaviour. In such a milieu, it should not be surprising that Tudor and Stuart writers measured Gaelic Irish practices against the perceived norms of English society. Many of these planters, endowed with such notions of what a barbaric society should look like, found aspects of native Irish society wanting.[70]

One particular feature of Irish farming that was to attract the admonitions of many commentators was the supposed widespread practice of transhumance. This was seen as indicative of nomadism, which was more typically associated in sixteenth-century travel literature with far flung tribes in Asia Minor such as the Scythians and the Tartars. Spenser went as far as interpreting the practice of transhumance as proof that the Gaelic Irish were descended from the Scythians themselves. Barnaby Rich, arguing against those who thought that the conduct of planters was too severe, pointed out that the Irish preferred to 'live like beastes, voide of lawe and all good order' and that they were 'more uncivill, more uncleanly, more barbarous and more brutish in their customs and demeanures, then in any other part of the world that is known'.[71]

Many colonizers found justification in their endeavours with the contemporary European belief in the right to acquire land that was not been productively utilized according to established norms of European mercantile economies. The Roman law *res nullius* held that unoccupied or under-utilized land remained the common property of humanity until enterprising people brought it into productive use, following on from which they might become its owners.[72] Sir John Davies asserted that

> if themselves [the native Irish] were suffered to possess the whole country as their septs have done for many hundred of years past, they would never (to the end of the world) build houses, make townships or villages or manure or improve the land as it ought to be; therefore it stands neither with Christian policy nor conscience to suffer so good and fruitful a country to lie waste like a wilderness.[73]

This 'wilderness' encountered by Davies was not a real one, but an ideological construct. From an English perspective, native societies in Ireland and further afield in Virginia and New England had failed in their God-given duty to cultivate the landscape properly – a failure linked to a lack of true religion.[74]

Henry Sidney, before his tenure as lord deputy, had spent the years 1553–6 as ambassador for Queen Mary in the Spanish court, and would probably have become, at the very least, acquainted with the Spanish colonial activities in the New World. With this in mind, it is of interest that Sidney's appointment as lord deputy coincided with the first practical proposals for settlements in Ulster to be carried out with the aid of private enterprise. The conditions specified in such schemes were very similar to the grants given by Spain to her conquistadores.[75] In 1610, when justifying the transplantation of natives during the course of the Ulster Plantation, Sir John Davies cited the example set by the Spanish who 'lately removed all the Moors out of

Granada into Barbary without providing them with any new seats there'.[76] The most significant source of Spanish influence on planters in sixteenth-century Ireland was Richard Eden's partial translation of Peter Martyr Anglerius' *De Orbe Novo*, a work that recommended that Englishmen should emulate the example of the Spanish in the Americas. Eden was a student of Thomas Smith, which would suggest a probable familiarity on the part of the latter with the work.[77] According to Canny, the English were aware of the harsh treatment by the Spanish of peoples in their colonies who did not measure up to their standards of civility, strengthening the conviction that they were justified in their own severe treatment of the Gaelic Irish population.[78] One settler in Delbhna Eathra, Matthew de Renzy, criticized the Dublin administration for being too lenient towards the native population in Ireland, warning that it would bring a weakening, if not an overthrow, of the conquest.[79]

The English colonial mind compared the levels of civilized behaviour among the native societies on either side of the Atlantic. Differences in settlements, housing, dress and agriculture were highlighted in a manner to justify colonial endeavours at the expense of native populations, whether in Ireland or in America.[80] Indeed, propaganda tracts portrayed both countries in similar patronizing terms, though at the same time highlighting the benefits of moving to new lands endowed with temperate climes, extensive productive farmland, an abundance of woodland, and rivers and seas swollen with fish stocks.[81] The practice of transhumance and the shelters used by its practitioners invited comment from some English writers on the similarity between Gaelic Irish houses and those of Native Americans. Thomas Morton, for example, was to observe that 'the natives of New England are accustomed to build them houses much like the wild Irish'.[82] De Renzy commenting on the size and economic potential of the River Shannon observed that it 'might be made more famous to these parts ... than the river of Plate in America, or the river of Nilus in Africa'.[83] Overt comparisons with the Americas, however, were few and far between as it was not easy to sustain practical comparisons between the Gaelic Irish and the Native Americans, for in Ireland colonists and natives mingled closely together in a manner that diluted cultural differences.[84] This was recognized by contemporaries, with Sir Francis Bacon considering the settlement of Virginia as 'an enterprise in my opinion differing as much from this [the settlement of Ireland] as Amadis de Gaul differs from Caesar's Commentaries'.[85] The principal challenge to English hegemony in early modern Ireland, indeed, came not from the Gaelic Irish, but from the Old English communities in the south and east of Ireland, who eschewed any valid comparison with Native Americans. More importantly, the concept that the presence of English settlers in Ireland could be compared to Spain's colonies in the Americas remained largely unexplored, as such comparisons would have denied the legitimacy of Ireland's status as a kingdom under the English crown. It would also have undermined the efforts of successive administrations to govern Ireland by the means of legal institutions as well as question the very ability of English common law to survive in a country in which it had been planted centuries beforehand.[86]

English commentators also looked to current international relations for the justification of colonial endeavours. Sir Humphrey Gilbert, for example, asserted that the Irish were susceptible to foreign aid as 'all nacyons doe naturallie mislike forraigne subjectyone ... all conquered people obeying rather for feare than throughe love as may p[ar]tlie appeare by Naples, Myllane, Cecill [Sicily]'.[87] At times of tensions between England and Continental powers, there was always the nagging fear that Ireland would be invaded as a means to attack the exposed western seaboard of England. Walter Raleigh reflected upon this strategic weakness in 1593, opining that 'We are so busied and dandled in these French wars, which are endless, as we forget the defence next the heart'.[88] English officials saw a similarity between their defiance of Spanish oppression in the Netherlands and their campaign for civil reform in Ireland. Philip, the son of Sir Henry Sidney, had viewed the assertiveness of Catholic powers with consequent loss of liberty on the European mainland with despondency, but argued for the spread of the royal prerogative across Ireland as liberty there had already been lost through the machinations of Gaelic Irish and Old English lords. Neither 'wicked Saracen nor yet cruel Turk' so oppressed the 'poor commons' as did these lords in Ireland who imposed their capricious rule.[89]

Conclusion

From the mid-sixteenth century onwards, Ireland experienced a series of formal and informal plantations that inaugurated a protracted and convoluted process of cultural, economic and political change. It has been estimated that 150,000 immigrants arrived in Ireland between 1586 and 1700, possibly as many as had moved from Spain and Portugal from 1500 to 1650 to establish colonies in Latin America.[90] Numerous authors wrote on the subject of anglicizing the Gaelic population in the early modern period. They were inspired by previous colonial endeavours such as the expansion of the Roman Empire and the Anglo-Norman conquest of Ireland centuries beforehand. However, the extent to which these precedents and analogies successfully contributed to the process of colonization can be questioned. The classical emphasis on order and symmetry exemplified Elizabethan concerns for the maintenance of social hierarchy and order. Nonetheless, in the face of political, geographical and economic realities, aspirations for the spread of civil reform, and in turn the crown's writ across Ireland, were difficult to realize. Indeed, civil and religious reform was clearly not a major motivation for individual planters, with some English clergy and laity objecting to the pursuit of profit by some of estates at the expense of the social and religious agenda as originally enunciated in the preamble to colonial ventures. John Long, Protestant archbishop of Armagh during the 1580s, reminded London officialdom that 'subjects have souls as well as bodies' and criticized those who 'by sword and law' would shed the blood of those who, 'for lack of better teaching, could never be better'.[91]

CHAPTER 3

English interventions in early modern Offaly

Introduction

In the early modern period, west and south Offaly encompassed a number of native lordships, polities that were defined in terms of both people and territory according to the norms of Gaelic Irish society. Through the late sixteenth and early seventeenth centuries, these lordships, each in turn, were subsumed into baronies, forming the basis of an English-style county or shire. From then on, these baronies underpinned the county structure, supported by an administration headed by a sheriff and local justices of the peace. These baronies survive today, in effect preserving the extent of the various lordships as they existed in late sixteenth-century Offaly (fig. 3.1). The O'Carrolls of Éile Uí Chearbhaill originally controlled the baronies of Clonlisk and Ballybritt in southwest Offaly, while their neighbours to the north, the O'Molloys of Fir Cheall, held sway over the three baronies of Eglish, Ballyboy and Ballycowan. The MacCoghlans of Delbhna Eathra dominated the largest barony of all, Garrycastle, while the Foxes of Muintir Thadhgáin were pre-eminent in the smallest, Kilcoursey.[1]

Strategic importance of these lordships

The strategic importance of these territories in the Shannon basin was recognized as early as the 1540s by Edmund le Fay, who ventured into Éile Uí Chearbhaill and Delbhna Eathra at that time.[2] This was again acknowledged in official circles in 1580, when the defence of crossing points along the Shannon was considered as part of a proposal for establishing fortifications along Ireland's coastline and estuaries. Locations considered along the river for fortification included a site below Clonmacnoise, possibly Raghra (presently known as Shannonbridge), Banagher and Meelick.[3] Matthew de Renzy, a German settler living in Delbhna Eathra in the years leading up to the plantation of 1620, observed that 'as long as the heart of a kingdom is not purged or cleanst from the infections (out of which all rebellions sprung) the members of it can never be sound'.[4] The midland territories such as Éile Uí Chearbhaill and Delbhna Eathra contained some of the most important routes in the kingdom, linking Connacht and Munster with the east and north of the country. This strategic reality was recognized by army commanders such as the earl of Tyrone, Hugh O'Neill, in 1599, the Cromwellian general, Henry Ireton, in 1650 and the Jacobite general, Patrick Sarsfield, in 1690, all of whom passed through the region on military campaigns.

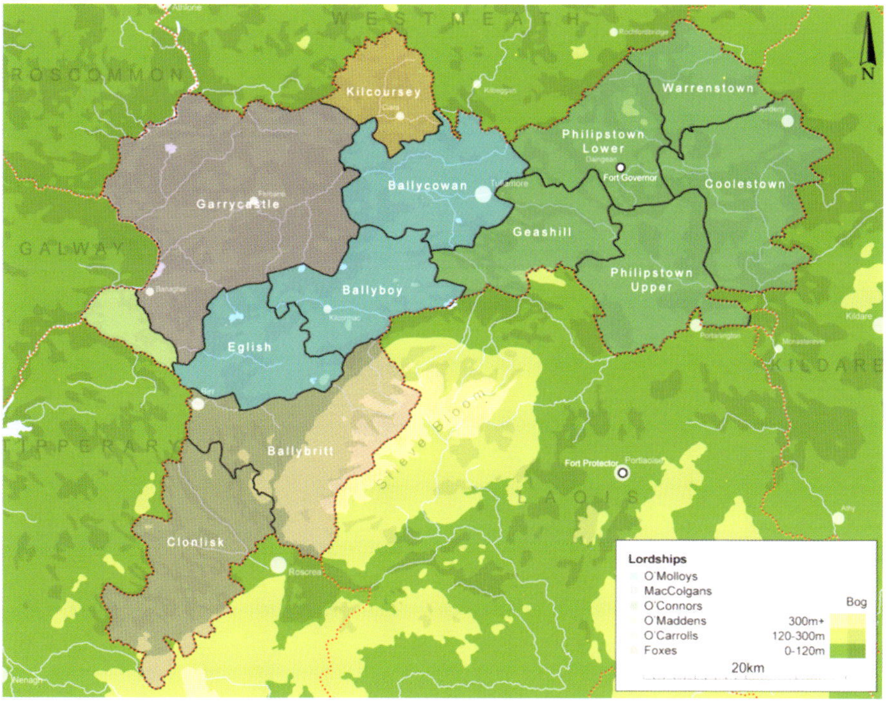

3.1 Native lordships of late medieval/early modern Offaly (prepared by Conor McDermott and Hugh Kavanagh).

Early English military campaigning in the lordships

The first wave of English settlers in the Offaly lordships since the thirteenth century arrived in the 1540s during the reign of Queen Mary. In 1547, a crown garrison by the name of Fort Governor was established in the O'Connor lordship in the east of what is now Offaly, with land in the surrounding districts set aside for soldiers with the intention of encouraging the garrison to become self-sufficient. The following decade saw the wholesale confiscation of land from leading native elements in this area. This paved the way, in 1557, for the first formal scheme of plantation to be implemented in the country. Fort Governor (now named Philipstown) became the seat of administration for a newly established county called King's County. A mixture of native Irish, Old English and New English settlers took up patents for estates across the original territories of the native lordship there.

This focus upon the confiscation and plantation of lands in east Offaly saw the original O'Connor lordship being rent asunder, though the territories in west and south Offaly, namely those of the O'Molloys, the Foxes, the MacCoghlans and the O'Carrolls, were to remain free from plantation for the rest of the sixteenth century.

English officialdom, however, was not shy in pursuing its agenda of civil and religious reform – the establishment of a permanent English garrison at Fort Governor now brought these Gaelic territories within the sphere of English influence. Through the sixteenth century, these lordships were to experience English military campaigns, the destruction of monasteries, the confiscation of monastic lands, the trickle of English settlers into the area, the policy of surrender and regrant, and the administration of English justice in areas where Brehon law had previously prevailed.

In west and south Offaly, military interventions were to be a feature of relations between the native aristocracy and the government in the sixteenth century. The nature of crown rule at this time was characterized by English-born lord deputies assisted by standing armies, but constrained by lack of time and resources, allowing only periodic military campaigning rather than the conquest and settlement of planters.[5] As early as 1537, the then lord deputy, Lord Leonard Grey, took the castles of Eglish and Birr in a campaign against Donough O'Carroll, a claimant to the O'Carroll lordship. This eventually led to an agreement in 1538, followed by a treaty in 1539 between the O'Carrolls and the crown, by which Donough's rival, Fearganainm, was acknowledged as chief of Éile Uí Chearbhaill. In return, the O'Carrolls would pay tribute for their territory, provide a fixed number of soldiers each year for the crown's use and facilitate the passage of the lord deputy and his forces through the lordship.[6] Such agreements were of little practical value, but brought the native lordships into the realm of common law, which could allow for the forfeiture of estates in the event of a rebellion or an intervention in a succession dispute. Indeed, the crown's interests in Éile Uí Chearbhaill were to strengthen with Fearganainm's successor, Tadhg O'Carroll, who was received by Henry VIII in London in 1542, seeking the status of tenant-in-chief. Such a move was calculated by Tadhg to acquire the same legal footing under the crown as enjoyed by his more powerful neighbours, the Butlers of Ormond.[7]

But it was not only the O'Carrolls who were at the receiving end of English military campaigns. The Annals of the Four Masters mention that in the years 1540 and 1548, English forces raided Delbhna Eathra; in the latter year forcing the MacCoghlans to demolish castles at Banagher, Moystown and Cloghan, lest they were invested by English troops.[8] The same source records that in the latter year churches throughout west and south Offaly were also subject to raids by English garrisons. The monasteries located at Kilcormac in Fir Cheall and Seir Kieran in Éile Uí Chearbhaill were burnt and destroyed by a combination of English and O'Carrolls in 1548,[9] while in 1552, the English garrison from Athlone plundered Clonmacnoise, leaving neither 'a bell, small or large, an image, or an altar, or a book, or a gem, or even glass in a window, from the wall of the church out, which was not carried off'.[10] In 1557, the O'Melaghlins from neighbouring Westmeath and the English of Athlone demolished a castle at Raghra (Shannonbridge), resulting in tensions between the MacCoghlans and O'Melaghlins.[11] The same year also saw tensions rise between the crown and the O'Carrolls, when the latter gave sanctuary to Brian O'Connor Faly, whose lordship in east Offaly had just been the subject of the Marian plantation. As a consequence, the lord deputy of the time, Sir Henry Radcliffe, brother of the earl of Sussex, led a military campaign to 'plague, punish and prosecute with sword and fire', briefly occupying some O'Carroll strongholds including Leap Castle.[12] Indeed, for several years after 1557, an English garrison was established in the grounds of Meelick friary on the Galway side of the River Shannon bordering Delbhna Eathra, confirming the strategic importance of this waterway.[13]

The incursion of English legal norms into the Offaly lordships

Crown policy, however, was not completely engrossed in military solutions and sought more peaceful and politically expedient ways of consolidating English control in Ireland. The policy of surrender and regrant saw native lords surrendering their lands, which were then returned under secure title recognized by common law. This was facilitated by the 1541 Act of Kingly Title, which elevated the lordship of Ireland into a kingdom, sharing the same crown as England.[14] Many of these Gaelic lords were knighted, with some acquiring substantial titles like the earldoms of Thomond and Tyrone. In return for this benevolence on the part of the government, the native landowners pledged allegiance to the crown, embraced the principle of primogeniture and accepted the use of common law. This policy was pursued at a time of fiscal rectitude, and was seen as an expedient and more economic way of securing the advancement of English interests in Ireland, rather than engaging in expensive and protracted military campaigns. This policy was to remain a popular one, on and off, through the sixteenth and early seventeenth centuries. Initially, the government was primarily concerned with the most powerful of lords such as the O'Briens and O'Neills but, as the sixteenth century progressed, smaller lords such as the O'Carrolls and MacCoghlans increasingly made agreements with the crown, and after 1603, agreements were also made with politically insignificant landholders.[15]

This policy was realized in Éile Uí Chearbhaill in 1551 when Tadhg O'Carroll, son of Fearganainm, submitted to the crown as tenant-in-chief and was knighted in return by the lord deputy, Sir William Brabazon, at Limerick. Shortly afterwards, he was also granted the title of 'Lord Baron of Ely'.[16] In 1567, Tadhg's brother and eventual successor, William Odher, was knighted by the then lord deputy, Sir Henry Sidney, again at Limerick. However, unlike his brother, William was not to be rewarded with a baronetcy.[17] In 1578, Sir William O'Carroll, on surrendering his territory to the crown, received it back in a charter enrolled in the Irish chancery. He was acknowledged as tenant-in-chief in return for a payment of £100 per annum and for providing twelve horsemen and twenty footmen when required.[18] One of the legal successors (to be recognized under common law) named by William in the entail of

1578, Calvach (or Charles) O'Carroll succeeded to the lordship and was knighted by lord deputy Sir John Perrot in 1585.[19] In 1600, Sir Charles was murdered while following a delicate balancing act between the crown and native interests when the Nine Years War was at its height. His lands were subsequently granted to his son John, but the honour of knighthood was given to another son known by the name of Mulrony on the coronation day of James I, 24 July 1603. This acceptance of primogeniture presented a direct challenge to the native custom of passing chiefry lands from one elected chieftain to another, as now the lands were to remain in the direct line of the grantee. By this time, however, the O'Carroll lordship was considerably weakened, not only due to succession disputes but also by the military and legal aggrandizement of the Dublin government, paving the way for the final annexation of Éile Uí Chearbhaill into King's County in 1605.[20]

The O'Carrolls were not the only native family in Offaly to play a part in this process of assimilation. The chief of Delbhna Eathra, Art MacCoghlan submitted to the crown in Athlone in 1551, in the process obtaining a pardon, along with a patent for his lands.[21] Around 1570, his successor, John MacCoghlan was knighted by the lord deputy.[22] Later, in 1581, Sir John surrendered his possessions in Delbhna Eathra to the crown, and received them back the following year to be now held by knight's service. In addition, Sir John, instead of being styled 'Chief Captain of his Nation' was now appointed as seneschal of Delbhna Eathra.[23] As seneschal, Sir John was expected to uphold the interests of the crown in the region; he was one of those notified by the lords justices in 1583 to watch out for the fugitive earl of Desmond in the aftermath of his rebellion.[24] Sir John's recognized status as local grandee necessitated his invitation to a sitting of parliament in Dublin in 1585.[25] His younger son, also called John, succeeded after the father's death in July 1590 and was subsequently knighted by the earl of Essex in 1599 for service in the queen's name during the Nine Years War.[26] As expected of English landowners, Sir John sought and was granted the right to hold a market in Banagher in 1612, long before the town was incorporated in 1628 as part of the plantation of Delbhna Eathra.[27] In Muintir Thadhgáin, Hubert Fox, along with four other members of the Fox family, surrendered their secular and spiritual holdings in 1599, allowing the introduction of a court baron and leet, with Hubert as seneschal, an appointment designed to undermine the older Gaelic traditions of redress in the lordship.[28] It has been argued that the long-term success of the surrender and regrant policy was due to such minor political figures because it was with the cooperation of these men that the Dublin administration was able to consolidate English local administrative practices across the counties.[29]

In the late sixteenth and early seventeenth century, English influence in the midland territories was clearly advanced through the administration of common law in areas where, until recently, Brehon law had prevailed. This was facilitated by the subsuming of the various lordships into King's County, with Fir Cheall and Delbhna Eathra in the early 1570s, Muintir Thadhgáin in 1591 and Éile Uí Chearbhaill in

1605.[30] When a native lordship became shire ground, local officials such as sheriffs and justices of the peace were appointed to administer justice according to the precepts of English common law. Indeed, in the case of Éile Uí Chearbhaill, the stated rationale behind its annexation into King's County lay in consequence of crimes being carried out there with impunity due to the territory not been shire ground.[31] Even as early as 1575, however, the head of this territory, Sir William O'Carroll, attended sessions held by the lord deputy, Sir Henry Sydney in King's County. This was not primarily a concern on Sir William's part to ensure greater conformity with English legal norms, but was an attempt to curtail the claims of the palatinate court of neighbouring Ormond, which, through the years had sought to extend its jurisdiction over Éile Uí Chearbhaill.[32] William's successor, Sir Charles O'Carroll, called in 1589 and 1595 for Éile Uí Chearbhaill to be added to King's County in the face of continuing Ormond pressure to impose their palatinate jurisdiction on the lordship.[33] Hence, the policy of civil and religious reform could be pursued not only through formal schemes of plantation, but by more gradual government intrusions facilitated by military incursions and the policy of surrender and regrant.

English settlement in west and south Offaly before plantation

It would be wrong to suggest that the plantation schemes of 1619 and 1620 were primarily responsible for the arrival of British settlers into these native territories. Individual colonists were taking up parcels of land much earlier than the actual plantation schemes, as early as the 1580s.[34] These newcomers came from a range of ethnic (Gaelic Irish, Old and New English) and social backgrounds (noblemen, officials, merchants, military officers and other private individuals).[35] However, these newcomers did not necessarily take up residence in their new acquisitions.[36] The majority of grantees were land speculators, with a short-term interest in the acquiring and selling of leases on monastic properties. The Carmelite priory at Kilcormac was dissolved and leased first to Con O'Molloy, a local notable in 1550, though in 1567 the lease was granted to Henry Cooley.[37] The crown leased the monastic lands of Seir Kieran in Éile Uí Chearbhaill to a succession of English gentlemen and officials, along with 'loyal' natives, John Croft in 1552, John O'Carroll in 1566, William O'Carroll in 1578, Lucas Dillon in 1586 and William Taaffe in 1604.[38] A gun turret at the southeast corner of the former Augustinian Priory church at Seir Kieran may date to either John Croft's or John O'Carrolls' occupancy, as an inquisition dated 1568 mentions *una turris parva*, a small tower (figs 3.2, 3.3).[39] The leasing of Seir Kieran to the O'Carrolls in the 1560s and 1570s highlighted the benefits of befriending a government. Speculators were selling their new lands to newcomers, opening up the region to British migrants such as John Briscoe of Srah Castle and Thomas Morres at Ballycowan, who took up residence in the O'Molloy lordship of Fir Cheall in 1588

3.2 Gun turret recorded as *una turris parva* in 1568, built against the southeast corner of the dissolved Augustinian priory church at Seir Kieran.

and 1592–3 respectively.[40] These gentlemen built residences on their properties, a tower house in the former case and possibly a fortified house in the latter.[41] Matthew de Renzy bought a tower house and a small estate from a member of the MacCoghlan clan at Clonony near the River Shannon, sometime in the early 1610s. This German settler described the lordship as

> pleasant, but very wast & waunteth the manurance of industrious inhabitants, for these that lieu ther are ... voyd of civility both in howses, apparel, & all other manners: and better store they are with eydle people then ther labours can be able to maintayne.[42]

Hence, before the plantations of 1619–20, there was a trickle of settlers into the Gaelic lordships of west and south Offaly, which hitherto had fallen beyond the scope of the mid-sixteenth-century plantations in the east of the county.

3.3 Interior of gun turret at Seir Kieran with gun ope embrasures evident. Note the remains of a vaulted roof with traces of wicker centring.

The plantation schemes of 1619 and 1620

A more thorough subjugation of the lordships in west and south Offaly finally got underway with the establishment of two plantation schemes, the first in August 1619 that covered Éile Uí Chearbhaill (along with Co. Longford), the second in October 1620 for Delbhna Eathra, Fir Cheall and Muintir Thadhgáin, along with Co. Leitrim, O'Melaghlen's country in Westmeath and Iregan in Co. Laois.[43] The alleged purpose of these schemes was to compel the midland lordships to conform to the norms of contemporary English society. It was envisaged that the newly arrived planters, by their example, would draw the indigenous population to the benefits of civil living and the succour of reformed religion. To ease this cultural transformation, the natives were to be assimilated into a new system of landholding, creating country estates based on English models. The native aristocracy were deprived of all their lands apparently due to lack of proper title, though by the terms of the plantation schemes they were to be restored to 75 per cent of their original property under the terms of English tenure.[44]

The proportions of the undertakers, which ranged from two hundred to one thousand acres of profitable land, were smaller than the proportions granted in Ulster because the British administration learnt from past experience that large grants of land were inimical to the interests of the plantations.[45] Only a minority of undertakers granted one thousand acres or more were to hold their lands by knight service, and were also required to build a castle within a bawn. The majority of undertakers, granted less than one thousand acres, were to hold their lands by common soccage, a tenure without severe military obligations. Still, these undertakers were required to build strong houses on their holdings. The nature of the building involved was commensurate with the size of the land grant. Undertakers granted between six hundred and one thousand acres were to build a strong house with a bawn, while those granted less than six hundred acres were to build a good stone house. These undertakers were obliged to fulfil their obligations within three years.[46] The larger undertakers, of six hundred acres or more, were also to have local jurisdiction over their tenants. Each of these larger proportions was to be created a manor, with a court baron to deal with tenant disputes, while those of one thousand acres and more were to have a court leet as well, to deal with minor criminal offences.[47]

In Ulster, it was envisaged that a whole spectrum of British society would be transplanted, together with a stringent military role for the undertakers and their British tenants. Under the midland plantations, only a thin spread of British landowners was contemplated, with a vague military role, which amounted only to the stipulation that the few undertakers with the largest proportions were to build castles. These undertakers, by example of their own lives, were to inspire the local population to civility and the state religion. This agenda was also to be supported by the introduction of English forms of tenure, estate organization, settlement and education.[48] Also in contrast to Ulster, the midland undertakers in general were not required to settle tenants of British origin on their lands. Indeed, the introduction of British tenants was only a peripheral aspect of the midland plantations.[49] They were expected, however, to grant leases to native tenants, with conditions designed to promote anglicization.[50] The plantation scheme sought to eradicate any trace of the old lordship, as natives were prohibited from using Gaelic titles such as the 'Great O'Carroll', or to yield the traditional dues of 'cup and maintenance'.[51] As a result, no Gaelic lord ever again assumed the chiefly role or demanded undivided allegiance from his people. Tenants were to build their houses in clusters and not in a dispersed manner; they were also encouraged to build a chimney in their houses and to lay out a garden and orchard. The leases were to follow the contemporary English practice of three lives (or twenty-one years) and to be based on acres, the English standard measurement and not the Gaelic unit, the cartron. Novel agricultural practices were to be introduced, encouraging the development of a market-oriented agricultural sector; tenants were expected to sow a quantity of hempseed as a commercial crop, while the commoditization of farmland was to be encouraged, with each tenant of sixty acres expected to enclose ten acres with a bank.[52]

Despite the earnest aspirations of the planners, a commission report in 1622 covering the plantation scheme for Éile Uí Chearbhaill and Longford indicated that many of the undertakers were of insufficient means to become productive landowners. These individuals were only too willing to sell out at the earliest opportunity, and it is likely that they had solicited these grants of land with a view to making a quick profit.[53] Less than one third of the same undertakers had made some attempt to fulfil their building requirements. Some were engaged in building a new house as stipulated in the plantation scheme, while others were repairing existing castles. Other undertakers had materials ready for building. In general, however, the buildings were not completed within the stipulated three years, and on the majority of the proportions no attempt was made to fulfil these building obligations.[54]

The situation in Delbhna Eathra, Fir Cheall and Fox's Country was even less satisfactory. The report covering these areas (along with Leitrim and Iregan) stated that there was little residence and no building to report.[55] One of the major weaknesses in the plantations was the poverty of many undertakers, which prevented them from fulfilling their obligations of residence and building. Many of the undertakers were from the army, which was in financial crisis at the time. These army officers may have received proportions in lieu of pay to remedy their perilous state, despite the fact that they lacked the financial wherewithal to develop their lands according to the conditions of the plantation. As a result, these individuals, keen to sell and make a fast profit, clearly undermined the principal objective of establishing a stable landowning class of British origin in these lordships.[56] The plantations of the midland territories produced fewer new castles and bawns than was the case in the Ulster Plantation, where Nicholas Pynnar felt able to claim that 107 castles had been built.[57]

Mac Cuarta states that the contribution of the plantation schemes to the long-term viability of planter society was less than that made by informal migration of settlers, which was a feature of the years pre- and post-dating the plantation.[58] The real contribution of the Jacobean plantation schemes was the creation of a large group of landowners who were keen to sell their lands, thus increasing the fluidity of the land market in west and south Offaly.[59] Undertakers who were willing to sell did not lack a market of ready purchasers for their lands, as enterprising newcomers such as de Renzy and Laurence Parsons were keen to expand their holdings.[60] While de Renzy held only two hundred acres in Offaly in 1622, by 1641 his son held 1,226 acres in the same county. Similarly, the Parsons family, who were granted one thousand acres in Éile Uí Chearbhaill under the plantation scheme for the area, had by 1641 extended the family property to over 5,400 acres there.[61] Thus, while the schemes in their own right failed to attract British settlers, the partial dismemberment of native lands opened up the region to less formal movements of settlers in the post-plantation era.

The new settler society made a significant contribution in terms of investment and enterprise to the economic development of west and south Offaly during the 1620s and 1630s. Despite the problems of compelling undertakers to build houses, investment in building was certainly a feature of economic activity. Native and planter landowners alike built brand new residences according to the latest fashions, while the pre-plantation practice of adapting existing castles for use as settler residences continued. For example, Birr Castle, which once belonged to Teige McCalloghe O'Carroll, was taken over by Sir Laurence Parsons as his residence and subsequently adapted to his needs as a country gentleman and local grandee.[62]

The establishment of villages and towns was also encouraged in the new dispensation, as nucleated populations not only facilitated the growth of industry and civil living, but also created a market for the produce of the new country estates. Kinnitty was granted a market in 1619, while other market settlements were established in Banagher (1612) and Birr (1620), also known as Parsonstown. The latter two settlements were eventually incorporated as boroughs in 1628 and by 1672 respectively.[63] The limited evidence would suggest that settlers were concentrated in a few places rather than being evenly scattered across the midland territories. John Bramhall, a Protestant clergyman, wrote an account of a journey to Lord Deputy Wentworth in 1634 in which he

> travelled fifty miles to the old Burre or new Parsons Town before I met with any remarkable footsteps of a plantation or at least any society of planters. This only town I found yet in all my journey fit to accommodate a traveller, having tradesmen in it of all kinds.[64]

According to a rental taken in 1641, Birr contained at least thirty settler households.[65] The building of a house in the English fashion was a condition of tenement leases in the town, and tenants were also expected to engage in municipal works such as paving streets and waste disposal.[66]

Local landlords could play a prominent part in encouraging the development of local market economies. Sir Laurence Parsons received the grant of a weekly market for Birr in 1620 along with two fairs per year, and was granted a further two fairs subsequently. He encouraged the development of industry in the area by inviting a Huguenot glassmaker, Abraham Bigo, to establish a glass factory on the outskirts of the town at Clonoghill in 1623. Parsons died in 1627, but the legacy of his patronage lived on. An assessment of 1641 showed Éile Uí Chearbhaill to be of greater fiscal value than any other area in Offaly (in fact, it accounted almost for one third of the whole county).[67]

Out in the country estates, substantial tenant farmers invested in farm buildings, such as barns and limekilns, while lesser tenants restricted themselves to building dwelling houses. The productivity of farmland was improved by settlers introducing new methods of fertilizing, with the use of marl and lime. Attempts were also made by settlers to drain the extensive bogs in the area.[68] Cattle and sheep rearing, along with the growing of corn, were common agricultural activities. Planter farmers introduced new strains of English cattle and sheep onto their lands, as Irish stock was reckoned to be very small; indeed, in west Offaly, some large-scale cattle farmers were rearing cattle for the Dublin market.[69] A by-product of this pastoral activity was the prevalence of tanning throughout the region, arising from the supply of cattle-hides and the ready availability of bark from nearby woodlands.

Despite less emphasis being placed in the Jacobean schemes on establishing a large British population, depositions taken in the aftermath of the 1641 uprising reveal that settler society in the midlands was indeed broadly based, and in no way confined to landlords. Planters included servants and apprentices, who were young single people living within the households of their masters. There were skilled tradesmen, including carpenters, clothiers, masons, smiths and tanners, as well as shopkeepers and innkeepers. Migrant workers such as the Huguenots were involved with the glassworks near Birr. There was also a small professional group, which consisted mostly of clergy, though there was a schoolmaster, Thomas Mitchell, of the freeschool at Birr. The most numerous group, however, was the tenant farmers.[70]

Clearly, fundamental social, economic and political changes were wrought upon the Offaly landscape, but if the Jacobean plantations were not primarily responsible, then what was driving such changes? Raymond Gillespie suggests that change in most localities, whether planted or not, appears to have been brought about by an incipient capitalism that encouraged the adoption of new foodways, fashions and furnishings, and consequently new values that informed relations between natives and newcomers as both groups manipulated the new market economy, developing commercial skills unrelated to religious or ethnic background.[71] This is evident in the archaeological record, with an increased volume in goods recovered from excavations, including imported pottery, tobacco pipes, wine glass and glass bottles. The plantations in Ireland were not necessarily responsible for driving the social and economic change that swept across the country in the early modern era; likewise, on the other side of the Atlantic, there was a substantive population living all year round in Newfoundland by the end of the seventeenth century, despite the weakness of the formal English plantations on that island in the early 1600s.[72]

CHAPTER 4

The human landscape of early modern Offaly

Introduction

Unfortunately, detailed surveys made for the Jacobean plantations of the midlands have not survived.[1] These documents would have provided scholars with a more thorough insight into the nature of the physical environment that the newly arrived settlers would have encountered. The utilization of published primary sources and published histories, pollen analysis and cartographic sources, however, ameliorates the lack of detailed surveys to a certain extent. De Renzy, writing in a more positive mood a few years before the advent of the plantations in the area, remarked upon 'a goodly country as any may be had … with all manner of commodities as fish, fowl, wood & water'.[2]

The topography of west and south Offaly is quite varied, containing different landscapes and environments. To the southeast, the Slieve Blooms, with their almost treeless landscapes covered by blanket bog and rough pasture, form a common border with Co. Laois. These mountains, consisting of Devonian Red Sandstone and Silurian Shale, range in elevation from 130 to 510m above sea level.[3] Such an environment contrasts with the floodplain of the River Shannon to the west. Here, along the fringes of that great meandering river, the wet meadows of the callows create a rich mix of herbs and grasses along with willow and alder trees. Such trees adapted to waterlogged conditions also grow on the peripheries of the extensive raised bogs found across all of Offaly. In between these two extremes, the topography of the county varies from rolling to gently undulating countryside, where drier limestone soils prevail. The lordships of west and south Offaly were located within the catchment basin of the River Shannon, where tributary rivers such as the Brosna, the Little Brosna, the Camcor, the Clodiagh, the Silver and the Tullamore flow generally westward and eventually drain into the Shannon. Indeed, many of these rivers have their water source in the Slieve Blooms. After the Shannon, the Brosna is the principle river in the region (fig. 1.2).

Gaelic-Irish estate organization

Generally speaking, Gaelic lordships or *oireacht* consisted of the chiefry lands or demesne of the lord, with the surrounding territories ruled on the lord's behalf by his kin-related subordinate lords, the *uirríthe*. In west and south Offaly, a tower house was

4.1 The Offaly landscape is dotted with the remains of castles – in the foreground are the vestiges of Togher Castle, with Doon Castle a short distance away in the background.

located in the core territory of the lord, with associated houses, cabins and ancillary buildings. In the vicinity of the tower house was the lord's own estate, consisting of a number of ballybetaghs that made up the *uirrí* or demesne lands and the *lucht tighe* or mensal lands, which were held for the provisioning of a lord's household, as well as ancestral church lands. Such settlements had proto-urban functions and often went on to become market towns with administrative functions under English rule. The lord also held other castles throughout the lordship with specific functions such as to control strategic routeways or the gathering of taxes and tribute. The kinsmen, brothers and cousins of the lord played a core role in gathering money and food rents, as well as coordinating raids, defence and hospitality when necessary. These *uirríthe* also resided in tower houses, creating focal points of settlement in their respective territories (fig. 4.1). These minor lords in turn were supported in the running of these territories by local clan or sept leaders. This 'local gentry' resided in their own ballybetaghs, and fulfilled the necessary ceremonial, military and administrative obligations at a local level. The ballybetagh itself was comprised of a number of townlands. The townland was the primary land unit, surviving the erosion of native territorial organization in the sixteenth and early seventeenth centuries to become the standard basis of landholding in the post-medieval era.[4]

The conditions of the plantations covering the midland territories encouraged tenants to build in clusters, and not in a dispersed manner, inferring the general lack of nucleated settlement at the time. While the Down Survey of 1657 illustrates nucleated settlement in this post-plantation landscape, many of these settlements were probably medieval in origin. The survey depicts clusters of houses surrounding medieval churches and castles at Ballyboy, Garbally, Cully and Rathrobbin in Fir Cheall, while in Éile Uí Chearbhaill, groups of houses are associated with castles at Curralanty and Clonlisk. Given the stylistic nature of the Down Survey, it would be wrong to use these depictions as a complete account of either the number of nucleated settlements within an area or the number of houses within a particular settlement. However, such depictions at Ballycowan and Srah (in the townland of Ballydrohid) in Fir Cheall are labelled 'Castle & Towne', indicating that nucleated settlement could be found with tower houses as their focal points. In 1620, Luke Gernon, an Englishman, described a settlement in Co. Limerick similar to what would have been found in the Offaly landscape:

> In every village is a castle, and church, but bothe in ruyne. The baser cottages are built of underwood, called wattle, and covered some wth thatch and some wth green sedge, of a round forme and wth out chimneys, and to my imaginacōn resemble so many hives of bees, about a country farme.[5]

Pastoral farming

Approximately 70 per cent of the total land area of Co. Offaly is now devoted to pastoral activity; however, pollen analysis has revealed that early modern livestock was not reared on the smooth, treeless meadows that are prevalent today, but in an environment dominated by a mix of meadow grasses and hazel scrub.[6] Agriculture in the Gaelic lordships of the sixteenth century was predominantly pastoral and self-sufficient, with cattle considered the principal form of wealth, featuring prominently in dowries, jointures and even mortgages. Indeed, cattle were still used occasionally as a medium of exchange.[7] Transhumance played an integral role by which cattle were taken to more distant pastures on hills, mountains and bogs.[8] This practice of semi-nomadic pastoral farming attracted the ire of English propagandists who saw it as conducive to laziness and licentiousness, as well as providing places of refuge for rebels and criminals. In Spenser's *View of the present state of Ireland*,[9] one of the two principle characters, Irenaeus, observes that 'There is one use among them, to keep their cattle and to live themselves the most part of the year in bollies, pasturing upon the mountain and waste wild places, and removing still to fresh land as they have depastured the former days'.[10] Such accounts failed to recognize that the grazing rights in these marginal locations were normally related to the amount of land held in cultivated areas adjacent to lowland settlements.[11] Through the course of the seventeenth century, cattle-raising was to be intensified, with landowners in Ireland responding to market opportunities in England, with significant exports of tallow, hides, butter, barrelled beef and cattle on the hoof.[12] Sir William Petty, the chief surveyor behind the Down Survey, estimated in 1672 that across the country as a whole, only five hundred thousand acres of land was under tillage, compared with seven million acres of grassland.[13]

Tillage land

It would be wrong, however, to underplay the importance of tillage in agriculture in this period, with oats, barley, wheat, rye and some legumes being cultivated.[14] Cultivated areas could be farmed in common, sometimes subdivided into separate strips and plots that were redistributed periodically.[15] In the Tudor wars of the second half of the sixteenth century, it was standard practice among English troops to destroy crops in recalcitrant lordships, depriving the rebels of an important food source. In neighbouring Co. Laois, during the Nine Years War in 1599, Fynes Moryson described English troops destroying crops to the value of over ten thousand pounds, observing that

> it seemed incredible that by so barbarous inhabitants the ground should be so manured, the fields so orderly fenced, the townes so frequently inhabited, and the high waies and paths so well beaten as the Lord Deputy here found them. The reason whereof was that the Queens forces during these warrs never till then came among them.[16]

Agriculture in Éile Uí Chearbhaill seems to have revolved around corn and cattle. The Down Survey of 1657 describes the land of the barony of Clonlisk, one of the two component baronies in the original O'Carroll lordship, as 'for the most part ffertill, consisting of arable, meadow and pasture with good brush wood and timber trees', though Loeber believes that only one fifth of the lordship as a whole was profitable.[17]

The enclosure of the landscape

As well as illustrating the importance of arable farming, the account of Moryson, above, intriguingly alludes to well laid out enclosures for tillage in Co. Laois at the end of the sixteenth century, though whether these were of a temporary or a permanent nature is not known. Accounts provide an impression of a largely unenclosed landscape in Ireland, with the exception of parts of the south and east, and in areas surrounding the larger urban centres. Co. Kilkenny was described in 1598 as possessing 'the most show of civilitie of any other of the border counties, in respect of the fayre seats of houses, the number of castles and the Inglysh manner of inclosure of their grounds'.[18] An engraving of the siege of Cahir Castle in Co. Tipperary in 1599, subsequently published in *Pacata Hibernia*, illustrates both substantial and insubstantial field enclosures in the surrounding landscape, including wattle fencing. In among the fields stand trees singly or in pairs.[19] This recalls an entry in the Down Survey for the barony of Ballycowan in which the land is described as 'arrable, meadowe and pasture adorned with pleasant groves', though there is no explicit evidence for the widespread enclosure of farmland in early modern Offaly. As mentioned in the previous chapter, the plantation schemes of 1619 and 1620 stipulated that each tenant of sixty acres was expected to enclose ten acres with a bank, suggesting a general lack of enclosure across the countryside.[20] The enclosure of farmland was to be found in some areas of Gaelic Ireland, however; for example, in the O'Conor lordship of north Roscommon, a church enclosure at Carns is surrounded by a system of relict earthen boundaries that may be medieval.[21]

Overall, though, the imposition of new estate structures across early modern Ireland saw the basis for the first systematic planning of field systems. A 1598 map of an estate at Mogeely, Co. Cork, belonging to one of the more prominent planters in Munster, Sir Walter Raleigh, depicts an ordered pattern of fields bearing names such as 'the Parke Close' and 'the Barly Cloase'.[22] Archaeological evidence for the process of enclosing the early modern landscape has been uncovered elsewhere: the excavation of a farming settlement in Baltrasna, Co. Meath, revealed at least three adjacent rectangular field enclosures, aligned on a north–south axis and defined by large drainage ditches, up to 6m in width and 1.5m in depth. The few finds from the ditch and associated features suggest that the field system had been laid out in either the seventeenth or the early eighteenth century.[23] Certainly, in the late seventeenth century, economic conditions dictated by the 1663 and 1667 Cattle Acts, which banned live cattle exports to Britain, encouraged a move away from pastoral farming towards tillage. This, in turn, provided a greater incentive to enclose land so as to prevent cattle encroaching upon crops.[24] Writing in 1682, Sir Henry Piers gave an account of local farming practices in Westmeath, where tillage ground was enclosed though pastoral land was left open.[25] As late as 1709, however, Thomas Molyneux described open countryside without enclosures between Kilconnell and Athenry in east Co. Galway, suggesting that the process of enclosing the Irish countryside was a prolonged affair that was not concluded until the eighteenth century, the rate of enclosure varying regionally.[26] Unfortunately, the extant cartographic and documentary sources for Co. Offaly do not allow for a detailed analysis of the rate of field enclosure in the area during the seventeenth century.

The raised bogs

Raised bogs are commonplace in Offaly, covering 34 per cent of the total land area of the county.[27] There are extensive tracts of such bogland across Garrycastle and adjoining areas of Eglish, Ballyboy, Ballycowan and Kilcoursey. De Renzy described Delbhna Eathra as 'an island in itself & that no arable land of it doth meet with any other country but by only bogs & woods, [and] water'.[28] A comparison of the modern extent of bog with a county map in William Petty's *Hiberniae Delineatio* (1685) illustrates that, despite major reclamation and industrial peat extraction, the extent of bogland has essentially remained the same in the last three hundred years or so (fig. 4.2).[29] In the early modern period, peat would have provided the chief fuel for the bulk of the population, with the environment also providing opportunities for hunting, the collection of reeds for thatching, bog timbers for structural purposes and herbs for medicinal needs. The topographical files of the National Museum of Ireland are peppered with references to finds of bog butter, with the butter often contained in wooden vessels and buried in the peaty layers. As well as woodlands, the boglands also provided the local population with a refuge from raids and attacks, an important consideration given the sporadic uprisings and military campaigns that consumed the region through the course of the sixteenth and seventeenth centuries.[30]

Forestry

The forests of Ireland were the subject of much comment by Tudor and Stuart writers, who considered these sylvan environments as wildernesses that needed to be brought into the realm of civil society. These forests attracted attention either as a source of quick profit for adventurers, the strongholds of recalcitrant rebels, woodkernes and tories, or the lairs of wolves.[31] Estimates of woodland coverage in Ireland at the start of the seventeenth century range from one-eighth of the total land area to just 2 per cent.[32] The woods in Ireland *c.*1600 lacked the variety of trees that can be found in today's woodland. The only evergreens in the country at the time were holly, juniper and yew, while the broad leaved species were dominated by oak, with hazel, birch, alder and, to a lesser extent, ash, also to be found.[33]

The Civil Survey (1654–6) utilized labels such as 'pasturable wood', 'woody pasture', 'underwood' and 'copps', indicative of wood management and woodmanship.[34] But it is precisely in this period that the excessive exploitation of woodland, principally to supply staves for barrel-making and charcoal for iron smelting, brought about the disappearance of Ireland's forests. In this regard, it is pertinent to acknowledge that the felling of woodland will rarely obliterate a tree species, as woodland will regenerate even when cleared repeatedly. What changed in the seventeenth century was that these woodlands failed to grow back as they had done in the past. It is thought that the decline of the Gaelic order brought about changes

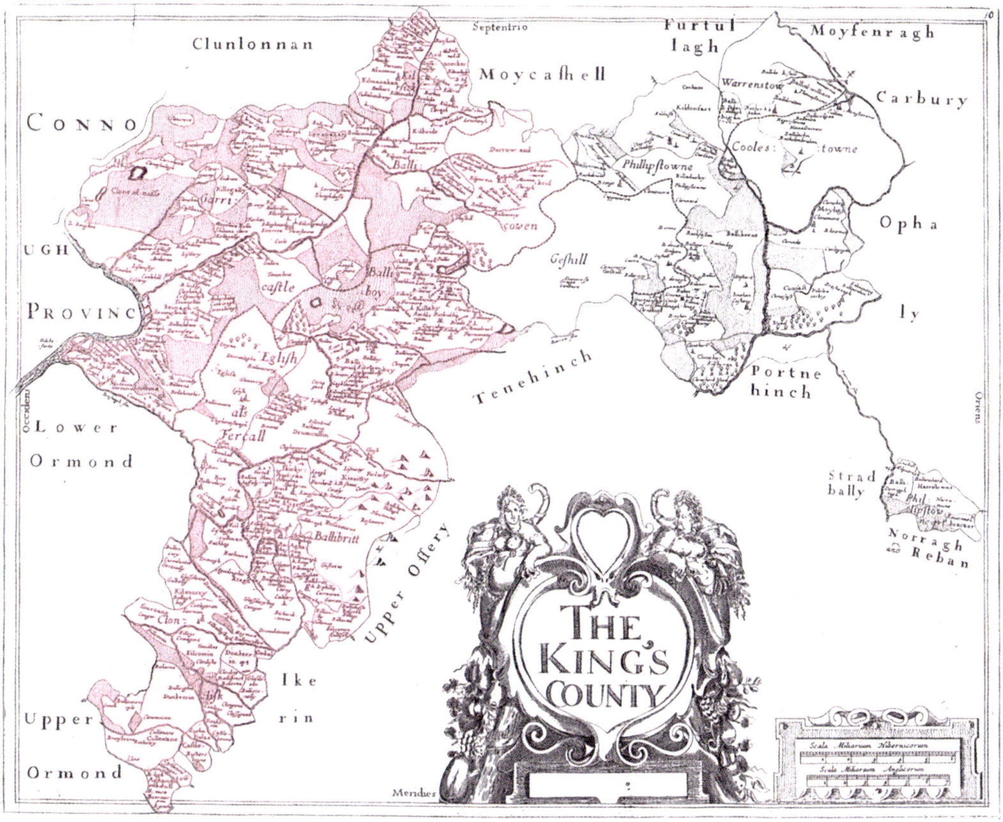

4.2 William Petty's map of present day Co. Offaly; published in *Hiberniae Delineatio* in 1685 (but based on survey work carried out in 1655–7). The area highlighted illustrates the portion of the county affected by the Jacobean plantation schemes of 1619–20. The areas stippled indicate the extent of bogland in the mid-seventeenth century.

in the way woodland and pasture was managed. Cattle encroaching on newly opened tracts of woodland, consuming newly grown grasslands, would have crushed young tree saplings and hence prevented woodland regeneration.[35] From the native perspective, the loss of such woodland could be seen as a metaphor for the collapse of the Gaelic order, as is evident in the lament poem *Cill Chais*.[36]

Cad a dhéanfaimid feasta gan adhmad
Tá deireadh na gcoillte ar lár
[What shall we do without timber
The last of our woods is gone]

Tracts of woodland would have been a feature of Offaly in this period, as evidenced by the numerous townland names in the county bearing the words *Ros, Doire* and

Coill, all of which mean wood or forest.[37] The O'Molloy lordship of Fir Cheall was noted for its extensive woodland, with a sixteenth-century commentator, John Dymmok, describing Fir Cheall as 'a place so stronge as nature could devise to make yt by wood and bogge, with which yt is environed'.[38] In a military campaign of 1599, the earl of Essex spent a whole day manoeuvring his troops from Durrow to Ballycowan in this lordship, a distance of only 6km as the crow flies, due to the dense woodland between the two locations.[39] In 1632, an inquisition refers to 'the greate woode of Fercall'.[40] William Petty's map of King's County of 1685 illustrates discrete tracts of woodland across Fir Cheall in the vicinity of Screggan, Broughal and Dowris. Apparently, traces of this woodland could still be found near the latter two locations at the turn of the twentieth century.[41] Inspection of the first edition of the Ordnance Survey six-inch series does not reveal any explicit evidence for such ancient woodland in Broughal or Dowris, with tree coverage in these areas confined to demesne landscaping, though, of course, such woodland may have been integrated into formal schemes of demesne parkland in the eighteenth and nineteenth centuries.

Pollen analysis carried out at Mongan Bog close to Clonmacnoise indicates that there were extensive oak woods in the vicinity certainly up to 1650.[42] These woods were mentioned as being used as a bird sanctuary to cultivate young goshawks, both male and female, half of which were to be delivered to the bishop of Meath for the purposes of falconry. Unfortunately, by 1622, indiscriminate tree-felling in these woods forced these birds of prey to vacate the locality, as the species required undisturbed woodland for its habitat.[43] Despite the depletion of this woodland, oak pollen values remained relatively high in Mongan Bog and did not fall until around the eighteenth century.[44]

Specific accounts of woodland in early modern Offaly, however, are few and far between. The surveys for the Jacobean plantations of 1619–20 are lost, though some lists of barony totals survive, divided according to land quality, such as 'profitable wood' and 'unprofitable wood and bog'. As 'unprofitable bog' is a separate category in these lists, 'unprofitable wood and bog' has been interpreted as woodland growing on bog or rocky ground unsuitable for either timber or pasture.[45] In the territory of Éile Uí Chearbhaill, the two categories of woodland, profitable and unprofitable, in an approximate manner, represent respectively 9.46 per cent and 9.15 per cent of the total land area, giving a high total of 18.61 per cent.[46] This percentage is appreciably higher than other parts of the country. Later in the seventeenth century, the Civil Survey of 1654 reveals a rough and approximate account of woodland coverage as percentage of the total area for other parts of the country such as the baronies of Muskerry, Co. Cork (11.4 per cent), Slieveardagh, Co. Tipperary (10) and St Mullins, Co. Carlow (9); however, other baronies such as Owneybeg, Co. Limerick (18.5) and Duffry, Co. Wexford (24) were comparable to Éile Uí Chearbhaill, even after decades of intensive timber exploitation.[47]

A major limitation of the Down Survey maps, produced in the mid-1650s, is that the vast acreages of land in Protestant hands were left unsurveyed. Nonetheless, this source can be used to identify the presence of surviving woodland. A perusal of the barony and parish maps of the Down Survey (1657), which survive for certain areas of west and south Offaly, reveal a landscape dominated by arable and pastural farmland, with discrete pockets of bog and woodland. The Cromwellian surveyors described the land in the barony of Clonlisk as 'for the most part ffertill consisting of arable, meadow and pasture with good brush wood and timber trees'. Compared to the relatively extensive woodland detailed in the earlier plantation surveys of 1619–20, however, the Down Survey parish maps covering Clonlisk indicate more limited woodland, with the parishes of Kilcolman, Kilcomin and Shinrone only containing some woods. In a parish adjacent to Shinrone, namely Kilmurryely, stood a little wood at Galbally, while twenty acres of a wood stood in the vicinity of Donough O'Carroll's household at Ballybrack in Roscrea parish. That such small areas of woodland merited attention from surveyors, whose brief was to identify profitable and unprofitable acreages, suggests that the landscape in the O'Carroll lordship was predominantly open by the mid-seventeenth century. In this respect, the parish of Cullenwaine was described with very little wood appearing in it, while the parish of Castletown, in part mountainous, was covered by no wood at all, but open pasture. Woodland was not even mentioned in relation to other parishes in the barony of Clonlisk, such as Finglas. This bears out John Feehan's comment in relation to the neighbouring barony of Ballybritt (also in Éile Uí Chearbhaill) that woodland on the Offaly side of the Slieve Blooms was scarce by the mid-seventeenth century, in contrast to the great tract of forestry that existed on the far side of the mountain range in Co. Laois.[48] While the unsustainable clearance of trees in Éile Uí Chearbhaill and elsewhere for agriculture and the timber industry was a major factor in the deforestation of the region, the practice of grazing animals would have prevented their regeneration, creating the open landscape that typifies Offaly today.

Communications

The communications system in Ireland at this time was not well regarded, with coastal and riverine routes being seen as the best means of long-distance transport. Sir George Carew, writing in 1600, stated that he had to retain a crompster [galley] 'to waft victual from Corke to Gallwaye'.[49] With strategic and economic concerns in mind, a Highway Act was passed in 1615 that required each parish annually to appoint two parishioners to act as surveyors and each farmer to send two able-bodied men, a horse team and tools to work on the roads on six days between Easter and summer. The running of this system was placed into the hands of county administrations in 1634. The road system in general, however, continued to be poorly developed in Ireland.[50] A complaint was made in 1623 that 'the ways are not passable as being smooth nor repaired, not yet much frequented by carriers, wainmen and like industrious men here so common'.[51]

Eskers – sinuous ridges of sands and gravels – were originally deposited by glacial meltwaters. These ridges weaving through the region facilitated communications across a landscape, which up to the seventeenth century was covered by bogland and forestry. Given Offaly's central location within Ireland, eskers such as Eiscir Riada and the Slighe Mór became well noted in documentary sources, allowing travel across long distances.[52] However, other communication routes were also opened up by the creation of passes through the woodland and wooden trackways across the bog, as illustrated on early modern copies of a mid-sixteenth-century map of east Laois and Offaly.[53] While most peatland in Offaly is now bereft of medieval and post-medieval layers due to extensive commercial milling, wooden trackways that can be roughly dated to the sixteenth and seventeenth centuries are not unknown. In the townlands of Lisdermot and Straduff, northwest of Lemanaghan in Delbhna Eathra, a trackway of gravel and wood dating to around the fifteenth or sixteenth century was found crossing the width of Corhill Bog for over 400m.[54] Due to the poor state of communication routes overland, one would expect rivers to have provided an important means of transportation. This is clearly highlighted by the fact that all the principal early modern settlements in west and south Offaly were located on rivers: Birr on the Camcor River and Banagher on the Shannon. A map of Banagher dated *c.*1630 illustrates a pair of rowing boats on the Shannon, which emphasizes the role that rivers offered as an expedient means of transport over long distances (fig. 4.3).[55] As well as providing routes for transport and communication, rivers were important as sources for drinking water and waste disposal. The currents of rivers also offered a potential source of power for flour mills, ironworks and other industries. Fishing rights were jealously guarded in this period, with weirs very much documented in leases and grants of property. One such weir, apparently of stone construction, is illustrated in Michael Richards' 1691 map of Birr (fig. 7.24).[56]

Conclusion

The landscape of Offaly is quite varied, with the mountains and low-lying peatlands occupying either end of a topographical spectrum, with gently undulating or rolling pastoral and arable countryside in between. Contemporary information on the appearance of the Offaly countryside is sparse, though pollen analysis and cartographic research has mitigated to a certain extent this dearth of knowledge. The mild climatic conditions, which encourage grass growth for around 270 days of the year, favoured a predominantly pastoral economy. Pollen analysis indicates that livestock were not reared on well-maintained pastures like today, but in an environment dominated by a mix of meadow grasses and hazel scrub. Arable farming was also an important activity. The break-up of the Gaelic-Irish landholding system and its replacement with English-style country demesnes saw the creation of estates whose

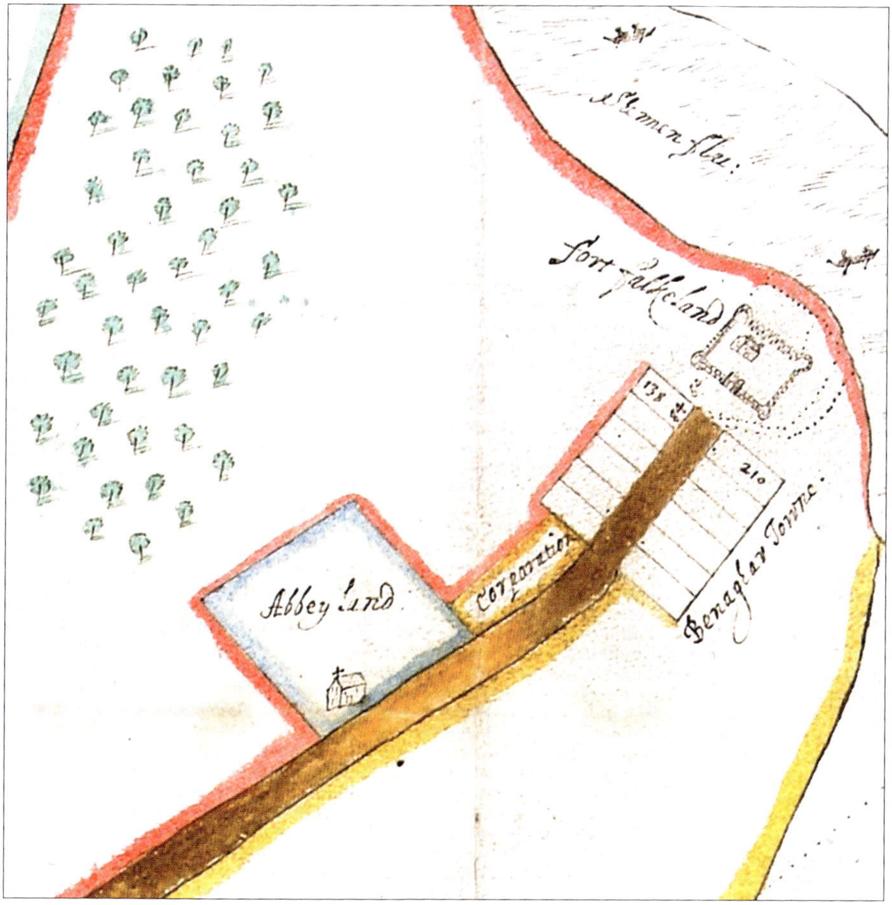

4.3 Map of Banagher, *c.*1630 (National Archives, London, MPF 1/268(6)).

produce was created for cash profit in a market economy. The imposition of these new estates also saw the basis for the first systematic planning of field systems enclosed by permanent hedgerows.

More marginal landscapes, such as bogs, mountains and forestry, attracted the attention of contemporary observers, whether to emphasize the non-productivity of these landscapes according to the norms of a capitalist economy, or to highlight the fact that these areas offered sanctuary to both rebels and wolves. Changes in land management during the seventeenth century prevented the regeneration of forestry, allowing for the landscape to become more open than it had been in the medieval period. Comparing official surveys in 1619–20 and 1655–7 illustrates the general depletion of woodland in one lordship, Éile Uí Chearbhaill. Due to the poorly developed nature of roads, especially in areas with raised peatland and woodland, natural routes of access such as rivers or eskers were utilized. Settlement, whether nucleated or dispersed, for the most part appears to have concentrated on the rolling or undulating countryside free from forestry or bog. Survey work by the Irish Archaeological Wetland Unit of the raised peatlands in Offaly, however, revealed a small number of timber hurdles and trackways of general late medieval/early modern date. The likelihood of hunting camps similar to early medieval and prehistoric examples cannot be dismissed. Even with the advent of a capitalist mercantile economy, there was still a level of self-sufficiency dependent on whatever resources were available in the local environment. Hence, landscapes such as forestry, river meadows and bogs provided sources for fuel, building material and hunting. The predominant bedrock in the area, either limestone or sandstone, was also sourced by the resident population for a variety of buildings through the sixteenth and seventeenth centuries. These buildings are the focus of analysis and discussion in the following chapters.

CHAPTER 5

The tower house: an old building in a new world?

Introduction

Tower houses are one of the most common archaeological monuments in the Irish landscape, suggesting the widespread popularity of the castellated building across the social spectrum of late medieval and early modern Ireland. Conleth Manning estimates that 1,200 tower houses remain in varying states of preservation, of the 3,000 that were originally built.[1] Taking into account the numerous sites of demolished castles depicted on seventeenth-century Down Survey maps and the nineteenth-century Ordnance Survey maps, David Sweetman suggests a higher figure of around 3,800 tower houses.[2] Alternatively, on the basis of another seventeenth-century source – the Civil Survey – it has been proposed that 7,000 tower houses were erected, a radical figure suggesting that Ireland was one of the most heavily castellated countries in Europe.[3] Tower houses certainly proliferated in some areas – just over four hundred castles, the majority of which were tower houses, have been recorded in Co. Limerick alone, the heart of the earldom of Desmond, though it is suggested that only two hundred were perhaps in use by the mid-seventeenth century.[4] Despite their large numbers, the distribution of tower houses is rather uneven across the country: there is a relatively low number of tower houses in south central Ulster and north Connacht, when compared with the numbers to be found in Munster, Leinster and south Connacht, suggesting a greater diversity in the nature of Gaelic elite settlement. In areas lacking tower houses, the Gaelic lords, and their dependent physicians, poets and brehons, lived in houses probably made of timber, clay and wattle, surrounded by bawns made of sods, and judging from Richard Bartlett's maps of settlements in Ulster *c.*1601, such structures could be quite substantial.[5] Indeed, in areas with lakes, crannogs appear to have seen continuous usage right into the seventeenth century.[6] In the Offaly lordships, tower houses were the predominant elite residence around 1600; Éile Uí Chearbhaill had at least forty-five castles, compared to the eleven surviving tower houses today, while de Renzy counted twenty-eight castles in Delbhna Eathra, with only eight upstanding examples at present (fig. 5.1).[7] Rolf Loeber has compiled documented dates for the building of Gaelic castles across Ireland between 1370 and 1600, commenting that dated castles in Delbhna Eathra, with few exceptions, originate from the second half of the sixteenth century, reiterating the statement of a late eighteenth-century observer that

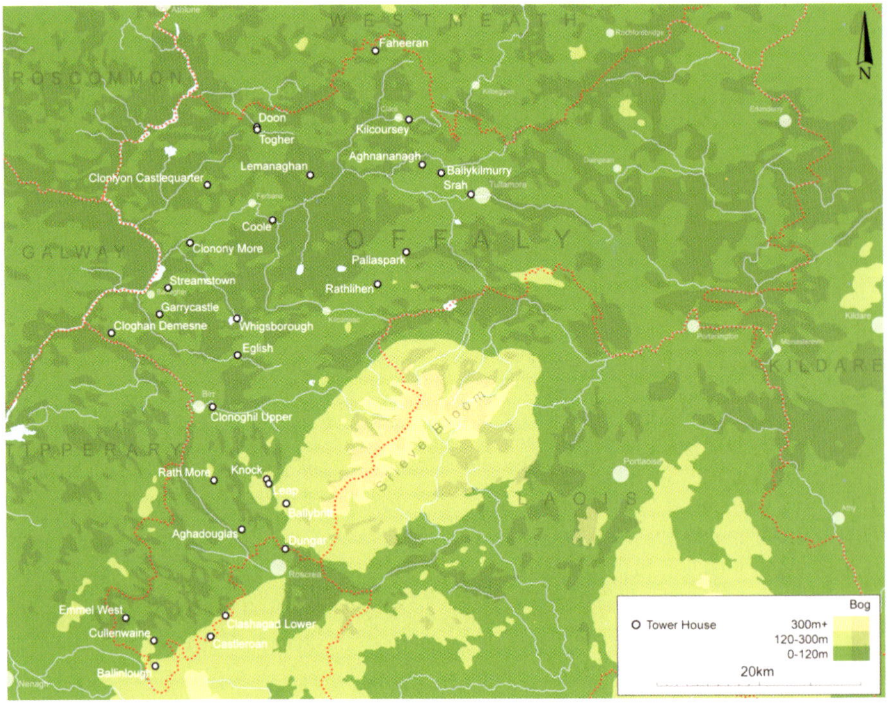

5.1 Distribution of tower houses in west and south Offaly (prepared by Conor McDermott and Hugh Kavanagh).

this territory 'abounds with ruins of the MacCoghlan's castles, [which] all have Latin inscriptions showing that they were built in Elizabethan times'.[8] This ties in well with fieldwork carried out by the Archaeological Survey of Ireland in Co. Offaly, where the majority of the forty-three tower houses recorded date to the late sixteenth and early seventeenth centuries.[9]

This chapter introduces the reader to the basic layout and form of tower houses in the region, as well as discussing their cultural and social background. While these tower houses are now rather dark, dank forlorn ruins, such buildings could be contrived by landed families, both native and newcomer, to create comfortable living spaces embued with notions of gentility and civility. The remains of these buildings allow for a consideration of the spatial arrangements and furnishings of the hall and other chambers that were considered necessary in wealthy late medieval and early modern households. Features such as the parapets of tower houses, ancillary hall buildings and bawns are also discussed in detail. Such features were integral to the principles of castle architecture in a defensive and metaphorical manner, becoming motifs of lordship itself. Gender relations within elite households in the period are also touched upon, before the chapter finally considers the defensive attributes of tower houses and their associated bawns.

5.2 View of a MacCoghlan tower house at Coole. Matthew de Renzy described the castle in 1620, then in the hands of Sir John MacCoghlan, as 'a very good castle and pleasant land and meadows about it'.

The tower house in west and south Offaly

While tower houses were built in both Gaelic Irish and Anglo-Irish lordships between the fifteenth and the seventeenth century, it is clear that the origin of this architectural form is to be found among the original colonial families who were accustomed to living in masonry castles since the late twelfth century. It is not certain how tower houses evolved in their earliest phase of development, which was probably in the fourteenth century, though it has been suggested that the earlier Anglo-Norman donjons of the thirteenth century, as well as the halls within larger castle complexes, or the freestanding hall houses also of thirteenth-century date, may have been a source of inspiration.[10] The cylindrical tower houses at Dungar and Rath More in Éile Uí Chearbhaill may indeed have been inspired by the thirteenth-century donjon of similar shape at Nenagh Castle in the neighbouring lordship of Ormond. Whatever their cultural origins, the native lords and gentry clearly saw such buildings as appropriate to their needs – the vertical, and in many instances hierarchical, arrangement of rooms, possessing a homologous relationship with the social order of late medieval Gaelic Ireland.[11]

The general layout and form of tower houses has been outlined by various authors over the years.[12] The examples in west and south Offaly for the most part share the attributes of tower houses found elsewhere in the west and south of Ireland, possessing a rectilinear plan (with the exception of the cylindrical examples found at Dungar and Rath More), extending three to five storeys in height, with the roofline crowned by crenellated battlements (figs 5.2, 5.3). Entry was typically gained through a double-centred doorway, protected on the outside by an iron grill known as a yett or grate. There was one to two chambers on each floor, with smaller chambers built into the thicknesses of walls. Access to the upper floors was usually via a spiral stairwell ascending from one corner of the tower house to the battlements. The upper floors were provided with larger, more ornate windows, fireplaces and garderobes. Windows came in a variety of shapes and sizes, but were typically flat-, round- or ogee-headed, with the larger examples divided into separate lights by mullions and transoms. Vaults could be placed over the ground and second floors, built using wickerwork matting. Not withstanding certain regionalisms, there appears to have been little innovation in the appearance of tower houses between the late fourteenth and mid-sixteenth century, highlighting a pronounced degree of stylistic conservatism on the part of their builders. On the basis of form, layout and the treatment of discrete architectural features such as window and door surrounds, it is difficult to differentiate between a tower house built in 1440 and one built a hundred years later, without the aid of documentary sources or tree-ring dates. It is only in the late sixteenth century that changes occurred, with the insertion of larger square-hooded windows, the provision of in-built fireplaces served by tall chimney stacks, the impediment of movement along the battlements with roof gables now built flush with the walls below, as well as the removal of vaulting. The incorporation of date-and-initial stones is also a feature of some of these later tower houses. A number of examples can be found across the midlands including Garronmaconly, Co. Laois, and Behamore in north Tipperary.[13] Fieldwork and documentary evidence suggests that many of these tower houses were also accompanied by ancillary halls, sometimes built of stone, in other instances of timber. Both the tower house and accompanying buildings would be protected by a walled courtyard or bawn.

The tower house form, though differing in details and layout, was also known in northern Britain. When John Briscoe of Crofton Hall, near Thurby in Cumbria, moved to Fir Cheall in the 1580s, he lived at Ballydrohid in Srah Castle, a tower house that was an architectural form also to be found in his homeland.[14] It is not known what stood at Crofton Hall in the sixteenth century (all that remains of its nineteenth-century successor is an attractive gate entrance and stable block), but a few stand-alone tower houses are to be found elsewhere in Cumbria, typically sixteenth century in date and located near the Scottish border.[15] The best examples are those built by the Grahams at Brackenhill (either built or occupied by the family in 1586) and Kirkandrews (built by 1552) (interestingly, in an effort to quell feuding

5.3 The tower house at Dungar, which was in the hands of Rory O'Carroll and his wife Finola O'Brien in 1640 (© National Monuments Service: Department of Arts, Heritage and the Gaeltacht).

in the border country, this family were deported to Ireland in the sixteenth century).[16] Like their Irish counterparts, these Cumbrian tower houses possessed ground floors that were covered by barrel vaults and lit by narrow loops. The upper floors, provided with fireplaces and larger windows, were reached via a newel stairwell. Given the close proximity to the border, Scottish influences are evident in these two tower houses, with openings framed by simple roll-mouldings, the roof gables decorated with crowstepping, and the battlements in each instance carried on a moulded and corbelled projection.[17] Kirkandrews is also provided with a bawn-like enclosure known as a barmkin (laid out as late as 1827, though possibly replacing an earlier barmkin).[18] As well as protecting the tower house, these barmkins may have contained ancillary buildings such as kitchens, brewhouses and other farm buildings.[19] According to Peter Ryder, though, evidence of such enclosures associated with towers of any form is slight in Cumbria and Northumberland.[20]

There are twenty-nine upstanding examples of tower houses recorded in west and south Offaly, and these have survived to varying degrees of preservation. On the basis of their preservation, these tower houses can be divided into three groups. Only seven have survived to the extant that their internal spaces can be more or less fully reconstructed: Ballinlough, Dungar and Leap in Éile Uí Chearbhaill, Clonony More, Coole and Doon in Delbhna Eathra, and Srah in Fir Cheall. Another nine have fared less well, often only reaching first-floor level: Ballybritt, Cullenwaine and Rath More in Éile Uí Chearbhaill; Ballykilmurry, Eglish and Rathlihen in Fir Cheall; Clonlyon Castlequarter and Togher in Delbhna Eathra; followed by Kilcoursey in Fox's Country (fig. 5.4). The ruinous nature of this group prohibits complete reconstruction of their original room layouts, but their extant walls with surviving architectural features offer a valuable corpus of material to compare with the first group. The third and final group is composed of eleven sites with only ephemeral traces of what were once tower houses. This group consists of Aghadouglas, Castleroan, Clashagad Lower, Clonoghil Upper and Knock in the O'Carroll lordship; Faheeran, Lemanaghan and Streamstown in Delbhna Eathra; and Aghnananagh, Pallaspark and Whigsborough in Fir Cheall. Two other tower houses were not available for survey: Emmel West, a fully preserved tower house in Éile Uí Chearbhaill and Garrycastle, a partially upstanding building in Delbhna Eathra.

In addition to these tower houses, there are sixty known sites of castles in west and south Offaly. They have been identified through documentary sources, various editions of the Ordnance Survey, seventeenth-century cartographic sources such as the Down Survey barony and parish maps, surviving place-names and local tradition. There are generally little or no upstanding remains of these castles, which precludes more specific classifications for them. In certain instances, however, historical documentation suggests that most of them were probably tower houses or fortified houses. Despite obvious limitations, cognisance of such sites allows for a more meaningful appraisal of the early modern archaeological landscape.

5.4 MacCoghlan tower house at Clonlyon Castlequarter, with various floors and vault exposed.

The tower house in plantation society

Whatever their actual numbers, it is clear that the construction of tower houses involved a considerable outlay of resources. In the 1570s, tower houses in Co. Down such as Mahee Castle and Narrow Water cost £300 and £361 4*s*. 2*d*. respectively to build.[21] Forty years later, in the Irish midlands, de Renzy reckoned that the 'meanest' castle could not be built for less than £600 or £700.[22] This compares to substantial country residences in England that could be built for under £2,000 in the same period.[23] Sir John Davies, one of the chief architects of the Ulster Plantation, reckoned that in Gaelic society only the chieftains were builders of stone castles, and that 'never any [other] particular person ... did build any stone or brick house for his private habitation'.[24] Contrary to Davies' opinion, of the forty-five castles in Éile Uí Chearbhaill in *c.*1600, only nineteen (42 per cent) were on O'Carroll demesne land.[25] This level of castle building on lands not directly held by the dominant chief sept suggests that other classes such as freeholders, galloglasses, poets and chroniclers in Éile Uí Chearbhaill embraced the use of tower houses. The number of freeholders in Gaelic lordships varied much, but nonetheless constituted a substantial portion of the upper social levels in native society. Many of these freeholders or minor septs were holders of church lands, which often functioned as buffer zones between rival chiefs, as they carried with them the right of sanctuary. In Delbhna Eathra, Melaghlin O'Dalaghan, whose family originally had come into the lordship as 'church men', built Lisclooney Castle in 1556. Intriguingly, this castle was described in 1620 as built 'uppon a church wall', and a 'fine and stately seat of a castle ... English-like seated with a fine parke neare it and goodly meddows belonging to it upon the Shenen [Shannon] side'.[26]

To be an elite man in Offaly in the early modern period was to be at the centre of a social milieu that embraced a series of discourses on issues such as lordship, honour, traditional rights, loyalty to the crown, religious affiliation and ethnicity – discourses that were neither real nor fantasy, but were part of a complex ideological package that guided both the mundane and ceremonial in a substantive manner. The occupation of tower houses in sixteenth- and early seventeenth-century Offaly has to be placed against a social and ideological background that was being transformed. This period can be characterized as an anxious time for the native elite, whose power base was under threat from the expansionist tendencies of a Tudor state that sought to centralize authority in the workings of a government, located both in London and in Dublin. The experience of the O'Connors in east Offaly, who were decimated by successive military expeditions and land confiscations, would not have been lost on their neighbours. Gaelic-Irish lordships legitimized their power and authority by upholding certain values perceived as 'ancient' and 'traditional', which were embedded in the land and in past custom. It has been suggested that native elite families resisted English concepts of spatial ordering by constructing tower houses based on traditional spatial grammars.[27] In Offaly, power and authority were certainly under stress, and on the verge of being transformed. It could be argued that the widespread construction of tower houses in this period was an effort to make the existing native social order appear natural and unchanging. The building of a tower house at Rathlihen by the O'Molloys, a short distance southwest of *Mullach Croiche* (Mullaghcrohy), the traditional inauguration site for that ruling family, may have signalled a more explicit assertion of their standing in local society.[28]

With this in mind, it is significant that the planters who arrived into Offaly with the implementation of plantation schemes after 1619 moved into the same buildings. This appropriation of native lordly residences, however, was not only due to fiscal considerations, saving the newly arrived settlers the expense of erecting new residences. By usurping the previous owners and establishing their households in the same tower houses, these new arrivals showed themselves ready to adopt the mantle of the local landed elite, forming a corner stone in the emergent county administration. The use of old castle fabric emphasized permanent presence and linear succession on behalf of the newcomers, and demonstrated in a material way that planters could adopt native concepts of elite material behaviour.

Spaces of genteel identity, polite disposition and comfort

A series of profound changes marked the early modern era in Ireland, culturally and architecturally, from late medieval times. The different ethnic groups – Gaelic Irish, Old English and New English – proved very receptive to classical traditions and humanist thinking that were propagated under the influence of the Renaissance. These intellectual trends, however, were not simply reflected in novel architectural forms, with tower houses being characteristic of the late medieval period and fortified houses being architecturally representative of the other. What changed was the use of new discursive rules in the treatment and perception of architecture in the physical and cultural landscape. In this process, old buildings such as medieval castles came to carry quite different meanings that could be actively deployed in the construction of elite identities in the early modern period.[29] It was not necessary to completely reject late medieval gothic and adopt Renaissance classicism. The English traveller, Thomas Dineley, on his tour around Ireland *c.*1680, drew a number of tower houses that were still occupied and integrated into newer buildings.[30] Later in the same decade, in 1686, it was observed how 'several builders in Ireland have incommoded their new houses by striving to preserve some incurable or smoky castle'.[31] Clearly, new ideas on social identities and class could be projected onto the older edifices. Evidence of this can be found in the similarity in the form and style of date-and-initial stones, with their Roman capital lettering, that appeared on tower houses from the mid-sixteenth century onwards and those found elsewhere in contemporary northern Europe, suggesting that these stones were an integral part of a neo-classical architectural genre inspired by the Renaissance.[32]

Many scholars have regarded tower houses as uncomfortable spaces, with outdoor activities such as managing estates, hunting, visiting friends and neighbours, involving people in pursuits away from such interiors.[33] Those who do, have cited early seventeenth-century accounts of these castles, from the perspective of foreign travellers (such as Ludolf von Münchhausen in 1591, Luke Gernon around 1620, William Brereton in 1634 and Bouillaye le Gouz in 1644), whose accounts portray a lifestyle very much at odds with notions of polite disposition and gentility as understood by these visitors.[34] It would appear that scholars for the most part have accepted the testimony of these commentators in confirming the archaic nature of tower house architecture by the standards of the time. Such observations, however, can be misleading, as lifestyles informed by notions of gentility and polite disposition could still be played out within these castellated buildings.

The status of guests governed ease of access to specific areas within the early modern tower house, with the status of rooms, communicated by scale, position, furnishings and decoration that attested to the munificence of the owners. The best furniture, pottery and hangings were reserved for the more important chambers in the castle, serving not only the needs for domestic comfort, but also impressing upon guests the wealth and connections enjoyed by the resident family. Even if the built environment was not sophisticated by the norms of early modern Europe that is not to say that the Gaelic Irish and New English families did not enjoy luxury furnishings that were more sophisticated than the physical settings in which they were placed. Rich stucco ceiling decoration of the Renaissance period is found in the great upper hall and various other chambers in Bunratty Castle, testifying to a lifestyle of grandeur and refinement that one would expect of the O'Briens, the earls of Thomond.[35] It is important for scholars to realize that a lifestyle informed by notions of gentility and polite disposition could indeed be played out within these 'medieval' buildings. One late Scottish example, Coxton Tower, built near Elgin in 1644, contained a single chamber on each of its four floors, arranged from bottom to top as the cellar, common hall, principal hall and private apartment. Despite living in a castle like Coxton Tower, Sir Alexander Innes was described as 'one of the first gentlemen in Scotland, being a graceful person and of fine natural parts'.[36]

Notwithstanding the static, unchanging appearance of these gothic tower houses, the identities of their inhabitants were in a constant state of flux, which could allow for conceptual changes in how various chambers within these tower houses were used. It is important to recognize that identity and social values, like architectural styles, shifted from one building to another, from one place to another, or from one moment in time to another.[37] De Renzy was very much a man of learning, well versed in several European languages including Irish.[38] This individual, like many other settlers in the area, readily occupied a tower house at Clonony More, previously owned by a native. It is unlikely that these settlers (most of whom were of gentry stock) would have readily foregone their standards of social etiquette and simply conformed to a lifestyle that they would have considered archaic or even barbarous. Planters in one of the flagship projects, the Londonderry plantation, reused the tower houses of the displaced O'Cahans at Limavady and Dungiven.[39] Indeed, Edmund Spenser, author of the *Faerie Queene* and apologist for English colonialism, also inhabited a tower house on his estate at Kilcolman in Co. Cork. Excavations there have unearthed evidence of improvements made during the tenure of the Spenser family (*c.*1588 to before 1622) including the construction of a large parlour wedged between the tower house and great hall.[40] The vertical arrangement of chambers in tower houses could be adopted for early modern concepts of spatial ordering and class identity. A hierarchical arrangement of rooms continued to be the norm in the aristocratic houses of Tudor and Jacobean England, with halls and great chambers offering a focus for daily activity with service chambers at one end of the house and more private withdrawing chambers at the other end or on the floors above.[41] In tower houses, these arrangements were simply vertically rather than horizontally arranged. The success of this conceptual, rather than physical reordering can be seen in the longevity of these tower houses that continued to house both native and colonist alike through the early modern period.

The hall

> We are come to the castle already. The castles are built very strong, and wth narrow stayres, for security. The hall is the uppermost room, lett us go up, you shall not come downe agayn until tomorrow. ... The lady of the house meets you wth her trayne. ... Salutations paste, you shall be presented with all the drinkes in the house, first the ordinary beer, then *aqua vitae* [whiskey], then sacke [white wine], then olde-ale, the lady tastes it, you must not refuse it. The fyre is prepared in the middle of the hall, where you may solace yor.selfe till supper time, you shall not want sacke and tobacco. By this time the table is spread and plentifully furnished wth. variety of meates, but ill cooked and without sauce. ...When you come to yor. chamber, do not expect canopy and curtaines.[42]

Luke Gernon's 1620 description of the uppermost room in a Limerick tower house serving as a hall parallels the evidence in west and south Offaly where the hall is located on the highest floor of many tower houses. One of the finest examples is to be found at Leap Castle, which is not surprising given its status as one of the chief households of the O'Carrolls, remaining so until the Cromwellian confiscations of the 1650s (fig. 5.5). In this chamber, all except one of the window embrasures are set

5.5 High end of the hall chamber in the tower house at Leap. This castle, known as *Léim Uí Bhanain* or *Baile Uí Chearbhaill*, was the principal seat of the ruling branch of the O'Carrolls.

5.6 Reused sixteenth- or seventeenth-century chimneypiece in the modern wing adjacent to the tower house at Leap (© National Monuments Service: Department of Arts, Heritage and the Gaeltacht).

into reveals. The reveal openings possess punch-dressed pointed arches, chamfered with elaborate stops. The surrounds of the window openings themselves are punch dressed and chamfered, with ogee- and round-arched heads possessing recessed spandrels. There is a subtle spatial hierarchy, with two-light windows in the main body of the room and single-light windows at the lower end, where people gained entry. A more explicit demonstration of this spatial hierarchy can be seen in neighbouring Ormond. A rather ornate window, now ruined but originally embellished with tracery, is placed at the upper end of the hall at Lackeen Castle, Co. Tipperary, one of the chief households of the O'Kennedy Fionn. Such windows are rather unusual for tower houses, as they are more commonly found in contemporary religious buildings. A parallel for this window can be found in the Augustinian abbey in nearby Lorrha, a religious centre that enjoyed O'Kennedy patronage in the late medieval and early modern periods.

Unlike other tower houses in the region, there is no inbuilt fireplace in the hall chamber at Leap, suggesting that a centrally placed hearth heated the room, paralleling Luke Gernon's description of a Limerick hall where the fire was prepared in the middle of the room. Support for this interpretation is found with the lack of garret space over the O'Carroll hall – this allowed the smoke to escape through an aperture in the original roof. This does not necessarily mean that the O'Carrolls were oblivious to the merits of an inbuilt fireplace as evidenced by the flat-headed example with a joggled lintel in the great chamber on the second floor. A chimney stack in one of the modern wings adjoining the tower house also contains a number of reused fireplaces of early modern date, which may have originally heated chambers within the tower house before its substantial refurbishment by the Darby family in the eighteenth century (fig. 5.6). One suspects that there was a cultural resonance to the display of a central hearth in the hall chamber compulsive enough to override any concerns for the lack of a proper fireplace. Such a tendency was exhibited among the Anglo-Irish as well – in a tower house occupied by the Shortalls at Clara, Co. Kilkenny, a central hearth originally occupied its main upper hall, even though a fireplace was provided on its second floor.[43] The lord deputy, Sir Henry Sidney, when writing to the queen in 1567, commended one of Leap's owners, Sir William O'Carroll 'for civill and bountifull entertayninge me, for obedience and conformity, such a one, as I never founde the like of anny of the Irisherye'.[44] Here, within the castellated surrounds of Leap Castle, even the queen's representative could find it possible for an Irish chief to live a lifestyle shaped by notions of gentility and civility.

This hierarchial spatial grammar, with a greater emphasis on the upper end of the hall chamber, can be seen at a number of other Offaly tower houses such as Clonony Castle in Delbhna Eathra. Here, the hall chamber has poorly preserved remains of windows, which saw alteration probably as the result of nineteenth-century renovations (fig. 5.7). The only extant original window is a chamfered single-light ogee-headed window dressed with fine regular punching in the corner close to

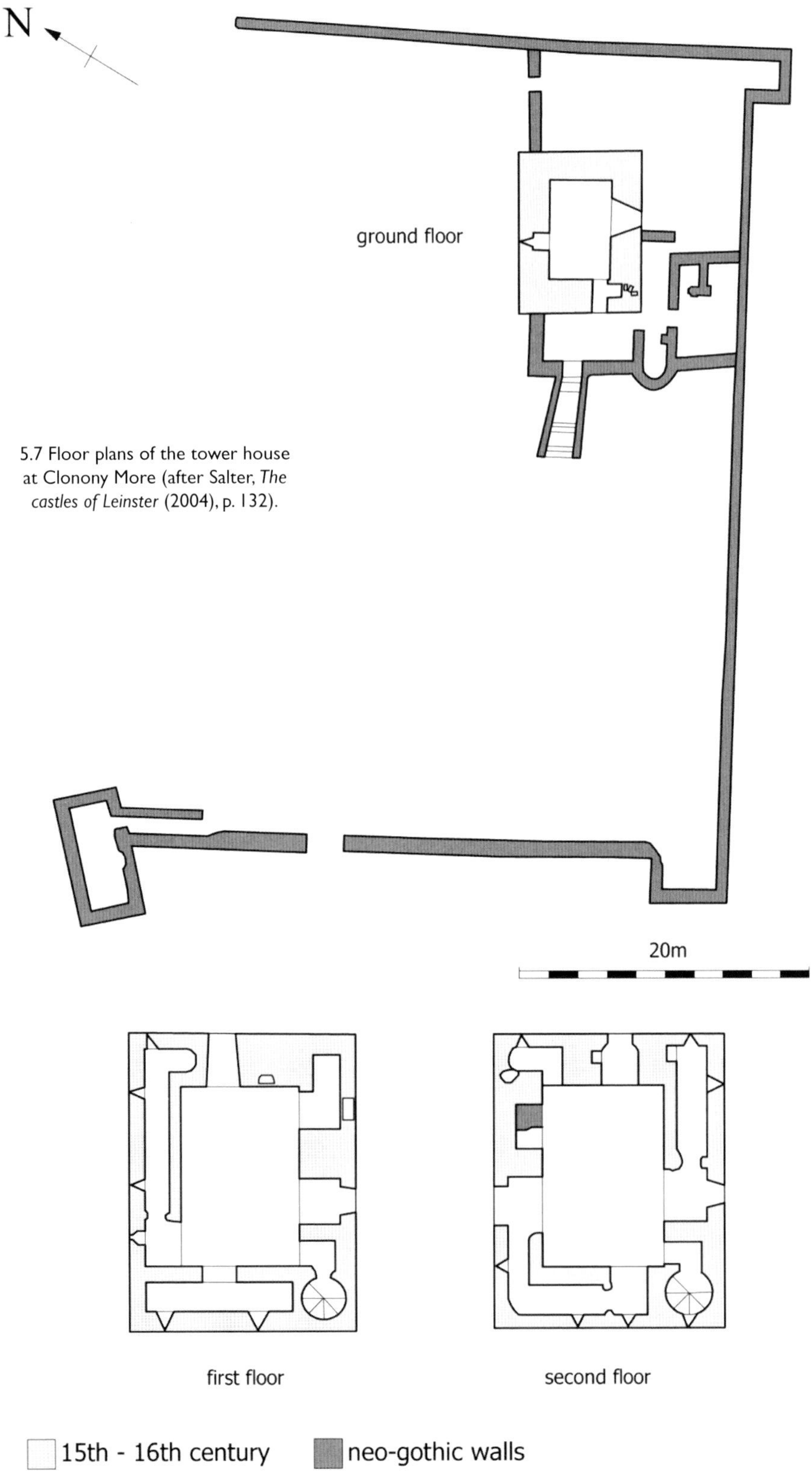

5.7 Floor plans of the tower house at Clonony More (after Salter, *The castles of Leinster* (2004), p. 132).

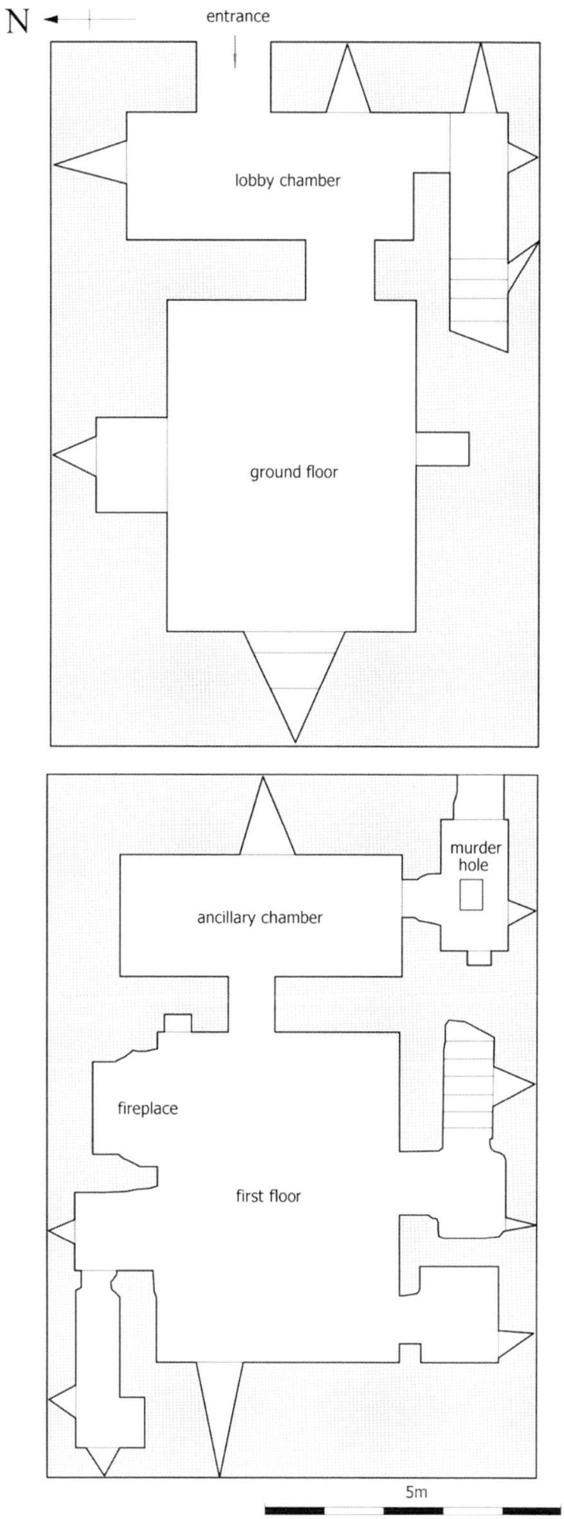

5.8 Floor plans of the tower house (Doon Castle) at Esker (after Salter, *The castles of Leinster* (2004), p. 134).

the stairwell entrance. There are indications that twin-light windows originally lit the rest of the chamber. At Doon, the more ruinous nature of the castle prohibits identification of the hall chamber; however, the principal chambers on both the first and second floors are provided with an ornate ogee-headed window with an accompanying fireplace at the end of the room furthest from the entrance (fig. 5.8). In the case of Leap, Clonony and Doon, the greater emphasis given to architectural features at one end of the hall chamber creates a staged progression, from first emerging into the light of the chamber from the narrow, dark confines of the stairwell, followed by crossing the chamber itself to the focal point of the room, the fireplace and large window reveals, where members of the household could be reading bardic poetry or Latin treatises among themselves and their associates. The importance of spatial arrangements in these hall chambers can be seen at Dungar, where the builders went to the trouble of building a hall chamber of rectilinear plan inside a cylindrical tower house (fig. 5.3). In a room of circular plan, it would have been more difficult to create hierarchies of space than in a room of rectilinear plan. Indeed, the experience of the hall and the experience of another important social space – the church – in terms of layout and movement, may not have been dissimilar. The hall was divided into an upper and lower end; likewise, the church was divided into a chancel and nave.[45]

As the hall chamber in the tower was enclosed within the immediate household of the lord, access to the hall could be more exclusive. The relative smallness of the hall chamber in the tower house, compared to the larger freestanding halls in the accompanying bawn, would very much reduce the scale of feasting and hospitality. Clearly, these hall chambers were spaces where discourses of power and status could be played out at a more intimate level than would have been possible in the ancillary hall in the bawn.

As these halls were used to demonstrate lordly munificence, the decline of native lordship from the sixteenth century onwards brought about the eventual demise of the hall itself. In general, later tower houses lacked architectural embellishments that signalled the elevated status of halls in earlier examples, such as floors supported by vaulting, windows with carved rear arches, window seats, windows with ornate heads, ornate arcades and high ceilings. The hall, as such, was becoming less visible in later tower houses.[46] There is also historical evidence that the hall within tower houses had fallen out of use by the early seventeenth century – in a 1639 inventory of Bunratty Castle, the furnishings in the Great Hall were only worth £2 compared to the value of over £52 placed on furnishings within the new dining room that was built in the castle during the tenure of the fourth earl of Thomond (fl. 1581–1624).[47]

The other chambers

Field survey and documentary evidence suggest that the Irish tower house, spatially speaking, could be self-contained. As such, various activities – eating, sleeping, entertaining guests – could be simply contained within various chambers in the one building. In this more domestic arena, the family would spend their leisure activity, including the entertainment of the more important guests. Pastimes would include singing, dancing, storytelling and feasting. Board games were favourites in a household, as revealed in inventories, with games such as chess, backgammon, Fox and Geese and Nine Men's Morris.[48] It is clear that, while the hall chamber facilitated the reception of guests and offered the principal room in which family members and their more esteemed guests could gather for meals, other chambers fulfilled less public roles.

The lack of documentary sources, such as contemporary building accounts and contracts, household inventories and other relevant writings, from either native or colonial sources, prohibits an exact reconstruction of room use in such tower houses. Keeping in mind the evidence elucidated from other scholarly work on early modern architecture in Ireland and Britain, however, these other chambers can be interpreted as chambers to withdraw to from the hall, and, as such, were designed to cater for the daily needs of a wealthy household in the early modern period. Such rooms could fulfil the functions of a great chamber, a withdrawing chamber, a parlour, a bedroom

5.9 View of Clonony Castle. The Annals of the Four Masters record the death of James MacCoghlan, prior of Gallen, at the castle of *Cluan Damhna* in 1519, and the taking of the castle of *Cluain-Nona* in the course of a struggle between the MacCoghlans and the O'Molloys in 1553.

5.10 Floor plans of the tower house at Kilcoursey (after Salter, *The castles of Leinster* (2004), p. 136).

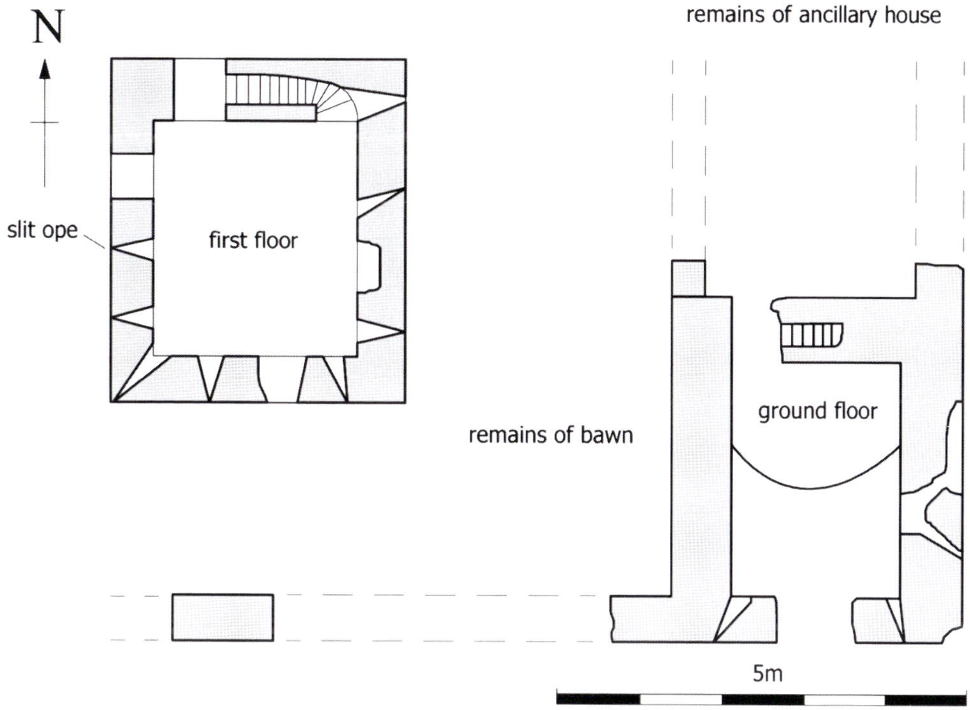

chamber or a privy chamber. These chambers have been termed private, though these rooms were not private in the sense of a domestic retreat in the modern manner. Important political functions could take place in such rooms. Personal ties and connections were central to the flow of political power in the late medieval period. The family and household were a microcosm of political order and, as such, these rooms saw status and power played out at a more intimate level.

Some tower houses possess a rather simple floor plan with one room accounting for the total area, except for the provision of mural stairwells, garderobes and bartizans. The floor plans at Ballinlough, Dungar and Kilcoursey follow this simple plan (fig. 5.10). Clonony More follows this trend to an extent, though it makes greater use of mural chambers cut into the thickness of the walls at first- and second-floor levels (fig. 5.7). These provided the occupants with more differentiated space. Both Dungar and Clonony More have seen significant adaptations since 1700, involving both the blocking and enlargement of windows, along with the insertion of fireplaces (figs 5.3, 5.9). This has complicated the interpretation of these buildings. Ballinlough, however, possibly of early seventeenth-century date, appears unaltered, which allows a more faithful reconstruction of the internal layout, with the hall chamber occupying the highest level, the third floor (fig. 5.11). Even with the excellent preservation of a building, however, it has to be accepted that the attribution of particular roles to certain chambers is tenuous, given the lack of independent verification. Bearing this in mind, the following arrangement is tentatively suggested for Ballinlough. The ground floor is occupied by a chamber, which could have served as storage space or quarters for servants and lesser members of the household. In turn, the first floor is provided with a bedchamber with an accompanying garderobe chamber built into the thickness of the wall. A great chamber or parlour, heated by a fireplace of basic appearance, is located on the second floor, while the hall chamber is located on the third floor with access to the pair of bartizans. Thus, from top to bottom, the following sequence of rooms can be envisaged: cellar, bedchamber (with garderobe), great chamber/parlour and hall. This is an articulation of a spatial hierarchy, which underpinned the social hierarchy of a household, giving physical expression to discourses on class identity and familial relations.

Other tower houses possess more complicated internal arrangements, with the living area on each floor divided into a principal chamber and a subsidiary chamber, along with a number of other mural passages. The internal arrangements at Leap Castle were completely transformed by the Darbys in the eighteenth century (fig. 5.12). Fortunately, the hall occupying the highest floor was left untouched, though the other floors were adapted to meet the needs of an eighteenth-century gentry family. This rebuilding saw the insertion of large neo-gothic windows and the removal of partitions, creating more open spaces. Examination of the present layout of the castle suggests that the first and second floors were originally divided into a principal and subsidiary chamber, while the hall occupied the total area of the third

5.11 View of Ballinlough Castle from the north.

5.12 The interior of Leap Castle has been heavily altered by the Darby family since the eighteenth century, resulting in the original ground floor being raised, leaving space for a semi-basement, in which a brick-vaulted wine cellar was inserted (© National Monuments Service: Department of Arts, Heritage and the Gaeltacht).

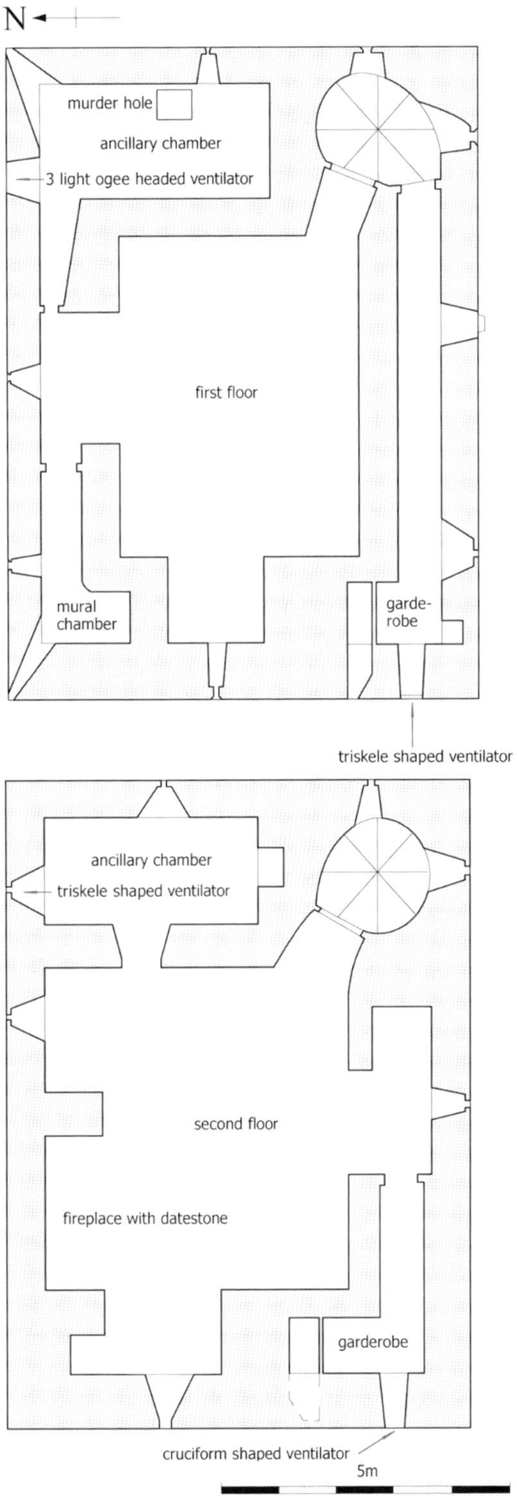

5.14 View of a ground-floor window in the west wall of the tower house at Coole.

5.13 First- and second-floor ground plans of the tower house at Coole (after Fennelly, 'An analysis of the tower houses' (1997), pp 83–4).

5.15 View of ground-floor windows in the tower house and adjoining hall at Srah Castle.

floor (fig. 5.5). The tower house at Srah also preserves a hall, which covered the total area of the upper floor, while the first and second floors were each subdivided into a principal and subsidiary chamber.

The tower houses at Coole and Doon are quite interesting in respect of the provision of domestic chambers (figs 5.8, 5.13). In each instance, the main chambers at first and second floor are provided with ancillary chambers along with garderobe chambers, creating a suite of rooms replicated on each floor, but independent of each other. Such an orderly arrangement of rooms – a principal chamber followed by withdrawing chambers and garderobes – is symptomatic of a social etiquette that regulated access to the more private spaces of a household. According to Faulkner, the most remote apartment would be reserved for the most select occupant and difficulty of personal access was an indicator of rank, so that the chamber of the highest-ranking male (the lord of the household) would be located in the deepest space.[49]

At the other end of the spectrum, the shallow position of a ground-floor chamber in relation to the rest of the tower house suggests a greater degree of accessibility than would be the case with other chambers. At Kilcoursey, there is exceptionally poor provision for lighting, with only the bare remains of a window embrasure now remaining in the ground-floor chamber there. The ground-floor chambers in other buildings were lit by crude, slit opes, as is the case at Aghnananagh, Ballinlough and Dungar. These small, rather primitive-looking lights have been seen as an appropriate architectural response to a chamber located at ground level. A position at ground floor would render this area of the building most vulnerable to attack. The sparse nature of the chamber itself also suggests a utilitarian purpose, providing a storage or service area for the apartments above. The presence of a vault over such a chamber, as is the case at Kilcoursey, is seen as a means of limiting any fire started by attackers in the ground floor area. A functional interpretation, however, solely dictated by needs of defence and security, does not allow for a more comprehensive and meaningful appreciation of how tower houses were used. Ground-floor windows with dressed surrounds, and of comparable size to windows in more elevated chambers, are to be found at Clonony More, Coole and Srah. The ground-floor chamber at Clonony More possesses a chamfered single-light ogee-headed window in the north wall, with jambs tapering to take account of the base batter. A similar window, along with the remains of a round-arched slit ope (now blocked), light the ground-floor chamber at Coole (fig. 5.14). The same chamber at Srah is particularly well served. Though preserving a rather heavily modified simple rectilinear ope in the south wall, the north and east walls are equipped with a pair of fine twin-light, cusped, ogee-headed windows dressed with rough punching and linear drafted margins. In both instances, the mullion is missing (fig. 5.15). The use of windows comparable to those lighting domestic quarters on the upper floors suggests that ground-floor chambers at Clonony More, Coole and Srah could be utilized as accommodation, say, for the lesser members of the household such as servants, rather than solely for storage. The ground-floor chamber at Coole was equipped with three wall presses, which suggests a concern to provide for the requirements of a living space rather than simply a cellar. Wall presses are typically found in domestic spaces such as halls, withdrawing chambers and bed chambers, and presumably they were used to store household items.

How were these rooms decorated and furnished?

Today, most tower houses are in a ruinous condition, their dark and dank rooms, linked by narrow stairwells and corridors, creating a foreboding, almost claustrophobic atmosphere that emphasizes the insecurities of late medieval Ireland that demanded the need for defensive strongholds. This has coloured modern perceptions of how tower houses were actually used by their occupants. The chambers within 'restored' tower houses are today presented as largely bare-walled and bare-ceilinged, with the odd piece of furniture including an occasional bed and tapestry. The exposed rubble walls, while covered in whitewash, are left bare rather than given a smooth plaster finish. Such restorations fall short of how the landed elite contrived the furnishing and decoration of chambers in an effort to create comfortable living spaces. This problem has also been observed in Scotland, where castles had their external harling removed to make the buildings look more 'authentic'.[50] In Offaly tower houses, there is clear evidence for wall finishing, with most if not all of the internal spaces, such as the halls, chambers, stairwells and passages, finished with a smooth coat of render. This render would have obscured every feature of the stone structure, including, in many instances, the dressed surrounds of fireplaces, doors and windows. The punching evident on such dressed stone provided a key for the plasterwork. Unlike many recently restored late medieval interiors in Ireland, it is unlikely that whitewashed stone rubble walls ever formed a deliberate decorative finish, even in the short term.[51] However, finished walls as well as decorative stonework did receive whitewash. Covering the interior walls with such a bright colour was a necessary device to lighten the room as much as possible. This was important in the context of rooms provided with the small opes typical of tower houses.

Polychrome wall paintings are less common than those found in ecclesiastical contexts, but have been identified in a number of castles, including four tower houses: Barryscourt, Co. Cork, and Ardamullivan, Ballyportry and Urlanmore (collapsed in 1999), all in the south Galway/north Clare area.[52] Despite their location in a domestic context, the paintings are religious in nature and include the Passion cycle, the Pietà, the Madonna and Child, and a number of saints such as St Michael the Archangel, St Christopher and St Sebastian.[53] The absence of limewashing or other colour paints over wall renders in Offaly tower houses does not necessarily mean that interiors were not painted, as such coatings can be highly sensitive to exposure and neglect. Given these circumstances, the survival of intact limewashed domestic interiors is unknown in Ireland.[54] Yet the extant archaeology and documentary evidence, such as household inventories, points to a vigorous use of colour, achieved with the application of paint on both walls and furniture, along with colourful wall hangings such as tapestries and portraits.[55] Contemporary English inventories record that rendered walls were commonly painted in various colours, based on themes imitative of textiles, tapestry and panelling. Wooden wall panelling itself is a feature of early modern architecture in England, though it is a somewhat rare survival in Ireland, with examples preserved at Myrtle Grove in Youghal, Co. Cork, and Tintern Abbey, Co. Wexford.[56]

Household inventories have been invaluable in identifying the nature of furnishings in Old and New English households, but little information has come to light as to how Gaelic Irish households were furnished.[57] A rare document of native provenance survives from early modern Offaly. In his final days, the then lord of Delbhna Eathra, Sir John MacCoghlan, drew up his will on 10 July 1590 in the presence of witnesses in the house of Solomon MacEgan in Coole. According to the terms of his last testimony, all his movable goods – corn, chattels and furniture – were to be distributed among various members of his family, including dishes, pots, flagons and vessels as well as those made of pewter. Six vessels called, in English, 'tonna' and two cups bought and made in the name of Sir John were specifically not to be divided up in the final distribution.[58] His epitaph in the Annals of the Four Masters records that 'There was not a man of his property, of the race of Cormac Cas, who had better furnished or more commodious courts, castles, and comfortable seats, than this John'.[59] While the will does not specify individual pieces of wooden furniture, there was a range of such pieces to be found in tower houses in general, with a difference between items provided mainly for functional purposes (benches, stools, boxes, work-tables) and those provided for display and the promotion of status (the master's chair, dining tables, display cupboards, storage chests, bedsteads). The latter pieces of furniture were elaborated upon to reflect the aspirations of their owners, with chairs and chests graced with heraldry, and beds adorned with rich cloth hangings. Such furniture was typically made from oak, ash, elm and sycamore, though more luxurious native (walnut and spruce) and imported (cypress, yew tree and juniper) woods were also used.[60]

The parapets of the tower house

Turning to the exterior, the tower form emphasizes verticality, drawing the eye upwards. The base batter found along all sides of the building accentuates this verticality. Turrets, crenellation and chimney stacks crown the roofline. As the visitor reached the doorway, he or she must have become aware of standing directly underneath a panopoly of castle defences – the crennellation, bartizans, machicolations, arrow loops, gun opes. While these features suggest an architectural grammar that could very much act as a metaphor for lordly power and authority, they were also critical for providing the backdrop for the staging of social discourse. Approaching a castle as a guest invoked a set of social and cultural connotations. The guest trusted the host to abide by the rules of hospitality, a need accentuated as the guest came up to the entrance within the range of crennallated parapets and gun opes. There was a collectively shared vision of ideal conduct, in which hospitality was celebrated and meanness condemned. In addition, the actions of a man also reflected upon the character of the household in general.[61]

Parapet levels have not survived unscathed, with only the castles at Srah, Ballinlough, Clonony More, Dungar and Leap preserving their roof lines (figs 5.3, 5.9, 5.11, 5.12, 5.16). Only Clonony More, Ballinlough and Leap appear to have possessed crenellation, with the latter two examples crowned with simple oblong merlons. At Clonony More, the profile is more irregular, but the corners of the parapets rise above stepped crenellation decorated with string-coursing. The coped and moulded chimney stacks found at Srah, Ballinlough and Clonony More are

5.16 View of the tower house with adjoining hall at Srah Castle, which in 1588 belonged to John Briscoe, an early English settler who hailed from Crofton Hall in Cumbria. He had married into a local Gaelic family, the Kearneys.

unnecessarily tall, advertising a level of internal comforts unknown to most people. Also at Srah and Clonony More, a string-course defines the parapet level from the walls below. In both cases, sitting on this string-course are regularly spaced drain holes called weepers. The presence of such drainage features provides a clue as to why battlements are so poorly preserved on the Offaly examples. The wall-walk or alure behind the battlements is typically sloped to allow for the dispersal of rainwater. Even though the sloped wall-walk is usually keyed to take the vertical stress of the battlements, there is still an inherent instability, which results in the dislodging of the parapets over time.

The parapets, with their crenellation, roof turrets and machicolation boxes, were integral to the principles of castle architecture, both in a defensive and a metaphorical sense. The metaphorical importance of the parapet can be clearly illustrated in a Scottish courtier's advice to his son not to build his house without battlements, as the resulting edifice would be construed as demeaning to the family's heritage, undermining their standing in society.[62] The castle could be interpreted metaphorically as the lord's body at a time when the body was a social metaphor for the lord and his household.[63] It was believed that the outward expressions of a man reflected something of his inner self, and, as such, communicated to others his integrity and sense of morality. One of the chief qualities required of a candidate suitable for election to chiefdom was freedom from physical deformities, which goes towards explaining why many participants in dynastic competitions found themselves blinded or emasculated by their opponents. If it is accepted that the tower house constitutes in a real and meaningful way the identity of its owner, then surely the throwing down of the building emasculated not only the building as a fortification, but also the authority and position of the same owner. Could the throwing down of castles mentioned in the sources actually refer to the toppling over of the battlements, emasculating rather than the completely destroying the tower house? In Scotland, the 'destruction' or 'throwing down' of castles typically involved the destruction of ancillary buildings and courtyards, the looting of goods and the burning of the roof rather than the wholesale destruction of the main building.[64] The demolition of a castle with its thick walls would have involved considerable expense in time and labour. It is of relevance here to note that Mark Girouard regards the word 'demolished' in early modern England as really meaning dereliction rather than wholesale demolition, as would be understood today.[65]

Lordly wards and gardens

These tower houses only formed a part, albeit an important one, of a greater complex, which included ancillary buildings. The walled courtyard or bawn framed social activity within and around the castle complex. The testimony of contemporary observers like Richard Stanihurst alludes to halls built adjacent to the tower houses of Gaelic Irish lords. According to Stanihurst,

> adjoining them [castles] are reasonably big and spacious palaces made of white clay and mud. They are not roofed with quarried slabs or slates, but with thatch. In the palace, they have their banquets but they prefer to sleep in the castle rather than in the palace becauses their enemies can easily apply torches to the roofs.[66]

The Elizabethan antiquarian William Camden described Irish castles as 'no more than towers, with narrow loop-holes rather than windows; to which adjoins a hall made of turf, roofed over with thatch, and a large fenced quite round with a ditch and hedge to defend their cattle from thieves'.[67] In Offaly, the prominent planter William Parsons wrote a letter in the midst of the 1641 uprising to his faithful neighbour, Teige Carroll of Rath More, in which he advised him that 'If you feare that your hall being fired maye doe your Castle any hurt, I pray pull all the thatch of it for feare of the worst the charge cannot be great and you must not value that now'.[68] As these accounts suggest, these halls were typically built of perishable material such as post-

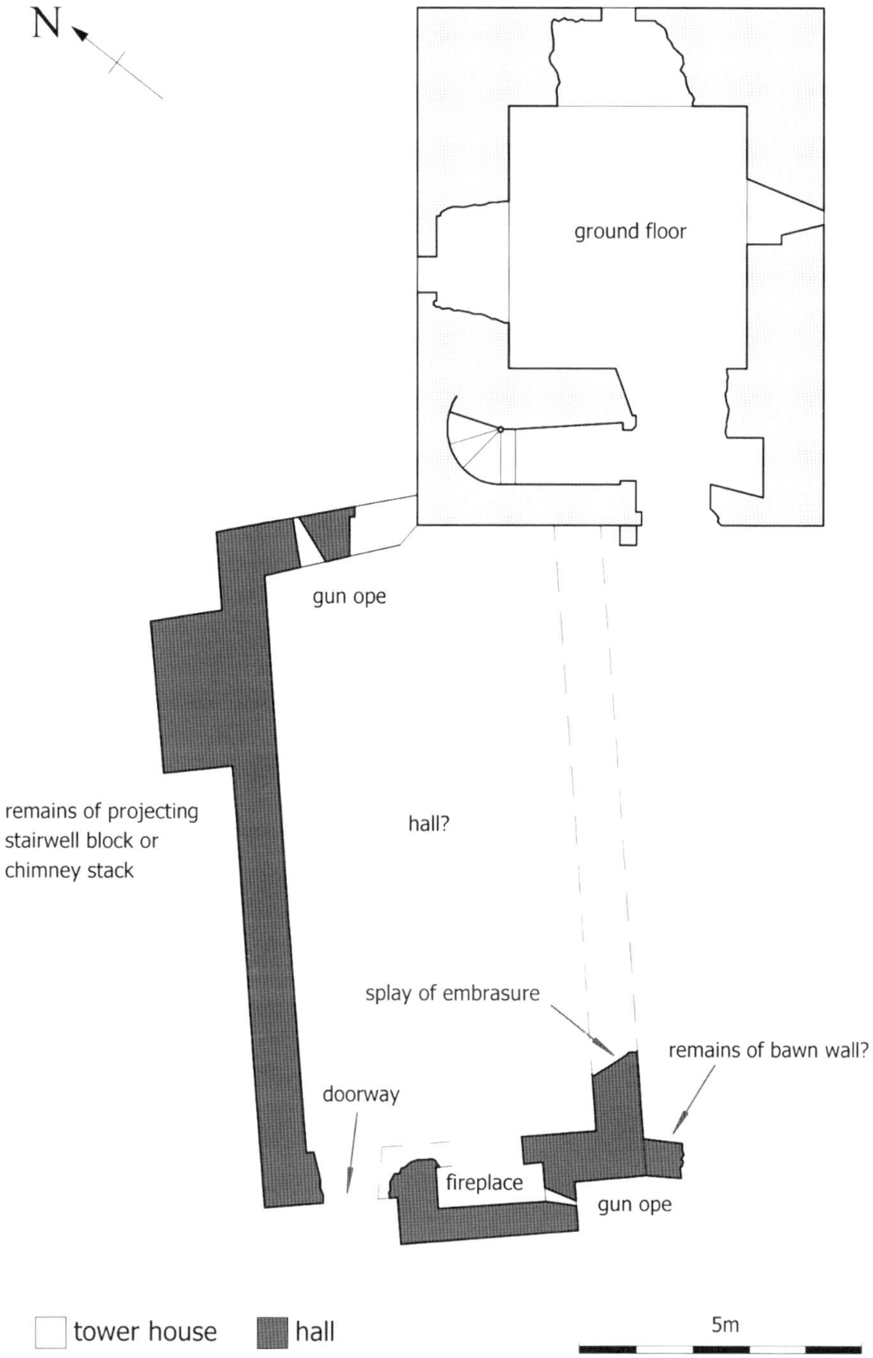

5.17 Ground-floor plan of the tower house and hall of Srah Castle (after Fennelly, 'An analysis of the tower houses' (1997), p. 54).

5.18 View of the fire-place in the west end of the hall beside Srah Castle.

and-wattle and clay, and roofed with thatch. As such, the archaeological evidence for such high-status buildings, even with excavation, can be quite ephemeral. The attached timber-framed hall and other buildings in the bawn at Barryscourt Castle, Co. Cork, were represented by the vestigial remains of thin clay-bonded stone walls, the ghosts of horizontal timbers edging patches of stones, and fragmentary clay flooring.[69] Often, the only evidence for the existence of such a hall are the creases of the roof left against the side of the tower house, one such example being the O'Carroll castle at Dungar.

Unfortunately, contemporary accounts typically do not provide any detail on the spatial arrangements within these halls, while native literature such as bardic poetry is more often focused on the generosity and hospitality of a particular lord rather than the building in which it takes place. The absence of documentary sources comparable to what can be found in England makes an interpretation of the built environment in a native lordly castle difficult, but there are some surviving contemporary observations. The German traveller, Ludolf von Münchhausen, in 1591 described the houses of the nobility as follows:

> Their houses are usually built in the form of a tower surrounded by a wall. Yet they do not live in those but keep them as a fortress. Nearby they keep a house, badly built unlike our farmhouses, where they light a fire in the middle. Right at the top is seated the man of the house with his wife, around them the servants according to their rank.[70]

This suggests that the internal arrangements to be found in a hall attached to a castle could have a homologous relationship with the social ordering of an early modern native lordly household, with the upper ends of these halls being the preserve of the lord and his immediate family.

There are the poorly preserved remains of a stone-built hall against the west wall of the tower house at Srah, which consists of a single piled house, one and a half storeys in height (figs 5.16, 5.17). Only the north wall, along with steeply pitched gables at the east and west ends, now survive. A fine fireplace was placed against the west gable, away from the tower house. This fireplace possesses an attractive limestone surround dressed with rough punching and linear drafted margins, surmounted with a mantelshelf (fig. 5.18). The remains of a window embrasure, greater in size than any other window evident in the house, lit the area immediately in front of the fireplace. There is no evidence for any partitions at ground-floor level, and in the context of the house being built right up against the tower house, it would be feasible that the ground floor of this house contained a hall, with the western end of the room as the focal point, heated with an elaborate fireplace and lit by a large window. There was no direct entry between the hall and the tower house, instead one had to walk out into the courtyard to gain access, an arrangement that somewhat distanced the immediate family of the lord who resided in the tower house from the comings and goings of the hall.

Another possible example of a stone-built hall separate from the main residence is located beside the fortified house at Ballycowan (fig. 6.29). Sir Jasper Herbert was granted the site in 1623, building the fortified house there in 1626 on the site of an earlier O'Molloy stronghold *Baile-mhic-Abhainn* that was burnt in 1557. The possible hall now only survives as a west gable end with a slight return of the south wall. The gable possesses a steep pitch and its scale would suggest that the building was originally two storeyed. However, inspection of the interior of the gable did not reveal any evidence of a first floor, whether in the form of corbels, joist holes or floor line. This invites a parallel with late medieval halls that contained a single floor open to roof level. The interior of the house was provided with a massive fireplace (H. 2.4m, W. *c*.3.3m, D. *c*.1.6m) with a flat arch of rubble construction. There are the remains of two substantial ovens located in the northwest corner of the fireplace. The larger oven has a damaged opening, though a sill with a slop-stone dressed with rough punching survives. A vault roofs the large interior of this oven (int. diam. *c*.1.5m). The smaller oven possesses an opening with jambs and lintel dressed with linear drafting and rough punching. The jambs and lintel also bear a rebate to hold a shutter. The interior of this oven appears to be circular (int. diam. *c*.1–1.25m) and roofed with a vault. This substantial provision for heating and baking suggests a scale of consumption commensurate with a lordly household of late medieval and early modern date that contained extended family members, retainers, servants and other guests. The nearby fortified house itself possesses a kitchen in one of the vaulted basement chambers equipped with an equally substantial fireplace (H. 2.14m, W. *c*.3.4m, D. 1.4m) with an oven (fig. 6.10). The fact that there are two substantial fireplaces with ovens at Ballycowan are indicative of the largesse of the resident family. An alternative explanation is that the hall with its elaborate cooking facilities was associated with the earlier O'Molloy stronghold, and that the functions of the hall were replaced by the construction of the fortified house in the 1620s with its own substantial internal kitchen arrangements.

Either way, servants, farmers, brewers and other agents of comparatively low status would observe the huge fireplaces and bread ovens of the kitchens, signifying to them that this particular lord embraced certain aristocratic obligations in offering appropriate hospitality to great hosts of people. This arrangement of the stand-alone hall in a castle complex had long antecedents in Anglo-Norman architecture, as is apparent with the thirteenth-century castles at Trim, Co. Meath, and Adare, Co. Limerick. The Desmond castles at Askeaton and Newcastlewest, again in Co. Limerick, were also provided in the fifteenth century with halls separate from the main residences.[71] This separation of castle and hall can be seen in Gaelic Irish lordships outside Offaly as well. At Aughnanure, Co. Galway, there stand the remains of a masonry hall in the outer ward of a sixteenth-century stronghold of the O'Flahertys on the shores of Lough Corrib.[72]

In the late medieval world, hospitality occupied a far more central position in legal, economic, social and political frameworks than in modern times, even though it operated between individuals in a private and personal manner. The practice of hospitality was an inescapable obligation that formed the nexus of people's most important relationships, making it fundamental and indispensable to the functioning of medieval Ireland.[73] Literary and historical sources suggest that a nobleman's honour and status were inextricably connected to displays of hospitality, with the maintenance of his reputation depending on his ability to continually provide gifts liberally and entertain generously throughout his lifetime.[74]

This emphasis on hospitality was to continue into the early modern period. In his *Playne and perfect description of Irelande*, published in 1577 as a section of Raphael Holinshed's Irish Chronicle, Richard Stanihurst conceded that, despite their 'barbarous custome', the Irish were 'great almsgivers, passing in hospitality'. Elsewhere, he notes that their homes were

> filled daily with a great throng of guests. [The Irish] are without doubt the most hospitable of men, nor could you please them more in anything than by frequently visiting their houses willingly of your own accord, or claiming an invitation from them.

In the same light, John Dymmok, author of *A treatice of Ireland* (1599), observed that they were 'great [with regards to] hospitallitye … [and a] kinde harted [people]'.[75] Hospitality brought individuals together under convivial circumstances, helping to form new alliances or cement existing relationships. In early modern Ireland, there was a cultural imperative, with the level of hospitality acting as a signifier of a guest's status, setting that person apart.

The archaeological evidence suggests that houses constructed either against or close to tower houses functioned as halls, designated for large gatherings, while the tower house itself was conceived as private space into which the household retreated in the evenings. Where the hall is freestanding and relatively separate from other accommodation, there is a sense that the communal activities of the hall were paramount: the freestanding hall is an inclusive space. When the hall is integrated into a suite of rooms, occupying the upper floor of the tower house, the emphasis on communality is very much reduced.

The general surroundings of tower houses could be used to demonstrate the power and munificence of a lord and create a suitable backdrop for the ceremonial reception of guests. There are earthworks in the vicinity of the tower houses at Clashagad Lower (two terraces flanking the approach to the castle), Cullenwaine (platforms defined by wide, flat-bottomed drains to the immediate west of the bawn) and Faheeran (a terrace to the north of the castle) that may be suggestive of garden landscaping. Unfortunately, there are no other extant surface traces of gardens in the vicinity of tower houses in west and south Offaly, but it is important to note that such formal gardens can be found through excavation. Dave Pollock excavated the bawn interior at Barryscourt Castle, Co. Cork, revealing a variety of features including the remains of a garden containing raised beds, presumably for flowers or hedging, along with a possible garden terrace, all enclosed by a wall that probably reached the height of the main bawn wall.[76] At Kilcolman Castle, Co. Cork, survey and excavation failed to reveal significant features in the northern area of the bawn, suggesting the presence of a walled garden, consisting of a kitchen garden on the east, near service buildings, and a pleasure garden on the west, overlooked by the tower house itself.[77]

A more nuanced understanding of how landscapes were manipulated may be required. Despite the lack of obvious earthworks, the actual settings of tower houses could have been used to frame natural features such as summits and waterways in an attempt to create composed surroundings. One of the chief reasons that 'watery landscapes' have gone unrecognized is that they utilize sites with bodies of natural water in front or around them, as is the case with tower houses at lacustrine locations such as Whigsborough and Pallaspark. The many MacCoghlan tower houses strung along the course of the Brosna can be seen in the same light. Such a natural setting would not attract comment from modern researchers except if medieval buildings like castles were placed in the context of other more obvious artificial landscaping. The use of precipitous locations may have had an earlier military intent, though which subsequently became an integral part of a composed landscape.[78] Large ornate windows in tower houses not only facilitated vistas of surrounding estates, but also acted as features to be seen and admired from below. The tower houses and castle sites at Castleroan, Clashagad Lower, Doon, Streamstown, Faheeran and Moystown Demesne may be examples of this process, utilizing the natural lie of the land in forming composed surrounds.

The gendering of the tower house

Castles have traditionally been interpreted as fundamentally masculine, reflecting the nature of the inheritance of land and power in late medieval and early modern Ireland through the male line, with marriage seen as a means to consolidate and improve the social, financial and political standing of a family. While many women could be perceived as simply pawns in such arrangements, these alliances could still provide women of ability to become involved in affairs outside the confines of tower houses. The frequency of obituaries in the annals for the wives of even minor lords gave recognition to the status of noble women within the native ruling classes.[79] In 1553, the daughter of O'Connor Faly, a native lord from east Offaly, travelled to England, 'relying on the number of her friends and relatives there and on her knowledge of the English language to request Queen Mary to restore her father to her, and on her appealing to her mercy, she obtained her father and brought him home'.[80] In 1576, Mabel Browne, the wife of Gerald Fitzgerald, eleventh earl of Kildare, played a key role in the running of his large estate, while he was under arrest in London. On the subject of his wish to see her in England, she replied: 'So I am sure if I shold depart the contrey all your doings here wold ron to wrack', and in so doing stressed her centrality and importance to the future of the earldom.[81] Women in the early modern period were also more actively involved, not only politically, but economically as well. The wives of native lords could retain goods that they brought to their marriage, with some entitled to receive income from their husband's lands for their own use. An example of this is the wife of MacCarthy Mór, who collected rent from his lands known as the Cáin bheag, or 'little tax'. Such women, therefore, had access to wealth and power independent of their male relatives.[82]

Tower houses as well as defensible strongholds were also family homes. It has been suggested by Mary McAuliffe and Allan Rutherford that the smooth running of the household was the responsibility of the lady of the castle.[83] The stocking of food and other provisions came under the remit of the female head as well as dealing with many of the servants and workmen. This view of the domestic/private domain been the sole preserve of the 'household wife' has been criticized as overly androcentric and stereotypical, ignoring the need for a more sensitive discussion of intra-familial relations at this time.[84] However, with regard to the gendered ordering of space inside castles, the identification of precise room functions has remained problematic, since it is difficult to identify with certainty any rooms other than the hall and garderobes.[85] The hall is usually perceived as a masculine space where the male head would have presided over the business of organizing political alliances and running country estates. The leading lady, however, may have ruled the activities of the household from this same chamber. Many eulogies to these noble women testify to their generosity and hospitality, acting in a complementary manner to the strength and determination of their husbands.[86] As mentioned earlier in this chapter, it is not without significance that, when visiting a tower house, Luke Gernon was greeted by a lady with a retinue of attendants in the hall, where she performed a core part in providing hospitality. Ceremoniously, she would taste a variety of drinks before presenting each of them to Gernon, taking responsibility not only for their quality but also for the well-being of the guest.[87] Ladies of the castle were noted in the annals as providers of great hospitality. The Annals of the Four Masters in 1524 record Gormlaith, wife of Aodh O'Neill, as 'a most bounteous and hospitable woman who has bestowed many gifts upon ... the literary men and ollaves', while in the same year Mór, wife of Donnchadh O'Brien, was described as 'a woman who kept a house of open hospitality'.[88] Such accounts were not merely complimentary, as the hospitality exhibited by these women was fundamental in the creation and maintenance of legal, social, economic and political relations. Women, as well as men, were inextricably bound to displays of generosity and hospitality that credited the honour and status of a noble household.

There is little evidence to suggest that women built tower houses themselves. The Annals of the Four Masters inform us that one Catherine, daughter of the earl of Desmond, constructed castles at *Beann-dubh* [Castle Salem] and *Dún-na-mbeann* [Dunmanway], both MacCarthy strongholds.[89] However, there are more references in the annals to women 'in their own house'. It is not clear how a lady would come to own a tower house, but these buildings may have been part of a dowry or could have been granted as life interest to widows. Property could also pass into female hands under more unusual circumstances. In Delbhna Eathra, Awly MacCoghlan, 'having stolen a beefe, wanted money to save himself from the gallows', sold or mortgaged half the share of Clonony to Mairgread Ní Coireacháin, wife of his elder brother Cohogry.[90]

One tower house in Delbhna Eathra granted as a life interest to a widow is at Coole, built, according to a stone inscription, in 1575 (figs 5.2, 5.19). A will made by Sir John MacCoghlan in 1590 bequeathed Coole Castle to his wife Sabia O'Dallaghan, 'as long as she should live unmarried', but if she was married it was to be restored to her son John (Oge) MacCoghlan.[91] Another stone plaque, now missing from the site, was apparently inscribed in Latin with the following incomplete details:

> This tower was built by the energy of Sir John MacCoghlan, knight, chief of his sept, at the proper cost of Sabia O'Dallaghan, on the condition that she should have it for her lifetime, and afterwards each of her sons according to their seniority, with her ...

5.19 Fireplace in the second-floor hall chamber of Coole Castle. The inscription on a date-stone over the right side of the fireplace suggests that the building of the tower house was interrupted, possibly during the rebellion of the sons of the earl of Clanricard in 1572, and resumed again in 1575 (© National Monuments Service: Department of Arts, Heritage and the Gaeltacht).

5.20 Triskele-shaped ventilator serving a first-floor garderobe in the west wall of the tower house at Coole.

This plaque was found at Lawrencetown, Co. Galway, in 1913, but it is suggested that the plaque was originally placed over the now missing doorway into the tower house at Coole or over the gateway of the bawn, if such existed.[92]

Roberta Gilchrist observes in relation to English castles that the rooms of a female household may have been characterized with better facilities, such as fireplaces and private garderobes, and made more hospitable by furnishings such as tapestries, room hangings and cushions.[93] Inventories of aristocratic women's possessions include tapestries, rugs and linen, in addition to clothes, jewels and books. Wills indicate that these luxury items were passed down through the female line, connected perhaps with the female role of providing hospitality. Bearing this in mind, it is pertinent to note that Coole is one of the more elaborate tower houses in Offaly, in terms of both layout and architectural adornment. De Renzy described Coole as 'a very good castle and pleasant land and meadows about it'.[94] In this tower house, the chambers on the first and second floors are provided with ancillary chambers along with garderobe chambers, creating a suite of rooms replicated at each level, but independent of each other (fig. 5.13). There is a greater sense of spatial differentiation in this building. For example, the loft chamber directly underneath the vault can only be approached from the stairwell via an ancillary chamber, whereas all the other principal chambers, both in this castle and in other tower houses in Offaly, are accessed directly from the stairs.

The garderobe chambers themselves are equipped with rather ornate ventilators carved in limestone, whose motifs are borrowed from both gothic and Insular art traditions. The first-floor garderobe in the southwest corner is provided with a triskele-shaped ventilator in the west wall, within a plain circular band, surrounded in turn with regular punching (fig. 5.20).[95] The second-floor garderobe chamber, also in the southwest corner, is equipped with a cruciform ventilator in the west wall, the opening defined by a plain band surrounded by regular punching (fig. 5.21). Besides these garderobe chambers, other chambers opening off the first-floor main chamber were provided with ventilators, such as a three-light ogee-headed opening with recessed spandrels, dressed with punching in geometric design in the north wall (fig. 5.22). Another ancillary chamber, this time at second-floor level, is ventilated by a triskele opening defined by a circular band of interlace set against a background decorated with punching (fig. 5.23). Such attention to detail is unparalleled in any of the other tower houses in Offaly, creating well-aired ancillary chambers within the tower house.

Such treatment, however, is also to be seen in the fenestration of the same building, with most windows possessing well-cut limestone surrounds covered in punch dressing forming geometric designs. The largest windows in the building are chamfered single-light ogee-headed opes with recessed spandrels, which contain various motifs, including knotted triquetras (fig. 5.24). Attractive angle loops are to be found in both the ancillary chamber and the mural chamber, which served the

5.21 Cruciform ventilator serving a second-floor garderobe in the west wall of Coole tower house.

5.22 Three-light ogee-headed ventilator serving a first-floor ancillary chamber in the tower house at Coole.

5.23 Another triskele-shaped ventilator and ogee-headed window at second-floor level in the tower house at Coole.

5.24 Another window serving the hall chamber on the second floor of Coole Castle. Note the knotted triquetra motifs within the spandrels of the ogee-shaped lintel.

first-floor main chamber (fig. 5.25). As this chamber was more likely to be reserved for the sole use of the household, the lesser chambers opening from it could have been used as bedchambers and closets, offering a greater degree of privacy for the lady of the castle, their retainers, friends and servants. The ancillary chamber is lit by a four-light ogee-headed and round-arched angle loop in the northeast corner, while

the mural chamber is lit by an angle loop with both lintel and sill sharing an ogee-headed profile with recessed spandrels in the northwest corner. While such loops could be interpreted as purely defensive responses, allowing for the corners of these towers to be covered by firearms, surely in peacetime the occupants of these chambers with their retinue could gaze upon 'the pleasant land and meadows' as well as gardens.

The fine fireplace in the second-floor chamber bears a stone plaque directly over the mantelpiece with an inscription in Irish *Seagha Macochl do tindscain o seo suas * 1575 **, which translates as 'John MacCoghlan began from here up * 1575 *' (fig. 5.19).[96] This clearly ascribes the construction of the castle to a male, reinforcing the typical conception of castles as masculine entities. However, such buildings as discussed above could be administered or owned by women. In the instance of Coole, Sabia O'Dallaghan's husband built the castle for her. In England, female households in castles shared certain distinctive characteristics such as gardens, private chapels, enhanced solar blocks and private galleries or walks between these features.[97] Gilchrist is of the opinion that, to medieval women, seclusion in separate households, chapel closets and gardens was a mark of prestige, from which they managed estates, maintained social networks and exercised considerable social and economic power.[98] The chief castle of Sabia's husband, Sir John MacCoghlan, was at Cloghan, *c.*10km to the south.

5.25 Angle loop serving a mural chamber on the first floor of Coole Castle.

Could the 1590 will of the same native lord and the Latin inscription originally over the entrance to the tower house or bawn at Coole acknowledge the reality that his wife and her retinue were already secluded in a separate household, the architecture of which was more elaborate and ornate? This would certainly have paralleled the situation in late medieval England, where the female accommodation in castles was better heated, more amply furnished and provided with greater numbers of garderobes.

While such a gendering process is only beginning to be investigated in Ireland, it is clear that any building can be ascribed with varied understandings, dependent on the social status and gender of the observer. Tadhg O'Keeffe admits that the documentary evidence for the identification of spaces solely reserved for women is non-existent, but the complexity of corridors in many of the great castles such as Trim might be ascribed with a gender significance.[99] The deepest chambers of the castle, defined by their difficulty of access, may well have been for the elite females within a household. There seems little doubt that aristocratic women were spatially secluded for at least part of their lives, with female chastity and fidelity essential to patrimony. This did not necessarily mean a loss of autonomy, limited communication or lower prestige, however, as can be testified by the actions of women in the political and economic spheres of early modern Ireland.

Tower houses in Offaly suggest that spatial seclusion based on gender was not as heavily pronounced as in the great castles such as Trim or Bunratty. The relative ease of access to most chambers in the Offaly tower houses calls for a more nuanced appreciation of the gender ordering of a household. While the architectural features at Coole can be presented as an explicit metaphor for the feminine identity, it would be wrong to suggest that other tower houses were bereft of gendered spaces. As mentioned above, common architectural features and layouts link all the tower houses in the study area. Each of these buildings contained a household with men, women, boys and girls, with attendant servants, again male and female. Despite the ascription of castle architecture as a metaphor for the masculine identity of the head of the household, the very activities of such gender-mixed households through various discourses must have ascribed particular spaces and chambers with socially constructed notions of what counted for masculine and feminine, in both an explicit and an implicit manner. Members of the household and visitors, on the basis of gender, could have a different understanding of what space was allowed to them and what was forbidden, and with this went different understandings of how to behave.

The tower house as centre of an agricultural estate

Tower houses were first and foremost the centres of agricultural estates that provided the economic surpluses necessary for the support of a lineage-based society. The proliferation in castle building suggests the presence of disposable wealth, presumably derived from agriculture and trade. After the economic dislocation of the fourteenth century, Ireland, in line with the rest of Europe, focused on specialized production, which in Ireland's case meant a focus on pastoral farming, with its products filtering into the food and leather industry. The land and climate was more suitable for the raising of cattle than for tillage, potentially increasing the amount of profitable farmland. This saw an expansion in the economy during the fifteenth century, which allowed for the proliferation of castle building, along with the building of many parish churches and friaries.[100]

Like their Old English counterparts, native lordly groups enforced building expenses on their territories in a practice called musteroon. The O'Dunne inquisition of 1607 in neighbouring Co. Laois mentions the

> works and customs of cutting and drawing wood and timber, and also of building, repairing and keeping staunch the castles, halls and bawns belonging to O Doyne from time to time, which the jurors say was done of compulsion and not of right.[101]

The ability of a native lord to build castles depended on such customary duties, whereby tenants provided services to build and maintain lordly residences. A listing of the duties and customs due to O'Reilly in 1585, paid by 'the gentill and others of the barony of the Cavan' included 'all manner of chardgis both for workmen, stofe and labourers, and victuals, for the buildinge and maintaininge of his castell of the Cavan, and all other necessary romes and offices about the same'.[102] In Delbhna Eathra, de Renzy observed that the castles built by MacCoghlan were constructed 'uppon the countrie charge as their custom is so that he laid out no monie'.[103]

The activities of a large agricultural estate could not be confined within the four walls of a tower house. Byres, outhouses and kilns would have been necessary to provide for the demands of pastoral and arable farming, while the construction of accommodation and a kitchen house may have been necessary to cater for farm workers who worked in the fields of the outlying demesne lands. In an era characterized by small-scale raiding and family feuding, it may have been necessary to provide protection for these farm complexes. Such protection would have come in the form of bawns. As such, the bawn framed the social activity within and around the castle complex.

As centres of agricultural estates, ease of access to surrounding resources was paramount. As mentioned before, nearly all tower houses in the region are located in pastoral farmland. In areas such as Delbhna Eathra, where there are extensive tracts of bogland, many of these tower houses are reasonably close to such wetlands, where peat could be extracted for fuel. In no instance, however, were tower houses placed on the edge of bogs for strategic purposes. Some of the tower houses are located beside major rivers such as the Shannon or the Brosna, which would have contained fisheries, an important consideration when there were so many days of abstinence in the Christian calendar. In an area of the country in which extensive raised bog and woodland would have made travel difficult, waterways played an important role in communications. One group of castles, some belonging to MacCoghlans and others to their freeholders, are situated either on or near the north bank of the River Brosna (Moystown, Lisclooney, Clonony More, Faddan More, Bellmount, Ballysheil, Ballyclare, Gallen, Kincora, Coole, Kilcolgan More, Lemanaghan and Ballycumber). Sometimes castles were placed close to passes or toghers through woodland and bog. The tower house at Esker, known as Doon Castle, sits on the ridge of a famous esker, the Eiscir Riada, a route that allowed communication between Dublin and the Shannon river basin. The O'Carroll castle at Birr (Townparks) was at the conflux of several important routeways; to the southeast ran a route along the Brosna river valley towards Roscrea and further afield into Ossory; several routes ran southwest into Munster across the plain of north Tipperary; while other routes ran north into Delbhna Eathra and northeast into Fir Cheall.

With a preference for location on good agricultural land, easy access to the natural resources of the area including fisheries, peatland and woodland, as well as proximity to important communication routes, tower houses pinpoint nodes of settlement across the various lordships in the early modern period. Documentary and cartographic sources, along with pollen analysis, can be useful in reconstructing the appearance of landscapes in a general sense, yet little survives to suggest the original appearance of the countryside in the sixteenth century. An exceptional case may be found at Cullenwaine, one of the chiefry demesnes of the O'Carrolls. A short distance to the north of the bawn is the parish church of Cullenwaine. Straddling the area between the castle and the church lie relict fields with droveways and associated tofts that may have contained farmsteads. A possible windmill mound lies to the northwest of the bawn.

'Gleaming white castles and ramparts': tower houses as defensive entities

The development of bastioned forts manned by professional soldiers paid from royal coffers was important for understandings of castle architecture in sixteenth-century England because they contributed to a separation between the categories of 'military' and 'social'.[104] While such forts were known in early modern Ireland, the concept of a private defensible residence remained a popular one across the island for both native and colonial elites. The tower house provided a modicum of defence for its household in a society in which small-scale raiding and intra-family feuds provided the *modus operandi* for political life. The martial culture of Irish lordship meant that rulers had to demonstrate their ability to rule through the incursion and plundering of neighbouring lordships. Incursions were so central to notions of nobility and political legitimacy that a special form of literature existed to record them, the *caithréim*, which listed the various military triumphs achieved by a lord.[105] This aristocratic martial valour was also suitably expressed by the castellated appearance of tower houses, graced with narrow windows and projecting bartizans, and crowned by crenellated battlements and machicolation boxes.

Most tower houses were located in relation to the labour and economic resources of the surrounding area rather than adhering to more military-minded concerns for defensible locations. Whigsborough is a notable exception, where the wall footings of a single turret are all that remain of a castle on an island in Lough Coura. A government survey of 1550 noted that on this lake

> there is a fast Iland that no man can cume unto but by bote & reputed for a verye fast place, having a greate wo[o]d & moche mo[o]re & bogge, where O'Connor [Brian, chief of O'Connor Faly] had his chiefe refuge all the tyme of his exile, where are two messuages.[106]

A hundred years later, in August 1652, one of the last Confederate commanders to surrender in Ireland, Col. Richard Grace, made his final stand at the same castle, where his forces were besieged by a parliamentary force under Col. Sankey, who possessed a culverin and a mortar. Sankey described the castle as being located on a very strong island in a great lough, a fort with a stockade in the water, ramparts well flanked twelve feet high, and within the fort a castle.[107] A large number of artefacts testifying to such military activity were found at the castle in July and August 1847, including portions of brass and iron helmets, parts of gun and pistol barrels, large cannon shot, portions of match and flint gun locks, leaden pellets, curious horse trappings (both iron and brass), crossbow bolts and polishing stones. Other artefacts found included a silver sixpenny bit and some copper coins of Queen Elizabeth I, a French coin of Louis XIII and several base coins of James II, with numerous iron keys, knives, scissors, spoons and smoking pipes. Sherds of pottery and glass bottles, 'all of old pattern and fashion', were also recovered, along with several curious bronze pins or fibula.[108]

A number of tower houses are located on elevated spots that allow the tower to rise above and dominate the surrounding landscape, but not to the extent that they are rendered impregnable. Good examples include Ballykilmurry, Clonlyon Castlequarter, Clonoghil Upper, Faheeran, Rath More and Streamstown, which utilize the contours of a gently rolling or undulating landscape. Certain tower houses were constructed on elevated sites, which could provide a modicum of defence. Doon is on a rock outcrop at the west end of a ridge, providing extensive views of the surrounding countryside. Leap is on a vein of rock that runs along the edge of a ridge west of the Fuarawn river, commanding an impressive position, while Clonony More is also situated on a rock outcrop, though not as elevated as the previous examples.

5.26 The entrance to the tower house at Srah is covered by a combination of defensive features – battlements, machicolation and bartizan.

The location of such tower houses on bedrock had the added advantage of prohibiting any attempt by attackers to undermine the tower walls by mining. Indeed, the rising of tower walls from impregnable bedrock may have acted as a metaphor that the base on which a family's status was built on was just as solid as the rock on which the castle itself was supported.

The tower houses could be equipped with defensive features that offered the household a certain degree of protection. Standing in front of the doorway into the tower house itself, the visitor must have been aware that he or she was covered by a variety of defensive features such as the machicolation box and bartizan. Machicolation and bartizans can be found in six tower houses in west and south Offaly: Ballinlough, Srah, Clonony More, Emmel West, Garrycastle and Leap. These features are often found in combination with each other, with the machicolation box covering the area in front of the ground-floor entrance, while bartizans at opposing corners allow for each side of the building to be covered (fig. 5.26). These machicolation boxes and bartizans contained apertures at floor level through which to drop objects such as rocks. In addition, gun opes in the walls of the bartizans afforded sniping positions from which to cover the ground in the vicinity of the tower house.

The façades of these tower houses could also be dotted with gun opes. The remains of a tower house at Kilcoursey, which forms the southeast corner of a bawn, has numerous gun opes. The ground-floor chamber is equipped with four gun opes, two each in the east and south walls respectively, covering the ground outside the bawn (fig. 5.10). The first-floor chamber is provided with six gun opes, two in the south wall, one directly in the southwest corner, one in the west wall and two in the east wall. With the exception of the one gun ope in the west wall, all the other opes covered areas outside the confines of the bawn. Srah also saw the ample provision of gun opes in each side of the building, numbering ten in total. The provision of so many gun opes in rooms usually considered as domestic clearly indicates that tower houses were an architectural genre in which domestic comforts were married with defensive (and indeed political) realities. The endemic feuding between native elites through the sixteenth century, plus conflicts between native and colonial interests, which enveloped the Offaly region periodically throughout the early modern period, encouraged the continued popularity of such castellated residences. That said, the gun ope did not always receive such unbridled acceptance within the confines of the tower house. At Ballinlough, which is covered by sixteen gun opes in its bawn wall, within the tower house itself there are only two such opes. A window in the north mural stairwell is provided with a gun ope underneath the sill, while another one is located in the west wall of the third-floor chamber. The tower house at Cullenwaine possesses a possible gun ope in the north wall of the ground floor, covering ground outside the bawn. Even in the massive edifice of Leap Castle, besides the bartizan, only two gun opes were present, one in the west wall of the passage leading from the third-floor chamber to the bartizan and another in the west wall of the mural passage

5.27 Double-centred doorway at Ballybritt Castle. This is the site of an O'Carroll stronghold that was sacked in 1432, and which together with Leap Castle was a principal seat of the ruling branch of the family throughout the sixteenth century.

5.28 Main façade with double-centred doorway at Doon Castle in Esker. Matthew de Renzy noted that Doon Castle was 'builded by the Englisch and throwne downe by the Coghlans and of the ruins an other built in place by the Nugents'. From at least as early as 1620 through to 1641, it was held by Owen Mooney, who was dispossessed and transplanted to Co. Clare in the 1650s.

in the northern roof turret. At Clonony More and Coole, there are no traces of gun opes whatsoever, illustrating that the defensive requirements of a tower house varied from location to location, from household to household.

Thus the panoply of machicolations, bartizans and gun opes along with the battlements could make anyone approaching the tower house vulnerable. The doorway itself was defended from unwelcome visitors. An iron grill known as a yett or grate commonly protected the doorway itself. Evidence for the former presence of a yett comes in the form of a rebate cut into the surrounds of the door to hold such a feature. The grill itself would open and close on hinges provided in one jamb. The yett was secured by a metal chain, which was controlled via a hole in the opposite jamb from the inside of the tower house. Evidence for these yett rebates can be found at Ballinlough, Ballybritt, Srah, Emmel West, Doon and possibly Leap (figs 5.27, 5.28). While no yetts survive in Co. Offaly, examples have been found in tower houses elsewhere, such as Cregg North, Co. Cork, and Clonbrock Demesne, Co. Galway.[109] Indeed, an example of a surviving wooden door may be found at Bourchier's Castle, Co. Limerick, with a gun ope placed centrally within it.[110]

5.29 Murder hole covering a corridor leading to a mural stairs in Doon Castle.
The ceiling retains traces of wicker centring.

The lobby room itself is a liminal or transitional space where entry did not necessarily mean unhindered access to the rest of the tower house. The vulnerability of unwelcome guests was accentuated once inside the lobby, which was flanked by a guardroom and covered by a murder hole in the vault above. Such murder holes, typically plain rectilinear openings, can be found at Ballinlough, Srah, Clonony More, Coole, Emmel West and Doon (fig. 5.29). Depending on the internal layout of the tower house, these murder holes were accessible from either the principal chamber or the ancillary chamber on the first floor. The murder holes covered the confined space of these lobbies within a deadly range of fire, a particular advantage when assailants found themselves trapped within these confines if exits from the lobby chamber could be closed off.[111]

At least thirty tower houses or potential tower house sites in west and south Offaly were originally surrounded by a bawn. There is extant evidence for bawns defined by both earthworks and masonry walls. The general condition of these enclosing features can be described as poor, with bawn walls typically surviving as wall footings, and then only forming incomplete circuits. At a time when vernacular architecture was dominated by the use of perishable organic features such as post-and-wattle, timber, clay and mud, the extensive use of masonry, albeit of roughly coursed rubble construction, implied the control of manpower and resources expected of a Gaelic Irish lordly family. The original appearance of these walls would have been much different from their forlorn look today. The walls would have been covered in harling or external rendering, usually whitewashed. A sixteenth-century Irish poem refers to 'the fair castle with its shining sward … white-walled rampart amongst the blue hillocks, it seemed to me if I could reach that house I should lack nothing'.[112] While bawn walls were typically no more than walled courtyards housing buildings necessary for the function of an agricultural estate, these walls could be provided with defensive features such as corner towers, mural towers, bartizans and machicolation. Such features would have presented a martial appearance to the outsider, increasing the defensive capability of the bawn. The location of bawns on natural heights such as hill slopes and ridges would have accentuated the domineering appearance of such sites; for example, Aghadouglas and Castleroan in Éile Uí Chearbhaill.

Five (possibly six) tower houses in the study area were originally surrounded by rectilinear bawn walls, built of roughly coursed limestone rubble – Eglish and Rathlihen in Fir Cheall, Kilcoursey in Fox's Country, Castletown and Cullenwaine in Éile Uí Chearbhaill and Garrycastle in Delbhna Eathra. One of the better preserved examples is at Cullenwaine, which appears to have been amended and extended over time (fig. 5.30). This bawn was equipped with defensive features that allowed the sides of the bawn to be protected by covering fire. Placed almost centrally within the north wall are the remains of a gun turret, which has been adapted to form two sides of a modern gateway into the bawn area. The surviving east and west portions of the

5.30 Bawn at Cullenwaine, a stronghold of the O'Carrolls. A survey of 1604 described it as 'a thatched castle and bawn, an orchard'. After the attainder of Tadhg O'Carroll in 1606, the castle and lands passed to John King. By 1641, it was held by John Carroll, though, following his transplantation to Connacht, it was granted to John Desborough, a Cromwellian planter. In 1660, Cullenwaine was restored to John Carroll.

original turret structure (which show the beginning of a curve) are each provided with a gun ope. The dressed corbel stones of a now-disappeared bartizan are located at the northeast corner of the bawn, while the wall footings of a cylindrical gun turret are extant at the southeast corner. Along the circuit of the bawn there are a number of gun opes, two surviving in the east wall, with two other possible examples in the north wall. A portion of the south bawn wall close to the southwest corner preserves an upper and lower row of joist holes separated by string-coursing, possibly to support a wall-walk.

The best-preserved evidence for earthwork bawns appears where tower house builders reused the banks and ditches of earlier ringforts.[113] The poorly preserved wall footings of an O'Carroll tower house at Clonoghil Upper, on the outskirts of Birr, are located within a circular enclosure (diam. 37m east–west) defended by a bank, with traces of a fosse and counterscarp. The dimensions and location of this earthwork (the site is on a slope overlooking the Camcor river) suggest the reuse of an early medieval ringfort, though this would need to be clarified by excavation. The banks may have supported a masonry bawn wall as there are the fragmentary remains of such a wall projecting from the north-west corner of the tower house. At Castleroan in Éile Uí Chearbhaill, the poorly preserved remains of a polygonal bawn wall (dims 40m north–south, 36m east–west) with traces of an external base batter surround the site of a possible tower house. There are no indications of a gatehouse, with a simple gap in the southeast side representing the only entrance. There is a remnant of an embrasure for a gun ope in the north wall. This bawn wall, in turn, is surrounded by a series of earthworks; a berm, bank, fosse and counterscarp. The site is located on the slope of a hill overlooked by higher ground in the manner of a ringfort, again suggesting the reuse of an earlier site. The partial remains of a polygonal bawn wall (dims 31m north–south, H. *c.*2.5m, T. 1m), with the exceptional number of sixteen gun opes, surround another tower house in neighbouring Ballinlough, which in turn is surrounded by a berm and a substantial fosse (fig. 5.31). Again, this site shares morphological and location criteria associated with early medieval ringforts. The use of polygonal bawns at Castleroan, Ballinlough and indeed Rath More, also may illustrate the continuity of high-medieval building tradition among the O'Carrolls, as examples of polygonal walled enclosures built by the native elite in the thirteenth and fourteenth centuries are known elsewhere across the country.[114] Outside Éile Uí Chearbhaill, this time in Fox's Country, there are the remains of a potential tower house in a reused ringfort at Faheeran. The building is off-centre within a sub-circular platform (dims *c.*35m north–south by *c.*45m east–west) defended by a substantial fosse to the south and west with ephemeral traces of the same fosse on the other sides. A causeway crosses the fosse to the southwest.

There may have been cultural and political motivations for the location of tower houses on earlier ringforts, though practical considerations can be involved. The existing earthworks cut down on the amount of labour and resources required to renovate the defences, while the elevated location of some of these ringforts was certainly defensively appropriate. Earthwork defences of curvilinear plan, however, could be constructed *ab initio* as well, their layout not being governed by a pre-existing ringfort. One largely destroyed O'Molloy tower house was built on the northern shores of Pallas Lough overlooked by higher ground. Here, the O'Molloys appear to have constructed a tower house on a raised area (dims 69m east–west by *c.*60m north–south) surrounded on all sides by elaborate earthen defences except along the shoreline, creating a semi-circular plan. The defences consist of a bivallate arrangement of banks and fosses (fig. 5.32).

There is no doubt that concerns for defence played a part in the design of tower houses in the various lordships of west and south Offaly. Scholars in the past have interpreted the development of castle architecture revolving around two competing needs: domestic comfort and defensive invulnerability. However, when castles are interpreted through either a military or a social lens, there is the danger of essentialism, which searches for a set of fundamental principles that can applied to castles as a whole. The debate as to whether castles were military or residential is

5.31 Aerial view of Ballinlough Castle with the partial remains of a polygonal bawn overgrown with vegetation (© National Monuments Service: Department of Arts, Heritage and the Gaeltacht).

essentially misguided, because the social status of both the builder and the building was rooted in both. The assumption of a dichotomy between domestic and military imposes modern preconceptions of castle architecture on late medieval and early modern society in Ireland.

Conclusion

While scholarship in the past has focused upon castles from a typological or evolutionary perspective, there is rarely an exposition of how these buildings were used by occupants or viewed by spectators. Tower houses were not erected simply to passively fulfil particular roles, such as the provision of defensible accommodation or to 'reflect' social status. Such buildings were active in these roles, yet they also allow more in-depth interpretations of early modern society. Castles were major statements of their proprietors' identities, acting as backdrops in front of which and through which multiple identities were articulated and negotiated. Tower houses, like other aspects of material culture in early modern Offaly, were all involved in the creation and manipulation of evolving social structures. Individuals possessed an implicit understanding of the spatial ordering that they encountered; creating a stage for appropriate modes of conduct and behaviour. This understanding of spatial organization may be likened to that of language. Tower houses possessed a social ordering that gradually unfolded itself to the visitor. Stops and pauses, successive staging and movements, could allow for the communication of certain mentalities, meanings that underpinned relations both within a household and in society at large. In general terms, certain rooms were accessible to a greater range of individuals than others. While estate workers and tenants could come and go in the service areas, access to the private chambers may have been restricted to immediate family members, their guests and personal servants. Thus, the spatial arrangement of chambers could express in a real and meaningful way the social ordering of late medieval and early modern society.

A series of profound changes marked the early modern era in Offaly as culturally and architecturally different from late medieval times. It is significant, however, that tower houses continued to be occupied after the collapse of the native autonomy and the subsequent establishment of British settlers in the region. New discursive rules were applied to the inscription of architectural forms on the physical and cultural landscape. In this process, old buildings such as tower houses came to carry quite different meanings that could be actively deployed in the construction of elite identities. It is important to note that social identities in the early modern period were constructed around the way buildings were viewed, rather than simply changing the architectural style of buildings from late medieval gothic to Renaissance classicism. Despite the poor preservation of interiors and the limited survival of

5.32 Bi-vallate earthen bawn at Pallas Lough. Francis Blundell was granted the 'moiety of the castle, town and lands of Pallaice' in 1613. By 1629, it was the property of Theobald O'Molloy and was to remain in O'Molloy hands until at least 1641, when Neale O'Molloy was resident there.

documentation, it is clear that the interiors of these tower houses were not necessarily the dark and bare abodes described in the commentaries of foreign travellers. Accounts from both Old English and Gaelic households indicate that the chambers within these castellated buildings could be furnished to a standard acceptable for civil and genteel living, comparable to the more fashionable fortified houses that came into vogue among natives and newcomers in west and south Offaly in the early decades of the seventeenth century.

CHAPTER 6

The fortified house: a colonial bastion?

Introduction

As was seen in the previous chapter, tower houses were to remain an integral part of the built environment right through the seventeenth century. Indeed, it would be incorrect to say that the tower house ever went out of use in Ireland, given the number integrated into the plans of eighteenth- and nineteenth-century 'grand' houses.[1] The early modern period in Ireland, however, witnessed wide-ranging cultural, social, political and economic change, which transformed aspects of the material culture including architecture. The native lordships in early seventeenth-century Offaly could not and did not remain oblivious to such changes. One obvious material manifestation of the new epoch was the rise of the country house, albeit in its earlier forms possessing defensive features that would not have looked out of place in tower houses. Such buildings were material expressions of mentalities, whose ambiguous nature, allowed for the negotiation and manipulation of various identities such as class and ethnicity. The families behind these fortified houses, both native and newcomer, were certainly aware of the importance of how gentility and polite living could be structured, both in the environs of and in the interior of such houses. As Girouard points out, they were power houses in which affairs of the estate, parish, county and indeed, at times, country, would have impinged upon the concerns of the occupants.[2]

In this chapter, such themes are discussed, bearing in mind not only the external elevations and plans of these fortified houses, but also the various rooms that were to be found within them, such as the hall chamber, the great chamber, the withdrawing room, the parlour and bedchambers along with their furnishings. Cognisance is also taken of the surrounding bawns and gardens, which were to play a fundamental role in framing the central composition of early modern country estates. Exploring how these places gave meaning to the lifestyles of these occupants allows for the consideration of other issues pertinent to the understanding of early modern society, namely the impact of classicism and gender politics. Finally, the defensive capabilities of fortified houses are placed against the background of a society in which there was no clear separation between 'military' and 'social'.

Introducing the fortified house as an architectural genre

There is greater variation in the plan and form of fortified houses than is the case with tower houses.[3] Houses of L-plan, T-plan and U-plan are well known across the country. Houses with more basic oblong plans are embellished with tower projections, themselves rectilinear, circular or bastion-shaped. Doorways come in a variety of shapes, either flat-headed, double centred, semi-circular or semi-elliptical, allowing access to the interior of these buildings. Windows take a variety of forms and sizes, though most are flat-headed, with the larger examples divided by mullions and transoms and crowned by square hood mouldings. In some buildings, the window surrounds appear to have been of timber rather than cut stone, precluding the identification of original forms. External string-coursing can highlight the different floors of these buildings, though in many cases this form of external decoration is limited to a single string-course defining the parapet level from the rest of the façade. The gable ends can be quite steep, sometimes rising into a chimney stack. In other instances, the chimney stacks themselves project from the gable ends or from the rear wall of the house. Chimneys can be grouped in rectangular stacks or set diagonally, sometimes panelled and crowned with a stone cornice.

Despite the greater provision of well-lit domestic accommodation in fortified houses, various defensive features found in them can be paralleled with those of tower houses. These include the small ground-floor or basement windows, the provision of gun opes throughout the façades, doors secured with large bolts, protected on the outside by a yett set into an external rebate and secured from within by a chain passing through an opening in one of the door jambs. Indeed, the vicinity of the entrance could be protected by the combination of a machicolation box at parapet level and gun opes inserted into the door jambs. A bawn wall embellished with a gatehouse, flanking gun turrets and numerous gun loops defended the approaches to many of these houses. The walls of these buildings vary in thickness from 70cm to over 2m, typically being built of roughly coursed limestone or sandstone. Both the internal and the external wall faces of fortified houses were originally rendered with a skin of harling that protected the masonry from rainwater.

The distribution pattern of these houses across Ireland is fairly random, though with empty patches, notably Cavan and Monaghan. There is a more or less continuous belt in the Shannon basin, taking in northeast Galway, south Roscommon and the adjoining parts of Longford, Westmeath and Offaly. Tipperary is rich in these houses and there are significant concentrations in Co. Cork, along the Blackwater valley and the coastline.[4] Maurice Craig was of the opinion that the total number of fortified houses including fragmentary remains was around two hundred, though far more houses have been destroyed over time, while many others lie hidden under the accretions of later building.[5] Recent analysis by Sharon Weadick suggests that 448 fortified houses and nearly five hundred other possible examples were built through

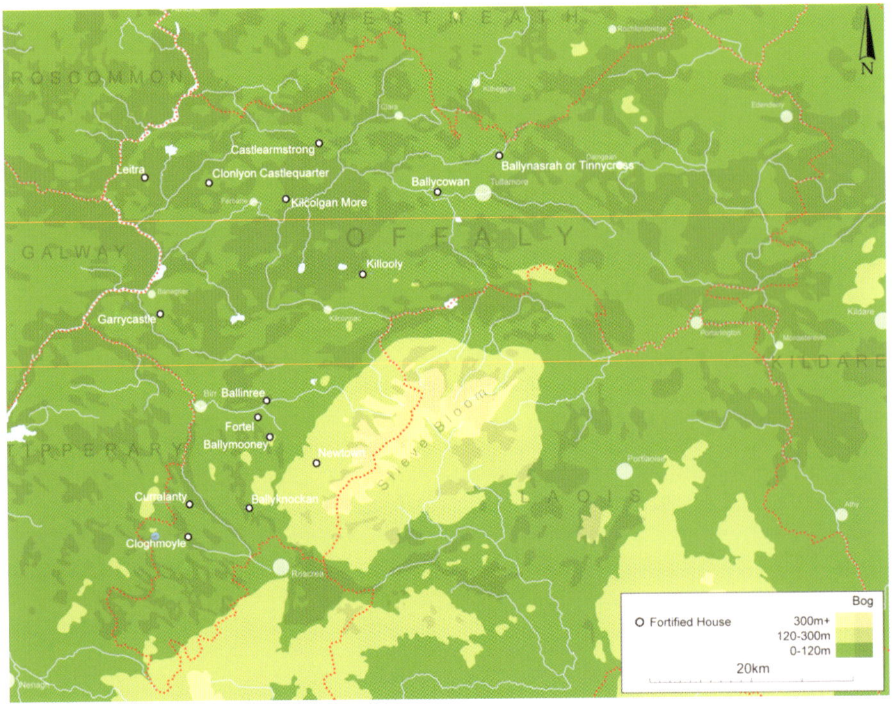

6.1 Distribution of fortified houses across west and south Offaly (drawn by Conor McDermott and Hugh Kavanagh).

the seventeenth century; a remarkable level of building that reflected a class of landowners undergoing transformation.[6] The latter figures are given credence when over one thousand country seats in Scotland are either wholly or partly dated to the sixteenth and seventeenth centuries, and even these probably only represent a fraction of the numbers originally built in that country.[7]

There are seventeen examples of fortified houses across west and south Offaly that have survived to varying degrees (fig. 6.1). Like the tower houses in the previous chapter, these buildings can be divided into three groups on the basis of their preservation. Only three have survived to the extent that original exteriors and internal spaces can be interpreted, namely Ballycowan in Fir Cheall, and Castlearmstrong and Leitra in Delbhna Eathra (figs 6.2, 6.3). Another ten have fared less well: Annaghmore, Cloghmoyle, Curralanty, Fortel, Newtown and Ballymooney (in the townland of Oakley Park) in Éile Uí Chearbhaill, Clonlyon Castlequarter and Garrycastle in Delbhna Eathra, and Srah and Killooly in Fir Cheall (fig. 6.4). The ruinous nature of this group of fortified houses precludes complete reconstruction, but their extant walls and surviving architectural features provide a valuable corpus to compare with the first group of houses. The third group consists of sites where there are no traces of the original house, though turreted bawns have survived. This

6.2 Ballycowan Castle lies on the site of an earlier O'Molloy stronghold, *Baile-mhic-Abhainn*, which was burnt in 1557. The property then passed into the hands of a succession of owners – Thomas Morres in *c.*1589, Sir Jasper Herbert in 1623 and the earl of Mountrath in 1666.

6.3 Façade of the fortified house at Castlearmstrong.

group consists of Ballinree and Ballyknockan in Éile Uí Chearbhaill, Ballynasrah in Fir Cheall, and Kilcolgan More in Delbhna Eathra. Fortunately, in the case of Kilcolgan More, there are a series of photographs in the Magan Collection held by the Offaly Historical and Archaeological Society that depict Kilcolgan Castle as it stood at the turn of the twentieth century. As mentioned above, there are sixty known sites of castles in west Offaly. They have been identified through documentary and cartographic sources, including an analysis of place-names and local tradition. There are generally few or no upstanding remains of these castles, precluding more specific classifications for them, but they were probably either tower houses or fortified houses.

Origins

The advent of fortified houses in early modern Ireland is considered an appropriate architectural response to the political and social instabilities of the time.[8] It is an architectural form strongly associated with the incoming waves of English and Scottish settlers, who were being settled in confiscated lands, as part of crown policy to advance civil and religious reform throughout Ireland. However, attempts to find buildings corresponding to the earlier plantations of the sixteenth century, notably those of east Laois and Offaly from 1556 onwards and the Munster Plantation of 1586, have proved to be difficult. The earliest known example of a fortified house was built in *c.*1589 by the archbishop of Armagh, Adam Loftus in Rathfarnham, Co. Dublin.[9] While there is a significant number of early modern buildings across Ireland, they seem to be post-1600 in date for the most part.[10] Indeed, any fortified house with secure dating invariably belongs to the first half of the seventeenth century, though their continued popularity into the post-Restoration era can be seen in the earl of Orrery's observation of 'the little old-fashioned flankers such as most noble men and gentlemen's houses have to this day in Ireland'.[11]

There have been a number of attempts to identify the origins of fortified houses across the Irish Sea. Parallels for a particular group of fortified houses characterized by basic oblong plans embellished with rectilinear or cylindrical corner towers, such as Kanturk, Portumna and Burncourt, have been sought in the southwest of England, where many of the undertakers involved in the plantation of Munster came from. Mount Edgcumbe in Cornwall (1546), and Lulworth, Dorset (1609), both of which possessed an oblong plan with round angle-towers, and Sherborne in Dorset, an oblong building with hexagonal angle-towers (commenced by Sir Walter Raleigh in 1592) possess ground plans that bear a striking resemblance to the above-mentioned Irish sites, raising the possibility that suitable progenitors for some of the Irish fortified houses can be found in the building traditions of the West Country.[12] These particular English examples, however, have been regarded as much flimsier than the

6.4 Remains of the fortified house at Annaghmore. This fortified house is poorly preserved but appears to consist of a single-pile building with two floors. There are two towers – one at the northeast and one at the northwest corner of the building. The O'Carrolls held this site intermittently. With the onset of plantation, the property was granted to Sampson Theobalds (or Theobald) in 1621.

Irish examples, owing more to Spenserian knight errantry than to serious defence, expensive one-off toys with little to do with everyday living.[13] Instead, builders and artisans in consultation with their patrons may have drawn inspiration from medieval traditions of castle building in Ireland. The O'Carroll manor house at Curralanty was provided with cylindrical corner flankers at each corner, a layout paralleled by thirteenth-century castles at Carlow and Terryglass, Co. Tipperary. This castle form was to continue in use right through the medieval period, with later fifteenth- and sixteenth-century examples in evidence at Dunmoe, Co. Meath, and Enniscorthy, Co. Wexford. Other fortified houses, such as Burncourt, Co. Tipperary, or Portumna, Co. Galway, whose flankers were rectilinear, could look to fifteenth-century tower houses such as Bunratty Castle, Co. Clare for inspiration.

In Ulster, where there was a greater concentration of British settlers, English and Scottish influence is seen as contributing more significantly to the development of the manor house. English settlers arrived into Ulster bringing tall, compact houses with bay window units carried to the full height of the building. Unfortunately, the more important Ulster examples have been destroyed. However, bay windows are found in an L-shaped house at Dunluce Castle, Co. Antrim, another house at Castle Curlews, Co. Tyrone, and a tower house at Donegal.[14] No such bay windows have been found in Offaly, though Castlearmstrong (probably MacCoghlan) was provided with a rather crude oriel window (fig. 6.5). The tradition of defensive building was still current in early seventeenth-century Scotland. Scottish architectural features, including crow-stepped gables, conical-roofed turrets, commonly supported on moulded corbel courses, and rounded stair-turrets containing a newel stairwell (often corbelled out from the face of the building at high level), can be found on fortified houses in Ulster such as Monea Castle, Co. Fermanagh. Many of the Scottish settlers came from the western areas of lowland Scotland, where a large number of early modern castles possess these features.[15] While few Scottish settlers were involved in the Offaly Jacobean plantations, it is curious that the east tower of Ballymooney Castle is crowned with a crow-stepped gable.[16] Indeed, the bawns at Ballinree and Newtown were provided with only two flanking turrets at opposite corners, a layout that has been regarded as Scottish in inspiration.[17] It may be no coincidence that the original grantee of Newtown, Sir William Sinclair, was of Scottish origin.[18] Admittedly, though, in areas covered by the Ulster Plantation, a number of bawns such as Brackfield and Salterstown, both in Co. Derry, show this plan to have been built under English auspices,[19] and it has been pointed out that small rectilinear field forts with round flankers at opposing corners were previously utilized by English troops during the Nine Years War in the same region.[20]

Craig regards such Scottish details as limited in extent and mostly superficial, pointing out that there was little difference between the fortified houses occupied by the Gaelic Irish/Old English population and those built by the more recent settlers.[21] Many of the finest and earliest fortified houses in the country are indeed associated with Gaelic Irish or Old English landholders such as Kanturk Castle, Co. Cork (MacDonagh-MacCarthy, lord of Duhallow), and Portumna Castle, Co. Galway (Richard Burke, fourth earl of Clanricard). The formal origins for the fortified house, then, remain rather ambiguous. This may reflect, however, the intellectual and social milieu in which these buildings were conceived of, rather than the partial preservation of buildings or documentary sources. The tastes and aspirations of the period did not radiate from a single source; instead they reflected the experience and preferences of a number of individuals from different backgrounds: native Irish, Scottish, Old English and New English.[22]

Close examination of settler homes may betray details of native craftsmanship. Tully Castle in Co. Fermanagh is interpreted as possessing a plan and style based on Scottish buildings familiar to its Berwickshire owner, though particular building details such as the wickerwork centring for the ground floor barrel vault and solid mortared supports for the angle turrets of the main block are indicative of native craftsmanship.[23] A number of fortified houses in Offaly, namely Ballycowan, Castlearmstrong and Ballymooney, possess architectural features that attest to the

6.5 Oriel window in the south wall of the fortified house at Castlearmstrong.

strength of native architectural traditions in the new colonial dispensation, such as the use of double-centred doorways, vaulting with traces of wicker centring, machicolation boxes and bartizans. Irish craftsman were apparently commonplace on building sites, as evidenced in the comments of one Vincent Gookin in 1665.[24] This can be seen in Offaly, where the leading undertaker Sir Laurence Parsons, in his reconstruction of Birr Castle in the 1620s, employed native masons all bearing local names such as James Bourke, Brian McHugh Coghlan and John O'Hogan.[25] English and Irish grantees in Offaly, such as Parsons, faced with an obligation to build a fortified residence within a specified period, had to improvize, exchanging concepts of architectural design with others and employing locally available craftsmen. Hence, the influence of native building traditions, even in the most elaborate and novel residences in appearance, cannot be dismissed.

This tendency for manor house forms to be tailored to local circumstances can be seen in contemporary English colonial settlements in North America. In colonies like Newfoundland or Maryland, the homes of the gentry were quite modest compared to those in England and Ireland. The hall of the 'mansion house' of the first Lord Baltimore in his Newfoundland settlement at Ferryland was revealed to be a modest building of stone construction, originally two storeys and measuring only 11m by 7m. It was part of a complex of buildings that were arranged around a cobbled courtyard that served the needs of the general population in that settlement.[26] Archaeological investigations in Maryland of the homes of Leonard Calvert (governor) and John Lewger (provincial secretary) revealed timber-framed houses of relatively small size, essentially two-unit farmhouses with a central chimney. However, by local standards such houses were large. Little is known on the original appearance of the governor's residence, though in 1647 it was described as a 'large fram'd house'. The provincial secretary had also constructed a timber-framed building on a stone sill (16m in length by 6m in width), its apparent modesty obscuring the significant investment, given that wage rates in Maryland were triple those in England. Another prominent settler, a Captain Cornwallis, had written proudly to the second Lord Baltimore in England, the then non-resident proprietor of the Maryland colony, that he was building a one-and-a-half-storey house with brick fireplaces and cellar 'toe encourage others toe follow my example', explaining that 'heithertoe wee liue in cottages'.[27]

Problems in the interpretation of fortified houses

The plantation conditions covering west and south Offaly specified that each native or undertaker who received one thousand acres or more under the schemes was obliged to construct a castle to certain specifications (to be constructed of stone or brick, and to be thirty feet long, twenty feet broad and twenty-five feet high, with a bawn two hundred feet in compass). Undertakers of six hundred acres were to build a strong house of stone or brick with a bawn, while those with less than six hundred acres were to build a good stone house. Gaelic Irish grantees in the last two categories were not obliged to construct any buildings. These conditions of building were to be fulfilled within three years.[28]

These obligations, while specifying three separate categories of housing – castles, strong houses and good houses – fail to provide an adequate description of each architectural type. It could be argued that such an elaboration in the plantation instructions was unnecessary, as the categories may have been self evident to contemporaries. In the minds of the planners, there was a clear correlation between scale of building and social status. The planners of the Jacobean plantation schemes envisaged the creation of a new civil society in which landowners occupying castles with over one thousand acres were to become the leaders of a community in the process of anglicization. Landowners of more middling stature were required to build only a 'strong house' or a 'good stone house', implying that their status in the new plantation did not befit residency within a 'castle'.

Archaeological fieldwork in west and south Offaly has identified a series of fortified and non-fortified houses that could fulfil the description of 'castle', 'strong house' and 'good stone house' respectively. The correlation of extant sites with documentary sources, however, reveals a more ambiguous picture. Across Europe, documentary references to castles in medieval and Renaissance sources are quite vague.[29] In Ireland, medieval sources are notoriously opaque about building forms, as both the compilers and the readers of the documents implicitly understood terms like *fortalicium, munitio, mota, turris* and, of course, 'castle'.[30] In light of this, it should come as no surprise that Jacobean planners in the Irish midlands did not feel that they had to elaborate with great detail on the various forms of buildings outlined in the schemes. This lack of distinction between castles and houses is also evident in early modern Munster.[31]

Contemporaries could perceive fortified buildings as houses despite the martial appearance of these structures. Kilcolgan Castle, a fortified house defended by a massive bawn with bastion-shaped gun turrets, was described in 1650 as 'a faire house belonging to Terence Coghlan'.[32] At Birr, an O'Carroll castle along with a complex of other buildings including a gatehouse, flanker and dungeon, all protected by a bawn, was acquired by Sir Laurence Parsons in 1620.[33] The residence is described as a house in a number of written, pictorial and cartographic sources in 1643, 1668 and *c.*1691,[34] and alternatively as a castle in 1643, 1650 and 1689.[35] This clearly illustrates the interchangeable and ambiguous manner in which early modern observers used terms like castle and house to describe the one building, and acts as a cautionary note in identifying particular building types from the documentary sources. This ambiguity in the contemporary usage of such terms merely reflects the implicit nuanced understandings of architecture that were perceived as obvious or taken for granted at the time.

The great variability in the form of fortified houses challenges typological approaches that seek to place these buildings into defined categories. The difficulty of generalizing seventeenth-century house plans is highlighted by the examples of six houses in neighbouring Co. Roscommon. In this group, there are various house plans: one simple rectangle with stacks at each end, one rectangle with two cylindrical towers at adjacent corners and stacks at each end, one rectangle with an L-projection containing a staircase, one rectangle with stacks at each end serving corner-fireplaces as well as a full height projection at the front, and two that consist of three blocks set corner-to-corner, making a U-plan, also with end stacks, four to each house.[36]

The chronology of these buildings can present challenges in the absence of detailed documentary sources or date stones. The latter can be problematic as date stones often commemorate a phase of refurbishment rather than actual construction, as is the case at Barryscourt Castle, Co. Cork, and Shrule Castle, Co. Laois.[37] Cut stone detail in the surrounds of doors, windows and fireplaces is the best and often the only available indicator of style and date, though again fortified houses in Co. Offaly at Curralanty, Leitra, Newtown and Ballymooney were provided with timber door and window surrounds, which have largely disappeared. In many instances, the only available chronological indicator is the general rule of thumb, which holds that the further back in time the more massive the construction, which is a rather unsatisfactory guide.[38] However, whether coincidentally or otherwise, most, if not all Irish fortified house with dates attached were built before 1641.[39] An armorial plaque over the entrance to Ballycowan Castle records its construction in 1626.

The internal spatial arrangements in seventeenth-century houses can rarely be fully recovered due to the prevalence of timber partitions.[40] In consequence, these fortified houses usually survive as empty shells completely bereft of the chambers that once would have contained the daily activities of a landed household. Only occasionally are the positions of these timber partitions revealed, outlined as impressions in surviving plaster rendering. It has been suggested that the partitions in some houses created internal layouts similar to those in late medieval houses, with timber-formed cross-passages that divided the interiors into upper and lower ends.[41] The situation is further complicated by the lack of documentation that can be used to interpret the spatial arrangements in such buildings. As Toby Barnard observes, without substantial documentation, 'trends are at best gauged impressionistically'.[42] Moreover, the extant evidence can mislead researchers. While the names of rooms on plans and inventories suggest single purposes, in reality many interiors had still to be used flexibly. As a result, beds could still be found in parlours and halls as late as the mid-eighteenth century. Indeed, after an owner died, especially when possessions were about to be dispersed, articles may have been shifted from their original locations and piled in more convenient places. Items may also have been omitted from probate inventories, either because they were reserved for family members, because they had already been removed or because they were considered of little worth.[43] This acts as a cautionary note against rigid interpretations of space in early modern households, where a single chamber could serve multifarious functions.

The fortified house in plantation Offaly

The construction of fortified houses in the early decades of the seventeenth century in Offaly has to be placed against a social, political and ideological background undergoing transformation. This period can be characterized as an anxious time for the Gaelic-Irish lords, whose power base was under threat from English officials who sought to regularize their status according to the norms of common law and civil living. Moving into the subsumed lordships was a thin sprinkling of British landowners who, by example of their own lives, were to inspire natives to embrace civility and reformed religion. Such an agenda was to be supported by the introduction of English forms of tenure, estate organization, settlement and education. Social interaction between natives and newcomers through various means such as economic activity and the running of local government, however, allowed for the reciprocal exchange of ideas on social habits and customs. Such exchanges transformed both cultures, with both groups adjusting their cultural practices in the new environment.

In this environment, the chief native families in west Offaly sought to maintain their political and social standing as they redefined their political, economic and social organization. There was a need among the native elite to redefine and present themselves as landlords in the English tradition, given the expansive agenda of the colonial order. This included the commutation of traditional dues and services to standardized money rents, which encouraged the development of an early modern capitalist economy and the consolidation of colonial commercial interests in the native lordships. It would be wrong, therefore, to view the process of anglicization in the Offaly lordships as simply creating categories of 'them' and 'us', or 'native' and 'newcomer'. English colonial discourse and its contestation by Gaelic Ireland was characterized by a level of complexity and inconsistency that created fluid and intricate relations between the different ethnic groups.

The fortified house in Offaly is a material expression of certain mentalities whose ambiguous and fluid nature allowed the negotiation and manipulation of the various identities now commonly evaluated in archaeological discourse. Diverse and fluid concepts of identity such as ethnicity, class and religion were expressed in a variety of media including buildings (as well as verbal communication, dress, writing, eating habits, deportment). James Delle has argued that spatial forms were integrated into the processes of domination, resistance and collusion in early modern Ireland, though the evidence in Offaly strongly points to mutual hybridization between native and colonial populations.[44] In areas of English settlement in North America, hybridization certainly took place. This process can be gauged from both historical and archaeological sources. A household inventory of 1719 describes the contents of the household that belonged to the last chief of the Wicomococo people in Virginia, William Tapp. He owned livestock, books and other household goods identical to those listed in the inventories of contemporary English settlers.[45] Another native settlement on the Rappahannock River (the Owings site) was occupied in the late seventeenth to early eighteenth century, and produced English material culture along with quantities of handmade pottery. Originally interpreted as a site occupied by an African American married to a Chesapeake Native, reassessment suggests that it was more likely to have been inhabited by a hybridized Wicomococo family. This site typifies the challenge facing archaeologists in trying to identify the ethnic background of a site from this period.[46]

As mentioned in the first chapter, architecture is invested with a range of meanings by knowledgeable social agents for whom the investment is often unconscious or implicit.[47] Such meanings are not random concepts; on the contrary, the creation, maintenance and negotiation of such cultural meanings requires that expression of these follows strategies that are intelligible to social actors.[48] So it should come as no surprise that leading families in Offaly, both native and planter, were introducing novel architectural forms across the county; forms that followed a common spatial and aesthetic grammar. While the colonial elite adopted traits from the native gothic tradition, the overall novel forms of buildings demonstrated in a meaningful manner that the values and concepts that underlay what it meant to be a member of the local landed elite had been transformed. In essence, there was realization of *realpolitik* that saw planter and native elites develop strategies of cooperation in economic, cultural and social spheres for the mutual benefit of all concerned.

The arrangement of space and form in a fortified house in Offaly

Fortified houses were required to meet the multifarious needs of the immediate household, combined with the owner's public obligations and the demands of a large agricultural estate. Movement within a fortified house was important for setting the stage for various discourses, as it defined the social status of both the occupant and the visitor. As the visitor came to understand the house by moving through its corridors, stairwells and chambers, so reciprocally the household came to know the social status and identity of the visitor. Of the seventeen fortified houses recorded in west and south Offaly, only three have survived to the extent that their internal arrangements can be subject to analysis. As the elite created architecture in which discourses on identity and power could be expressed both implicitly and explicitly,

6.6 Ground- and first-floor plans of the fortified house at Castlearmstrong (after Salter, *The castles of Leinster* (2004), p. 128).

the form and layout of these fortified residences would have been of utmost interest to these families, possessing a homologous relationship with the social and cultural values of the elite.

The fortified houses in Offaly illustrate a greater diversity in form and layout than neighbouring tower houses. As mentioned above, the inspiration for such houses did not radiate from a single cultural or ethnic influence, but instead reflected the experiences and aspirations of individuals from different backgrounds. In Offaly, there were a number of plans such as the plain oblong (Srah, Castlearmstrong and Leitra) (fig. 6.6), the oblong equipped with round corner turrets (Curralanty, Annaghmore and possibly Killooly) (fig. 6.7) and the oblong with projecting block (Ballycowan, Fortel and possibly Clonlyon Castlequarter and Newtown) (fig. 6.8). Ballymooney Castle in its incomplete state presents a challenge, as its sprawling façade is without parallel in Offaly. Incorrectly termed a house of U-plan,[49] it certainly appears that the two tower blocks did project from an extensive accommodation block, which appears to have spread either side of these towers (fig. 6.9).

The ground floor or semi-basement level of these fortified houses typically contained storage spaces, cooking areas and parlours for the servants. In the absence of surviving internal arrangements and appropriate documentary sources such as plans and surveys, it is difficult to identify the location and scale of the hall chamber,

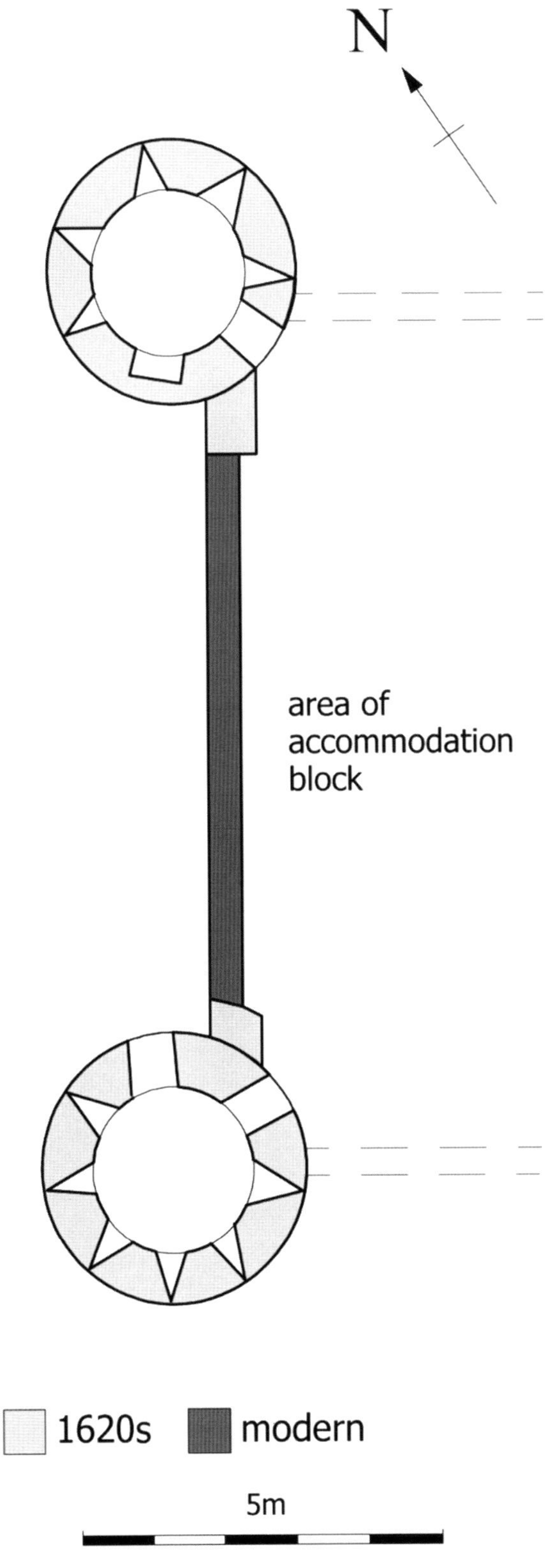

6.7 Ground plan of the fortified house at Curralanty (after Salter, *The castles of Leinster* (2004), p. 133).

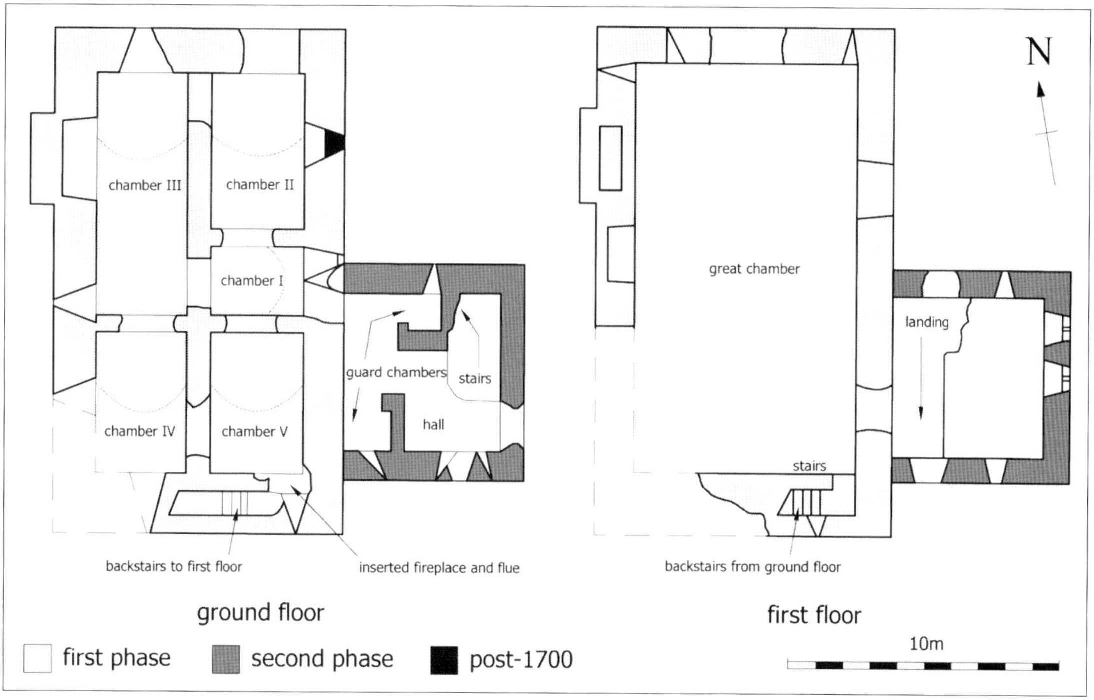

6.8 Ground- and first-floor plans of Ballycowan Castle (after Salter, *The castles of Leinster* (2004), p. 126).

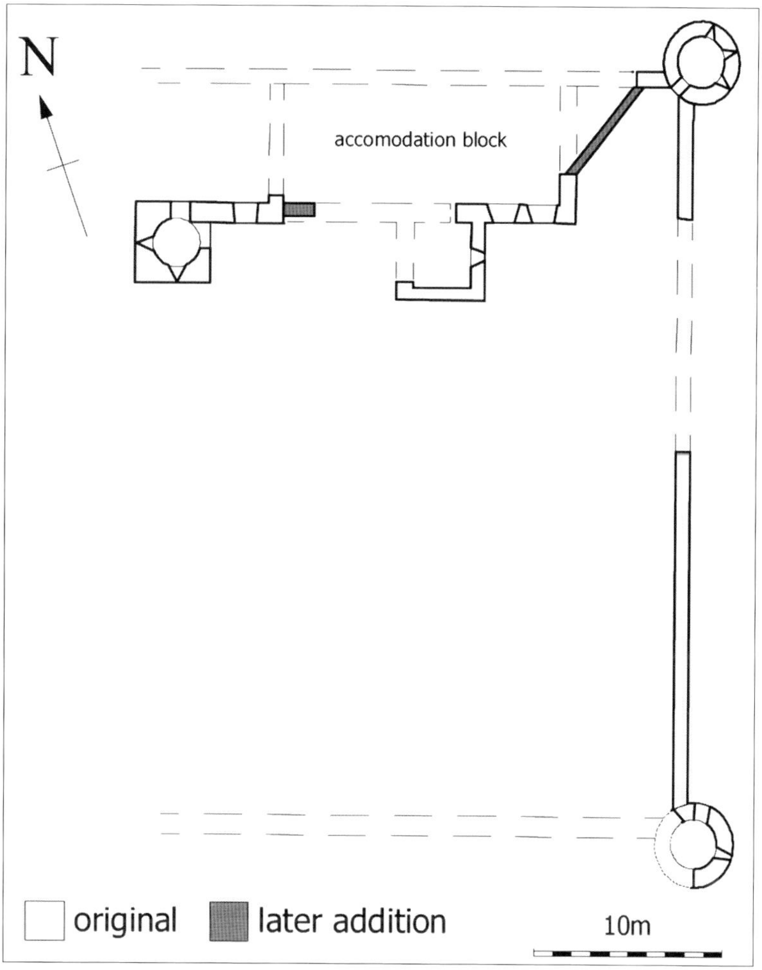

6.9 Ground-floor plan of Ballymooney Castle in the townland of Oakley Park (after Salter, *The castles of Leinster* (2004), p. 128).

6.10 Vaulted kitchen in the basement of Ballycowan Castle (chamber III).

which was increasingly marginalized in early modern society. On the first floor were the principal chambers such as the great chamber and the chief withdrawing room, bequeathing the first floor with the status of *piano nobile*, while the second floor contained more private chambers for members of the family, such as parlours, bed chambers and closets. The substantial roofs of these buildings could contain garret rooms for the use of more junior members of the family or servants. In this regard, it is pertinent to note that the Civil Survey of 1654–6 records that the larger houses in the town of Kilmallock, Co. Limerick, had a single room on the top floor, suggesting use of that level as a dormitory.[50] All floors of the house would be amply lit, though the largest windows were typically confined to the first floor. As well as in the kitchen, fireplaces could also be found in the great chamber and a variety of other chambers such as the parlours and bedrooms. A commonplace feature of houses in this period was for a wooden stairwell of dogleg or open-well type to be contained in the projecting block. Wooden flooring was used throughout, though in the instance of Ballycowan and Castlearmstrong, vaulting supported by wicker centring is a feature of some chambers, whether on the ground floor or in upper chambers (fig. 6.10).

The walls of these buildings, constructed with roughly coursed limestone or sandstone rubble, were usually first rendered with a base coat of rough-textured lime mortar mixed with hair, fine gravel and other material, and sometimes finished with a final skim coat of finer lime plaster bound with hair. While this rendering fulfilled the role of protecting wall fabric from climatic attrition, it also played an important

6.11 Façade of Kilcolgan Castle at the turn of the twentieth century, from the north. A date stone of 1649, now missing, was located over the original gateway to the bawn. By 1650, the site was described as a 'faire house belonging to Terence Coghlan' (Magan Collection, Offaly Historical and Archaeological Society, vol. 4.061).

6.12 View of internal wall rendering in the northeast gun turret of Ballymooney Castle. Note the in-situ timber lintels.

6.13 Ballycowan Castle from the east. This fortified house was built in two stages, with the main block constructed first, followed by the tower. Above the main entrance is an armorial plaque bearing the date 1626 and a dedication to Sir Jasper Herbert and his wife Lady Jane Finglas.

6.14 Ballycowan Castle from the northeast.

decorative function.[51] The external rendering could receive further elaboration around windows and corners, where surrounds (either block-and-start or recessed) and quoin stones where made out using finer render as at Fortel, Ballymooney and Kilcolgan More (fig. 6.11). Such treatment was used elsewhere in the country: Castlecuffe, Co. Laois, and Brazeel House, Co. Dublin.[52] There are excellently preserved traces of both internal and external rendering at Annaghmore, Ballycowan, Castlearmstrong, Curralanty, Fortel and Ballymooney. At Curralanty and Ballymooney, internal rendering still preserves traces of whitewash, which suggests that the internal walls within these buildings were coated in a bright white in order to brighten rooms (fig. 6.12).

Many of the fortified houses in Offaly are poorly preserved with incomplete elevations; however, a number remain to provide at least a silhouette of their original form. These houses, in contrast to tower houses, are typically gable ended. One of the defining characteristics of their external appearance is the steeply pitched gables that rise to a well-built chimney stack. These stacks are stoutly built, often crowned with a moulded cornice and coping above that. A fine example of these chimney stacks rising skywards above the surrounding estate can be found at Ballycowan, where individual and grouped stacks are defined with quoin stones and crowned by finely dressed coping (figs 6.13, 6.14). String-coursing could be used to draw the

6.15 The main entrance to Ballycowan Castle is a doubled-centred doorway with punch-dressed limestone surround in the form of three orders. A recessed square hood springs from the outer order, while the two inner orders support double-centred arches.

6.16 The main entrance into Ballymooney Castle possesses a rebate for a yett or grate with two metal fittings in the north jamb of the doorway, possibly the remains of hinges for the grate.

attention of the external viewer to various floor levels within these buildings. In Offaly, the fortified houses at Ballycowan, Fortel and Newtown possess such string-coursing (fig. 6.14). These stout, robust buildings, like their tower house predecessors, draw the eye skywards with their steeply pitched slated roofs crowned with tall chimney stacks rising from behind a parapet, the parapet itself highlighted by string-coursing. The steep pitch of these roofs, inclined between 45 and 65 degrees, was encouraged by the use of oak shingles, which was more durable on steep roofs, though slates and tiles could also be used for roofing.[53]

It appears from the surviving remains that these fortified houses were entered at ground-floor level. Of the four fortified houses that preserve their original entrances, three possess punch-dressed and chamfered limestone surrounds surmounted by a double-centred arch (figs 6.15, 6.16). These doorways are invariably equipped with a recess designed to hold an iron grill or yett over the doorway, as was the norm with the earlier tower houses. The iron hinges for such a yett are preserved at Ballymooney Castle. It is to be presumed that the doors themselves were wooden, and swung on a hinge. Again at Ballymooney Castle, a rather crude hanging eye designed to carry the hinge, is to be found inside the north jamb of the doorway. These doorways would be further secured by a bolt, as indicated by the presence of boltholes just inside the jambs at Ballycowan and Ballymooney. The main entrance at Leitra had no finely wrought door surround, remaining as a poorly preserved rectilinear opening (fig. 6.17). Here, a flat-headed doorway, solely of timber, may have defined the entry point into this building.

6.17 The entrance into the fortified house at Leitra consists of a poorly preserved flat-headed doorway with no dressed surround in the east side of the building.

The use of name plaques or armorial devices became a feature of early modern elite residences in Co. Offaly. Adorning the ground-floor entrance to Ballycowan Castle is a finely carved armorial plaque of limestone bearing the Herbert and Finglas coats of arms along with a motto that resonated with the prevailing ethos of the time: 'By God of might, I hold my right'. Above the plaque is an inscription, stating that Sir Jasper Herbert and his wife Lady Jane Finglas built the house in 1626 (fig. 6.18). Another armorial plaque once graced an O'Molloy residence in Derrydolney, carrying the family coat of arms and the following inscription (figs 7.15, 7.16):

> This house was erected by Philip Molloy and Mary Molloy his wife in the yeare of our Lord God 1684 in the three & thirteeth [sic] yeare of the reign of Charles the II by the grace of God King of England Scotland France & Ireland Defender of the faith.

Armorial plaques such as these were hitherto only to be found in churches and graveyards, commemorating the dead, so the use of such devices within the secular realm may have relevance for our understanding on the rise of individualism in early modern Ireland.[54]

6.18 Above the ground-floor entrance in Ballycowan Castle is an inserted armorial plaque of limestone with the motto 'By God of might, I hold my right'. Above the armorial plaque is an inscription, which states that Sir Jasper Herbert and his wife, Lady Jane Finglas, built this house in 1626 (© National Monuments Service: Department of Arts, Heritage and the Gaeltacht).

The façades of these fortified houses were punctuated by both symmetrical and asymmetrical arrangements of windows. Indeed, both arrangements could be found in one building, as at Ballycowan (figs 6.13, 6.14), though symmetry is particular noticeable at Leitra and Newtown, where there is consistency in the placing and size of windows (figs 6.17, 6.19). The windows came in a variety of shapes and sizes but were typically flat-headed, though segmental arched windows were found at Castlearmstrong. In general, the window openings in the Offaly examples were fitted with wooden frames; for instance, at Newtown the slots for the lintels and sills of

6.19 Sir William Sinclair from Roslin in Scotland was granted the town and lands of Newtown in the plantation of Ely O'Carroll in 1621. It was sold to William Parsons of Birr in 1637.

wooden window frames can be seen. Flat-headed stone window surrounds dressed with punching can be seen at Srah, Castlearmstrong, Fortel and the gatehouse at Kilcolgan Castle. Such treatment is indicative of masons influenced by late medieval vernacular building traditions in Offaly during this time. The wrought window and door surrounds of stone in fortified houses could be treated with a delicate dressing of punching or linear drafting. As with the punch-dressed windows in earlier tower houses, it can be assumed that this dressing made it easier for rendering or paintwork to adhere to the surrounds of these openings. Indeed, the punch-dressed surrounds of the double-centred doorway at Ballymooney Castle are still partially covered with plaster rendering.

Unlike tower houses, where the ornamentation of stone window surrounds underlined the social hierarchy of chambers within, there are generally no such cues available to the external observer of fortified houses. However, it is quite apparent in many of these houses that the largest windows, typically on the first floor, served the principal chambers. This can be seen at Castlearmstrong, Ballycowan and Ballymooney (figs 6.14, 6.20). The symmetrical arrangement of equal-sized windows at Newtown obviates such nuanced architectural ordering, which is an extraordinarily early precursor of a trend in Georgian architecture that placed a strong emphasis on consistency of fenestration to obscure the spatial hierarchies within.

The great chamber

In line with developments in fifteenth- and sixteenth-century England, the hall was supplanted by the great chamber, which became the ceremonial focus of the household. While the hall chamber remained a feature within these fortified houses, its primacy was been gradually eroded by a growing tendency of different elements of the household to dine in other chambers of the house due to greater demands for privacy, comfort and state. Johnson suggests that domestic comfort must be seen in the context of other cultural shifts at the time, including the secularization of culture, changing patterns of social display and the rise of civil etiquette.[55] The hall was maintained as a room of entrance, but now more usually used as a servant's dining room or common area, as is the case at Ballycowan, where the hall was now relegated to the status of a lobby area containing a grand open-well staircase of stone ascending to the first floor.[56]

Bearing in mind the provision of more elaborate fireplaces and windows of greater size in the first floors of the fortified houses in west Offaly, it should come as no surprise that the great chamber was at this level. This is to be found in similar buildings across the country, such as the Purcell residence at Loughmoe, Co. Tipperary.[57] At Myrtle Grove in Youghal, Co. Cork, the main room on the first floor in a house of Elizabethan date is heated by an elaborate oak chimneypiece that reaches to the ceiling.[58] The location of the principal chambers at Ballycowan, Castlearmstrong, Kilcolgan More and Ballymooney at first-floor level had the effect of creating a more refined and impressive entrance, with visitors required to ascend to the great chamber to gain access to the more private chambers of the household. In early modern England, improved techniques of joinery allowed the production of the open-well wooden staircases decorated with fine carving and painting.[59] At Ballycowan, while an open-well stone staircase in broad flights allows access up to the great chamber from an entrance lobby, it is unclear if chambers on the above floors were accessed via a fine wooden staircase, the only evidence for ingress to such higher levels being a narrow mural stairwell in the thickness of the south wall (fig. 6.8). The means of progress to the principal chambers in the case of Castlearmstrong and Ballymooney, however, was via the narrow confines of a stone newel stairwell, which recreated an experience in movement and light that was to be found in tower houses, testifying to the strength of native architectural traditions in early modern Offaly (figs 6.21, 6.22).

The chief function of the great chamber in fortified houses was as a dining area for members of the family and their guests. The same chamber also catered for music,

6.20 Ballymooney Castle is one of the finest examples of a plantation period residence in Co. Offaly. It was built *c.*1622 and was the property of Donell O'Carroll until his dispossession due to his role as 'Marshall for the rebels' in the 1641 uprising. In 1657, he was transplanted to Connacht and by way of final settlement received 1,100 acres in the barony of Costello, Co. Mayo (© National Monuments Service: Department of Arts, Heritage and the Gaeltacht).

6.21 The western tower of Ballymooney Castle originally contained a newel stairwell (now robbed out), which facilitated access to the three floors and attic of the main accommodation block.

6.22 The newel stairwell in the fortified house at Castlearmstrong facilitates access to the first and second floors through double-centred doorways, before continuing to attic level.

dancing, the displays of drama and masques; for the lying in state of dead relatives before funerals; for playing card and board games between meals; and for family prayers, especially in houses with no chapel. The latter was an important consideration when well-maintained churches of whatever denomination were few and far between in early modern Offaly. While the relatively small size of fortified houses such as Annaghmore, Leitra and Newtown could preclude the use of the great chamber for the congregation of large groups of people, it is certainly the case that the buildings at Ballycowan, Castlearmstrong, Kilcolgan More and Ballymooney could cater for the elaborate hospitality and display required of a landed gentry family. Given its status, the great chamber had to be suitably provided with fine furniture such as tables and cupboards, as well as chairs and stools covered in rich embroidery.[60]

Portumna Castle in neighbouring east Co. Galway is a fine example of an early modern elite household. Despite being burnt in the early nineteenth century, rare plans of the internal arrangements from the mid-eighteenth century have survived, allowing the reconstruction of the spatial ordering of an early seventeenth-century aristocratic household in the Irish midlands.[61] The absent fourth earl of Clanricard, Richard Burke, who built Portumna in the years before 1617, resided in England, and so it should come as no great surprise that the internal arrangements followed the fashion favoured across the water. In these aristocratic houses, the great chambers were usually provided with an adjoining withdrawing chamber, with either the owner's bedchamber or best bedchamber beyond it. At Portumna, there were two parallel suites of such rooms on the first floor, one suite presumably for the family, while the other served the needs of important visitors.

When in such elite spaces, it was important that appropriate conduct was followed, which underscored the social standing of the occupants. When certain principles of social etiquette were not abided by, such behaviour could be construed by contemporaries as deliberate slight to the occupants of the fortified house. Visitors could call to a landed household, and whether on official business or making a courtesy call, they would have all carried away with them a report of the hospitality received there and whether appropriate standards of polite conduct were abided by. The lord deputy in the 1580s, Sir John Perrot, was criticized for 'the strict and pinching parsimony' of his household, where shabby liveries, scanty commons and barely adequate 'ffyre or candle throughout the yeare', all detracted from the dignity of a viceroy with 'the like most miserable & strict orders. Not beseming his place'.[62] The hosts themselves, of whatever ethnic background, would not have been insensitive to the impressions made on their visitors, creating receptions in architectural surroundings that would do credit to their social standing. In such social interactions, however, there was a responsibility upon the guests to respect the conventions and boundaries of a particular household, giving due care and reverence to the occupants and goods within. When another lord deputy, Thomas Wentworth,

6.23 The tower of Ballycowan Castle contains a lobby area allowing access to the ground and first floors of the main block. Above the lobby area is a single small room on each of the upper floors, providing parlours or bedchambers for the household of Sir Jasper Herbert.

held his inquisition into crown title in Connacht at the residence of his rival, the earl of Clanricard, in Portumna, the castle and its contents were treated with a pointed lack of respect, with the earl's son complaining of Wentworth 'casting himself in his riding boots upon very rich beds'.[63] The same lord deputy in turn was equally concerned with protocol in Dublin Castle, limiting access to the rooms of state, issuing the following instructions: 'that upon days of meeting none but noblemen come further than the drawing chamber; the gallery only free for those that be of the council, and that all their servants stay in the great chamber'.[64]

The other chambers

During the sixteenth century, withdrawing chambers gradually began to serve some of the functions that were originally the preserve of other chambers. Such withdrawing rooms were conceived of as rooms to withdraw or retire from the great chamber. These withdrawing chambers in essence became the private sitting, eating and reception rooms for the occupant of the bedchamber to which they were attached.[65] Bearing this in mind, the configuration of main and ancillary chambers evident on the upper floors of Castlearmstrong, Ballycowan, Kilcolgan More and Ballymooney could have served such a function (figs 6.6, 6.8, 6.9, 6.23). 'Bedchamber' is a term that first became common in the mid-sixteenth century, underlining the fact that such rooms were no longer used as bed-sitting rooms, as chambers had been in the late medieval period, but were now mainly used for sleeping.[66] Notions of gentility encouraged the trend towards sleeping areas separate from areas reserved for daytime activities. Such an ideal was slow to spread, given the difference in opinion in Co. Clare as late as 1713 between Catherine O'Brien and her father-in-law, Sir Donough O'Brien, who insisted that she should not erect a field bed in the parlour.[67]

Parlours fulfilled roles as informal sitting and eating rooms; indeed, on contemporary plans, they were called dining parlours. Big houses often had several parlours, though no such chambers have been irrefutably identified in any of the fortified houses in west and south Offaly. A small winter parlour, often near the kitchen, was a common feature from at least the early seventeenth century. Such an arrangement is apparent on the ground floor of a fortified house at Coppinger's Court, Co. Cork.[68] On the same floor in Portumna Castle, a little and a great parlour both opened off the main hall directly above the basement kitchen.[69] This use of multiple parlours parallels the situation at English residences. An account by Sir William Cecil in 1553, when he was living in Wimbledon, suggests that he and his family normally ate in the parlour, possibly with upper servants or his wife's retinue, but on more formal occasions moved up to the great chamber. This was a common arrangement in seventeenth-century elite households, but in some great houses the parlour was exclusively the room where the upper servants dined, an arrangement that may also have been found in the medieval period.[70] Parlours grew proportionately more important, until by the end of the sixteenth and beginning of the seventeenth century their ceilings and fireplaces were often not much less elaborate than those in the great chamber above, as is the case at Ormond Castle at Carrick-on-Suir in Co. Tipperary.[71]

The fortified houses in west and south Offaly were also provided with in-built kitchens and other service chambers. Fireplaces equipped with small ovens can be found in ground-floor chambers at Ballycowan, Killooly and Newtown. This contrasts with tower houses where, in many instances, the principal kitchen may have been located exterior to the tower itself, though still within the bawn complex, as testified by the excavation of the tower house at Barryscourt, Co. Cork.[72] These ovens were not necessarily heated by proximity to the main fireplace, as they could be independently heated by the burning of wood within their own cavities. The temperature of these ovens was then usually gauged by the changing colour of the interior, and when sufficient temperatures had been reached, the embers were swept out, and bread or other foodstuffs placed into the oven.[73] The oven was subsequently sealed, though unfortunately none of the examples in the fortified houses in Co. Offaly preserve their original openings. At Ballycowan, the ground floor of the main block is occupied by a vaulted lobby from which are accessed four other vaulted chambers, one of which, possessing a massive fireplace, was certainly the kitchen (fig. 6.10). The other three chambers could have fulfilled the roles of larder, buttery and pantry, respectively. These service chambers were provided with a narrow backstairs that allowed direct access to the lower end of the great chamber on the first floor, keeping the coming and going of servants away from the main stairwell.

How were these rooms furnished?

At Curralanty and Ballymooney, internal rendering preserves traces of whitewash, which suggests that the bare walls within these buildings were coated in such a fashion in order to brighten rooms (fig. 6.12). Building accounts for Birr Castle in 1626 recorded various sums of expenditure to plaster its interior.[74] Such rooms were further embellished by the provision of fine furniture, wall panelling, paintings, fabrics and other items such as vessels of pewter and silver. While Kilcolgan Castle no longer survives, an antiquarian drawing of an elaborately carved chimneypiece found there depicts an architrave crowned with Jacobean-style strapwork reminiscent of the Fox tomb at Rathreagh, Co. Longford.[75] Differences in the willingness to participate fully in the consumption of fashion and luxury arose more from income and personality than from ethnic or religious considerations.[76] The principal chambers could be well finished, as seen at Portumna Castle in the early nineteenth century before it was burnt down. Daniel Beaufort in 1808 observed a 'very fine room in which the antient ceilings, wainscot & broad stucco frieses have been preserved. The arms over the chimneypiece are of James I or Charles I'.[77] The more important chambers in these fortified houses impressed their viewers mainly through the number and quality of textiles used to ornament the surroundings. Turkey carpets were placed over tables, while generous amounts of expensive fabrics, gathered in abundant folds, screened beds and windows. Tapestries were hung on the walls, often depicting tales of classical origin. These tapestries were supplemented, and sometimes replaced, by pictures or wooden panelling, carved and inlaid. Indeed, fine dark oak panelling or wainscoting covered all the rooms on the first floor of Myrtle Grove in Youghal, Co. Cork. The household of John Skiddy, a Waterford merchant in 1640, contained no fewer than ten paintings, though whether these depicted ancestral, familial, religious, political, allegorical or topographical themes is not certain.[78] An elaborate stucco ceiling could surmount a painted or plasterwork frieze. Such a frieze (*c.*1630) is preserved in what is known as the 'muniments room' in Birr Castle, festooned with zoomorphic heads, foliage and fruits of the vine.[79] Very few such examples from the first half of the seventeenth century survive in Ireland.

6.24 Hollow House at Ballynasrah was the residence of the de Renzys in the late 1600s. Three circular turrets, with the fragmentary remains of a fourth, define the corners of a bawn.

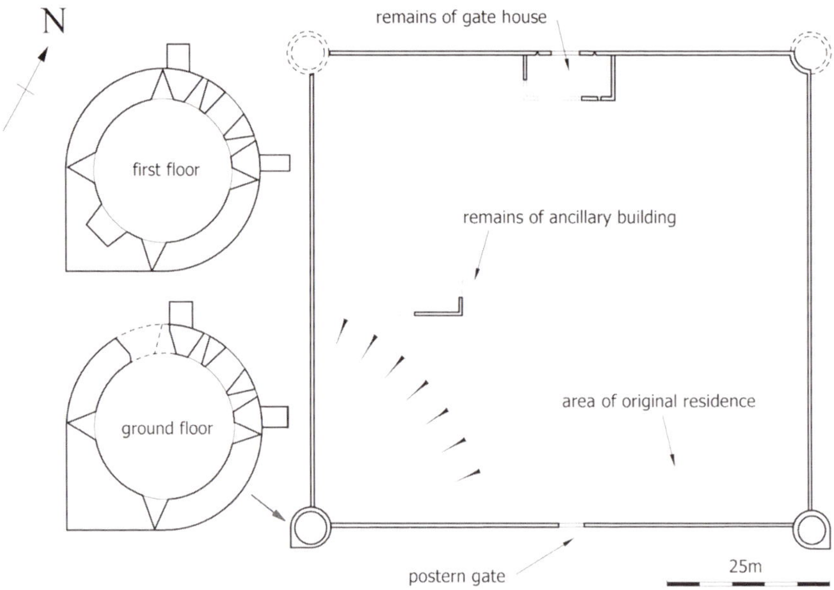

6.25 Plan of bawn at Kilcolgan More (after Salter, *The castles of Leinster* (2004), p. 137).

Another frieze in a fortified house in Mountlong, Co. Cork, albeit in a fragmentary state, contains figures from scriptural or sporting scenes.[80] Windows themselves could be filled with coloured glass depicting heraldic images. In some houses, it appears that the colours of upholstery and hangings in yellows, reds and greens were being coordinated by the owners.[81] The provision of well-furnished chambers in early modern households was fundamentally more important than had been the case in the late medieval period, as status and power had now come to be articulated by the amount and quality of furniture and other furnishings rather than by the number of servants and retainers. The early modern period saw an increase in consumption, in the complexity of house design, in the number of rooms with specialized functions, and in the cultivation of exclusivity and privacy, which saw family and servants increasingly segregated.[82]

The bawn

Fortified houses in Ireland are commonly surrounded by a bawn. In some cases, the house was placed centrally within the bawn, while in other instances it formed one side of the enclosing structure. In west and south Offaly, eleven of the seventeen fortified houses possess evidence for a surrounding bawn, while two other sites with no traces of either a tower house or fortified house (Castletown and Moyally) have considerable bawn defences. Of the sixty castle sites recorded in the study area, a combination of documentary sources and archaeological fieldwork allowed for the identification of ten that were surrounded by bawns (Annaghmore, Ballindarra, Ballynasrah, Behernagh, Broughal, Erry, Kincora, Moystown Demesne, Shinrone and Birr) (fig. 6.24). While many of these sites were probably tower houses, others may have been fortified houses. The bawns were invariably rectilinear, built of roughly coursed limestone or sandstone rubble. There is not one bawn whose original circuit remains unscathed, though the scale of the enclosures could be quite considerable. A massive bawn, measuring 74 by 65m externally, encloses the site of the original MacCoghlan residence at Kilcolgan More, with walls 4 to 5m in external height (fig. 6.25), while the extant walls at the O'Carroll stronghold at Ballyknockan, again 4 to 4.5m in external height, measure 58.5 by 73.9m externally.

Few examples of gates and gatehouses associated with these bawns survive in west and south Offaly. A local antiquarian in 1840 recorded the presence of a gatehouse at the bawn in Ballinree, but there are no upstanding remains of this building.[83] At Ballynasrah, there is a very fine round-arched gateway (H. 3.06m, W. 2.65m) with chamfered arch stones springing from crude capitals (fig. 6.26). Both the capitals and arch stones are dressed with punching and feathered margins suggestive of an early modern provenance. A pediment with coping and spiral finials above this gateway, however, suggests that the entrance may be a later reconstruction.

6.26 Round-arched gateway at Ballynasrah, with chamfered arch stones springing from crude capitals. Above is a triangular pediment with coping and spiral finials.

6.27 View of the postern gate and the remains of a machicolation box at Kilcolgan More. To the left can be seen the remains of a bee-bole that would have contained a hive.

Another round-arched gateway with dressed surrounds on both arch and jambs is found in the north bawn wall of the tower house and fortified house complex at Garrycastle. This gateway allowed access to a three-storey gatehouse with machicolation overlooking the entrance. The use of machicolation is paralleled at Kilcolgan More, where a postern gate in the south wall of the bawn is protected by an overhead machicolation box (fig. 6.27). Kilcolgan More also possesses the fragmentary remains of a gatehouse, off-centre in the north bawn wall. Judging from photographs taken at the turn of the twentieth century, the building may have been a couple of storeys in height.[84] The gatehouse has largely disappeared, but on each side of the gateway there is a blocked embrasure that originally served a gun ope. The current remains also suggest that a vaulted chamber flanked each side of the central corridor through the gatehouse. A datestone bearing the year 1649, now missing, was apparently located over the gateway.[85] Set centrally within the external façade of the gatehouse was a rather fine gateway built of ashlar fabric, where a round arch of classical proportions rose from imposts, creating a dignified entrance befitting the gentility and civility of the MacCoghlans (fig. 6.28).[86]

As well as protecting the main residence, other buildings may have lain within bawns. There is little upstanding evidence for such buildings in Offaly, though at

6.28 View of the classical gateway into Kilcolgan Castle (© National Monuments Service: Department of Arts, Heritage and the Gaeltacht).

Ballymooney the gable ends of two ancillary buildings surmount the east bawn wall adjacent to the southeast and northeast corner turrets, while at Kilcolgan More the remains of another ancillary building forms part of the south bawn wall, with a ground- and first-floor fireplace served by a huge chimney stack and the remains of a machicolation box overlooking the postern gate. At Ballycowan, the gable end of a rather large hall-like building is located a short distance from the fortified house (fig. 6.29). The evidence in Offaly parallels the situation across Ireland, where little remains of ancillary buildings within bawns besides the chance survival of gables on top of extant bawn walls, suggesting that many of these ancillary buildings were built along with their respective bawns in a single phase. Even with excavation, like at Brackfield, Co. Derry, Castlederg, Co. Tyrone, and Portora, Co. Fermanagh, subsequent use of bawn areas over time can erase material indications of early modern occupation.[87] The massive bawns at Ballyknockan and Kilcolgan More were occupied subsequently in the nineteenth and twentieth centuries by the homes, outhouses and gardens of ordinary farmers, which obliterated surface traces of early modern use. The occasional historical source elsewhere in Ireland can be more forthcoming. A claim made by Sir Hardress Waller in the aftermath of the 1641 uprising described his 'castle and manor house' at Castletown, Co. Limerick, as possessing a series of outbuildings, namely a dairy, a wash-house, a brewhouse, a malthouse, a turf-house, kennels and a pigeon house.[88] Other buildings to be found in bawns included stables, bakehouses, storehouses and living quarters for servants.[89]

Despite the martial ambience of turrets flanking these bawns, such structures were amenable to providing extra accommodation for the household. A survey of the Ulster Plantation in 1618–19 by Nicholas Pynnar records an undertaker's bawn at Derrywoon, Co. Tyrone, with four flankers, two of them having 'very good lodgings in them'.[90] Thomas Raven's 1622 depiction of the Mercers' Company bawn at Movanagher, Co. Derry, depicts corner flankers with large mullion-and-transom windows attached to both residence and bawn, suggesting the provision of ample accommodation within their circular spaces.[91] There is material evidence in the field as well. Two of the four square corner flankers surrounding Tully Castle, Co. Fermanagh, preserve fireplaces, while the southeast flanker in the O'Sullivan Beare stronghold of Carriganass, Co. Cork, is provided with a fireplace and a large window.[92] At Kilcolgan More, Co. Offaly, the southeast and southwest flankers were provided with five chambers in all, each heated by a fireplace (figs 6.30, 6.31). Each of these chambers, whether on the ground or upper floors, was separately accessed from the interior of the bawn by a doorway flanked on either side by flat-headed windows. The presence of these doorways at the upper floor levels suggests that elaborate timber lean-to boardwalks were used to facilitate access. The surviving turrets at Ballymooney contained two storeys, each with separate access from the ancillary buildings that they were attached to (fig. 6.20). The first-floor chamber of the southeast turret was provided with a small and a large flat-headed window, as well as a slit ope.

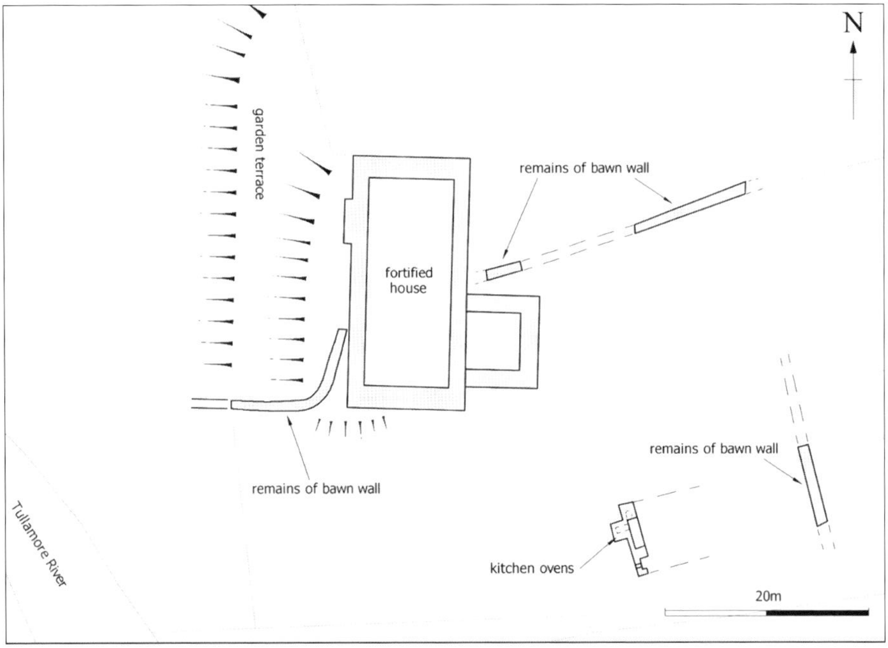

6.29 Plan of Ballycowan fortified house, kitchen and bawn (drawn by James Lyttleton and Hugh Kavanagh).

6.30 Southwest turret from the interior of the bawn surrounding Kilcolgan Castle. This three-storey turret was accessed at each floor level through round-arched doorways. These entrances were flanked on either side by flat-headed windows. The ground and first floors are visible in this view.

6.31 Fireplace along with an embrasure for a gun ope in the ground-floor chamber of the southwest gun turret at Kilcolgan Castle.

Polite garden landscapes

Garden landscapes associated with these fortified houses can offer an insight into the workings of polite society before the eighteenth century, but their potential is diluted by the poor survival of such gardens, a situation exacerbated by meagre documentary sources that fail to elucidate the layout, content and size of gardens.[93] The grounds of these fortified houses were designed to fulfil the functions of both power and pleasure, as gardens could be used to assert the status and wealth of native and planter gentry alike. Garden planning and horticultural matters were of concern in polite quarters as the principles of elite behaviour could be imparted through the gaze. The layouts of such gardens were planned as a form of mediation between the elite and common sections of society, as well as between 'Nature' and 'Culture', as they exemplified the triumph of civil order over unrestrained wilderness.[94] There was an appetite for rigid geometrical patterns created by bands of box, thrift, lavender or similar plants, and infilled with flowers or coloured earths such as gravel, brick dust and soot. Such designs, because of their complexity, were termed 'knots'. Topiary or the planting of small miniature trees like box or privet, then sculpted into ornate shapes, was also popular.[95] Such was their importance in early modern England that there may have been over five thousand such gardens created in that country from the early sixteenth to the early eighteenth centuries.[96] The setting of houses became increasingly important, particularly in the later decades of the seventeenth century, as the gaze required that the houses be viewed along definite lines of perspective from afar.[97] Individuals in early seventeenth-century Ireland were certainly becoming aware of the aesthetic principles behind landscape setting – in 1641, Lady Barrymore alluded to location and good prospect in relation to the rebuilding of Castlelyons in Co. Cork.[98]

The need for an unimpeded view of the house placed within a setting of gardens and parks required unobstructed views of the residences from a distance. Such requirements for the gaze had to be tempered by the political and social uncertainties of the time.[99] The most impressive garden remains from early modern Ireland are to be found in the Boyle residences of Youghal and Lismore, where extant garden terraces are surrounded by crenellated walls flanked with gun turrets.[100] Garden terraces were a feature of early modern landscaping, in many instances as a series of flights falling away from the residence. What is noteworthy here is that, despite learned exhortations to transform landscapes surrounding the residences of the elite into regulated symmetrical spaces devoid of 'barbaric' naturalism, many attempts at formal gardens were restricted to the confines of walled courtyards in the shadow of fortified houses. Bearing this in mind, though, some of the finest landscaped gardens in mid-seventeenth-century England were enclosed by high garden walls, such as at Wilton House in Wiltshire or Broome Park in Kent.[101]

It has been suggested that designed gardens have a better chance of survival when the residence itself was abandoned at a relatively early stage, precluding the inevitable altering or sweeping aside of these formal gardens in favour of later landscaping, reflecting changing fashions in subsequent centuries.[102] Many of the fortified houses in Offaly appear to bear little or no trace of subsequent adaptations, indicating abandonment at an early stage. Such desertions surely would have encouraged the survival of some traces of their associated gardens, but alas this is not the case. There has been a poor survival of garden features associated with fortified houses in west and south Offaly. A solitary garden terrace (H. *c.*1.5m, L 39m) flanks the west side of Sir Jasper Herbert's residence at Ballycowan overlooking the Tullamore River, while there are traces of a similar terrace running southwards from the southeast corner of Terence MacCoghlan's bawn at Kilcolgan More (fig. 6.29). In the external wall of the bawn there, also facing southwards into this defunct garden, is a pair of square bee-boles that once would have contained hives. Despite the apparent absence of garden features around fortified houses, traces of paths, flowerbeds and other features may lie preserved underneath the sod, requiring geophysical prospection and excavation to elucidate their nature and layout.

A more nuanced reading of the archaeological remains would suggest that the bawns themselves could have been used to frame the verdant scene, protecting valuable plants from the vicissitudes of climate, livestock and pilfering. Indeed, the flanking turrets, typically associated in the popular imagination with the grim defence of a household under siege, could have provided an appropriate platform for viewing garden arrangements. The circular plans and sizes of flanking turrets also lent themselves to the role of dovecots as instanced at Parke's Castle, Co. Leitrim, Carriganass, Co. Cork, and Ballynasrah, Co. Offaly.[103] Purpose-built dovecots of similar form are known in England, as well as in Ireland, as at Portanure, Co. Longford.[104] Dovecots were important accoutrements to a landed estate in England and Scotland, as they were legally a prerogative of the manorial gentry. Such a prerogative was a direct consequence of the pigeons' tendency to feed indiscriminately on the local grain crops, and thus represented a way of converting tenants' investment and labour into the owners' reserves of meat protein, especially during winter months, as an alternative to salted meat and fish. Dovecots also provided a source of manure for the gardens.[105] This highlights the danger of assigning definitive roles to spaces and features, which in reality could serve multifarious functions, transcending perceived boundaries between the military and the domestic. Associated with Lord Deputy Wentworth's palatial residence at Jigginstown, Co. Kildare, were raised walks from which the gardens could be admired. These same walks, as well as creating conditions appropriate to civil discourse, also served a defensive role, with their external faces lined with walling and covered with brick-built turrets in the corners.[106]

While Terence Reeves-Smyth accepts that some of the smaller plantation bawns might have contained gardens, he believes most of these bawns served as forecourts, and, as such, would have been treated in a manner typical of forecourts in contemporary England.[107] This would involve the placing of a wide path down the centre, a cross path and perimeter paths, the latter often running close to the walls. A comparable example was found with the excavation of the bawn at Tully Castle, Co. Fermanagh.[108] Indeed, Thomas Dineley's 1680s drawing of Ballyclogh Castle in Co. Clare depicts such a forecourt.[109] The resulting square or rectangular areas created by such arrangements were occupied, not with knots or parterres, but with grass plats, with the more pretentious households defining these plats with topiary, perhaps with a statue or urn in the centre of each. Few if any flowers would have been included in this arrangement.

The fortified house: where the late medieval meets the Renaissance

Changing tastes and ambitions can produce a change in image. In Girouard's words, 'the qualities of the courtier and the lawyer became more fashionable than the qualities of the soldier'.[110] Classicism made an appearance in the west midlands as early as 1567 with the construction of a bridge by the lord deputy of the time, Sir Henry Sidney, over the River Shannon at Athlone. Commemorating its construction was a memorial in the form of a pedimented entabulature, with a semi-circular central niche containing a dedicatory inscription, flanked on either side by a number of figurative and heraldic plaques.[111] Less than 30km away, the seventeenth-century residence of Terence MacCoghlan at Kilcolgan More no longer stands, but an antiquarian photograph depicts a building partly informed by classical principles of design, whose front and rear façade were punctuated with symmetrical fenestration (fig. 6.11).[112] In contrast to the stepped merlons of tower houses, the merlons of Kilcolgan Castle were designed as curvilinear gablets, echoing similar profiles at Portumna, Co. Galway, and Loughmoe, Co. Tipperary.[113] The ashlar-built gateway into the bawn itself was a fine classical arch rising gracefully from plain imposts (fig. 6.28). Not all residences built in Co. Offaly at this time, however, adhered to Palladian principles of design, which celebrated symmetry and harmony.

A branch of the O'Carrolls under Donell Carroll constructed one of the finest fortified houses in the county at Ballymooney in *c.*1622. Unfortunately, the south façade with two projecting towers are all that survive of this residence (figs 6.9, 6.20). The elongated plan of the building, with its many corners and towers, is unparalleled in Offaly. There is no regular arrangement of windows, while the entrance is placed to the side instead of commanding a central position in the elevation. The plan of the building is sprawling. Indeed, the entrance itself is more typical of late medieval architecture, consisting of a double-centred doorway with a punch-dressed limestone surround (fig. 6.16). There is a rebate for a yett, which could be closed over the doorway to reinforce the entrance. The area immediately surrounding the doorway was covered by a machicolation box, of which only a pair of dressed corbels survives. The presence of such archaic features at Ballymooney highlights the tendency for late medieval elements to persist in Irish architecture during the first half of the seventeenth century.

On entering the double-centred door into the fortified house at Ballymooney, people were met with a sight familiar to the occupants of tower houses: a stone newel stairwell. Other double-centred doorways opening off from this stairwell allowed access to the various floors of the main block. The stairs have been removed, but the impressions of the missing steps remain (fig. 6.21). In the Jacobean period, there was much emphasis on processional routes through the houses of the elite, which involved twists and turns. What is interesting in this case is that the O'Carrolls at Ballymooney felt comfortable to continue with approaching each floor of the house via the confines of a dark, narrow stairwell, recreating an experience in movement and light that was to be found in tower houses.

Such a marriage of traditional and novel design can be seen in a number of fortified houses across Ireland, such as Gowely, Co. Leitrim, with its spiral stairwell (built by the anglicized John Reynolds in the 1620s), or Dunasead Castle in Baltimore, Co. Cork, with its ogee-headed two-light windows (built by the English planter Thomas Crooke).[114] While the continued strength of medieval forms is initially surprising, it can be seen not only in Ireland but across the Irish Sea as well.

In England, the architecture of the period remained generally unresponsive to developments on the Continent. Indeed, in the reign of Elizabeth I, only one book on architecture was published in England, John Shute's *The first and chief groundes of architecture* (1563).[115] According to Girouard, there was no reverence for or feeling that classicism was a discipline to be learnt or that it expressed principles of absolute validity.[116] The owners of buildings, in the absence of architects in the modern sense, could have much influence with comparatively uneducated master artisans, in the design of their own homes.[117] This can be clearly seen with the wide range of fortified house plans in Offaly, where planning may have been informed by several minds rather than inspired by the one mind formally trained in the concepts of architectural design. Patrons, their friends and executive craftsmen could alter plans and elevations, with individual architectural features such as fireplaces, stairwells, windows, chimney stacks, plasterwork and panelling normally being designed by the craftsmen who erected them.

As a result, the overall impression from the surviving architecture of early modern Ireland is that builders were quite selective in their use of classical design. As a result, the influence of classicism was superficial, with classical ornamentation confined to openings and fireplaces. An illustration of Trinity College Dublin (*c.*1592), the Irish cradle of Protestant humanism, shows that entry into the institution was via a classical entrance, a rather ornate frontispiece flanked by pillars and large statues on either side of a round-arched doorway, finished with an entabulature and pediment above. And yet, the rest of the college complex followed the English late medieval tradition of the hall and ancillary buildings arranged around a fully enclosed courtyard.[118] It was only much later, after 1660, that whole plans and elevations came to be informed by classical precepts of symmetry and rationalism. It is a story that finds parallels in the English experience, where, despite the genius of Inigo Jones in the first half of the century, his countrymen were quite slow to adopt classicism wholly.[119] This selective attitude among the early modern elite towards gothic and classical elements can be seen in other European countries such as France and Denmark, where classical architecture was blended with the gothic tradition, suggesting that the adoption of classicism did not necessarily mean the setting aside of local technology, expertise and materials.[120]

The gendering of the fortified house

Men, according to early modern commentaries and advice books, were associated with the outside, running the country estate, presenting the public and political face of the household, while women were enjoined to stay indoors, maintaining the needs of the household.[121] The appearance of the main residence played an integral part in proclaiming to the public the patriarchal values of an early modern elite household.

The presence of martial features such as gun opes, bartizans and double-centred doorways protected by yetts and overhead machicolation boxes, has emphasized the military role of such houses, allowing for the personification of the fortified house in the same masculine terms as tower houses to the exclusion of the female perspective. This division between male and female roles, between public and domestic, was underlined by the surrounding grounds of such residences, where the bawns of fortified houses served as forecourts, with few, if any, flowers included in what has been considered a masculine arena with the forecourt serving as an outdoor extension to the hall, 'traditionally a male preserve' where visitors and tenants would be received by the head of the household.[122]

As mentioned above, Lady Barrymore was interested in location and good prospect in relation to the rebuilding of her residence in Co. Cork in 1641.[123] Given Lady Barrymore's interest in landscaping, gardens could be perceived as feminized spaces. The garden provided much of what was required to run the household, in terms of food and herbal cures, concerns that came under the remit of the lady of the house. There is an early seventeenth-century classical memorial at the altar end of Sligo Abbey, which contains a rather attractive carving of O'Conor Sligo and his wife Eleanor, countess of Desmond, kneeling facing each other. Beside the male head are various instruments associated with martial valour, such as a drum, a shield, a sword and a pike, while the lady of the household is provided with more domestic equipment including a shovel, which may allude to the more productive pursuit of gardening. Indeed, writers in the early decades of the eighteenth century often saw flower gardens as belonging to the domain of women.[124]

The role of women in elite households, largely implicit and ambiguous, was explicitly acknowledged at times of duress. This can be seen in the 1640s, when a number of households were led by female heads to hold out against attackers. One example in east Offaly was Lady Offaly's leadership in the defence of her residence at Geashill. Her residence was besieged several times, and on each occasion Lady Offaly, a widow since 1618, refused offers of safe conduct, asserting that there was 'no place safer than my own house', a course of action that proved to be the correct one, as each siege was subsequently lifted.[125] Lady Elizabeth Dowdall of Kilfinny, Co. Limerick, hired a soldier to train eighty men and then sent them out to attack confederate troops. In January 1642, she successfully led the defence of her castle in a siege that resulted in the loss of two hundred of the enemy. Such women were accustomed to administering the household in the years before the outbreak of war, as the husbands of many of them would have been absent for substantial periods on official business. For women like Lady Offaly or Lady Dowdall, the defence of their residences was probably a logical extension of managing household affairs in more peaceful times.[126]

Despite these individual cases, however, Margaret MacCurtain has highlighted the intensification of patriarchy through the seventeenth century, both in Protestant and in Catholic households.[127] There was a desire to restore women to their proper

6.32 Only the south gable end of a two-storey fortified house survives at Killooly, along with the remains of a bawn with a flanker at its northwest corner. Its owner was possibly Peter Saltonstall, the son of a prominent merchant and one-time mayor of London (1597–8), Sir Richard Saltonstall. He was granted lands here in 1622.

subjugated place in the family and to restore stability by returning authority to the male head of the household. Indeed, Catholic women were trapped by the prevailing influences of the Counter-Reformation, which emphasized centralization, regulation and control; a tendency mirrored both in clerical and in household structures.[128] Spatial arrangements within the fortified houses in Offaly, which could inform on the nature of social conventions governing the daily activities of an early modern elite household, are greatly lacking due to the rare survival of architectural and documentary evidence. Such an understanding could allow for the elucidation of how spaces in these buildings were gendered. As mentioned in the previous chapter, in the great castle complexes of the high medieval period, the female household was located in the deepest space of the castle at the greatest distance from the main ceremonial entrance. Contemporaries regarded the honour and patrimony of lordship as dependent on the impermeability of both the castle and the female body.[129] Bearing in mind the Puritan and Counter-Reformation ideologies, which encouraged the regulation and control of women, the more secluded chambers beyond the hall and great chamber, particularly on the upper floors of the fortified houses, may have similarly been considered as belonging to the domain of women.

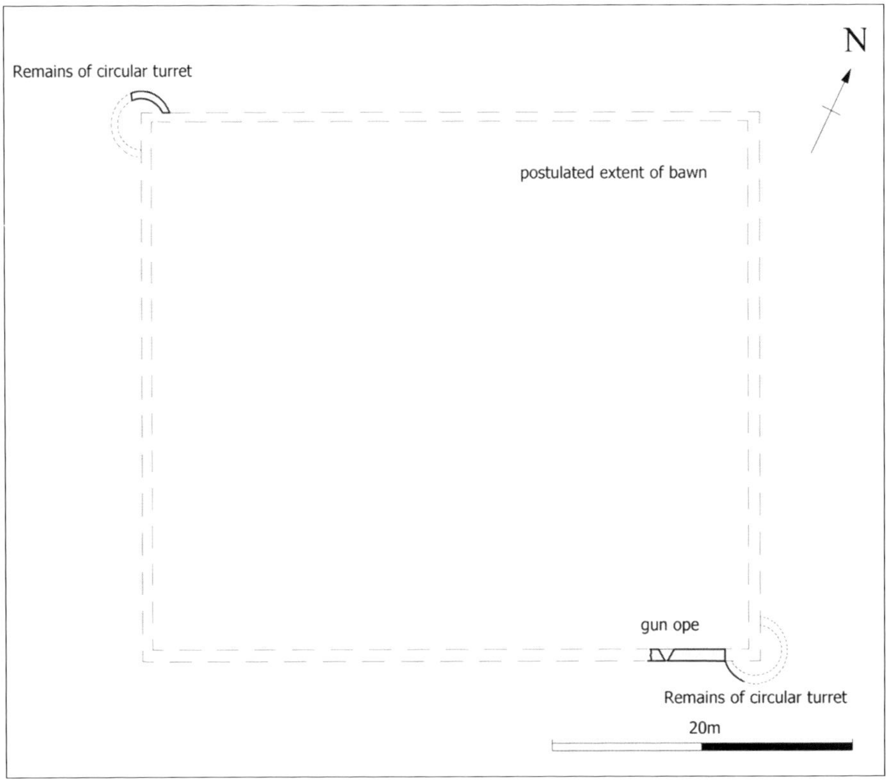

6.33 Plan of the bawn at Ballinree. Traditionally cited as Killyon Abbey, the archaeological remains at Ballinree indicate the former presence of a large fortified house. The house may have been built on or near the site of a former nunnery (drawn by James Lyttleton and Hugh Kavanagh).

Defensive qualities of fortified houses

Like the tower house, the fortified house provided a modicum of defence for its household in a society where religious and economic tensions characterized political discourse. As such, these fortified houses were equipped with various defensive measures such as gun opes, bartizans and machicolations, with perimeter defences provided by a gatehouse and bawn bristling with flankers and gun opes. In Co. Offaly, gun opes possess small rectilinear or circular openings, which are typically flush with the outer face of the wall, a type of opening developed after it was found that shot could be directed into interiors by openings with externally splayed surfaces.[130] Another version is also to be found at Ballycowan and at Ballymooney, where among the usual gun opes are a small number of slit opes whose long axis is horizontal, not vertical – a form that facilitated a greater range of view.

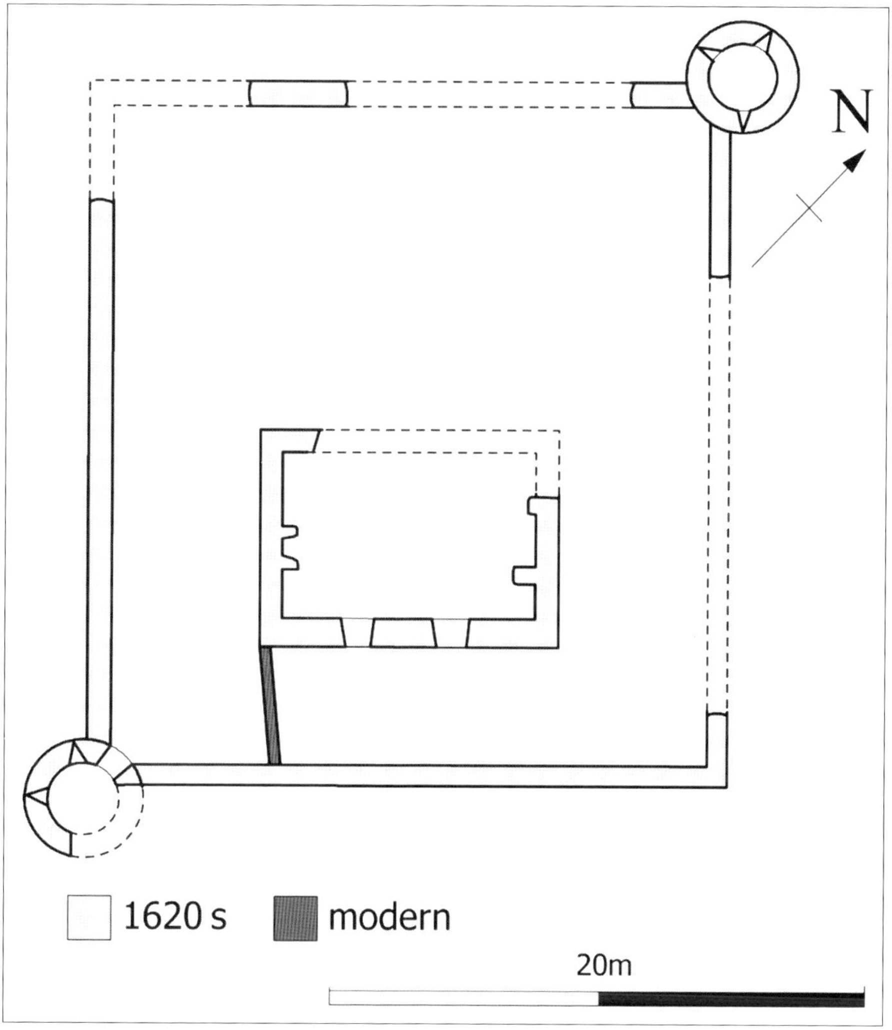

6.31 Plan of the fortified house and bawn at Newtown (after Salter, *The castles of Leinster* (2004), p. 139).

At Killooly, only one cylindrical gun turret survives, though other bawns were provided with a number of such turrets (fig. 6.32). The bawns at Ballinree and Newtown were provided with two flanking turrets at opposite corners (figs 6.33, 6.34) – the so-called Scottish Z-plan, which does not resemble a Z, but refers to the practice of placing flankers only at opposite corners, though still capable of commanding the length of all four walls. At Ballynasrah, each corner of the bawn is provided with four turrets. There are structural indications to suggest that the bawn at Kilcolgan More was also provided with a turret at each of its four corners. At the latter site, the turrets are atypical in that they are angled bastions with rounded flanks, paralleling Castle Ireton, Co. Tipperary, and Longford Castle, Co. Longford (fig. 6.25).[131] At Ballyknockan and Ballymooney, where two turrets survive, not at opposite, but at adjacent corners, comparative evidence with other bawns, and an appreciation of defensive principles, would suggest that at least one of the remaining corners was provided with a turret (fig. 6.9). At Moyally, there is an oval bastion flanking the northeast corner of the bawn, with a rectilinear tower projecting almost centrally from the east bawn wall. The stump of another bastion survives at the northwest corner. Earthworks are not typically associated with the perimeter defences of these fortified houses, though the bawn at Moyally was enclosed by a fosse that is visible along the west and north sides. The only approach to the fortified house at Annaghmore, which is located on a ridge of high ground in an area of low-lying marsh, is also defended by a fosse, *c.*20 to 30m to the southwest of the building.

Fortifications in contemporary North America were certainly inspired by the experience accrued through the construction and use of the bawn in Ireland. A number of fortified enclosures have been uncovered in Virginia, including Flowerdew Hundred, Jordan's Journey, Bermuda Hundred and Martin's Hundred. Hostilities with the native Powhatan confederacy in 1609–14, 1622–7 and 1644–5, and with the Susquehannocks in 1675–6, along with competition from European rivals, necessitated the fortification of these estate centres in the Chesapeake region.[132] Similar to the bawns at Ballinree and Newtown in Co. Offaly is Harbor View Fort (*c.*1645) in Virginia, where a wooden palisaded area 70m in length by 22.6m in width was covered by two cylindrical flankers at opposite corners, measuring 5 and 3.7m respectively in diameter, allowing for flanking enfilade fire.[133] Similarly, the fortified house at Clifts Plantation was enclosed by a wooden palisade defended at two opposing corners. This bawn was rather small, though, measuring 19m east–west by 17m north–south, the perimeter curtain walls only allowing enough space to facilitate access to the flankers. Lacking space to contain a courtyard and other ancillary buildings, the continued use of this bawn was impractical, and as soon as conditions stabilized for the occupants, the palisade was taken down.[134]

The location of most fortified houses in Offaly appears to have eschewed concerns of defence and security, with the main emphasis on cultivating the labour and economic resources of the surrounding countryside. In certain cases, the surrounding topography conspired to undermine the defensibility of sites with higher ground within musket shot of fortified houses and bawns, as at Ballyknockan, Ballynasrah, Killooly and Newtown. As a whole, fortified houses are typically located on undulating, rolling farmland, with examples at Ballycowan, Ballinree, Clonlyon Castlequarter, Fortel and Garrycastle occupying a slightly raised position that allowed the buildings to rise and dominate the surrounding landscape, but certainly not in a manner to render them impregnable. The location of the fortified houses at Annaghmore and Leitra on islands surrounded by impregnable wetland, connected

6.35 The fortified house at Annaghmore is provided with a number of gun-opes, including these examples in the ground and first floors of its northeast tower. Both gun opes possess roughly dressed surrounds with a circular opening (diam. c.9–10cm).

6.36 Embrasure of the ground-floor gun ope in the northeast tower of the fortified house at Annaghmore.

to the mainland by tenuous ridges of high ground, is rather exceptional. On dryland, the fortified houses at Castlearmstrong and Cloghmoyle occupy elevated sites, the former overlooking extensive bogland a short distance to the south, with the latter dominating the village of Shinrone to the northeast.

Edward Jope opined that some bawns were no more than walled farmyards, with little concern for the defence of the household, as at Muff, Co. Derry, where the main entrance to the house faces the exterior, and not, as would be expected, into the interior of the bawn.[135] The efficacy of gun opes and flankers has been called into question, with limited ranges of fire available from these features. Paul Kerrigan cited the fortified houses with bastioned angle turrets at Rathfarnham, Co. Dublin, Raphoe, Co. Donegal, and Manorhamilton, Co. Leitrim, as examples where the builder did not have a clear understanding of defence by flanking fire, as the faces of the turrets are not at an appropriate angle and are not covered by fire from the flanks of the adjacent turrets.[136] Most gun opes in Offaly, with their small openings, typically

9cm by 9cm, provided a limited range of vision and fire, an observation point completely obscured when a musket was placed into the firing position (figs 6.35, 6.36). Another important consideration is the resulting smoke from the discharge of gunpowder in these muskets and the potential danger from recoil in such confined spaces. The build-up of smoke from prolonged action could make positions from the inside of buildings, particularly flanking turrets, unbearable for defenders. Similar observations have been made on the military effectiveness of gun opes in Scottish houses.[137]

Such considerations may have meant that defences such as the gun opes, bartizans and machicolation boxes, with limited range of fire, were inadequate to stall attacks. In the aftermath of the 1641 uprising, the presence of fortified houses surrounded by their bawns in west and south Offaly failed to prevent the rapid overturn of plantation settlement there. Within the following year, the only surviving Protestant enclaves were in the south of the county, namely two strongholds at Birr and Knocknamese. Another factor that may have led to the exposure of most planter households to attacks was the overwhelming dependence on firearms to protect the precincts of these fortified houses. The demilitarization of society in the years before the 1641 uprising had reduced the number of muskets available to loyal sections of society. In Ulster, for example, where one settler in eight owned a musket in 1619, only one in thirty-three did so in 1630. Indeed, towns with substantial populations, such as Carrickfergus and Derry in 1631, reported only twenty muskets apiece for their defence.[138]

There is no doubt that concerns for defence played a part in the design of these fortified houses. Scholars in the past have interpreted the development of the fortified house as a transition between the castle and the freestanding country mansion, with the architectural genre being influenced by two competing needs, domestic comfort and defensive invulnerability. When these buildings are interpreted through either a military or social lens, however, there is a danger of essentialism, which obviates nuances in the contemporary understanding of architecture. As seen above, the application of the term 'castle' and 'house' to fortified houses was interchangeable and vague. There was no essential category of what made a fortified house a castle or a house, or indeed both, as it was a fluid concept to contemporaries in the early modern period. Indeed, the dichotomy of domestic versus military only had its beginnings in early modern Ireland, exemplified by the establishment of permanent army garrisons such as Fort Falkland in Banagher, Co. Offaly.

Conclusion

Fortified houses have not received the same amount of attention as tower houses. One reason for this could be the numerical superiority of tower houses scattered across the countryside when compared with the four hundred or so extant fortified houses in Ireland. Fortified houses are also more associated with newly arrived English and Scottish settlers, who were being settled in confiscated properties under the auspices of various plantation schemes. Such an association certainly would not have recommended the fortified house as an architectural form that merited appreciation and study in later times.

This chapter, while highlighting typological, chronological and documentary issues, illustrates that such buildings were an important medium through which complex and fluid relations between natives and newcomers could be played out, allowing for the transformation and maintenance of social, ethnic and gender identities. Thus, the appearance and layout of fortified houses were invested unconsciously or implicitly with a range of meanings that were intelligible to contemporaries. The provision of well-furnished chambers in early modern households (along with the deployment of classical ornamentation and the establishment of formal gardens) was fundamentally more important than had been the case in previous periods, as the status of an individual was no longer conveyed by large numbers of servants and retainers, but by the style and quality of objects and surroundings. Clearly, the values and concepts that underlay what it meant to be a member of the landlord class had now been transformed in Ireland. In essence, there was a realization of *realpolitik* that saw planter and native elites develop strategies of cooperation in economic, cultural and social spheres for mutual benefit. A greater sensitivity to the nuances of interpersonal relations between the different ethnic and confessional groups, as manifested in architecture such as fortified houses, allows for a more balanced understanding of a society where old certainties were giving way to new.

CHAPTER 7

Houses in early modern Offaly

Introduction

The buildings discussed in the previous chapters were designed to provide a level of defensible accommodation. Traditionally, scholars have regarded this as necessary, given the level of political and social instability in the early modern period. The present chapter throws light upon a corpus of buildings in Offaly that appear to have eschewed such concerns for the defence of the household (fig. 7.1). Besides the O'Carroll homestead at Ballybrack and the Parsons residence at Birr Castle, the buildings to be considered here belong to the latter half of the seventeenth century. To a certain extent, this parallels the situation in Scotland, where elite country houses, lacking defensive features, were not built until after the Restoration, with the landed elite until then preferring tower houses and fortified houses.[1]

Following the Restoration, the parapets, machicolation boxes, bartizans, double-centred doorways protected by yetts, and indeed the ubiquitous gun opes, disappear from the elevations of elite buildings in Ireland. Thus, there was a visible break with native gothic building traditions, which were intimately linked with the display and assertion of late medieval lordship. Service to the crown or influence with officialdom, rather than martial prowess and large retinues, now enhanced the standing of the landed elite within communities. Given the absence of these overtly martial features, however, a bawn wall would still have surrounded many of these 'non-defensive' buildings. The form and scale of these houses expressed, through a material medium, the concerns and aspirations of a section of early modern society in Offaly. These were predominantly British in origin, ranging in status from probably well-off farmers (such as Ballynamire, Ballytoran and Lisduff) to wealthy and influential gentry (as at Birr Castle and Lisclooney) (figs 7.2, 7.3).

Besides Ballybrack (which probably belongs to the first half of the seventeenth century), no houses are demonstrably native in origin (fig. 7.4). This is indicative of falling fortunes among the Gaelic Irish aristocracy in late seventeenth-century Offaly. The aftermath of the Cromwellian conquest and the subsequent Restoration saw the undermining of the native aristocracy like the O'Carrolls and O'Molloys to such an extent that by 1688 only a quarter of the land in Offaly was in Catholic hands.[2] Only a small number of substantial native owners in Offaly survived these tribulations – for example, Francis MacCoghlan of Kilcolgan, Terence MacCoghlan of Kincora, Owen Mooney of Doon, Arthur Molloy in Ballyboy and Owen O'Carroll in

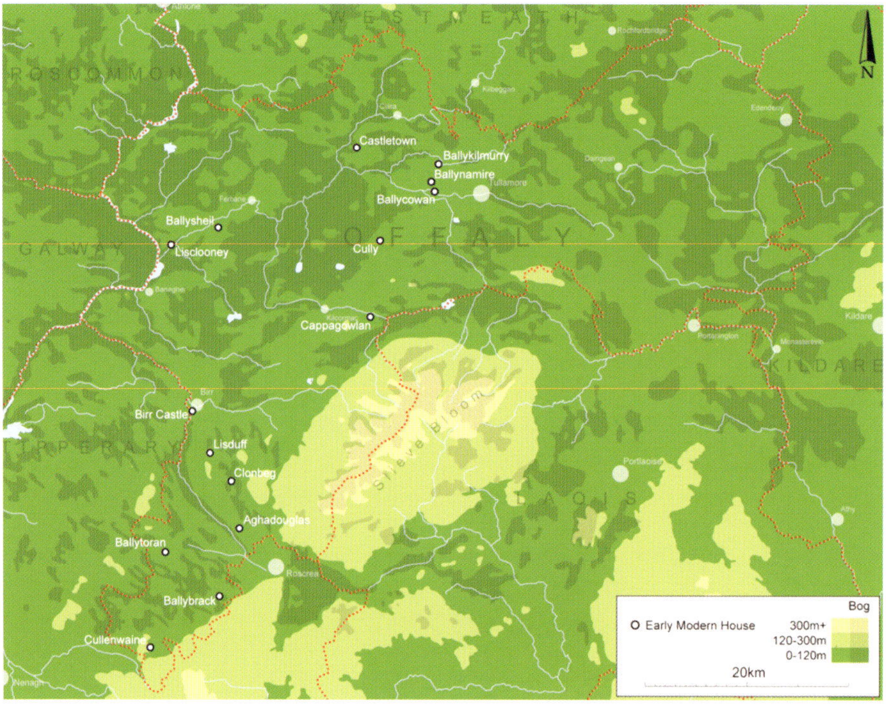

7.1 Distribution of early modern houses across west and south Offaly (drawn by Conor McDermott and Hugh Kavanagh).

Kilmaine.[3] Extant remains and documentary evidence suggest that the above proprietors, with the exception of Francis MacCoghlan and Owen O'Carroll, occupied tower houses; the former residing in a fortified residence within a formidable bawn, while only relict garden landscaping survives at the home of the latter. Thus, it can be said that, with some notable exceptions, the native landed elite deprived of their lands, went into economic decline. Stripped of their estates and landed wealth, it should come as no surprise that not one upstanding house of late seventeenth-century date can be definitively attributed to native proprietors. To an extent, this decline can be seen as part of a greater process, which saw the increasing marginalization of the aristocracy across Ireland and Britain, with their regional power bases being assimilated into a national political and cultural hegemony ultimately centred on London.

Introducing early modern 'non-defensive' architecture in Offaly

While there is variation in the forms and plans of these buildings, as would be expected in this period, most houses in Offaly are T-shaped in plan, with a rear

7.2 Front elevation of farmstead at Ballynamire, from the south. The first floor was in the attic space, presumably lit by dormer windows that have not survived. The central chimneystack with its diagonal chimney shafts is characteristic of seventeenth-century architecture, while the brick chimney shaft on the chimneystack to the left is a replacement inserted later but possibly before 1700.

7.3 Rear façade of residence at Lisclooney. In 1641, Hugh O'Dalaghan was the proprietor of Lisclooney, though following the Cromwellian confiscations, William Hamilton held the property in 1659. He built the present house sometime after 1665 on the site of an earlier castle.

7.4 Remains of the seventeenth-century T-plan house at Ballybrack. In 1639, Ballybrack was held by Donough O'Carroll, who was transplanted to the barony of Ballymoe, Co. Galway, in the 1650s, following the Cromwellian confiscations (© National Monuments Service: Department of Arts, Heritage and the Gaeltacht).

projection containing a wooden stairwell. At Ballynamire and Lisduff, however, there is evidence to suggest that access to the floors above was integrated into the main body of the house, in the manner of modern housing (figs 7.5, 7.6). This obviated the need for a projecting block, not only saving expense in materials and heating, but also allowing oblong houses to be erected. At the other end of the scale, both architecturally and socially, Birr Castle and Lisclooney have plans without extant comparisons in early modern Ireland. The former consists of an oblong block flanked by straight wings that, like two bent arms, project forward (fig. 7.7). Lisclooney has a rather sprawling plan, with an L-shaped main block with a central projection in the rear wall and another wing drawn out from the northeast corner at an obtuse angle, again at the rear (fig. 7.8).

Birr Castle merits further attention, as only three other examples of early seventeenth-century triple-piled buildings are known in Ireland: Portumna Castle, Co. Galway, and two houses built by Sir Arthur Chichester – Chichester House in Dublin and Belfast Castle, Co. Antrim.[4] Birr Castle's unusual plan may have been inspired by Warmwell Manor in Dorset, though the Parsons family had their roots in Leicestershire and Nottinghamshire.[5] Máirtín D'Alton has made an intriguing

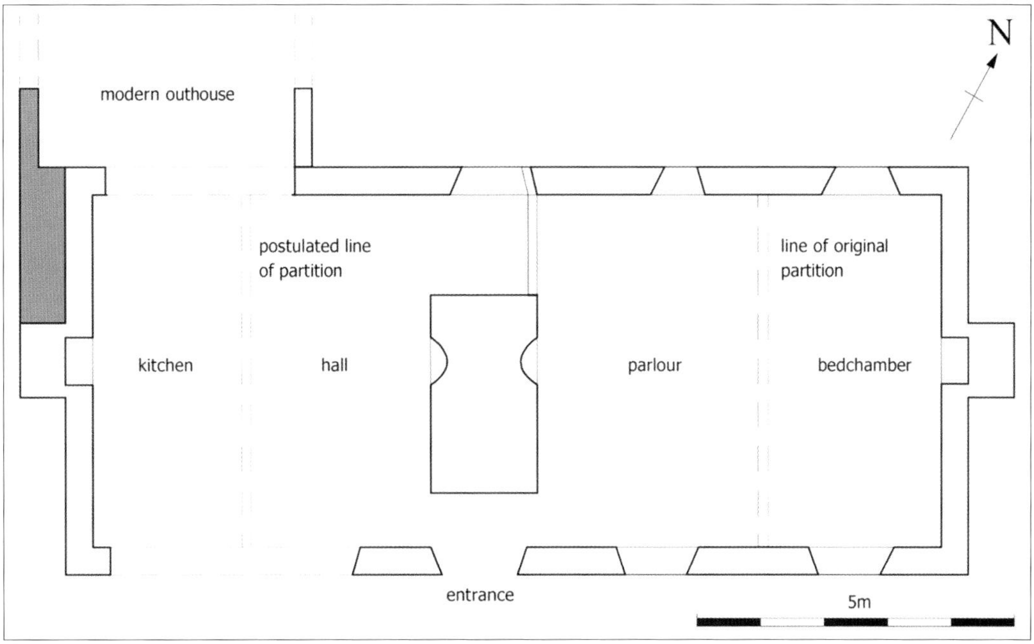

7.5 Plan of the farmstead at Ballynamire (drawn by James Lyttleton and Hugh Kavanagh).

7.6 Plan of the farmstead at Lisduff (drawn by James Lyttleton and Hugh Kavanagh).

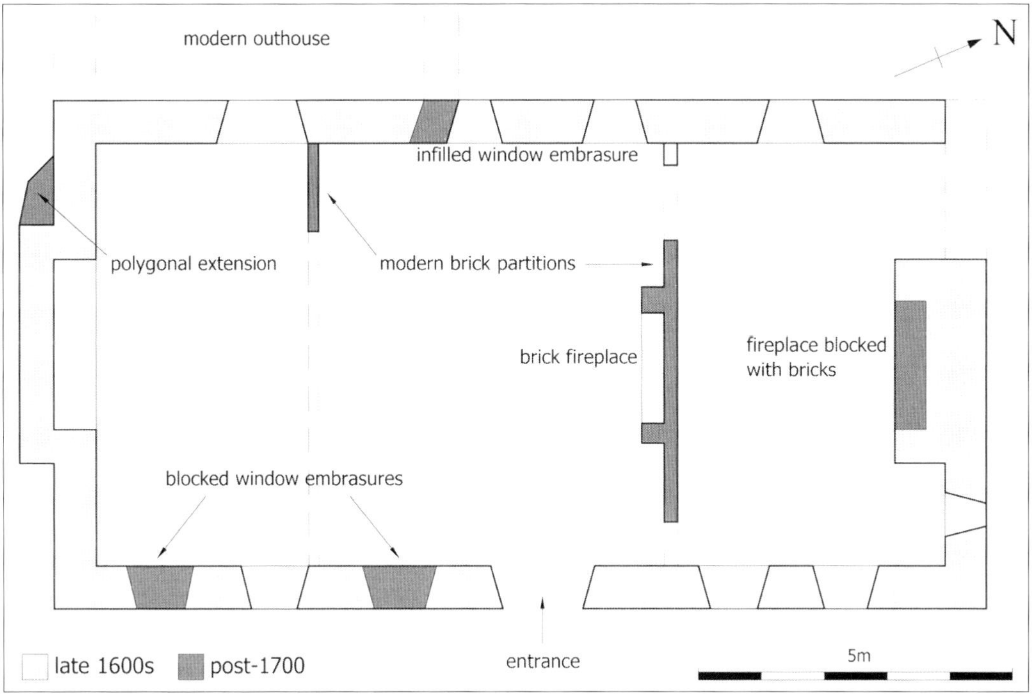

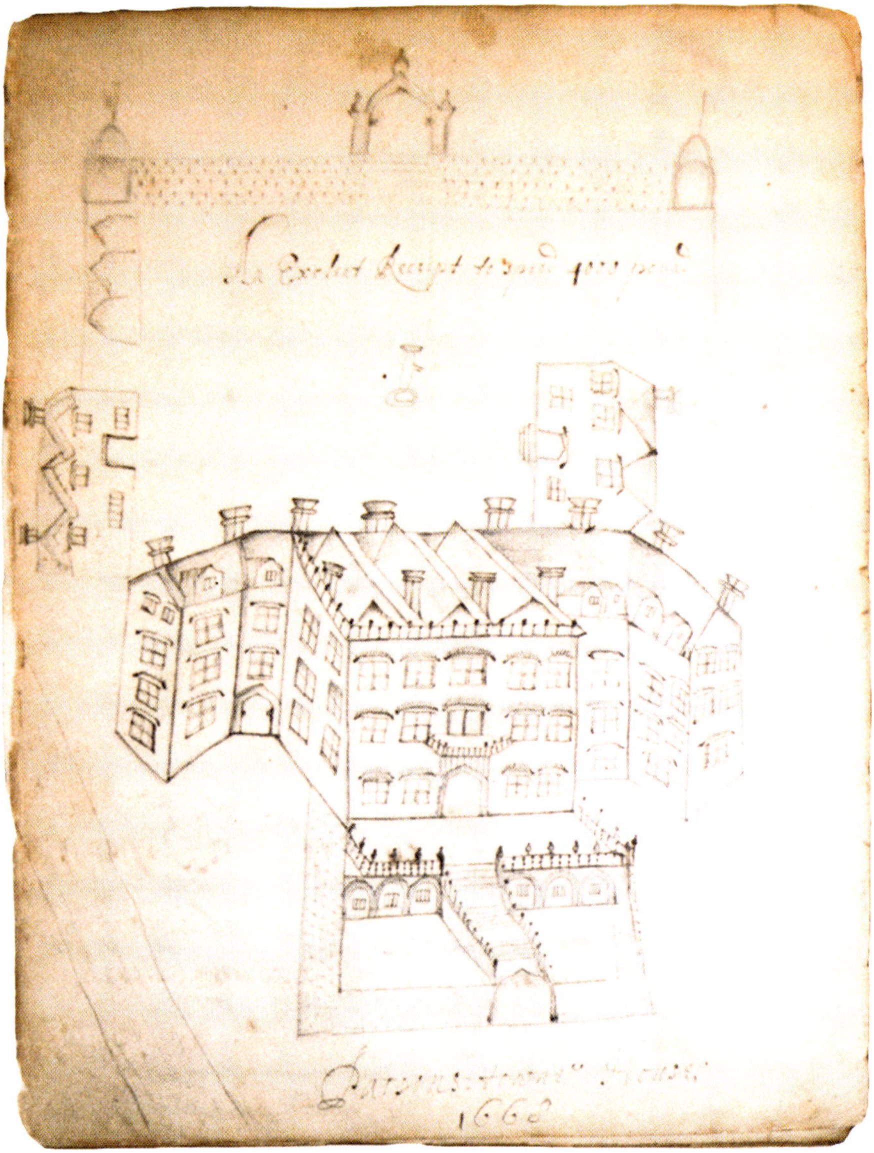

7.7 Depiction of Birr Castle and surrounding grounds from a southerly perspective, drawn by Lady Dorothy Parsons in 1668 in her recipe book (Birr Castle MS A17, 1668).

suggestion that an Irish parallel may be found in a panoramic painting *c.*1740 of the Cosby estate at Stradbally, Co. Laois.[6] The eighteenth-century Cosby residence (demolished *c.*1770 when Stradbally Hall was moved to its present location) forms the central composition – but to its side was an older house, possibly early

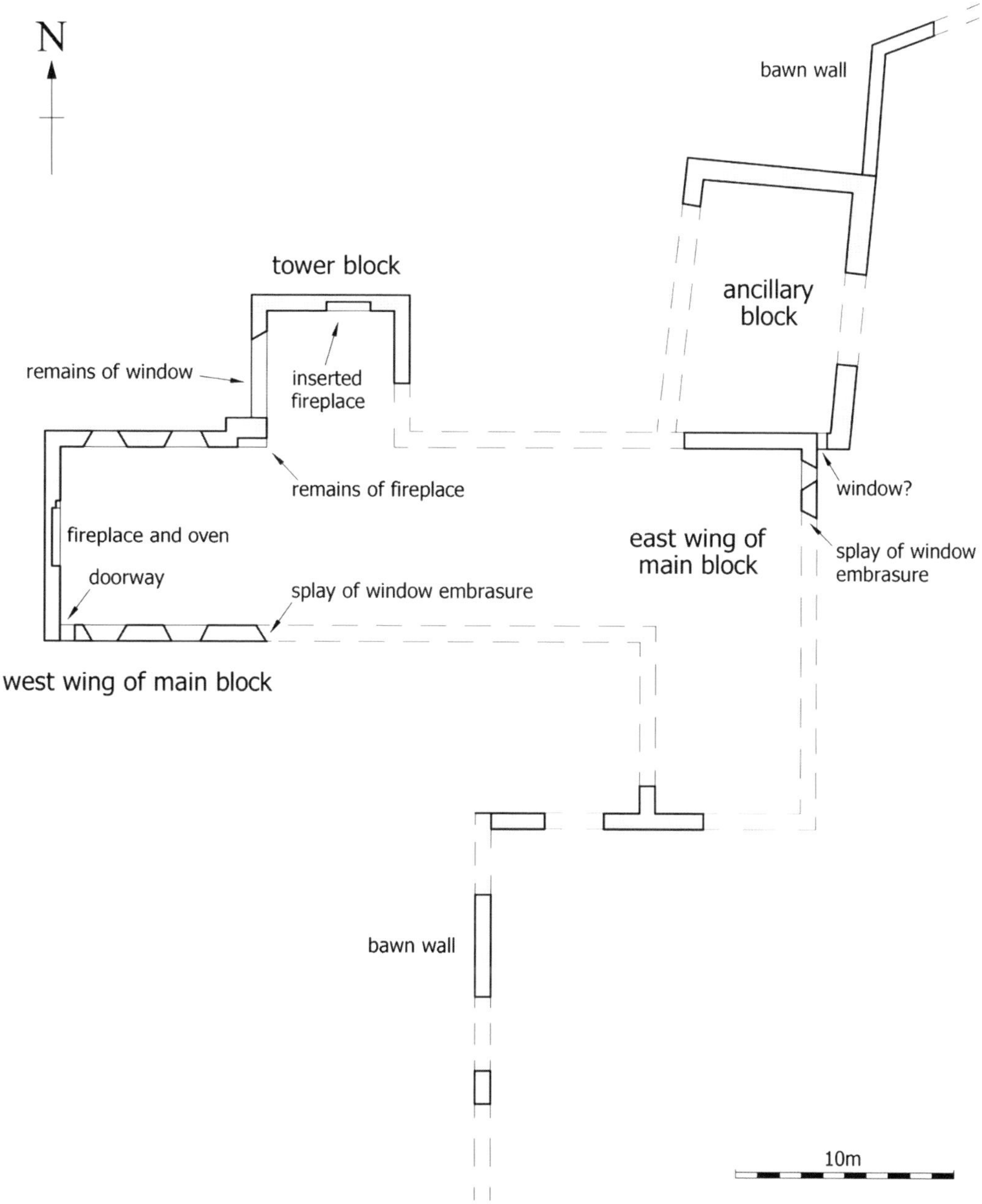

7.8 Plan of the residence at Lisclooney (drawn by James Lyttleton and Hugh Kavanagh).

seventeenth century in date, with a square gabled wing placed at an angle to it. By the time of the painting, a corresponding wing on the other side of the house may have been demolished or integrated into its eighteenth-century successor.

These houses, like fortified houses and tower houses, are built of roughly coursed limestone and sandstone rubble, with varying degrees of preserved internal and external rendering. Despite the appearance of brick chimney shafts, as well as ovens and chimney flues lined with similar fabric, houses of early modern date built wholly of brick are unknown in Offaly. In Ulster, in areas of more intensive English settlement, houses constructed of brick have been recorded, especially along the Lagan Valley, through north Armagh, in the Erne basin and central Cavan, as well as to the west and north of Lough Neagh.[7] Elsewhere in Ireland, large brick structures such as the five-storey house built into the northern recess of Bunratty Castle during the tenure of the fourth earl of Thomond (1581–1624) were more the exception than the rule.[8]

Due to the perishable nature of doorways, or their subsequent adaptation in these buildings, it is difficult to ascertain their original appearance. The best preserved examples at Ballynamire, Ballysheil, Lisclooney and Lisduff are basic flat-headed openings without dressed surrounds, in some instances with their embrasures and reveals still roofed with adze-cut timber lintels; openings that originally would have held door frames. The front entrance at Ballysheil, which was originally elevated and approached by a short flight of steps, was flanked by two tall and narrow windows, paralleling entrances to be found in other classically inspired buildings in this period such as Springhill, Co. Derry (*c.*1697).[9] Examples found elsewhere in the country of classically informed doorways with elaborate stone surrounds crowned with a pediment, or more typically with a swan-neck or segmental pediment, are unknown in Offaly (though the Protestant church at Durrow possesses a doorway with a classical entabulature surmounted by Grecian urns; see the following chapter). Birr Castle has undergone significant alterations since the early modern period, culminating in a mansion of neo-gothic appearance by the early nineteenth century (fig. 7.9). However, Dorothy Parsons' sketch of Birr Castle and its surrounding grounds in a recipe book dated 1668 illustrates a number of entrances, mostly with pointed, flattened arches, in the front façade of the main residence and in ancillary buildings facing into a rear courtyard. An exception is one ancillary building along the southwest side of the same courtyard with a flat-headed doorway (fig. 7.7).

The original appearance of windows in this corpus of buildings is largely a matter of conjecture, as timber window frames appear to have become increasingly popular. Timber casements, surrounds and fittings have perished, leaving bare openings. Only Ballybrack and Birr Castle preserve evidence of windows with wrought stone surrounds, with square hood mouldings still evident in the latter building (figs 7.10, 7.11). Where buildings have remained in continuous use, the original windows have been altered to a greater or lesser extent with the insertion of modern materials such as cement lining, concrete sills and sash windows (for example, Ballytoran). Where buildings have been abandoned at a reasonably early stage, such as at Lisclooney and Ballysheil, the reveals and embrasures bear adzed

7.9 Birr Castle has been altered by various generations of the Parsons family since the early seventeenth century. The present mansion contains the original O'Carroll gatehouse with a barrel-vaulted corridor surviving at basement level, along with the east and west wings, set at an angle to the main block, as depicted in Dorothy Parsons' cookbook of 1668. Also within the present building, though not in its original location, is a fine yew staircase of late seventeenth-century date with boldly turned balusters and a broad ramping rail that rises through three floors of the house (© National Monuments Service: Department of Arts, Heritage and the Gaeltacht).

timber lintels, as well as rebates and slots in the jambs of external openings to facilitate the insertion of wooden window frames. One of the windows lighting a ground-floor room at Ballysheil preserves a rare instance of an adzed timber lintel with a notch and tusk tenon at either end, for a window frame to fit into (fig. 7.12). Such a woodworking technique is typical of the late seventeenth and early eighteenth centuries.[10]

At Birr Castle, the surviving original windows in the east flanker possess stone square hood mouldings, confirming the veracity of Parsons' 1668 depiction mentioned above, which illustrates the use of square-hooded mullion-and-transom windows throughout the residence. Interestingly, these window surrounds could have

7.10 T-plan house at Ballybrack owned by Donough O'Carroll before the 1641 uprising.

been painted with a colour scheme, as a glazier called Roger Peirce was contracted in 1627 to 'colour and puttogh [putty] all my windows and doors and stairs now made ... and also to refresh again with colour and oil all windows, doors and stairs in my castle called the gatehouse'.[11] Bearing this in mind, it is of interest to note that mullion-and-transom windows of wood were decorated with external carvings at a late seventeenth-century residence at Eyrecourt, Co. Galway, not far from Banagher, raising the possibility that windows in Offaly were similarly treated.[12] There was space for innovative window styles besides mullion-and-transom windows, as exemplified at the O'Carroll residence at Ballybrack, where one of the ground-floor chambers is lit by a stone-cut, chamfered, segmental-headed slit ope with an attractive splayed opening of roughly dressed limestone (fig. 7.10).

Throughout the seventeenth century, it was fashionable to create false quoins and rusticated window surrounds in the rendering of exteriors.[13] In Offaly, a variation on the theme can be seen in the latter half of the seventeenth century; for example, at Ballysheil, Birr Castle and Lisclooney, where there are a number of windows that appear to have been surrounded by a recessed plaster border imprinted into the external rendering (figs 7.12, 7.13). Dormer windows were a popular feature of early modern housing, as is clear from pictorial and structural evidence. Parsons' 1668 illustration of Birr Castle depicts dormers in both wings of the residence, along with

7.11 View of the east wing of Birr Castle. Remarkably, the original square-hooded windows, as depicted in a sketch of the castle dated to 1668, have survived.

7.12 Recessed plaster borders surround the windows in the façade of Ballysheil. A timber lintel with a notch-and-tuck tenon at either end is preserved in the ground-floor window in the centre.

7.13 Recessed plaster borders surrounding the first-floor windows in the façade of the residence at Lisclooney.

7.14 An eighteenth-century drawing of Cloghan Castle depicts a three-storey structure with hipped roof and large windows set into wide round-arched embrasures, as well as a machicolation box at roof level. Abutting the building to the left is a gatehouse. The profile of the building, along with the solid stone partitions and the large window embrasures, are typical of tower houses in the region. The castle no longer stands, but the remains of it may exist below ground surface (courtesy of Lord Rossmore and the Irish Architectural Archive).

half dormers in the ancillary buildings to the rear (fig. 7.7). Remains at Ballysheil and Lisclooney indicate that the upper reaches of the surviving window reveals on the top floors have been lost, with the disappearance of the roof superstructure suggesting that these windows were half dormers. High-pitched, hipped or gabled roofs punctuated with dormers surmounted many buildings in this period, judging by surviving topographical drawings by Dineley in the 1680s or Francis Place a decade later.[14] Indeed, hipped roofs on elite buildings of the seventeenth century have been considered to be of Italian derivation, perhaps indicative of the interest in classical design at this time.[15] In Offaly, there are no extant examples of hipped-roof buildings, the elite residences of the gentry such as Birr Castle, Ballysheil and Lisclooney being gabled. However, an eighteenth-century drawing of the MacCoghlan stronghold at Cloghan village depicts a tower house with a hipped roof (fig. 7.14).[16] Holborn gables are not known in Offaly, with the Irish examples apparently restricted to Ulster, embellishing the roofs of residences at Waringstown, Co. Down, and Richhill, Co. Armagh.[17]

There is no surviving evidence for the nature of roofing, but it is probable that slate was the principal material. The 1668 sketch of Birr Castle reveals its roofs not to be covered by thatch, implying the use of slate; however, there is a suggestion that wooden shingles were used instead. In 1689, after Sir Laurence Parsons surrendered

Birr Castle to Jacobite forces, the victors quartered two companies there, who apparently stripped a shingle roof off the building for firing.[18] Wooden shingles and red tiles could be found across Ireland through the seventeenth century.[19] Redwood Castle, a residence apparently of seventeenth-century date, stood on the grounds of Charleville Castle near Tullamore. Redwood was described in the early nineteenth century by Lord Charleville as bearing:

> a ponderous and double roof, also of the same material, and covered with shingles of oak of more ancient date, procured from the adjacent bogs, which with occasional repairs repelled the beating storms for nearly two centuries.[20]

The use of bog oak to roof Redwood Castle prevented the usual shrinkage of shingles, which necessitated their relaying after a year. The size of shingles could vary, but those used to cover timber-framed houses at Moneymore, Co. Derry, measured two feet (61cm) in length, five inches (13cm) in width and one inch (2.5cm) in thickness.[21]

Chimney stacks projecting from steep gables or rear elevations of houses served fireplaces. Even where solid internal partition walls could support chimney stacks deep in the centre of a house, as at Ballysheil, there was a general inclination to concentrate stacks round the periphery of buildings. Even so, there is an emerging tendency in houses of lower status, probably associated with socially middling farmers (for example, Ballynamire), for a chimney stack with two fireplaces back-to-back to be located within the centre of the house, dividing the internal space into two areas, creating a plan known by scholars of vernacular buildings as the 'lobby entry' plan (fig. 7.5). These chimney stacks are stoutly built, often crowned with cornices and moulded stonework. Both diagonal and axial chimneys are known in this corpus of Offaly houses.

How many of these houses survive?

Fourteen early modern houses lacking defensive features have survived to varying degrees of preservation across west and south Offaly (fig. 7.1). On the basis of their preservation, these houses can be divided into three groups. Of the fourteen extant examples, only two have survived to the extent that original exteriors and internal spaces can be interpreted, namely Ballynamire and Ballysheil. Another five houses have fared less well: Ballybrack, Ballytoran, Birr Castle, Lisduff and Lisclooney. The ruinous nature of this group of houses (with the exception of Birr Castle, which has seen alterations over the centuries) does not allow complete reconstruction, but their extant walls, with surviving architectural features, allow comparisons with the first group of houses. The third and final group consists of seven sites with only ephemeral traces of what were once houses of early modern date. Indeed, due to their partial survival, the possibility of these buildings being the remains of fortified houses cannot be dismissed. This group consists of Ballycowan, Ballykilmurry, Castletown and Cully in Fir Cheall, along with Aghadouglas, Clonbeg and Cullenwaine in Éile Uí Chearbhaill.

The problematic nature of houses in early modern Offaly

A variety of challenges confront the student of early modern architecture in Ireland, with problems of abysmal preservation, poor documentary sources, subsequent building 'improvements', imprecise chronologies and unwieldy typological frameworks. As mentioned in previous chapters, documentary sources for early modern Irish architecture are poor, often with little or no references to the appearance of these buildings or indeed to how they were used. Material such as household inventories, wills and plans found in parts of Britain, Continental Europe and North America are unfortunately sparse in Ireland. Even where plans and inventories do survive, while the names of rooms may suggest specific functions, in reality many interiors were still used for a mixture of purposes. As mentioned in the previous chapter, beds were still to be found in halls and parlours in gentry residences right into the eighteenth century.[22] Indeed, contemporary drawings of country residences in Ireland prior to the 1680s are a rarity; even the royal country seat in Ireland, the Phoenix House on the outskirts of Dublin, has no known depiction.[23]

Scholars have commented upon the poor survival of buildings from the latter half of the seventeenth century across the island.[24] The establishment of large country houses set in open and exposed estates, bereft of defences, unfortunately condemned many of the new houses such as Lord Orrery's Charleville in Co. Cork to outright destruction during the course of the Williamite War in 1689–91.[25] This could explain why little architecture in Ireland from the late seventeenth century survives in comparison to what came before or after. Loeber has observed that practically all the known country houses of the post-Restoration period 'are ruined, or, more precisely, simply erased from the landscape, or changed beyond recognition', with some counties such as Offaly possessing remarkably few new country houses of this date.[26] Due to the strategic importance of Offaly, the county saw considerable action in the Williamite War, resulting in widescale destruction and dislocation. In such an unstable environment, it should not come as a surprise that few houses of the latter half of the seventeenth century survive. It is important, however, not to overemphasize the effects of sword and fire upon the built environment in this period. Another factor militating against a greater number of larger, more robust houses in this period could have been the comparatively low population in Offaly, as indicated by the 1659 poll-tax return.[27] Low population levels may have conspired against the levelling of high rents, thus reducing profits and restricting the capability of landowners to build or remodel their residences.

Even when early modern houses are identified on the ground, subsequent repairs and changing fashions have robbed façades of their early modern gloss. Owners in later centuries, in attempts to emulate more modish buildings, inserted inappropriate porches, doorways and sash windows, as well as remodelling chimney stacks with complete abandon, while the rearrangement of room partitions and the addition of new extensions obscured original house plans. This can be seen across Ireland, where buildings at first glance appear to be of eighteenth century or later date. The Turret (1683), in Ballingarry, Co. Limerick, is a good example of where an original form is partially obscured by such 'improvements'.[28] An Offaly example, Birr Castle, is a pertinent illustration of this process where, in 1803, the elevations of the castle were encased in a limestone gothic façade designed by John Johnson, which was further enhanced thirty years later when the central block was heightened by the addition of a storey after a fire (fig. 7.9).[29] In addition, other houses of the period could be obscured by later buildings placed to the front, such as at Newhall, Co. Clare, where the seventeenth-century gabled house with dormers and tall chimneys was concealed behind a Georgian front. The earlier house was converted into a kitchen, servants' and nursery wing for the mid-eighteenth-century house.[30] An example of this has been highlighted in Offaly at Cappagowlan, where a mid- to late eighteenth-century residence was added to the front of a single pile, gable-ended house of three storeys over basement. This original building was considered to be early modern, presumably on the basis of local information that a seventeenth-century date stone (exact year is not known) was uncovered during the course of renovations a number of years ago.[31] Unfortunately, enquiries failed to verify the existence of such a date stone and a detailed survey of the same building did not reveal any architectural features that could be attributed to before 1700.

Further issues of housing typology revolve around the study of early modern architecture in Offaly. In west and south Offaly, as mentioned in previous chapters, there are sixty known sites of elite residences, which have been identified by the Archaeological Survey of Ireland as 'castle sites' for the purposes of the county inventory. There are generally little or no upstanding remains of these sites, which can prevent the archaeologist or architectural historian from assigning more specific classifications. While the attribution of fortified houses or tower houses originally occupying these sites is generally correct, fragmentary remains on some sites may suggest a more ambiguous picture. The ephemeral traces of a 'castle site' at Cully suggest a house of early modern date rather than a tower house. Unfortunately, the lower courses of some walling cannot allow for identification of whether the residence was defensible or not. As mentioned in the previous chapter, at Derrydolney there is an armorial plaque embellished with the O'Molloy coat of arms recording the building of a house there in 1684 (figs 7.15, 7.16). No trace of the original house survives above ground. Indeed, the exact location of the house within the townland is open to debate. Again, there is a difficulty in determining a more

7.15 and 7.16 The O'Molloy armorial plaque and date stone from Derrydolney (1684) are carved on two blocks of stone.

7.17 The south façade of the residence at Ballysheil. This property was apparently held by the Sheele family in the period before their transplantation to the barony of Longford, Co. Galway, in 1654–8.

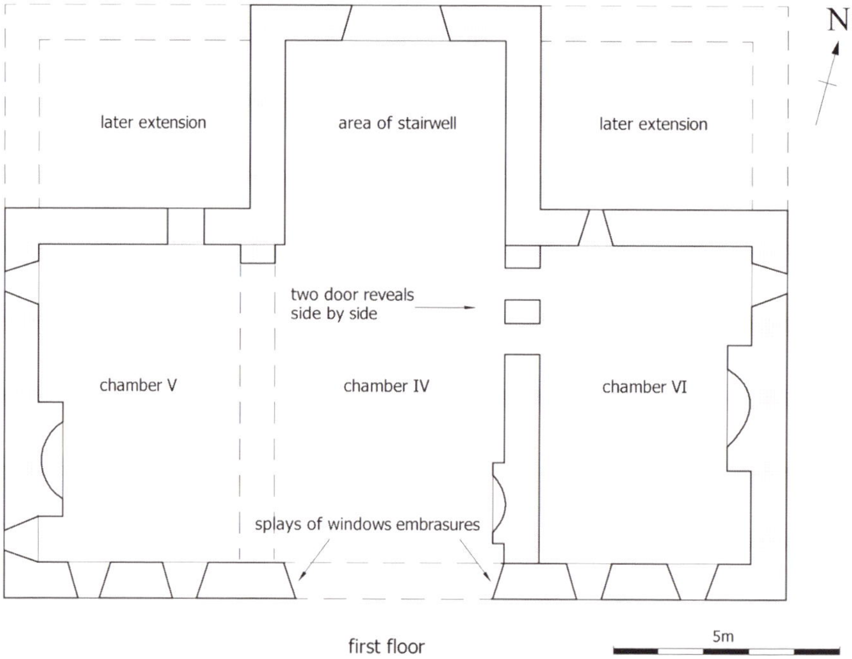

7.18 First-floor plan of the early modern house at Ballysheil (drawn by James Lyttleton and Hugh Kavanagh).

conclusive classification of this site, though the date of its construction in the 1680s would suggest (on the basis of comparative evidence in Ireland) that this O'Molloy residence was a manor house with no specific defensive features. As we have seen in chapter six, there was an ambiguity in how contemporaries in the early modern period defined castles and houses, with such attributions being fluid, and not necessarily contingent on the presence or absence of defensive features such as gun loops and machicolations. Birr Castle is a case in point. By 1668, it was clearly a country house, lacking defensive elements other than the front and rear courtyards. In addition, the description of Redwood Castle in Charleville Demesne does not allow one to conclude whether the building was a fortified house or not. Given that the house was built shortly after 1641, 'according to the fashion of that time', the possibility exists that it falls into the fortified category, but the issue remains unresolved.[32]

Another problem is a certain blurring in building traditions between the late seventeenth and early eighteenth centuries. After the troubles of the 1690s, there was little innovation in the design of houses, with no significant differences, if any, between a house built *c.*1680 and one built *c.*1720.[33] Indeed, Craig has highlighted country houses often T-shaped or L-shaped in plan, with the gables surmounted by massive stacks, the stacks usually flanked by small gable-end windows. He admits that their dating is elusive, spanning an even greater timespan, probably from 1660 or earlier to 1730 or later.[34] The fine residence at Ballysheil typifies such buildings that resist assignation by scholars to either side of the 1700 divide; its regular symmetrical fenestration centred on a slightly elevated doorway with side lights and solid partitions is suggestive of early eighteenth-century concepts of formal design (fig. 7.17). Its panelled chimney stacks and rear projecting stairwell block creating a T-plan, however, look back to early modern architectural traditions (fig. 7.18). One feature at Ballysheil that most exemplifies this 'blurring' is a piece of worked carpentry in one of the ground floor windows – an adzed piece of timber at lintel level with a notch and tusk tenon at either end – an example of woodworking that spans both sides of 1700 (fig. 7.12).[35] Indeed, it has to be said that features such as projecting chimney stacks and stairwell blocks, considered diagnostic of early modern architecture, continued to be built in Ireland into the eighteenth century.[36] Such projecting rear stairwells can still be found in English buildings through much of the eighteenth century.[37] The continuity of such features has been recognized by the Archaeological Survey of Ireland in Offaly. A heavily amended T-plan building with a rear projecting stairwell block within the confines of the O'Carroll bawn at Cullenwaine has been attributed by the survey to the late seventeenth/early eighteenth century.[38]

This apparent 'blurring' in the building traditions on either side of 1700 has created problems for the proper elucidation of the built environment in early modern Offaly. As mentioned above, a detailed survey of a building at Cappagowlan did not reveal any architectural features that could be attributed to before 1700, despite its

7.19 Façade of Knockarley House with symmetrical arrangement of doorway and windows, from the west.

dating by the Archaeological Survey as such. A number of other problematic houses in Offaly have been identified by the Archaeological Survey of Ireland as crossing the late seventeenth-/early eighteenth-century divide, namely Emmel West, Glassderry More, Knockarley and Tumbeagh (fig. 7.19).[39] These buildings, however, have not revealed any particular features that could be definitively dated to the early modern period. Indeed, they contained original features firmly ensconced within the eighteenth century and beyond. For example, Knockarley has been identified with original roof trusses considered by other scholars as seventeenth century. Nonetheless, inspection of these adzed timbers, held together with wooden pegs, suggests a provenance in the eighteenth century.[40] Indeed, the arrangement and size of the windows in the front elevation, which appear to be original, suggests an ordering rather Georgian in character.

The triumph of civil society in late seventeenth-century Offaly

Members of landed families in the early modern period may well have conceived of society in terms of 'degrees of people', with relations between the various social classes regulated by formal conceptions of status, lineage and pre-eminence. Such degrees or levels of social standing, which contributed to the proper functioning of society, were divinely ordained, a given of the natural, cosmological order. To be a gentleman was not simply a case of denoted status, as such status could only be affirmed by the demonstration of appropriate posture, countenance and disposition.[41] Humanism placed a value on education, with the cultivation of knowledge in the classics, where examples of civil virtue and nobility could be found. Humanistic thought also encouraged an appreciation of the dignity of man and his place in the universe, with an implicit value placed on the individual that was not predicated solely on one's relationship with God or with the community at large.[42] This appealed to those members of the new landlord class in Offaly who were keen to demonstrate a personal worth that was not dependent on noble (or indeed native) ancestry. As illustrated in chapters five and six, material culture, in terms of artefacts, documents, dress, buildings and landscape, played fundamental roles in the articulation of such concepts, which gave meaning to people's lives. People performed social identities, these performances being structured in a world that could be manipulated by architecture and documents.[43] Bearing this in mind, movement within the elite residence was critical in setting the stage for various discourses, which allowed for the social status of both the occupant and the visitor to be defined.

Internal arrangements in elite houses of late seventeenth-century Offaly

As discussed in the previous chapter, the medieval hall in the seventeenth century was increasingly marginalized by the great chamber as the chief ceremonial focus of the landed household. The hall on the ground floor was now relegated as a dining area solely for the servants of the household. In the early modern house, the principal chambers, the great chamber and chief withdrawing chamber were located on the first floor, a *piano nobile*, while the second floor could contain more private chambers such as the family parlour, bed chambers and closets. The substantial roof-spaces of early modern elite residences could contain garret or attic rooms for the use of more junior members of the family or servants. All floors of the house were amply lit, though the largest windows were typically confined to the first floor. Fireplaces could be found not only in the kitchen, but also in the great chamber and a variety of other chambers such as parlours and bedrooms.

One residence that most likely possessed such an arrangement was Birr Castle, home to the Parsons family, one of the pre-eminent planter families in Offaly. The 1668 sketch by Parsons of the residence as it stood at that time is informative (fig. 7.7). The presence of a balcony directly over the main entrance to the house suggests the location of the *piano nobile* on the first floor. The building was originally a gatehouse for an earlier O'Carroll castle there, which was heavily remodelled between 1620 and 1628. The sketch depicts a house of unique plan: a large oblong triple-piled building flanked by straight wings that turn and project at an angle. The same sketch depicts the symmetrical placement of square-hooded, mullion-and-transom windows throughout the building's front façades. Such an arrangement would suggest to the modern observer that the various rooms inside were organized in a regular and coherent fashion. However, even where elevations of early modern buildings were characterized by regular fenestration, such regularity was of a superficial nature, with rooms being laid out in a manner that bore no relation to the disposition of the windows. As an early seventeenth-century English commentator observed of elite housing at the time, residences were 'uniform without, though severally partitioned within'.[44] A description of one early modern residence in Offaly has borne out this observation. In the early nineteenth century, Lord Charleville wrote of Redwood Castle that:

> near where the gothic castle [Charleville Castle] now stands was the original mansion house, built shortly after the year 1641, according to the fashion of that time, with many small and ill-connected apartments, but on the whole not destitute of much comfort and convenience. The interior divisions were uniformly constructed by strong partitions of oak, probably the growth of the soil, and very liberally supplied.[45]

The house at Lisclooney echoes the contradictory mixture of symmetrical fenestration with irregular internal planning. Probably built sometime after the Restoration, this house, as mentioned above, possesses a rather sprawling plan (figs 7.3, 7.8). Unfortunately, the greater part of this house has been reduced to wall footings heavily obscured by rubble and dense vegetation, though the west end of the main accommodation block remains, preserving internal and external elevations from the ground floor right up to roof level. The internal rendering is exceptionally well preserved, compared to other examples of late seventeenth-century architecture in west and south Offaly (fig. 7.20). Indeed, original timbers survive in joist holes for flooring at second-floor level. But, given that most of the building complex is now missing, any interpretation of the spatial arrangements is limited. It appears from a detailed survey of the building that the principal accommodation of the household was located within the three-storey west wing, whereas the two-storey east wing and ancillary block more likely contained utilitarian spaces. The kitchen and other service chambers, such as the buttery and the pantry, are more likely to have been located in the rubble-choked ancillary block where a breached chimneybreast at first-floor level has revealed up to four separate flues, suggesting the presence of substantial fireplaces and ovens at ground-floor level there.

What is striking about the west wing at Lisclooney is a greater tendency towards symmetry and harmony, unlike buildings constructed a generation or two beforehand. The arrangement of the fenestration is balanced and symmetrical; the windows on the ground floor are just as large as those on the first floor, while the second floor half dormer windows are not that much smaller (fig. 7.21). None of the surviving six fireplaces in the west wing appear to be less or more grandiose than the

7.20 Ground-floor chamber in the west wing of the residence at Lisclooney. Note the well-preserved wall render.

7.21 Façade of the residence at Lisclooney, late seventeenth-century successor to an earlier O'Dalaghan castle. Matthew de Renzy wrote in 1620 that a 'fine and stately seat of the castle of Liscluna', then in the hands of Hugh O'Dalaghan, had replaced an even earlier castle called *Cul Fiamhaigh*, the ruins of which were still to be seen at the time within the parkland of its successor. The same writer described Lisclooney as 'one of the principalst seats' in Delvin MacCoughlan, 'Englisch-like seated with a fine parke neare it and goodly meadows belonging to it upon the Shenen side'.

other. One qualification is that the ground-floor fireplace in the west gable end is embellished with a stone- and brick-lined oven. Given that a substantial kitchen existed in the ancillary block, such a fireplace may have served the equivalent of a parlour. It can be seen that there is a rationalization or harmonization of architectural features within the house at Lisclooney. The primary effect of this process was to obfuscate the spatial hierarchies within. Architectural signifiers for more important spaces, such as the size and number of windows, were becoming less obvious – a process that was going to become more pronounced in the closing decades of the century.

Sub-medieval versus formal arrangements of rooms in elite homes

In England, under the influence of Palladianism, the asymmetrical arrangement of rooms that characterized much of Jacobean-period architecture was superseded by a symmetrical layout known as the formal plan, which grew in popularity after the Restoration, until by 1700 it had become more or less obligatory for genteel living.[46] Under the formal plan, the two most important rooms of the house, the hall and great chamber, were now arranged one behind the other. Suites of rooms or *appartements* could be arranged either side of these in a linear sequence for the use of family members and guests, with each successive room becoming more private and exclusive than the chamber before. The French sequence of chambers known as *antechambre, chambre* and *cabinet* roughly approximated to the English one of withdrawing chamber, bedchamber and closet. French influence can also be seen in the adoption of a new terminology, the saloon for the great chamber, cabinet for the closet and apartment for the set of lodgings.[47] In the formal plan, as each room of the apartment sequence was more exclusive than the last, the status of the visitor could be gauged not only by how far he or she penetrated along the sequence, but also by how far the occupant of the apartment came along it, and even beyond it, to welcome him or her.[48]

In Offaly, however, there is no surviving evidence that the landed elite were adopting such novel arrangements in the post-Restoration period. Bearing in mind that few country houses from the latter half of the seventeenth century are known in Offaly, it is necessary to look at trends outside the county. There were few houses purposely designed with the formal plan in mind, but one is Thomas Wentworth's creation at Jigginstown, Co. Kildare. Here, the lord deputy, the king's representative in Ireland, constructed in 1637 a country residence of a plan and scale appropriate to one of the king's principal courtiers. Jigginstown consists of a long building with a single storey over basement, flanked at either end by a small projecting wing. The basement is splendid, being an impressive fourteen bays long and two bays wide, roofed with brick rib vaulting. It was rare at this stage for brick to be used so extensively on a building project in Ireland. While only single storeyed, such an extensive plan could accommodate at ease a number of apartments with their linear sequence of chambers.[49] While it is commonly thought that the building was never finished, given Wentworth's premature departure, there is archaeological and documentary evidence that the house was finished and occupied intermittently until 1647.[50] The formal plan was also adopted in Kilkenny Castle, which was extensively remodelled in the early 1670s – state apartments were inserted into the first floor of the north wing of the castle, with the following sequence of rooms: great chamber/dining room (which served as an anteroom); drawing room/presence chamber (where the chair of state was placed on a dais under a canopy); state bed chamber; and, lastly, the duchess's closet. The sequence of apartments continued on the second floor with a long gallery that was adorned by portraits of various members of the monarchy and aristocracy.[51]

It seems, however, that courtly architecture did not make much of an impact on the wealthy settler families in Ireland, as no other building seems to have been inspired by Wentworth's creation. One of these wealthy families, the Percivals of Burton, Co. Cork, built one of the finest known residences in post-Restoration Ireland. Yet a plan of the house 'as it was before it was burnt at the Revolution by the Irish' during the course of the Williamite War, depicts a sub-medieval arrangement with direct entry into a ground-floor hall, separated from the dining room and drawing room by a central corridor. Beyond these more private chambers was a gallery, which ran down one side of the house.[52] Even as late as *c.*1710, a plan for a new residence at Conyngham Hall in Slane, Co. Meath, envisaged a great hall, great parlour and drawing room, illustrating that sub-medieval concepts of planning were still in vogue among the Protestant ascendancy at this time.[53]

Innovations in the classic mould outside the formal plan: Ballysheil

While Loeber has observed that little is really understood of spatial organization in late seventeenth-century houses in Ireland, the formal plan appears to have made limited impact upon domestic architecture in this period.[54] It would be misleading, however, to suggest that architectural design remained static. In the latter half of the seventeenth century, gentlemen and army officers were developing the knowledge to create whole plans and elevations that were classically informed. This was in contrast to earlier generations, when classicism was limited to inserting appendages such as door surrounds and chimneypieces to buildings that were essentially sub-medieval in character, illustrating only a superficial appreciation of the principles at work behind the architectural style. Classicism, with its precise rules of ordering, was eventually embraced because it expressed in a visible manner the seventeenth-century idea that reason was the foundation for the ordering and functioning of the universe, and everything therein.[55] Classical architecture in an Irish context also could be seen as an assertion of superior English and Protestant values that also celebrated simplicity and rationalism.[56] A more mature command of classical architectural grammar can be seen in one Offaly residence – Ballysheil – where a fine example echoes the symmetry and proportions that were to be found in elite homes of the following century. Its tripartite arrangement of rooms replicated on each floor, with a centrally placed entrance at ground-floor level allowing access into a hall or vestibule, expresses a rational use of space that looks to Palladian principles of harmonious design (figs 7.17, 7.18).

Despite this, certain features place Ballysheil within the milieu of early modern design. The building possesses a central rear stairwell projection that creates a T-plan, an arrangement that was quite popular in the early modern period. This stairwell faced the main entrance and was visible immediately to the visitor once inside the hall. It is obvious that such stairwells gained a more dramatic setting internally by being positioned opposite the entrance, a layout derived from the hall-and-cross-passage house type. This spatial arrangement remained ingrained in English house design during the sixteenth and seventeenth centuries.[57] The steeply pitched gables rising to tall slender chimney stacks are decorated with blank arcaded stone panelling. Such decorative features were popular in England during the middle decades of the seventeenth century. Similar panelling can also be found in Ireland at this time, such as at Brazeel (probably 1630s) and Oldbawn (*c.*1635), both in Co. Dublin, and Richhill, Co. Armagh (possibly *c.*1670).[58] As mentioned above, one of the ground-floor windows possesses a piece of timber at lintel level with working that can be found in the late seventeenth century (fig. 7.12).[59]

Despite the presence of such features, Ballysheil also looked to the future. This arrangement of a central hallway with the stairwell providing the main focus of attention is resonant of Sir Roger Pratt's seminal architectural creation in England, Coleshill House, begun *c.*1650. This house saw the last vestige of the medieval hall being relegated to the basement. Instead of providing a dining area for the servants, the hall was now used as a primary reception area where the grand stairs was located. Such an arrangement followed Continental practice, where this hall space could now be used as a vestibule or antechamber, in effect evolving into the modern concept of a hallway.[60]

The internal layouts of houses in the seventeenth century came to be increasingly segregated. Whereas the sight of many servants and retainers bustling about in the hall had been used to convey social status, by the mid-seventeenth century, architectural commentators such as Sir Roger Pratt and Roger North were advising on the relegation of service chambers such as the kitchen, buttery and pantry to basement level, linked to the principle chambers on the floors above by a backstairs, thus rendering the household servants invisible, so that 'no dirty servants may be seen passing to and fro by those who are above, no noises heard, nor ill scents smelt'.[61] Such a process of segregation was underway in Ireland at this period: in 1672, three carpenters were contracted by the bishop in Kilkenny to build (or remodel) a residence that was to be provided with a 'drawing room' and back stairs.[62] At Ballysheil, while there is no evidence for a backstairs, a semi-basement, almost obscured by rubble, is evident under the east end of the house. This semi-basement area, however, has no obvious access to the floor above, nor is it provided with a fireplace, obviating its interpretation as kitchen space. Given the present condition of the building with the interior strewn with rubble, excavation would be required to elucidate whether a more extensive basement containing kitchen space and access is located under the house.

Whereas the architectural arrangement of the communal hall, with its upper and lower ends, had structured status in the medieval period, it appears that at Ballysheil space has become more neutral, less invested with architectural signifiers of status. The meanings of particular spatial arrangements could be more readily changed; one chamber in a symmetrical house looked very much the same as the next, with only the décor and furnishings within these chambers indicating their function and relative social position.[63] The ground-floor and first-floor chambers at Ballysheil, judging from the disposition of equally sized windows and fireplaces, are almost carbon copies of each other. No longer is it possible for the archaeologist to assign a gradation of rooms based on the size of chambers, windows or fireplaces. The well-proportioned front façade of Ballysheil, along with the symmetrical layout of rooms and windows, obfuscate the social hierarchies within (fig. 7.18). In contrast to earlier elite buildings like tower houses, the interpretation of these structures becomes less transparent from the position of the outside observer. In a country residence like Ballysheil, besides the hall acting as a vestibule, other chambers such as the withdrawing chamber and parlour are indistinguishable from the architectural spaces alone. One thing, however, is discernible at Ballysheil: the disappearance of the principal living chambers from the first floor. From the late seventeenth century onwards, the great chamber on the first floor gradually disappeared; once the hall ceased as a dining area for servants, the necessity for having reception rooms elevated onto the first floor was called into question.[64]

The relegation of servants and household staff to the basement and backstairs is symptomatic of greater changes within the household. By the end of the seventeenth century, the ancient ceremonies with numerous servant attendees had disappeared. The remaining servants were now more likely to be recruited from lower social classes than had been the case before, and also with a different ethnic and religious background, given the minority position of British Protestants. The departure of the servants from the hall was also accompanied by the departure of all the tenants and other visitors who used to eat with them in the hall. Such everyday hospitality was now commuted to the basement level, where the kitchens and servants' parlours were located. All this was in contrast to the communal and public activities of earlier houses. Such changes not only stemmed from a greater need for privacy, but also from other transformations that were taking place in the late seventeenth century.

Power was no longer centred on the display of a large retinue tied to a lord by links of service and hereditary loyalty. Instead, influence now stemmed from central government, administered and maintained by locally based institutions such as the county assizes or the local garrison. No longer were men of standing attracted to a particular lord in the hope of receiving protection and munificence. Now, under the protective umbrella of the nation state, grammar schools and universities offered positions in the legal profession, army and church.[65]

The increased importance of furnishings

According to Johnson, space had become more neutral, less invested with allusions of status, with fewer architectural signifiers. Now 'the meanings of the space were … defined by movable furniture, and were thus less fixed and more interchangeable'.[66] In these houses, status came to be expressed through the disposition of luxury goods such as chairs, other furniture and decorative items, rather than via the medium of the medieval hall.[67] The greater popularity of household inventories from the late sixteenth century onwards illustrates the importance of moveable material objects more than ever before. These were legal documents that listed, separated and valued particular goods according to their location in the house.

Household inventories for the period, despite their drawbacks, show an exuberance of material goods that furnished the various chambers in the elite households. Furniture such as tables draped in cloth, upholstered chairs and stools allowed for the comfortable composure of the occupants, creating along with tapestry hangings and paintings, the necessary setting for the establishment and maintenance of discourses on elite identity. In a nascent capitalist economy where the regulation of labour became increasingly important, timepieces were becoming popular. Between 1660 and 1680, at least seventeen watch and clockmakers were working in Dublin.[68] The wide range of fabrics listed in one Co. Cork residence testify to rooms endowed with sumptuous curtains, tapestries, carpets, quilts, embroidery and upholstery.[69] Luxuriant colours, folds patterns and textures embellishing these rooms would create spaces of gentility and comfort, appropriate to the owner's standing in local society. There are indications that the colours of upholstery and hangings were being coordinated, with inventories naming rooms by colour.[70] Within Birr Castle, though not in its original location, is a fine yew staircase of late seventeenth-century date, with boldly turned balusters and a broad ramping rail that rises through three floors of the house and was restored after a fire in 1832.[71] This stairwell was apparently placed in the house sometime between 1660 and 1681, and was described by Dineley on the latter date as 'the fairest staircase in Ireland'.[72] Dineley also mentioned that there was such an abundant supply of yew in Birr that the Parsons household contained 'windows, staircases, window cases, tables, benches, stooles and stooles [sic]' made from this sturdy timber.[73]

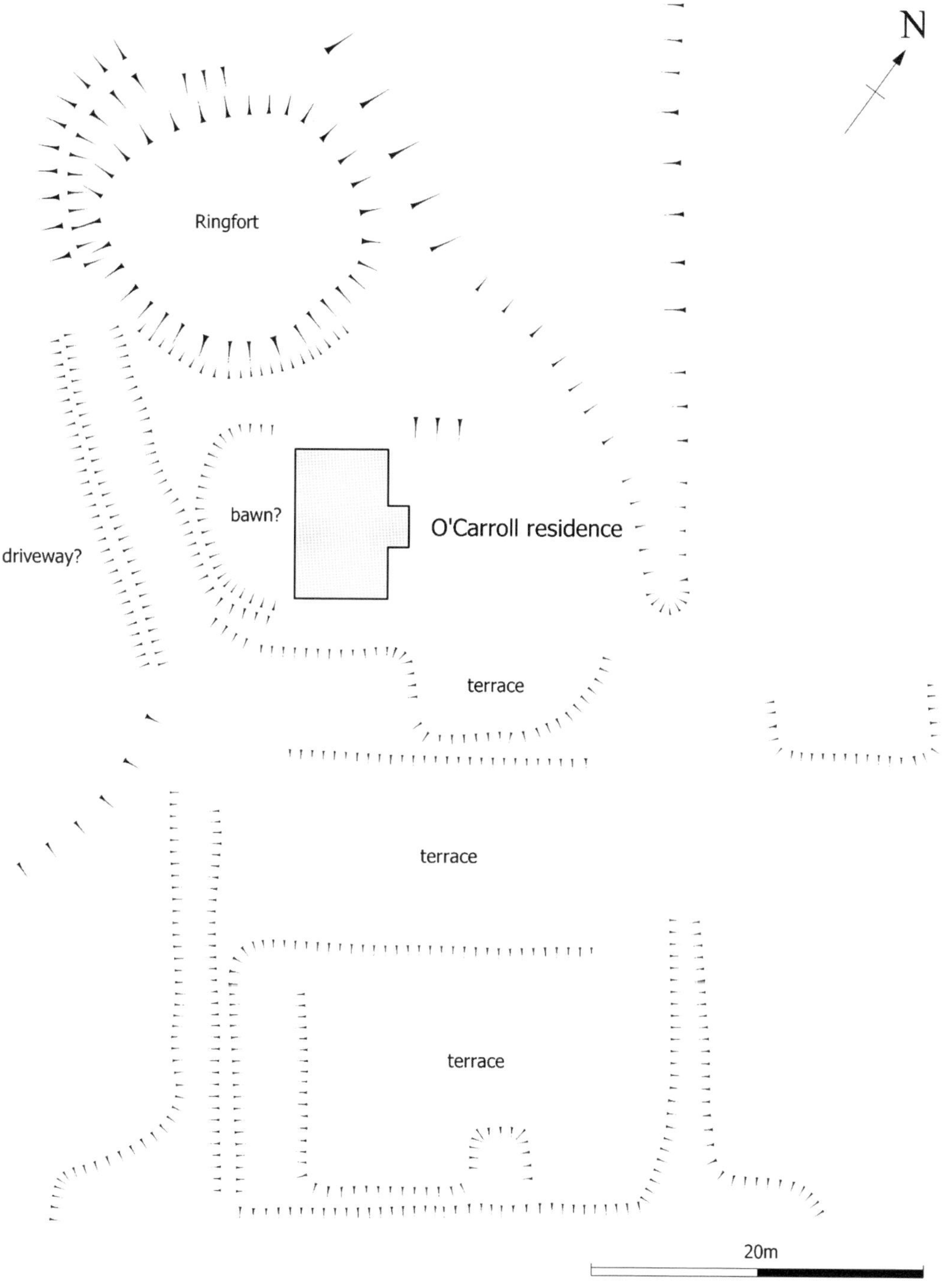

7.22 Sketch plan of garden terraces, with a possible driveway and bawn at Ballybrack (drawn by James Lyttleton and Hugh Kavanagh).

Gardens and parkland: the radiance of power

The creation of the appropriate genteel image, so important to the landed families in this period, could not be achieved by the style and decoration of the residence alone. Surrounding country houses, planned gardens acted as a form of mediation between the elite and the general population, as well as between nature and culture, with many writers in the period seeing such gardens as being endowed with utopian meanings or acting as complex metaphors for mortality and political agendas.[74] In an Irish context, the supposed indolence of the natives, failing to win nature away from unbridled growth as well as preventing the incursions of wild animals, branded them in the eyes of propagandists as mere barbarians, resulting in a landscape that blurred the distinctions between man and animal. By regaining control over unruly nature, sinners atoned and reformed themselves.[75] In an environment in which status and cultural identity were in a state of flux and subject to negotiation, it appears that landowners of native and planter origin adopted tenets of landscape organization that conformed to principles of civil improvement. The greater embrace of symmetrical plans and elevations of buildings encouraged the symmetrical design of the surrounding grounds, resulting in house, garden and estate being integrated with even greater care. Features such as terraces, mounts, ponds and canals were laid out in a symmetrical fashion, celebrating the role of harmony in structuring the country and cosmos. Unfortunately, there is little surviving evidence of such gardens in west and south Offaly. Where houses continued in use right through to modern times, such as Birr Castle, traces of early gardens have been obliterated through later landscaping. Where other buildings, like Lisclooney, were abandoned at a comparatively early stage, the chances for the preservation of garden features would appear improved, but alas this is not the case. Ironically, given the colonial ethos of such gardens, the only surviving examples are found associated with Gaelic Irish residences, namely at Ballybrack and Kilmaine, both of which are in what was formerly Éile Uí Chearbhaill.

At Ballybrack, there are the poorly preserved remains of a single-piled T-plan house, two storeys in height plus attic (fig. 7.4). While there is no definitive evidence for the dating of the house, a base batter and the partial remains of a stone newel stairwell, both associated with the rear stairwell projection, suggest construction in the earlier rather than the latter half of the seventeenth century. A consideration of the surroundings of this house, however, is more provocative and highlights the problem of dating relict garden remains in the absence of documentary and archaeological evidence. Running *c.*80m downslope from the house in a southerly direction is a series of terraces (fig. 7.22). Such an extensive garden, unprotected by any apparent bawn wall, or other enclosure, speaks of expansive garden design more typical of the late seventeenth and early eighteenth centuries than the comparatively small formal gardens that were found in the shadow of fortified houses and bawns a generation earlier. While there are traces of a possible semi-circular enclosure defined

7.23 Aerial view of Ballybrack house and early medieval ringfort. One of the garden terraces can be seen just to the right of the house (© National Monuments Service: Department of Arts, Heritage and the Gaeltacht).

by a slight earthen bank to the west of the house at Ballybrack, it is intriguing that a well-preserved ringfort only 30m north of the house was not appropriated for this purpose (fig. 7.23). Given the close proximity of the ringfort, however, and the fact that a hollow-way runs between the ringfort and the terraced garden, it is possible that the ringfort itself was integrated into the design of this formal landscape. This is not entirely fanciful, as the appropriation of ringforts as tree-rings became a feature of parkland designs in late eighteenth- and nineteenth-century Ireland.

The second example of a relict garden is the O'Carroll residence at Kilmaine, which survives as a platform surrounded by a fosse fed by a number of other fosses running at right angles to it and each other. Further survey work, including geophysical prospection, topographical survey and test excavation, is required to elucidate more information on the nature of the site, but the presence of these fosses and what the Ordnance Survey records as the 'the Old Bridge' straddling one of the them to the east of the residence suggests the presence of waterworks to decorate and

7.24 Michael Richards' map of Birr Castle (A), St Brendan's Church (F) and the adjacent town defended by earthworks in 1691. North is to the left (from Feehan and Rosse, *Atlas of Birr* (2005), 13).

demarcate different areas of the garden. Waterworks are often mentioned in contemporary sources and were a feature of other pleasure gardens in the Irish midlands. Longford Castle and Rathcline, both in Co. Longford, were enhanced with fishponds along with fosses to supply the necessary water.[76] Larger ponds were features of deerparks, but smaller ponds protected within the confines of gardens could be used to hold fish for consumption as well as for ornamental purposes.[77]

Given the lack of physical remains for formal gardens in this period, historical sources are all the more invaluable in elucidating their appearance. Unfortunately, documentary sources are generally reticent in elucidating the surroundings of these landed households. One exception is the Parsons residence at Birr, where a Dorothy Parsons sketch dated 1668 and Michael Richards' map of the town in 1691 illustrate the grounds that surrounded one of the more prominent planter households in post-Restoration Offaly (figs 7.7, 7.24). As mentioned above, the main residence at Birr Castle was originally a gatehouse that served an earlier O'Carroll stronghold enclosed by an irregular-shaped bawn on a height overlooking the Camcor River. The Parsons retained the outline of this bawn, constructing various outbuildings inside the perimeter with a well located within. Richards' map depicts two 'old castles' along its northern side, and these were probably associated with the earlier O'Carroll occupation. This bawn in effect became a rear courtyard, with the exterior side of the late medieval gatehouse now redesigned as the frontispiece to overlook the town to the south, as can be seen in Parsons' sketch. There is an irregular arrangement of paths within the rear courtyard leading to and from the residence and various outbuildings, testifying to the essentially utilitarian nature of the space within the old bawn.

By combining Parsons' sketch and Richards' map, it is clear that the approach between the front of the residence and the town was protected by a bawn of a more regular, rectilinear plan, presumably of seventeenth-century date. This bawn was defended by a pair of cylindrical towers, probably gun turrets, placed on the southern corners of the bawn facing the town's population. Richards' map depicts the bawn as being equally divided into two large courts, with the innermost one being further partitioned into two equal-sized areas by a division apparently less substantial than the bawn wall, though of what nature is not apparent. Parsons' sketch clarifies the nature of this division – there was an impressive terraced platform fronting onto the house, which allowed views of the courts beneath, as well as the church and town beyond. A balustrade, with finials rising from the handrail, defined the sides of this terrace. An arcade of round arches, each of which framed a small mullioned window, encased the rise of the terrace. Descending from the terrace to the lower half of the inner court was a flight of steps flanked by what appear again to be balustrades with finials. While not visible in Parsons' sketch, Richards' map depicts a pair of rectilinear parterres in the inner court, arranged either side of a central approach to the house. The same map also illustrates a more extensive garden to the north of the elevated house and rear bawn, away from the attentions of curious townsfolk. This garden contained three rows of parterres, laid edge to edge, creating a geometric arrangement of paths, interspersed among rectilinear beds of what one could only presume were flower beds, herb and vegetable plots possibly defined by box or thrift. Walled pleasure gardens, as these at Birr, provided shelter for valuable trees and flowers sensitive to climatic conditions, as well as from the attentions of trespassers. There is a remoulding of the immediate vicinity of Birr Castle, divorced from the surrounding landscape, creating an impression of exclusivity, dominance and permanence, concepts important to the assertion and maintenance of the Parsons' family identity.

Such gardens could be used to impress and overawe contemporaries whose reactions could differ according to experience and social background. Analogies were commonly made between the country estate and the kingdom, the former being viewed as a microcosm of the latter, with the well-managed estate providing an apt model for the nation at large. The value and attraction of such gardens cut across political and ethnic affiliations, as evidenced by the removal during the Williamite War of 'a load of cypress trees and tulips and other flowers, roots and herbs' from Sir

Laurence Parsons' gardens at Birr Castle for replanting in the aforementioned gardens of Kilmaine, which belonged to a prominent local Jacobite, Lieut.-Col. Owen Carroll.[78]

The increasing use of large glazed windows in the seventeenth century, whether as depicted in the 1668 sketch of Birr Castle, or in the surviving elevations of Ballysheil and Lisclooney, emphasizes the increasing importance of the gaze or view over the surrounding estate. In 1691, John Stevens, a soldier passing the fine late Caroline residence at Eyrecourt, Co. Galway, observed negatively that 'the house [is] large with a pleasant wood in the back of it; but no good prospect any way, nor any river near it'.[79] English literature in the troubled times of the 1640s and 50s compared the harmony and sereneness of designed royalist landscapes with the violent, chaotic wilderness where the crown's political enemies hatched plots.[80] These gardens could hold symbolic meanings, political or otherwise, where elements of the garden such as statues, parterres or trees could be manipulated to create meanings in either an implicit or an explicit manner, depending on the whim of the garden owners.

In Ireland, parks and gardens, as much as housing, furnishing, dress and diet, were interpreted as evidence of confessional, ethnic and social loyalties.[81] Indeed, the Irish demesne has been considered a good place to investigate the connection between symbolic violence and the conscious use of the landscape to convey lessons on the existing social order.[82] At Birr Castle, St Brendan's belfry dominating the townscape acted as a suitable backdrop to the terraced garden. This does not mean that the church was part of a passive background to the Parsons' garden walks, but it was a physical demonstration of how the family's status with its consequent notions of civility, gentility and polite behaviour were very much entwined with the agenda of civil and religious reform. The juxtaposition of castle, church and town underpinned in a very real way the success of such an agenda. Here in this constructed environment, social discourses of religious and civil reform and ethnic identity could be played out.

Geometric gardens, with their topiary and box-work, continued into the early eighteenth century, particularly with most members of the gentry. Gardens, like architecture, evolved, however, and at the same time new forms of gardens were embraced by the aristocratic and courtier circles with less emphasis on geometric parterres and more interest taken in neat gravel paths, grass lawns, hedges and formal arrangements of trees. From the 1720s, these elite gardens became more open to the surrounding landscape as they were surrounded not by high walls but by a sunken ditch or 'ha-ha', separating them from open parkland. However, it was only in the second half of the eighteenth century, under the influence of Lancelot 'Capability' Brown and others, that any house of importance stood surrounded by 'naturalistic' parkland interspersed with trees and surrounded wholly or in part by belts of woodland.[83]

The appearance of the 'ordinary' farmstead

Most of the buildings discussed up to now, whether houses, fortified houses or tower houses, were a product of a landed elite. Little trace of buildings associated with the lower social orders, whether native or newcomer in the early modern period, have been recovered in Ireland. Most archaeologists have explained this social bias in the architectural record by alluding to the perishable nature of the materials used in the construction of poorer homes: clay, sods and post-and-wattle. This situation is paralleled in Scotland, where, outside urban areas, very little survives of the homes occupied by the bulk of the population in the early modern era. Subsequent depopulation in the Highlands and the provision of estate cottages in the Lowlands means that such dwellings can now only be found through survey and excavation.[84] Even in England, it has been pointed out that the vast majority of one-hearth cottages recorded in a hearth tax in the late seventeenth century have now disappeared.[85] Similarly, in Virginia and Maryland, archaeological fieldwork consistently failed to find any trace of substantial buildings on early colonial settlement sites. Indeed, there was little evidence that solid framing more typical of English farmhouses of the time was erected either, and that a rudimentary, impermanent vernacular architecture, characterized by posts set into the ground, was more commonplace. Termed by archaeologists as earthfast or post-in-the-ground architecture, this type of construction was used right through the seventeenth century, transcending social class, and continued to be used into the eighteenth century. The unearthing of large numbers of nails, along with historical evidence, suggests the roofs and sometimes the walls of these structures were covered by thin oak planks known as clapboards. Although some were provided with brick chimneys, many were heated by wattle and daub stacks, perhaps with a little brick hearth where the heat was most intense.[86]

In Ireland, excavation has slowly but surely increased our knowledge of buildings occupied by the lower rungs of Irish society in the late sixteenth and seventeenth centuries. Archaeological fieldwork carried out in advance of the Cork–Dublin pipeline in the early 1980s resulted in the excavation of a T-shaped house at Drumlummin, Co. Tipperary, with a significant assemblage of pottery, stone, metal, glass artefacts and clay pipe fragments.[87] More recent investigations have included the three cottages on Sir Walter Raleigh's manor of Mogeely, Co. Cork, the five stone dwellings at Rough Point, near Killybegs, Co. Donegal, the sod-walled building with a post-and-wattle core at Movanagher, Co. Derry, and a timber-framed building with stone and earth-fast timber components at Blackrock in west Cork.[88] Excavations in advance of large-scale road developments have also uncovered evidence for timber-framed houses at Ballinvinny South, Co. Cork, and Danesfort, Co. Kilkenny, as well as a stone house at Annagh Hill, Co. Galway.[89]

A few non-elite buildings are still to be found in west and south Offaly, and these probably represent the homesteads of well-to-do farmers, comparable in status to the

English yeomanry, leasing land from the local landlord. The English yeomanry was made up of socially middling tenant farmers of reasonable security and wealth, who would occupy minor positions in the local parish administration, who took their political leadership from the gentry, but whose principal activity revolved around farming.[90] These farmhouses have been seen as epitomizing vernacular building (vernacular being defined as native building carried out by local people using traditional methods and materials).[91] Such a definition, however, could be applied wholly or partially to many of the elite buildings found in this period, such as tower houses and fortified houses. Indeed, one of the prominent scholars of vernacular architecture in Ireland included tower houses in his studies.[92] There is an ambiguous division between 'vernacular' buildings and the kind of buildings that are described as 'architecture'. As John Summerson succinctly puts it, 'as the "vernacular" ascends in quality, it catches the "architectural" idiom of more affluent buildings and more sophisticated craftsmen, and there is an area where either term is applicable'.[93] Implicit in these categories is a value judgment that renders vernacular buildings as less sophisticated modes of material expression. But the appearance and layout of these buildings can provide insights into the early modern world just as complex and nuanced as the manor house or the parish church.[94]

Problems in the study of early modern farmhouses

In Ireland, the extant homesteads of these farmers can be difficult to recognize due to the accretion of 'improvements' such as the insertion of new partitions and window and door surrounds, re-rendering, extensions and so on. Indeed, the general appearance of a late seventeenth-century farmhouse, such as at Shantallow on the outskirts of Derry, may not differ from a house of early to mid-nineteenth-century date.[95] At first glance, one of the Offaly examples at Ballytoran appeared to be a nineteenth-century farmhouse rendered with modern pebbledash (figs 7.25, 7.26). Closer inspection, however, revealed a pair of cement-clad diagonal shafts surmounting the south gable as well as the remains of a projecting block to the rear of the house, features typically associated with buildings of seventeenth-century date.

Another problem with these homesteads is the lack of evidence for ancillary buildings and outhouses that would have constituted the farm as a whole, as the residences of these socially middling farmers were not necessarily stand-alone buildings. Outhouses such as barns, stables, cowsheds, storage sheds and pig sties most likely featured. Some documentary sources suggest the presence of outhouses in the early modern period. A survey of northeast Co. Donegal in 1611 mentions an 'Irish barn of coples'. Problematically, knowledge of how these buildings were constructed, how they were fitted internally and how they were related spatially to homesteads is non-existent.[96] As part of a greater farm complex, the function and layout of early modern farmyards is fundamentally important to our understanding

7.25 Front elevation of late seventeenth-century farmstead at Ballytoran, from the west.

7.26 In the left middle-ground can be seen the ivy-clad remains of a block to the rear of the late seventeenth-century farmstead at Ballytoran. Also note the diagonal chimney shafts on the south gable in the left background.

of early modern agriculture. Across the Atlantic in Maryland, the typical household was accompanied by smaller buildings such as dairies, barns, storage sheds, hen houses and smoke houses that fulfilled various specialized functions.[97]

Documentary references to individual farms are rare and often of a vague nature, which hinders the proper elucidation of chronology and layout. In the absence of inventories or other documentary sources, dendrochronology has been offered as a solution for the identification of early modern households, given that oak timbers were a popular building material in the seventeenth century.[98] Such an approach, however, can be of limited value due to the potential for reuse of timbers from older buildings.

The morphology of 'ordinary' houses in early modern Offaly

Examples of late seventeenth-century Offaly farmhouses are to be found at Ballynamire, Ballytoran and Lisduff (figs 7.2, 7.5, 7.6, 7.25, 7.27). Each of these farmhouses is a single-piled building, three to six bays in length and one-and-a-half storeys in height, the upper storey occupying an attic or garret level. Roughly coursed limestone rubble is used in the construction of external walling, while more perishable organic material like timber was used for internal partitions. The front elevations of these buildings are characterized by centrally placed doorways surrounded by a regular arrangement of flat-headed windows, with the windows at garret level significantly smaller than those at ground-floor level. Less emphasis was placed on the rear elevation, where windows tended to be more irregular in size and location. These farmhouses were equipped with gable-ended chimney stacks, either flush with or projecting from the gable. These chimney stacks would serve both ground-floor and garret levels (fig. 7.28). Besides these gable-end fireplaces, there were other fireplaces to be found in the interiors of these homes. At both Ballynamire and Lisduff, there was a standalone chimney stack, centrally placed in the former, and off-centre in the latter. Within living memory, the houses at Ballytoran and Lisduff were thatched. Indeed, underneath the galvanized roof at Ballytoran is a layer of tough sod known as scraw, lying on a framework of modern roof timbers that originally served as underthatch. The roof at Ballynamire, with its low eves, was most likely thatched with dormer windows lighting the garret level.

In Craig's opinion, houses such as Ballynamire seem to foreshadow or represent early examples of simple stone-built farmhouses that were to be found scattered across the Irish countryside in the eighteenth and nineteenth centuries.[99] Berwick Hall, Co. Down, built *c.*1682–5 (fig. 7.29), and another example in Co. Kildare built about 1680, approximate to the original appearance of these Offaly farmhouses, testifying to the rise of a middling farming class in the Irish countryside by the latter decades of the seventeenth century, if not before.[100] The origins of such farmhouses,

7.27 Front elevation of the late seventeenth-century farmstead at Lisduff, from the east.

however, may be found in the early decades of the same century, if not earlier, as Thomas Raven's 1622 maps of the Ulster plantation settlements depict stone buildings, one and a half storeys in height, with dormer-gabled windows punctuating the roof (fig. 7.30). The roofs were generally gabled and slated or tiled, though several were thatched. Only a small number had gable chimneys, as they typically possessed a single chimney stack, along with entrance, placed in the middle. Other plantation surveys confirm that such buildings were frequently roofed with slates, tiles or thatch.[101]

Closer to home, Parsons' sketch of Birr Castle in 1668 shows two English-style houses of much smaller scale to the rear of the main residence, within the original bawn, on opposite sides of a courtyard. The building along the west side appears to have been one-and-a-half storeys with a gabled roofline. Chimney stacks embellished with moulded cornices and coping were placed at either end of the building to the rear. The interior was lit by square-hooded mullioned windows, their placement indicating that there was a hall-and-passage arrangement inside. Entry was gained via an off-centre doorway that presumably allowed access to the passage. Once inside this passage, one could enter to the hall to the left, the most important chamber in this house – its status marked by the largest window in the building, a five-light

7.28 Roofline of the early modern farmhouse at Ballynamire – the central chimneystack with its diagonal chimney shafts is characteristic of seventeenth-century architecture, while the brick chimney shaft in the foreground is a later replacement but possibly pre-1700.

7.29 Farmstead at Berwick Hall, Co. Down, built *c.*1682–5 (courtesy of Terence Reeves-Smyth).

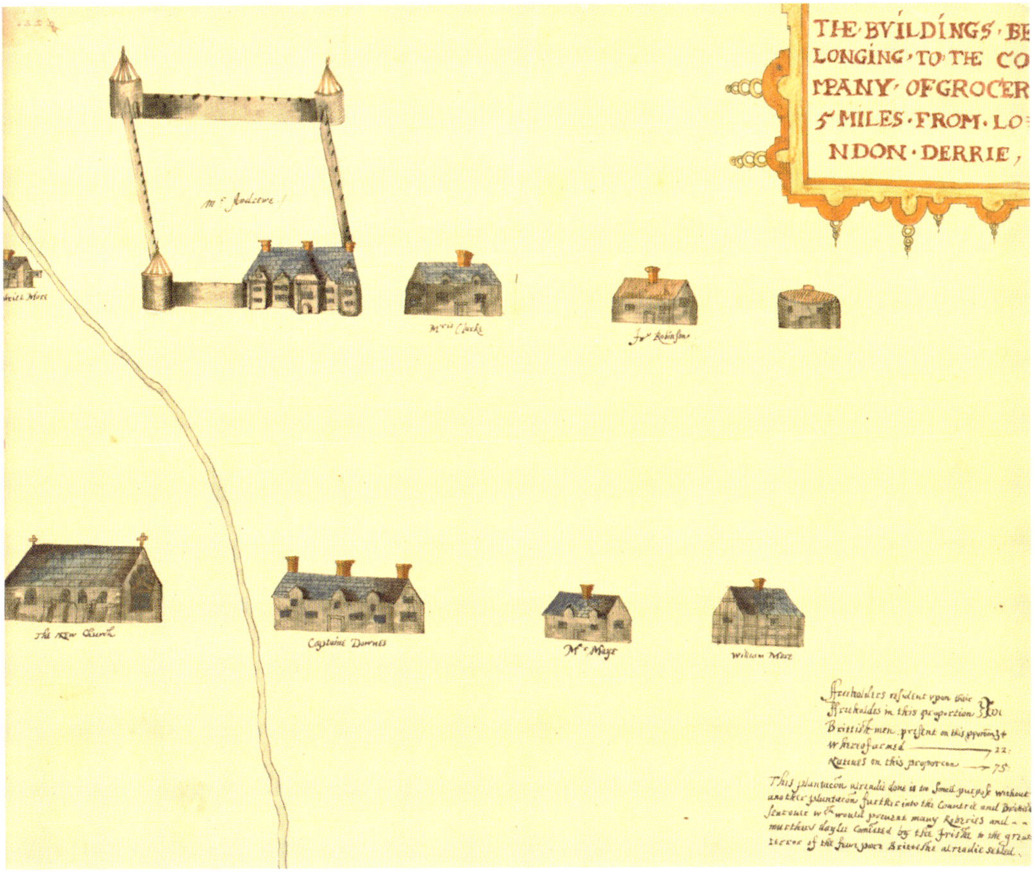

7.30 Thomas Raven's 1622 pictorial map of the Grocers' Company settlement in Co. Derry, illustrating manor house, church and village, the latter containing houses of different styles and traditions: timber-framed, stone- and clay-built (Trustees of Lambeth Palace Library, MS 634, fos 22v–23).

mullioned opening. To the right was a lesser chamber, possibly a kitchen; its lesser status deserving a smaller three-light window. The second building – placed along the east side of the bawn – is similar in appearance, though partially obscured by the main residence in the Parsons' sketch. It is two storeys with a gabled roofline, a chimney stack at one end and square-hooded windows of equal size on each floor. The windows possess mullions and transoms like the examples in the main house, while a short flight of steps leads to a four-centred arched doorway, possibly placed off-centre in the façade. These embellishments suggest a building of more importance compared to the house on the west side of the courtyard.

The general appearance of these two buildings is quite similar to the homesteads of the minor gentry or yeomanry in English midland counties such as Leicestershire, where the Parsons family originally came from. Their location to the rear of Birr Castle would suggest that these buildings were used to accommodate estate

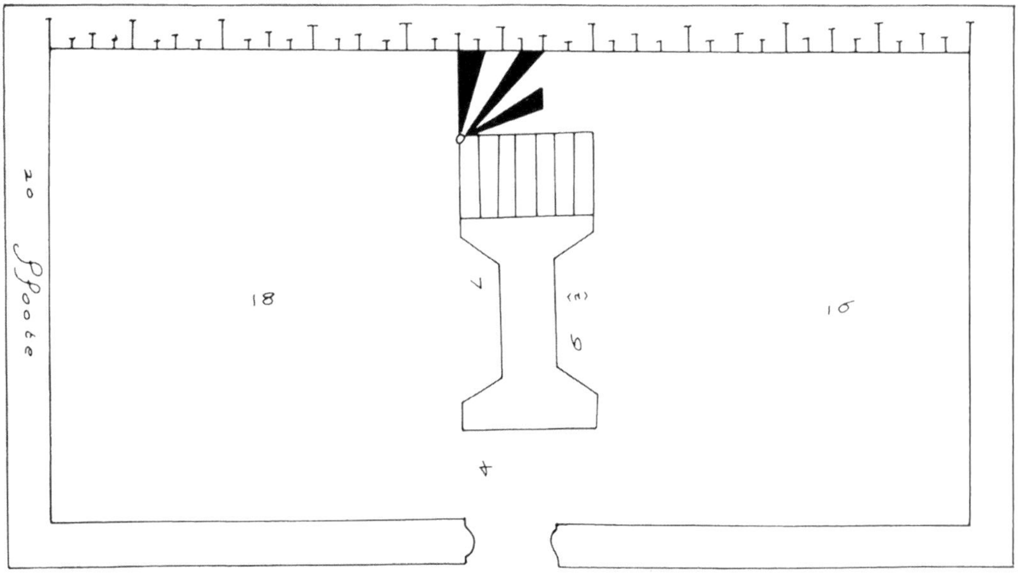

7.31 Ground plan of a small two-roomed tenant house envisaged for the Drapers' estates at Moneymore, Co. Derry, in 1615 (from Gailey, *Rural houses* (1984), p. 186, fig. 207).

employees. Their significance in an Irish context is the degree to which the English vernacular architectural tradition was making an impact in Co. Offaly by the mid-seventeenth century. The question remains, though, as to the extent to which these novel vernacular styles had spread beyond the walls of Birr Castle. Sir Laurence may have encouraged the spread of English building norms within the town by imposing a by-law in 1627–8 for the erection of chimneys. There are a number of buildings in Birr that may be of seventeenth-century date, albeit altered and re-edified in later centuries.[102]

While the farmstead at Ballytoran possesses a T-plan typical of seventeenth-century architecture, those at Ballynamire and Lisduff are oblong, heralding for the first time in Offaly the integration of the projecting rear stairwell block into the main body of the building, saving expense in both heating and materials. Such a feat, however, was achievable in Ireland by the early decades of the seventeenth century. Again, Raven's maps of 1622 depict a variety of buildings, including those of mass wall construction with no apparent projection containing a stairwell. Given that only the front elevations of these buildings were depicted, this particular cartographic source is not conclusive. The records of the Drapers' Company, one of the London companies involved in the Londonderry plantation, however, preserves the ground floor plan of a small two-roomed tenant house with a centrally placed chimney stack, presumably intended for their estate at Moneymore in 1615 (fig. 7.31). In the house, behind the chimney stack, two pairs of stairs are apparently depicted. As no cellar or attic is mentioned, it is likely that the draughtsman drew two alternative types of stairs; one a spiral, the other a dog-leg stair, illustrating that the integration of the stairs within the main body of a building was feasible by the early seventeenth century.[103]

The internal arrangements within these farmhouses

While medieval homesteads were characterized by non-partitioned interiors heated by hearths, houses in the early modern period saw the insertion of fireplaces served by chimney stacks, and the subdivision of living space into a number of rooms. The internal layouts within surviving farmhouses of this period can be difficult to interpret, as modern partitions are not necessarily based on original arrangements. Bearing this in mind, it is of interest to note that both Ballytoran (plaster wall boards) and Lisduff (nineteenth-century brick walling with timber bracing) possess a tripartite arrangement of rooms on the ground floor, paralleling the floor plan at the more elite residence at Ballysheil, possibly indicative of the middling sort emulating their social betters by the end of the early modern period. However, as Johnson cautions, such emulation was much more than a mindless urge to be fashionable, and involved an implicit decision to live life differently, representing a fundamental shift in the architecture and culture of ordinary people. Changes in the nature and appearance of houses accompanied changes in the nature of everyday life and social relations that took place in and around the same houses.[104]

Fortunately, an analysis of internal arrangements at Ballynamire can be more confident, as the original partitioning scheme can be reconstructed from standing remains (figs 7.5). The western half of the farmhouse is largely destroyed, except for the gable end, but it is probable that the house was a five-bay unit with two rooms either side of the central chimney stack. Opposed front and rear doorways facing directly onto this chimney stack created a lobby or reception area to the front and rear of the house. The appearance of the homestead at Ballynamire, with its lobby entries, thatched roof and dormer windows, can be traced directly to the arrival of British settlers in the opening decades of the seventeenth century. The earliest evidence for such lobby-entry houses with upper floors lit by dormer windows is to be found in the 1622 maps by Thomas Raven (fig. 7.30).[105] The above-mentioned ground plan of a small tenant house at Moneymore, Co. Derry, illustrates a small house plan, with a massive chimney stack in line with the entrance and a stairwell climbing to an upper floor between it and the rear wall (fig. 7.31). The evidence combined suggests that the hearth lobby plan is ultimately sourced from seventeenth-century England rather than from native building traditions. This could hardly have occurred much before 1600, for the type only emerged in England itself in the late sixteenth century by the insertion of a massive chimney stack in the cross passage of the sub-medieval vernacular house plan.[106]

7.32 The directly opposed entrances at Ballynamire, with cross-passage, are blocked by a chimneystack in the interior of the farmhouse. This creates lobby entries to the front and rear of the house, facilitating greater social segregation within the early modern household (see fig. 7.5 for plan).

Given the unmodified condition of the farmhouse at Ballynamire, it is pertinent to examine the internal layout where the communal activities of the hall were now dispersed among a number of rooms. Given the lack of documentary sources such as inventories, an identification of the functions ascribed to individual rooms here is tentative, bearing in mind that the same spaces can undergo changes in function over time. The front and rear lobby-entry at Ballynamire, as well as providing a form of entry which conserved heat, created 'reception areas' that needed to be negotiated by visitors before being admitted deeper into the house. The presence of lobby entries facilitated separation between different areas of the house, creating a greater sense of exclusivity among different elements of the household.[107] Given that there is a pair of rooms on either side of the lobby-entries at Ballynamire, a sequence of rooms can be postulated: hall and kitchen to one side of central chimney stack, with parlour and bed chamber on the other. While the front lobby allowed for the hall and parlour to be entered independently, the rear lobby allowed access to the hall only, as the remains of a stone partition cut off the parlour from here. The kitchen was used for cooking as well as as a dining area for farm help and servants, while the hall was maintained as a general living area, with the parlour beyond used as a withdrawing room. While spatial arrangements at garret level are not clear due to both poor preservation and the presence of dense ivy, fireplaces at this level in both gable ends indicate at least two rooms available for heated accommodation, such rooms serving as bedchambers for members of the immediate family. Any spaces at this level not provided with a fireplace could still serve the function of bedchambers for members of the family and servants, or alternatively could have provided storage space.

Houses such as Ballynamire were not necessarily built due to larger households, as enlargement was also a means to accommodate new activities such as entertainment, which had previously taken place outside the home. In England, communal entertainments were becoming less popular with the middling sort by the late seventeenth century. Instead, the well-to-do farmer and his wife may have given hospitality to guests of similar social standing inside their parlour, not only away from the attentions of servants or junior members of the family, but also at a remove from the outdoor culture of the village green and alehouse.[108] The segregation of space impacted upon the nature of intra-personal relationships in early modern society, as entrance arrangements were altered to provide increased control and facilitate social exclusion. Such separation with an emphasis on increased privacy can be related to greater social developments – more emphasis being placed on the individual, with consequent changes in community and household relations.[109] The presence of directly opposed entrances at Ballynamire (the cross-passage was now blocked by the central chimney stack) could allow for the careful social grading of a visitor (fig. 7.32). Social standing and the level of familiarity appropriate to a visitor could be demonstrated simply by who called at the front door and who automatically sought access through the rear door. Such a trend towards increased privacy is symptomatic of a greater emphasis on the individual than had been the case in medieval times. Consequently, this was to have a fundamental impact upon the household and community at large and can be seen as part of the process by which society came to be transformed by an expansive mercantile economy. In this new world, ties of hereditary loyalty and personal service, which were the hallmarks of Gaelic lordship, had no place, with more importance now placed on workers, free from feudal obligations, but ripe for the demands of a modern market economy.

Conclusion

While tower houses and fortified houses dominate the archaeological record of the early modern period in Offaly, such buildings preserve only a partial record of the built environment at the time. The importance of this chapter has been to elucidate less obvious buildings, which, for the most part, have escaped the attention of archaeologists due to problems of poor preservation, abysmal documentary sources, insensitive restoration, imprecise chronologies and unwieldy typological frameworks. A number of these buildings across west and south Offaly, eschewing defensive features, express the concerns and aspirations of families from a spectrum of social backgrounds, ranging from socially middling farmers to members of the gentry. Given the problems of poor documentation for the period at a local level, an archaeological analysis of such buildings plays a fundamental role in the elucidation of social processes in predominantly rural communities at this time.

The buildings analysed in this chapter demonstrate that despite being colonized a generation or two earlier, the territories of the old Gaelic lordships in the post-Restoration era continued to experience social change, with relations not only evolving between the native and newcomer, but also between the individual and the community at large. By the end of the seventeenth century, servants and tenants had finally disappeared from the hall, with such hospitality now commuted to the basement, in direct contrast to the communal and public activities of earlier households. Not only was the quest for greater privacy driving these changes in the use of space. Power was no longer centred on large retinues tied by links of service and hereditary loyalty. Instead, influence now stemmed from central government or the shire, with men no longer attracted to a particular lord in the hope of receiving protection and land. Changes were also occurring in the religious sphere, and while Protestantism appealed to only a relatively small proportion of the population (generally those of planter background), both the Reformation and the Counter-Reformation brought about radical transformations in the religious landscape in Offaly, which will be discussed in the next chapter.

CHAPTER 8

Churches, glebe houses and memorials

Introduction

While the political and institutional changes wrought by the Reformation in Ireland have been the subject of analysis and debate by historians, there has been comparatively little discussion on how this religious and intellectual turmoil impacted upon the material environment. Scholars such as Michael O'Neill and Olivia Horsfall Turner, however, have discussed the impact of the Reformation on church architecture using the seventeenth- and eighteenth-century diocesan visitations, while, from an archaeological perspective, Eamonn Cotter has looked at developments in religious architecture for the same period in Co. Cork.[1] Throughout the sixteenth and seventeenth centuries, the crown attempted to expand its jurisdiction based on the dual policy of civil and religious reform to win the hearts and minds of its Irish subjects. Civil reform involved inculcating adherence to the virtues of common law, along with an acceptance of contemporary English norms of how people should dress or build houses, as well as practise agriculture and industry. Religious reform was considered to be integral to this process, as contemplation of the individual's relationship with God would pave the way for the embrace of more public reforms. At the same time, the Counter-Reformation was gathering momentum, with an influx of Continental-trained Catholic clergy, not only stymieing the influence of Protestant ministers, but also introducing Tridentine reforms, which were no less committed to usurping or controlling aspects of traditional devotion. The Jacobean plantation schemes of 1619 and 1620 in west and south Offaly covered a number of dioceses (namely Clonmacnoise, Ossory, Killaloe and Meath) that contained a largely rural-based system of parish churches and dependent chapels (fig. 8.1). Sixty to seventy years earlier, a number of religious houses in the region had also been dissolved under government supervision, and their buildings, lands and revenues farmed out to local native magnates and other individuals considered deserving of government largesse.

A consideration of church architecture in this period is complicated not only by relatively low levels of church patronage and maintenance (when compared with earlier and later periods) but also by the poor survival of relevant documentary sources such as baptismal, marriage and burial records. As a result, scholars have tended to focus upon the church of the early and late medieval periods. In order to remedy this bias, churches and graveyards in west and south Offaly are discussed with reference to overall design and other features of architectural interest such as

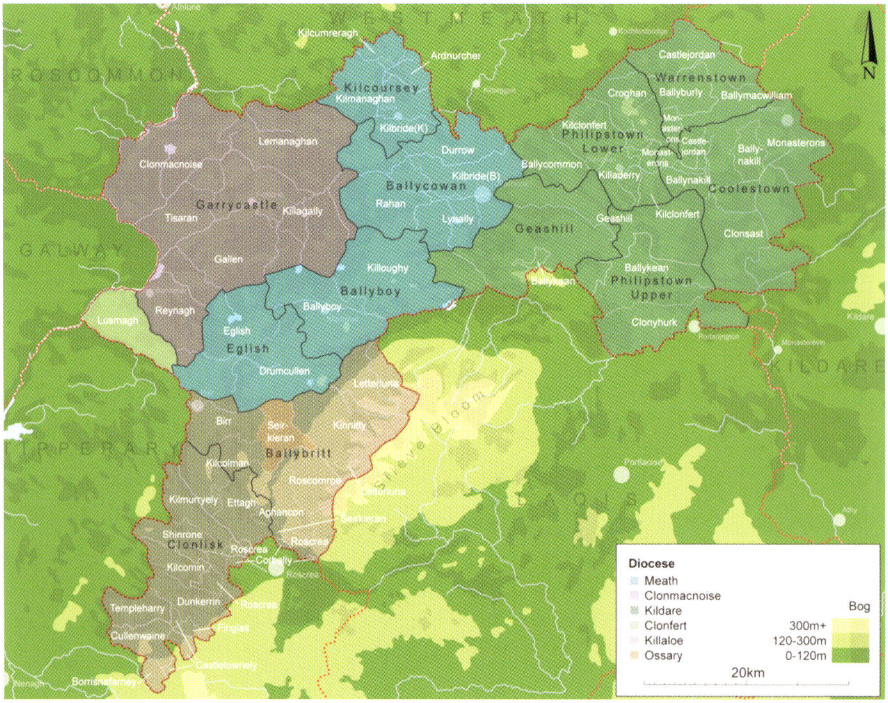

8.1 Map of the dioceses and parishes in Co. Offaly. Parish names are in white, barony names are in black (drawn by Conor McDermott and Hugh Kavanagh).

doorways, windows, armorial plaques and mortuary monuments. The Reformation and Counter-Reformation gave rise to theological and liturgical innovation, which were to have fundamental consequences for the maintenance and care of churches and graveyards. This chapter seeks not only to explore how such changes in the spiritual realm can be traced in the material arena, but also to place this process against the background of the cultural and social change being wrought by the decline of the old Gaelic lordships and the establishment of a new English and Protestant order in the localities.

Problems in the interpretation of early modern church buildings

Studies of religious practice and experience in this period are complicated by the nature of the surviving material. The vast majority of church sites in west and south Offaly simply do not preserve any evidence for continued use in the early modern period, with most sites indicating a hiatus between the early sixteenth and mid-eighteenth centuries; and do not receive any demonstrable patronage until the appearance of headstones commemorating families of socially middling status from the 1740s onwards. Of sixty-six sites surveyed in west and south Offaly, only

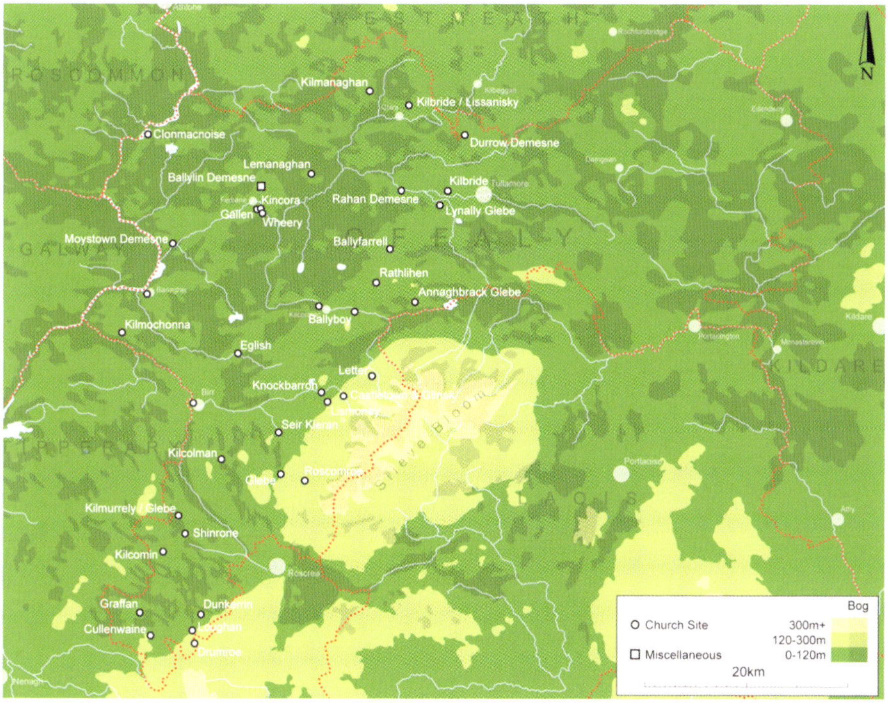

8.2 Distribution of early modern churches and related sites across west and south Offaly (drawn by Conor McDermott and Hugh Kavanagh).

seventeen exhibited material evidence, in terms of building fabric and commemorative pieces, of continuing religious activity between 1550 and 1700, illustrating the challenges of writing an archaeology of early modern architecture and social practice in Ireland (fig. 8.2). In a situation where the state discouraged public displays of the majority denomination, the material expression of that faith was greatly constrained. The combination of the dissolution of the monasteries, iconoclasm and periodic outbreaks of rebellions and war, followed by widespread confiscation and plantation, also conspired to create an environment that was not conducive to the patronage of church building and maintenance. Indeed, lay impropriators not attending to the repair of churches in Offaly also contributed to the decline.[2]

The exploration of early modern religious practice in an Irish context is also hindered by the poor survival of the documentary sources. The non-centralized nature of church administration, both Protestant and Catholic, in sixteenth- and seventeenth-century Ireland, coupled with extensive lack of organization at parish level, meant that documents created routinely in the rest of Europe, such as church court records, baptism, marriage and burial records, were either only produced intermittently or rarely preserved.[3] While over two hundred sets of churchwardens' accounts survive in England for the Tudor period, Ireland has but a single set, from St

Werburgh's parish in Dublin, for the most part dating from before the Reformation.[4] These problems are accentuated in native areas of the country, where little documentation other than entries in the annals and poetic eulogies have survived. In these annalistic entries, apart from the cause and place of death and burial, other details are rare.[5] There are no surviving depictions of church interiors at this time. The *Monumenta Eblanae*, a book of drawings illustrating church monuments in Dublin, is the only known contemporary portrayal of seventeenth-century memorials in Ireland.[6] This lacuna in documentary sources is particularly marked in Offaly, where the earliest parochial records for the county are the church vestry accounts of 1710 for the church at Ballyboy, with other parish records only surviving for the post-1800 period.[7] At diocesan level, however, a series of visitations involving periodic examinations of the clergy and churches in individual parishes were carried out for the Protestant dioceses of Killaloe and Meath.[8] Despite the terse nature of these visitation accounts, it is possible to ascertain to some extent the level of church maintenance in these dioceses in the seventeenth century.

The dissolution of the monasteries

The suppression of the monasteries and the confiscation of their properties and lands took place from 1536 onwards, gathering pace in the 1540s. In the Gaelic lordships, while the process of dissolution was slower, the native aristocracy could be just as eager to receive former monastic lands as well.[9] In due course, the Augustinian priories at Gallen, Durrow and Seir Kieran, as well as the Carmelite priory at Kilcormac, were dissolved in the 1550s and 1560s.[10] The properties belonging to these monasteries, including estates, tithes and other assets, were distributed to individuals from a variety of backgrounds: Old English, New English and Gaelic Irish.[11] These grantees, however, did not necessarily take up residence in their new acquisitions, as the majority of them were merely land speculators, with a short-term interest in leases of monastic property, keen to earn a fast profit by selling their new gains as quickly as possible. The subsequent history of the monastic houses in Offaly clearly illustrates a process whereby the properties fell into the hands of a succession of owners. The crown leased the monastic lands of Seir Kieran in Éile Uí Chearbhaill to a series of English gentlemen and officials, along with 'loyal' natives: John Croft in 1552, John O'Carroll in 1566, William O'Carroll in 1578, Lucas Dillon in 1586 and William Taaffe in 1604.[12] Similarly, the Carmelite priory at Kilcormac was dissolved and leased to a number of individuals, including Con O'Molloy in 1550, Henry Cooley in 1567, George Cooley in 1579, Thomas Lambyn in 1596 and Robert Leicester in 1603.[13]

With the suppression of the monasteries, and their buildings being given over to more profane uses, the performance of religious services therein may have been

8.3 Wooden Pietà reputedly of late sixteenth-century date in the Catholic church in Kilcormac. One local tradition holds that the Magawley family of Tremona brought the Pietà back from Italy. Another tradition records that the statue was brought from Spain to the Carmelite priory in Kilcormac before the Reformation. With the suppression of the priory *c.*1550, it was moved to the nearby church at Ballyboy, where it remained for a hundred years until the church was taken over and used as a stable by Cromwellian troops. It escaped destruction at the time by being hidden under a rubbish heap. It was subsequently buried in a bog for sixty years, until it was salvaged by one Fr Loughlin Lynam, parish priest of Ballyboy. Another version of the tradition holds that during the penal period the statue was buried for safety in nearby Derrydolney Bog, and that with Catholic Emancipation in the early nineteenth century it was resurrected and restored to Kilcormac.

rendered impossible. In this scenario, families may have relocated their internments with associated rituals and commemoration into parish churches unaffected by these closures.[14] It would be wrong, however, to presume that ruined monastic sites, despite their dissolution, did not continue to resonate with religious significance. Many of these monasteries were traditional burial grounds for members of the native elite, with generations of particular families buried in family tombs. The calendar of a breviary written by Malachy Ó Lachtnáin at Kilcormac in 1489 contains obituaries for various members of the O'Molloy family, including a number of chiefs of Fir Cheall between 1410 and 1577. Some of the entries allude to the burial of these individuals in the church of the Carmelite priory there. The founder of the priory, Aodh O'Molloy, was interred 'before the high altar' in 1454, and Calbhach O'Molloy was laid to rest 'at the third step, near the head of the choir on the north side' in 1476.[15] Such sites intimately associated with kin groups like the O'Molloys could continue to wield considerable attraction. Two decorative features associated with the site of the priory at Kilcormac – a wooden Pietà and a limestone crucifixion plaque – have been ascribed a late sixteenth-century date, indicating that they were donated sometime after the monastery had been dissolved *c.*1550 (fig. 8.3).[16] Despite the repeated complaints of Protestant clergy, people still preferred to bury their relatives in the consecrated grounds of suppressed abbeys and priories.[17]

The Reformation and Counter-Reformation finally gather pace

It was not until the opening of the seventeenth century that one discerns the workings of the Reformation and Counter-Reformation in progress, with doctrinal and liturgical differences beginning to establish deeper, more divisive roots in Offaly. There was a revival in the fortunes of the Catholic Church with the establishment of the Jesuits in Ireland in 1596, while Continental-based seminaries were producing an influx of well-trained priests into the country. In Spain and Portugal, no fewer than six colleges were established, with the prime but not exclusive role of training clergymen. The Council of Trent advocated the establishment of a more effective parochial system, the regular administration of the sacraments, the greater instruction of the laity in Catholic doctrine and the enactment of new regulations regarding the administering of baptismal, nuptial and funeral rites.[18] At the same time, opposition to the established Church of Ireland was growing among the bulk of the population. The Gaelic Irish, and in particular the Old English, became increasingly alienated from sources of political influence and patronage in Dublin and London. This, as well as resentment against recusancy fines, created a more distinctive Catholic polity in Ireland. The proponents of the Counter-Reformation could count on a popular distaste for Protestantism, partly on religious grounds, but also on political and even racial grounds.[19]

8.4 Stone window lintel with inscription, date and IHS monogram, now in rear wall of eighteenth-century mansion in Ballycumber.

The rate of spiritual renewal inspired by the Tridentine reforms in native lordships, however, was slower than in Old English areas. This was due to Continental-trained priests arriving later among the Gaelic Irish, while Tridentine decrees on marriage, funerals and baptism required more fundamental changes in cultural behaviour than was the case in Old English areas.[20] Aspects of secular lordship, which emphasized kinship and the value of extended lineages, as well as particular social norms that governed behaviour, had blended with religion, creating a world-view that could not be changed quickly.[21] Sir William Petty observed even as late as the 1670s that the religion of the poorer Irish was based on supernatural stories of saints and pilgrimages to holy wells; beliefs that could be traced back to the days of early Christianity and before.[22] While relics and miraculous images formed the focus of much popular devotion in early modern Ireland, there was a particularly strong tradition of holy places.[23] These sites were associated with saints' legends where the actions of a particular saint had sanctified a place. Such locations were scattered across the countryside and were usually the object of pilgrimages, with some attracting specific devotions. For example, the ruins of the medieval church of St Margaret in Wexford drew pregnant women.[24] Most holy places were less specific, however, and served as local gathering places. In Munster in 1617, for instance, people were observed to gather at 'supposed holy crosses and wells'.[25] Sixty-five holy wells, along with a number of sacred trees and rocks, have been recorded across all of Co. Offaly, and these are visible testimony to the strength of traditional devotion in the region, though by their nature it is difficult to quantify by morphological or documentary analysis alone the use of such sites in the early modern period.[26] Clearly, the parish church was not the specific and exclusive location of religious practice, as aspects of faith were played out in more mundane areas – people lived in a spiritualized world where the material and spiritual were not rendered separate to the degree that they are today.

To a certain extent, the receptiveness of Tridentine dictates seems to have depended on social standing. Sir William Petty observed that, while there was much 'superstition' among the poorer Irish, 'as for the richer and better educated sort of them, they are such Catholics as are in other places'.[27] Counter-Reformation doctrine was certainly permeating into the psyche of the native elite in west Offaly. Ballycumber House, an eighteenth-century mansion, is built on the site of an earlier MacCoghlan residence of which no trace survives except for the stone lintel of a flat-headed window that bears the following inscription: DERMOT . COGHLAN . MADE . THIS . CASTELL IN . ANNO . DNI . 1627. Left of the inscription is an IHS monogram in Roman capitals, with a cross possessing triangular terminals sitting on the cross stem of the H. Directly underneath the H is a V (fig. 8.4). The placing of the V underneath the H in the Ballycumber lintel is not without significance, representing radiating nails rather than the letter, though typically there were three nails rather than two. The IHS monogram was used elsewhere in Ireland; for example, the motif is present on a pair of armorial stones bearing the year 1612 in Carstown House, Co. Louth, a residence of the Plunkett families, one of the leading Old English families in the Pale. The armorial stone over the entrance to the house also bore a sculptured crucifix.[28] Recusants across Britain adopted the IHS monogram, with individuals such as Sir Thomas Tresham placing the monogram onto a date stone in his Triangular Lodge at Rushton, Northamptonshire. Indeed, such a symbol also came to be associated with one of the more prominent orders in the Counter-Reformation movement, the Jesuits.[29] For Dermot Oge Coghlan, who had been granted just over one thousand acres in the 1620 plantation of Delbhna Eathra, this monogram was an explicit assertion of a faith influenced by Tridentine doctrine, a display that could have drawn protest from his Protestant neighbours as well as sanctions from official quarters.[30] Among the more Puritan sections of Protestant opinion, it represented subversion, becoming closely allied with popery; however, it has been pointed out that the Arminian movement in the established church in England saw a rehabilitation of the monogram that to some extent restored its acceptability within Protestant circles in the early part of the seventeenth century.[31]

On the other side of the coin, Protestant reforms were beginning to take shape with the large numbers of British settlers arriving into the country following the conclusion of the Nine Years War and the Flight of the Earls. The implementation of plantation schemes like those in west and south Offaly saw a whole spectrum of British society being settled in the native midland territories. While the midlands never experienced the large-scale movement of British settlers as was seen in Ulster, Mac Cuarta argues on the basis of depositions taken in the aftermath of the 1641 uprising that planter society in places like Offaly was broadly based, and in no way confined solely to the landed elite.[32] This movement of British settlers into the country saw an influx of English and Scottish clergy after *c.*1610 who tended to the spiritual welfare of their countrymen, despite the fact that a large proportion of the reformed church's resources and income had been appropriated by secular proprietors. Settlers either brought clergymen with them or subsequently encouraged them to immigrate from across the water.[33] Plantation schemes included clauses for the endowment of lands to the established church so as to secure the proper maintenance of its clergy. In the midland territories, it was envisaged that church land would be deducted before the assignation of the appropriated proportions to undertakers.[34] In reality, only a miniscule amount of land was assigned to the established church in grants to various undertakers; for example, in Éile Uí Chearbhaill, only twenty acres was reserved for each of the parish churches of Letter, Shinrone, Birr and Dunkerrin, a woefully inadequate amount for the proper maintenance of clergy and their buildings.[35]

The inclination of the Protestant clergymen arriving from Britain ensured that by the 1630s the Church of Ireland's ministry was no longer ambivalent in doctrine as it had been in the sixteenth century. The introduction of foreign clergy with no knowledge of the Irish language, cultural mores and customs, of course, lessened the chances of converting the native Irish to Protestantism.[36] A rare example of an indigenous Protestant clergyman was Neal Malloy, the second son of Cosny Malloy, who entered Trinity College as a scholar in 1612. In 1616, he graduated with a BA, and in the following year was ordained and presented by the lord deputy to the vicarage of Fercall, where he was resident in 1622, and returned as a good preacher.[37] In the diocese of Killaloe, of which Éile Uí Chearbhaill formed the easternmost portion, it appears that attempts to develop an indigenous, Irish-speaking ministry had failed, while attempts to coerce the native population with anti-recusancy legislation had met a similar fate. Once conformity was no longer enforced from 1621 onwards, local attendance at church services fell away, leaving only a rump of New English parishioners. Just as the established church looked to English clergymen to perform pastoral duties, so it looked to incoming settlers to provide the parishioners.[38]

Spiritual changes affecting the material realm

A challenge facing the study of liturgy in this period is that religious beliefs were so integral to the individual's understanding of the world that most did not consider making explicit the assumptions on which their beliefs were based and on which they based their everyday lives.[39] In earlier chapters, Bourdieu's notion of *habitus*, that people tend to create and recreate the physical environment around them according to implicit notions of cultural norms, informed the analysis of secular buildings such as tower houses. Such notions can change from one generation to the next, or from one class to another, according to the different material conditions that people experience.[40] Within churches, these cultural norms (religious beliefs) are given explicit expression. The segregation of the congregation from the altar end, whether on the lines of gender or of social standing, was reinforced through the replication of ritual practices. At times of religious change, as was experienced in the early modern period, material culture can undergo a profound and, at times, dramatic, transformation.

The Protestant doctrine of justification by faith alone diluted the incentive for the patronage of church furnishings and fittings. Imagery, ornament and any object tinged with special curative, tutelary or apotropaic abilities was regarded as suspect, as it was likely to confuse the ignorant and lead people into idolatry.[41] Reforming clergymen could not support the concept of sacred spaces demarcated from the profane by ritual and decoration, with one Church of Ireland minister, Thomas Halstream, going so far as to say that prayer in the marketplace was as good as in any church.[42] This was to have repercussions for church buildings in Offaly; in 1552, English troops based at Athlone plundered the churches at Clonmacnoise.[43]

Before the Reformation, Mass was celebrated by the priest in the chancel, with the congregation either standing or kneeling in the nave area. From the later medieval period, a stone or wooden barrier known as the rood screen typically separated the nave and chancel. The congregation's only contact with the service was during the consecration of host and wine when the screen doors were briefly opened.[44] The Eucharistic liturgy was a drama in a language poorly understood, if at all, with the congregation acting in the role of passive observers.[45] This contrasted with the Protestant service, where the congregation was expected to participate in and to understand the proceedings. Protestant church services involved the communal rendition of prayers, interspersed with readings from the Bible, all to be concluded with the giving of a sermon. The Holy Communion, with its strong connections with Catholicism, was rarely celebrated.[46] As the new liturgy emphasized corporate worship (for the clergy and congregation to worship together), the focus of ceremony could be moved into the nave area, making the partitioned chancel redundant. The Dominican priest Richard Bermingham opined that the most profound effect of the Reformation in Ireland was that 'the Protestants have broken up the stone altars that were in our churches and altered the arrangement of the church in order that the marks of their original delineation should disappear'.[47] Rood screens were removed and fixed stone altars replaced by movable communion tables. Pulpits were erected in a prominent and more central position so that everyone could hear and see the minister. In these services, sermons could span a number of hours, necessitating the seating of the congregation. To remedy this, 'box-pews' were installed, each assigned to a particular family, with proximity to the preacher graded on social standing.[48]

Religious architectural development in early modern Offaly

There appears to have been either little or no development of religious architecture in Ireland during the sixteenth and seventeenth centuries.[49] FitzPatrick and O'Brien have amply described the dereliction and ruination of churches in west and south

8.5 South façade of the church at Kilmanaghan (© National Monuments Service: Department of Arts, Heritage and the Gaeltacht).

Offaly, suggesting a fundamental breakdown in the parochial system certainly by the late sixteenth century, if not earlier.[50] This would not have created conditions conducive to the patronage of church buildings. The lack of architectural development in this period in Ireland parallels to an extent the situation in Britain, where the conservative preferences of masons and builders for working in the perpendicular idiom, as well as sufficiency in the numbers of churches passed on from before the Reformation, may have been responsible for the hiatus in church building there.[51] Indeed, gothic continued to be considered an appropriate architectural style for church buildings in England right through the seventeenth century, and only became regarded as 'barbaric' in the reign of Queen Anne.[52] Another consideration behind the lack of novel architectural development may have been the zealous fervour of Puritanism that opposed the veneration of the church as a holy place, with the result that respect for the church as a building could be greatly diminished.[53]

Most of the church buildings in late medieval and early modern Offaly appear to have been quite rudimentary; a simple oblong block, with no belfry (fig. 8.5). The simplicity of most churches meant that for the most part the services of a skilled architect were not required. There was little in terms of innovative design, either in terms of planning or aesthetics. Instead, there was a focus upon the repair of existing church buildings with roofs, doors and windows being either repaired or replaced so as to maintain a protective environment for the interior of the church and the congregation. The now-empty chancel and nave windows were usually provided with bar holes and grooving to hold glass panes in place. The tribulations of the early modern period unfortunately have not allowed for the survival of in-situ glass panes in any of the Irish churches.[54] This too is paralleled in England, where the survival of pre-nineteenth-century glazing is more exceptional than normal.[55] While these churches in Offaly are now empty shells, exposed to inclement weather, such buildings, depending on the wealth and population of the parish, would have been suitably furnished to create an appropriate sense of solemnity and gravitas, as would be expected of a holy place.

An appreciation of how the interiors of churches were furnished in this period is unfortunately compromised by a combination of iconoclasm, the forceful appropriation of church buildings and poor documentary sources. As a result, little is known of how these church buildings in west and south Offaly were furnished. In general, fixed stone altars were removed and substituted by wooden movable communion tables. The only piece of seventeenth-century church furniture to survive in Offaly is a small side table currently in the modern Protestant church at Seir Kieran.[56] In form, it bears remarkable similarity to the earliest known communion table in Ireland, presumed to have been in use since 1610 at a church in Coolfadda in Bandon, Co. Cork, and now housed at another in Ballymodan in the same town.[57]

The walls of churches in west and south Offaly were more than likely rendered with harling on the exterior and finer plasterwork on the interior. In the absence of heating, external harling provided a means of weatherproofing and insulating the building from adverse climatic conditions.[58] The interior walls could be extensively decorated before the Reformation, both for aesthetic and for devotional reasons.[59] No such mural decorative work has survived in Offaly, possibly due to exposure to the elements once the buildings fell into dereliction. Another reason for lack of survival, however, could have been Protestant doctrine that entreated walls to be whitewashed, obliterating iconographical images from the views of the parishioners. While there is no surviving indication, documentary or archaeological, of how the internal plasterwork of churches in Offaly was dressed, late seventeenth-century churchwardens' accounts from Dublin suggest that the Protestant churches in the city were rather plain, mostly whitewashed inside and undecorated, except at Christmas, when holly and ivy were used.[60]

Protestant churches in Offaly in the age of the Reformation

Some of the churches in west and south Offaly that passed into the hands of the Church of Ireland bear material evidence of continued use and maintenance in the seventeenth century. Diocesan accounts record that the church at Durrow was in

8.6 Classical doorway, possibly of late seventeenth-century date, gracing the west gable of St Columba's Church in Durrow. The church was apparently rebuilt in 1802 and remained in use until 1880.

8.7 Church at Lynally Glebe from the northwest. This is a multi-period church with the western two-thirds built utilizing large blocks and antae typical of early medieval masonry churches.

8.8 The gateway in the graveyard boundary wall at Lynally Glebe is possibly early modern and may have served originally as the doorway in the west gable-end of the church.

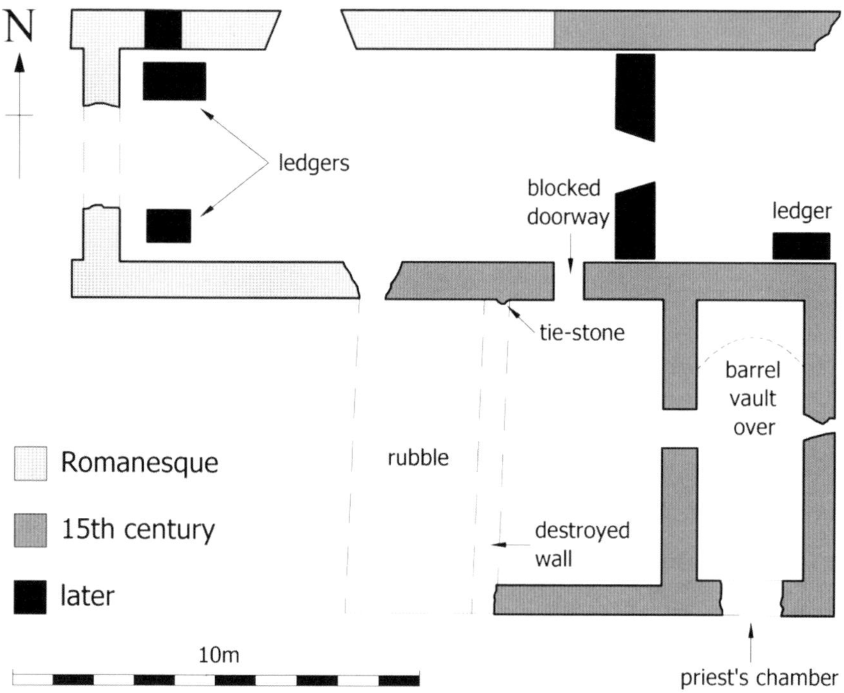

8.9 Ground plan of the church and priest's residence at Lynally Glebe. This early medieval church was extended eastwards by over 7.5m in the fifteenth century. The ground floor of the residential block may have been more extensive, with a second chamber accessed directly from the church via a narrow, pointed doorway. One room may have acted as a sacristy, while the other, together with the first floor, made up the priest's quarters (after FitzPatrick and O'Brien, *Medieval churches of Offaly* (1998), p. 135, fig. 127).

reasonable repair in the late seventeenth century. Unfortunately, it was damaged during the instabilities of 1689–91, though it was subsequently repaired, being described in 1693 as supporting a shingled roof, having two glazed windows and a clay floor, but no bells. The altar was provided with a reading desk, a pulpit and an unrailed communion table, but no font, carpet, linen cloth, chalice or flagon, and no registry for burial.[61] Today at Durrow, a fine entrance, possibly of late seventeenth-/early eighteenth-century date, graces the western façade of the church that was largely rebuilt in 1802 (fig. 8.6).[62] The flat-headed doorway is embellished with a scroll keystone and scroll brackets on either side of entrance. These brackets support an entabulature that is crowned with two ornate urns flanking a larger urn in the middle. Such a display of early modern craftsmanship is one of the finest and indeed earliest exercises in classical architecture in Offaly.

A classical doorway allowing entry into the church at Durrow was wholly suitable, given the belief at the time that physical and moral advances were displayed and furthered through the use of classicism. As such, commentators who advocated

English colonial endeavours in Ireland saw building as a means to assert the new civil and religious order in the face of native conservatism and backwardness. As well as secular buildings, churches could aptly embody the antiquity, eminence and superiority of clergy and patrons alike. The style of church architecture could be used to demonstrate the latest fashions, which embraced notions of gentility and politeness. In the process, the cultural and social dominance of the local landed elite could be demonstrated to the community at large.

Another Protestant church that also retains material and documentary evidence of use in the early modern period is the example at Lynally Glebe, where a number of grave memorials and mural plaques commemorate the landed gentry, both native and newcomer. This church has seen many accretions over the centuries, with pre-Romanesque and late gothic architectural features visible; however, it is interesting that the general appearance of the church was left largely unaltered in the early modern era, despite Bishop Dopping's 1682–5 description of the church as being in good repair with glazed windows, clay floor and shingled roof. Such a roof, with its wooden shingles, required continual maintenance, necessitating the removal of shingles from a disused chapel at Rahan in 1696.[63] Two burial vaults were inserted into the internal west end of Lynally Glebe in the late seventeenth century, while the entrance to the graveyard (a round-arched opening constructed of wrought keystones and jambs dressed with rough punching) may originally have graced the western entrance to the church where there is now a breach (figs 8.7, 8.8, 8.9).

One building that saw more investment and continued maintenance than any other church in Offaly is the parish church of St Brendan in Birr (fig. 8.10). Records for the diocese of Killaloe indicate that this church was somewhat remarkably undergoing repair in 1615, a number of years before the actual plantation of Éile Uí Chearbhaill itself.[64] Despite this, there is a strong tradition that Sir Laurence Parsons refurbished the church after his arrival in 1621 as one of the undertakers in the new plantation. Given that some of the ordinances enacted by Sir Laurence for the town of Birr included the collection of monies that ultimately went towards the maintenance of the church, it is more than likely that he was an improving landlord who took an active interest in the maintenance of his local parish church.[65] In contemporary Ulster, where British settlement was densest, landlords usually took an interest in the patronage of church building and repair.[66] Indeed, it was common for members of this social class also to contribute to the furnishings and ornaments, typically in the form of communion plate.[67] Richards' map of Birr in 1691 depicts St Brendan's as an oblong block with belfry to the west and transept to the south (see fig. 7.24). This transept (which no longer survives) could have served the Parsons family to accommodate their seating as well as their place of burial. Parallels for such transepts are to be found in Ulster and Scotland, where local landlords would erect or reuse transepts in a manner compared to the patronage of medieval chantries.[68] The present north aisle with gallery was added afterwards, more than likely in the eighteenth century, given the nature of the brickwork in the window reveals, as well

8.10 Early seventeenth-century belfry attached to the west end of St Brendan's Church in Birr before partial collapse in recent times (© National Monuments Service: Department of Arts, Heritage and the Gaeltacht).

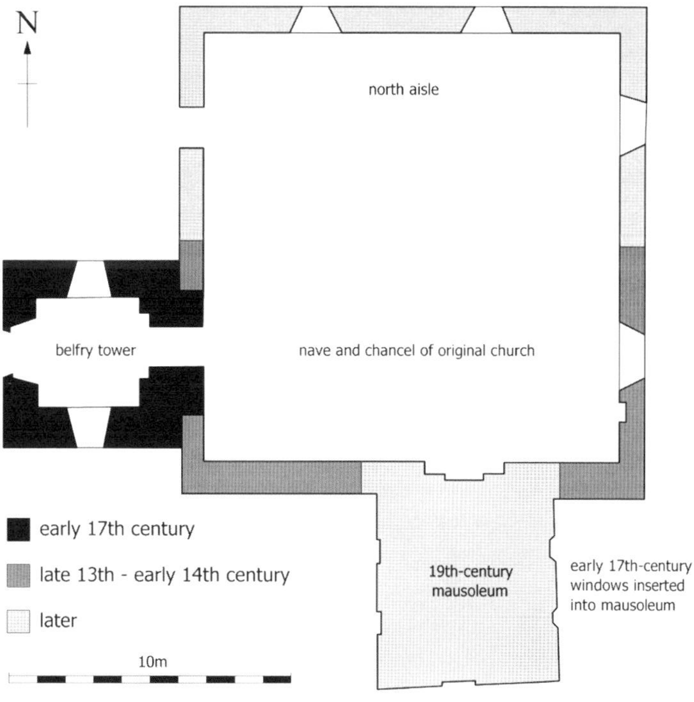

8.11 Plan of St Brendan's parish church in Birr (after FitzPatrick and O'Brien, *Medieval churches of Offaly* (1998), p. 112, fig. 105). Richards' map of Birr dated 1691 depicts the nave and belfry, along with a south transept that no longer stands. Sometime after 1691, the north aisle was constructed. In the early nineteenth century, the Parsons family constructed a mausoleum against the south wall of the nave. Blank single-light and twin-light round-arched windows with the square-hooded surrounds of seventeenth-century date were inserted into the walls of the mausoleum. These windows may have been sourced from the nave or transept of the church.

8.12 Round-arched doorway in the west wall of the belfry of St Brendan's Church. Note the blank armorial plaque above the entrance. In the nineteenth century, it was recorded that the plaque carried Sir Laurence Parsons' (d. 1628) coat of arms along with that of his wife.

8.13 Square-hooded, round-arched windows in the west wall of the later mausoleum attached to the south side of St Brendan's Church.

as the poor financial standing of the Parsons family in the aftermath of the Williamite War (fig. 8.11).[69] Intriguingly though, the pointed single-light windows with sandstone jambs and hood mouldings in the walls of this post-medieval aisle are thirteenth/early fourteenth century in date.[70] It may be the case that these windows are reused from the earlier north wall of the nave, though this still leaves the issue of where the large pointed window in the east end of the aisle originated. One possible source is the now-disappeared south transept.

The round-arched doorways in the walls of the belfry at ground level and the square-hooded, round-arched windows now inserted into a mausoleum built in the nineteenth century adjacent to the church (presumably appropriated from the church itself), provide a clue as to when the belfry was added and other improvements were made to St Brendan's (figs 8.12, 8.13). The limestone surrounds of these openings, dressed with linear tooling and rough punching framed by lines of more regular punching, are typical of native stonework in Offaly from the opening decades of the seventeenth century. It is pertinent to note that native craftsmen, all bearing local names, were employed by Sir Laurence in his reconstruction of neighbouring Birr Castle in the 1620s.[71] Given these circumstances, it is possible that these craftsmen were also engaged by Sir Laurence to construct the new belfry for St Brendan's at the same time as they were employed at Birr Castle, such is the similarity in the stonework evident in the church and in the stone surround of a round-arched gateway of 1620s vintage in Birr Castle (fig. 8.14).[72] Above the main entrance in the west wall of the belfry is a blank armorial plaque of limestone with the two helmets still visible, supporting the crests of an axe and a demi-lion respectively. From the helmets sprout elaborate mantling down both sides of the shield. There is no relief work apparent on the shield, though a nineteenth-century antiquarian recorded that the shield carried Sir Laurence Parsons' coat of arms impaled with those of his wife, surely a suitable embellishment that reminded all and sundry of their piety and good works in patronizing this church.[73] In Ulster, there is a strong association between benevolent landlords and the construction of belfries in the early modern period, an important consideration at a time when Presbyterian meeting houses and Catholic mass houses pointedly lacked such towers.[74] Belfries were added to existing churches in Maghera, Co. Derry, Magheralin, Co. Down, and with a rebuilt north aisle at a priory in Newtownards, Co. Down.[75] Such an edifice, dominating an urban settlement like Birr, was clearly calculated to articulate the hegemony of the Church of Ireland over temporal and spiritual matters.

More problematic is the parish church in Banagher, known as St Mary's or St Rynagh's (fig. 8.15). Commentators have regarded the present church as having been built in the seventeenth century on the site of a late medieval predecessor.[76] Unfortunately, there are no architectural features to support such a date. The only features now in the church that possibly pre-date 1700 (besides the memorial slab to Sir John MacCoghlan, dated to 1576–7) are plain flat-headed windows in the north and south walls at the east end of the church, with a plain segmental doorway and another flat-headed window above it in the west gable end. As at Kilmanaghan (fig. 8.5), these plain openings do not necessarily rule out a seventeenth-century date, though more convincing architectural evidence is required. Given the context of St Rynagh's history and location, however, on a rise overlooking the town, a corporate

8.14 Round-arched gateway in the south façade of Birr Castle.

8.15 St Rynagh's Church in Banagher from the southeast. According to a nineteenth-century antiquarian, there were several mural slabs commemorating the Armstrong family in the west end of the church then used as a vault. One of these slabs bore the name 'Grisell Armstrong' along with the date 'October 1680'. Another slab was inscribed with 'Armstrong 4 Brothers 1700'.

borough founded in the early seventeenth century, the maintenance or construction of a Protestant church on the site is likely. In 1624, a garrison fort known as Fort Falkland was established at Banagher, with an urban charter granted in 1628 to encourage settlement in the vicinity. A map of *c.*1630 shows the fort dominating one end of the main street, with regularly laid out burgage plots on either side of the street (see fig. 4.3).[77] The Protestant church and its surrounding land demarcate the far end of the town. Many towns in Ulster were similarly laid out, with the church positioned within the town at the opposite end of a street from a landlord's fortified residence, such as at Newtownstewart and Strabane, both in Co. Tyrone.[78]

The location of the most charged and potent symbols of civil and religious reform at either end of the main street was a self-conscious assertion of the new political dispensation that now existed in Offaly. In light of this, the rebuilding of St Rynagh's could have been necessary for both practical and symbolic reasons, serving the spiritual welfare of the burgesses and the garrison troops alike, who took up residence in this outpost of 'civility'. Parallels in the layout of plantation villages like Banagher and the earliest English settlements in America were recognized as early as

8.16 Clonmacnoise Cathedral from the northwest, with Temple Dowling in the right middle-ground. In the 1640s, the cathedral underwent restoration by the vicar general Charles Coghlan – work that is commemorated by a plaque bearing the year 1647 (© National Monuments Service: Department of Arts, Heritage and the Gaeltacht).

the 1950s, when Anthony Garvan compared the plans of the new towns laid out by English planters in the two areas.[79] John Reps regarded the early settlement of Jamestown as similar to the linear villages established in the Ulster Plantation, with James Fort serving the same function as the castle and bawn of the colonial settlements in Ireland.[80]

Glebe houses

Some late medieval parish churches preserve evidence that the clergy were accommodated within their hallowed precincts. Churches like Annaghbrack Glebe,

8.17 Wall footings of the residences for the deacon and the archdeacon at Clonmacnoise. Note the double-centred doorway in the graveyard boundary wall to the right.

Drumcullen, Letter, Kilbride (Kilcoursey), Kilcomin and Rathlihen preserve two-storey residences at their west ends, with barrel-vaulted ground-floor chambers. This is to be expected, as priests' residences in late medieval Ireland were commonly incorporated into the west gable end of parish churches.[81] At Clonmacnoise and Lynally Glebe, provision was made for more elaborate two-storeyed buildings that opened off the altar end, providing not only private chambers for the priests, but a sacristy as well (figs 8.9, 8.16).[82] The poorly preserved nature of these residences for the most part prohibits an accurate reconstruction, but the vertical arrangement of chambers lit by ogee-headed slit opes is very much reminiscent of tower house architecture. The deployment of a common architectural grammar, shared by tower houses and churches, is telling of an environment in late medieval Gaelic lordships in which secular and religious interests were intimately intertwined.

Given the general dereliction of churches in the early modern period, it is unlikely that the residences mentioned above continued to see usage. In 1622, the Protestant clergy in the diocese of Killaoe, of which Éile Uí Chearbhaill is part, complained that the lay impropriators deprived them of glebe land so that

> ye incumbent shall have no house nor place to build a house, but either must live in some poore hired cabin in danger of theyr lives, or in a victualling house not answerable to theyr calling: or be non-resident in repairing to some well peopled towne for safety and habitation.[83]

8.18 Glebe house at Graffan from the southwest. The architectural historian Maurice Craig considered this an enigmatic building – its thick walls and double-centred doorways made it archaic even in the seventeenth century, while the near-regular fenestration of the south wall looked forward to the eighteenth century.

8.19 Ground-floor plan of the glebe house at Graffan (after Craig, *Architecture of Ireland* (1989), p. 132, fig. 100).

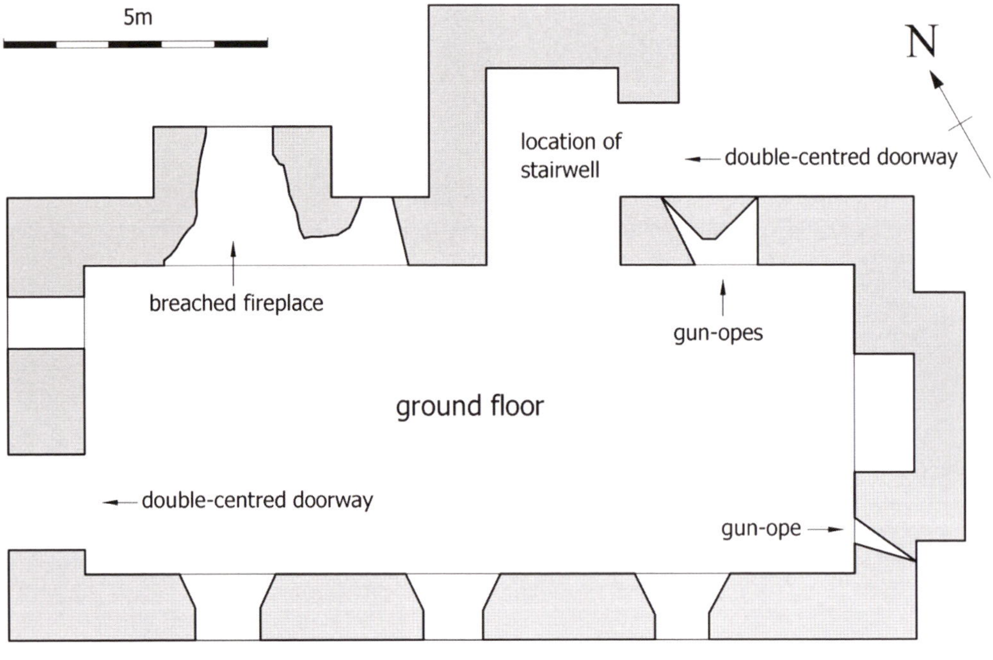

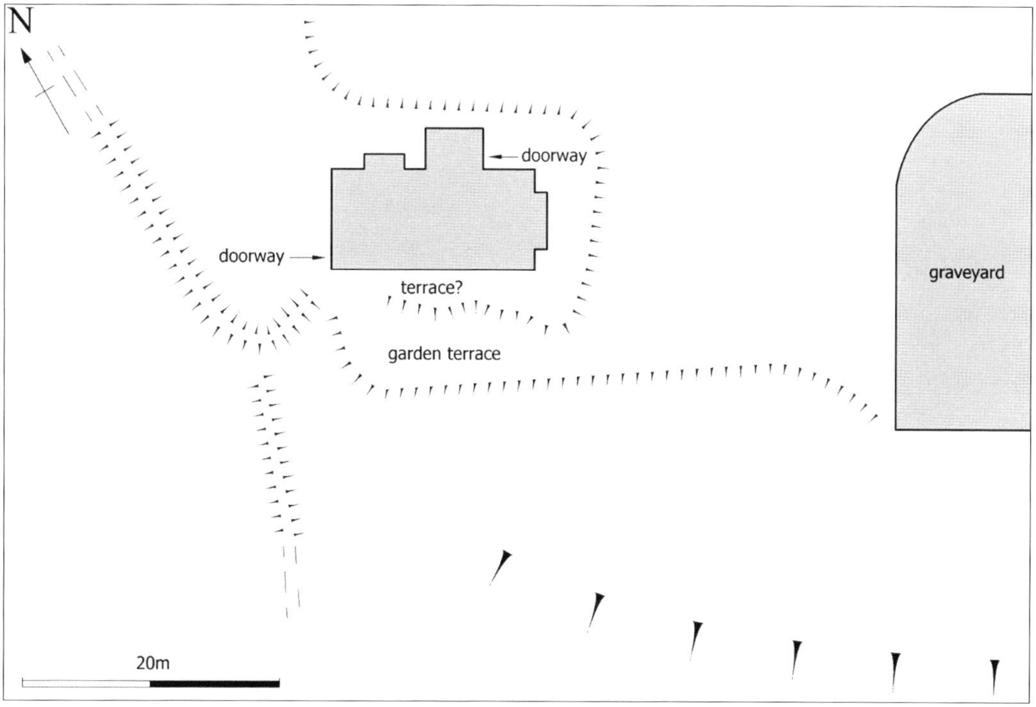

8.20 Sketch plan of the glebe house and grounds at Graffan (drawn by James Lyttleton and Hugh Kavanagh).

The clergy had seen the 1619 plantation scheme in Éile Uí Chearbhaill as a means to acquire glebe land, and petitioned to 'have assigned to them as of His Maties [sic] bounty some pportion of glebe land to be allotted in ye most convenient place'.[84] As mentioned above, however, only a miniscule amount of glebe land was assigned to the established church in grants to various undertakers.

Despite the problems stemming from impropriated benefices and poor revenues, in the ebullient property market of seventeenth-century Offaly, clergymen in the county could still develop substantial livings appropriate to their social standing; the memorials in Lynally Glebe to Thomas Coffy, the vicar of Fir Cheall is testimony to that. Earlier in the century, the Revd Marmaduke Clapham, vicar of Shinrone, lost his property at the outbreak of rebellion in 1641. In a deposition, he claimed to have lost monies, household goods, provisions, cattle and chattels at his farm, along with its yearly profit, together with church earnings, amounting to a substantial £1,000.[85] Similar levels of material loss were experienced by clergymen in south Ulster.[86] Clapham's glebe house and those of other clergymen in the period, in general, have not survived, depriving the archaeologist of the opportunity to analyse the degree to which the lifestyles of these clergymen were affected by developments in early modern architecture and society in general.

Yet, in Offaly there is some surviving evidence of early modern clerical accommodation. Besides the two-storey sacristy adjoining Clonmacnoise Cathedral, in the same complex are the wall footings of two conjoined buildings at the southeast corner of the graveyard boundary wall, designated on a 1739 map as residences for the dean and archdeacon.[87] As these buildings are not marked on an earlier plan of 1658, it has been suggested that the buildings may be of late seventeenth-century date.[88] Examination of these ephemeral remains concurs with this dating, as the more southerly of the two buildings was entered from the exterior of the graveyard through a double-centred doorway with a chamfered surround similar to a pair of doorways found in a seventeenth-century glebe house at Graffan (fig. 8.17).

This glebe house at Graffan in the parish of Templeharry is a unique survival. A number of commentators have interpreted the building as a glebe house, on the basis of its location just to the northwest of Graffan church and graveyard.[89] The glebe house is heavily obscured by ivy growth, though the overall plan of the two-storeyed building, an oblong block with projecting stairwell to the rear, is typical of seventeenth-century architecture (figs 8.18, 8.19). So too is the lack of mass walling for internal partitions, projecting chimney stacks, the asymmetrical arrangement of windows and the provision of gun opes. More unusual are the two double-centred doorways, one in the west gable end, and the other in the east wall of the projecting stairwell block. Craig considers this building rather enigmatic, given its thick walls and the double-centred doorways that make the building look archaic, even by the standards of the seventeenth century.[90] One only has to see Temple Dowling in Clonmacnoise (1689), however, with its double-centred doorway, to realize that late gothic traditions were still evident towards the end of the seventeenth century.

What is intriguing about the glebe house is that there is no clear indication as to which of these doorways acted as the principle entrance to the building. Typically, the principle entrance of a residence in this period was marked out in both size and splendour. At Graffan, there are two entrances of equal size and ornament, whose locations do not readily conform to what usually constitutes the front and rear of a house. While the location of an entrance in a projecting block can be seen in other buildings like Ballymooney and Ballycowan, no other building in Offaly possesses a second entrance in its gable end. The south elevation of the glebe house, with its numerous windows looking out over a garden terrace, would surely have formed an appropriate composition for the principle entrance. Instead, the two doorways are relegated to the opposite ends of the house (fig. 8.20).

One has to remember, however, that this was no normal residence; this was the household of a clergyman tending to the spiritual and material well being of his parishioners. The doorway in the stairwell block faces the church and graveyard, the spiritual heart of Templeharry parish. Tending to the spiritual cure of this parish church, any clergyman and his household would have had to contend with comings and goings of parishioners. This obviously would have created a tension between the demands of a vocation, and the form of social etiquette expected of a Protestant clergyman and his family at this time. There was an onus on the clergy, who were members of the landed elite, to provide a desirable model of civil living as an example to settlers and natives alike.[91] The location of one doorway in the stairwell block, allowing direct access to the church and graveyard, and the other doorway at the far end of the building, well away from the perambulations of the local congregation, may have been an architectural resolution to these competing demands, in which a local clergyman, while generally accessible to tenants and freeholders, could also preserve a level of segregation appropriate to his standing in civil society.

Catholic churches in Offaly in the age of Counter-Reformation

The prevailing political and religious environment in early modern Ireland necessitated the celebration of Catholic liturgy not in parish churches, but more discreetly in the houses of local Catholic notables, where tenants would assemble, with the priest being maintained by the same landlords. As a result, from the late sixteenth century onwards, there was domestication of the mass, with the ceremony being celebrated in the homes of gentry, tradesmen and farmers, running counter to the dictates of the Council of Trent.[92] In the view of the papal nuncio to Ireland, Giovanni Baptista Rinuccini, in 1645, confining such liturgies to a private setting, without the display and communal ritual associated with the parish, was unacceptable.[93] The Council of Trent dictated that religious activity be organized on a parochial basis with the priest as its focal point and the ritual of the church as its binding force. To the west of the River Shannon, in the diocese of Clonfert, a mass house, with an altar and statues, had apparently been established in every parish by 1641. Such mass houses could be quite substantial structures. In 1669, for instance, the Dominicans in Galway had built 'a large chapel and covered it with brick', while by the 1690s, Cork city was provided with a mass house that could accommodate four hundred people.[94] These public chapels certainly could be well furnished, such as the Jesuits' mass house at Back Lane, Dublin, which in the 1620s was described as being provided with confessionals, a pulpit adorned with pictures and a railed-off high altar, also enhanced with paintings.[95]

A number of churches were briefly reappropriated and restored in west and south Offaly to cater for the celebration of Mass, despite prohibitions against the public display of Catholic worship. These church buildings were typically patronized by members of the old ruling elite such as the MacCoghlans in years when the political environment was more favourable for Catholics. Generally, the repair or reconstruction of these churches took place in specific periods when Protestant hegemony was being openly challenged, such as in the 1640s, with the outbreak of widespread rebellion, and the 1680s, under the reign of the Catholic monarch James II.

One of the more prominent churches in Offaly is the cathedral at Clonmacnoise, a building that dates to the early tenth century.[96] The building has seen

8.21 West gable end of Temple Ciarán, Clonmacnoise. This oratory was probably one of the two churches in Clonmacnoise that were mentioned in 1621 by James Ussher, bishop of Meath, as being roofed. Bishop Dopping's account of Clonmacnoise in 1684 mentioned that the church was still roofed at that time.

extensions and improvements over the centuries, the last of which apparently took place in the 1640s (fig. 8.16). The interior of the cathedral bears a mural slab inscribed thus:

> CAROLUS COGHLANUS VICARIUS GENERALIS CLUANMACNOSE PROPRIJS IMPENDIJS HANC DIRUTAM ECCLESIAM RESTAURAVIT ANNO DOMINI 1647.[97]

This plaque celebrates the restoration of the cathedral by Charles Coghlan, vicar general of the diocese of Clonmacnoise following the Catholic appropriation of the building in the aftermath the 1641 uprising. Apart from this plaque and some contemporary internal plasterwork, however, nothing appears to have survived from this phase of restoration, suggesting that little or no work had been made to alter the general appearance of the cathedral. Given that this is the most important church building in northwest Offaly, the lack of truly innovative design in this period could point to constrained finances on the part of Charles Coghlan. Such restraint, however, may go beyond fiscal rectitude and suggest a need within native elite circles at the time to rehabilitate and celebrate the past cultural accomplishments of their ancestors.

8.22 Temple Dowling from the northwest. This is a two-period church, with the eastern two-thirds built utilizing large blocks typical of early medieval masonry churches. The steeply pointed east gable along with its round-arched window and evidence that the building was equipped with antae tie in with this early dating. This early medieval church was extended westwards by c.3m in 1689, though it is notable that this extension was also provided with antae, presumably in sympathy with the original.

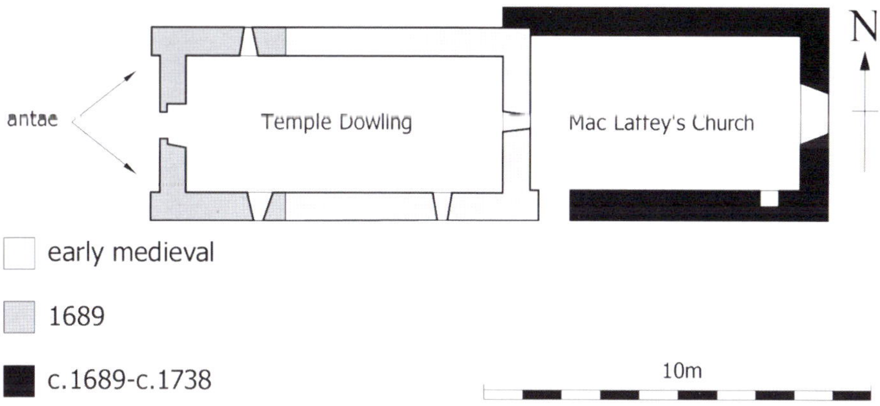

8.23 Plan of Temple Dowling and Mac Laffey's Church (after FitzPatrick and O'Brien, *Medieval churches of Offaly* (1998), p. 17). The historical and cartographic evidence shows that the former church was named 'Temple Hurpan' before its rebuilding in 1689. On a plan published in 1658 in the second edition of Sir James Ware's *De Hibernia et antiquitatibus eius disquisitiones*, it is called 'Temple Hurpan', as it is on a plan among the Ware manuscripts, based on a 1621 original. Bishop Dopping in 1684 referred to the church as 'Temple Hurpan als Mc Terpan, covered', indicating that it was roofed at the time. This church was first referred to as Temple Dowling on Blaymires' plan of 1738, with the caption 'Temple Doulin now a parish church'.

Just as the native landed families were well versed in old literary and oral traditions, such an appreciation of the past may have extended to physical monuments. A silver chalice has survived with the following inscription: *Ellinor Callinan P Sacello Sti Querani de Clonmacnoise me fieri fecit An 1647*, which translates as Ellinor Callinan had me made in the year 1647 for the Chapel of St Ciarán of Clonmacnoise.[98] It is probably not coincidental that 1647 was also the year in which the cathedral at Clonmacnoise was restored. Beside the cathedral is an early medieval oratory, St Ciarán's Chapel, now known as Temple Ciarán, the reputed burial place of the founding saint of Clonmacnoise (fig. 8.21). Such a chapel undoubtedly played some part in the celebrations surrounding the newly furnished cathedral. The chalice may therefore have been commissioned for use in the chapel or dedicated to the memory of the founding saint but intended for use in the newly restored cathedral. Temple Ciarán was probably one of two buildings at Clonmacnoise that were covered with a roof in 1621; it was certainly covered in 1684 when it was described as housing a reputed relic of St Ciarán, suggesting a state of reasonable repair through the seventeenth century. The continued maintenance of the oratory and adoration of the founding saint's relic highlights the persistence of traditional practices that had characterized religious devotion in the days when MacCoghlan lordship was pre-eminent.[99]

Temple Dowling is another church at Clonmacnoise and is so-called after Edmund Dowling, who is commemorated on a plaque above the entrance in the western façade (figs 8.22, 8.23). As well as bearing the Dowling coat of arms, the plaque is inscribed with 'M Edmund Dowling of Clondalare wh[o] build [sic] this chapel to the greater glory of God & use of his posterity 1689' (fig. 8.24). This plaque, given the Gaelic origins of the family, and more significantly the year that saw many churches being re-appropriated by resurgent Catholicism under the more benign rule of James II, suggests that the church was re-edified for the holding of Mass at this time. It is noteworthy that the practice of building mortuary chapels onto or close to parish churches by the Catholic elite was growing increasingly popular through the seventeenth century. Such chapels conferred exclusivity, not only through the expense incurred in their creation, but also through the manipulation of sacred space to create an arena that, while located in the graveyard, was to some extent aloof from the main church.[100] Bearing this in mind, could the re-edification of Temple Dowling suggest its adaptation as a mortuary chapel for the use of a local prominent family?

Temple Dowling is largely early medieval, built utilizing large blocks, the 'cyclopean walling', typical of masonry churches in that period. The steeply pitched east gable along with its round-arched window and evidence that the building was equipped with antae also agrees with this early dating (fig. 8.22). The Dowling armorial plaque celebrates the occasion on which Edmund extended the west end of the church by *c*.3m as well as heightening the east gable to accommodate a new roofline. While the double-centred doorway in the new west façade is derived from

8.24 Above the entrance into Temple Dowling is an armorial plaque of two limestone slabs set within a moulded frame, which carries the Dowling coat of arms with the motto *Fortis et egregius* (brave and distinguished) and the date 1689. Below the coat of arms is an inscription that states that 'M Edmund Dowling of Clondalare wh[o] build this chappel to the greater glory of God and use of his posterity 1689'.

late gothic traditions in the locality, it is intriguing that, overall, the new western façade recreates the appearance of an earlier medieval church with the steeply pitched gable and corner antae. These projections, which were originally designed by early medieval craftsmen to support the bargeboards of the roof, served no functional purpose in this instance, as the gable wall continues over the tops of the antae. It is obvious that functionality was not a concern here; instead, there was a clear desire to rebuild the front façade of a church in accordance with the architecture of the pre-Romanesque era, a period before the arrival of the Anglo-Normans.

Did these churches in Clonmacnoise – the cathedral, Temple Ciarán and Temple Dowling – just receive sympathetic reconstruction or is something fundamentally more important at work here; a conscious revival of past cultural accomplishments in the face of great social and cultural changes? It would be wrong to suggest that there was an intellectual or cultural propensity for native culture to remain inert, being solely attached to past allegiances and traditions, given the tremendous forces for political and economic changes that had been ranged against native society since the mid-sixteenth century. As mentioned previously, there is an

8.25 Kilcolman Church was apparently either rebuilt or refurbished by a member of the local gentry, Col. Oxburgh, in the late seventeenth century. This church stands on the site of a religious foundation reputedly established by St Colmán Niger in the sixth century. Note the inserted lintel of a twin-light round-arched window of seventeenth-century date in the west gable.

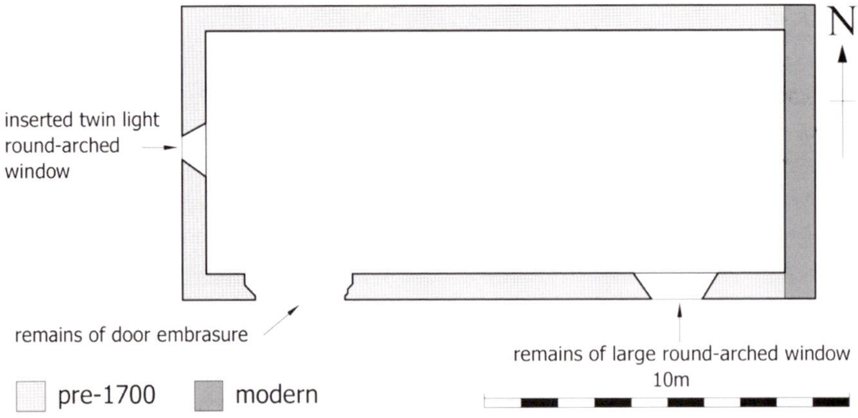

8.26 Plan of the church at Kilcolman (drawn by James Lyttleton and Hugh Kavanagh).

armorial plaque at Derrydolney in Fir Cheall carrying the O'Molloy coat of arms and an inscription acknowledging Charles II as king of Ireland and defender of the faith (figs 7.15, 7.16). What can be seen here is a partisan statement embodying allegiance to both the state and the established church. This particular family of native aristocrats, in a period that had seen the decline of native lordship, had redefined their interests and, in doing so, were enabled to amass the resources to build a new house, along with a fine heraldic plaque to commemorate the fact that they could do so.[101] The fact that the inscriptions on both the Dowling and the O'Molloy plaques are in neither Irish nor Latin, but in English, suggests a degree of assimilation into the British body politic to the extent that messages, whether supportive or subversive of the status quo, were mediated in a manner accessible to their Protestant neighbours, who were overwhelmingly of British origin. Indeed, Gillespie notes that even by the 1630s many of the native aristocracy were attempting to consolidate their position in the new dispensation by enrolling funeral certificates, which described their genealogy and heraldic arms, in the office of arms in Dublin.[102]

Another church that may have benefited from Catholic patronage, though nominally in the hands of the Church of Ireland, was the parish church of Kilcolman (figs 8.25, 8.26). In 1615, it was recorded as 'church downe, chauncell up', while another visitation for 1693 insinuates by omission that the church had gone out of use by then.[103] There is a tradition that the church was rebuilt or refurnished by a prominent local Catholic, Col. Heward Oxburgh, sometime in the second half of seventeenth century.[104] Undoubtedly, the church saw some improvements in the early modern period. The limestone lintel of a twin-light round-arched window was inserted into the west wall, decorated with linear tooling similar to that found on windows of comparable form and size in the early seventeenth-century belfry of St Brendan's in neighbouring Birr. Unusually, though, the embrasure for this window was designed solely for a single light, with the result that one of the twin lights is blocked with limestone rubble. Another anomaly with this window surround is that the lintel appears to have been placed into the wall in reverse position, with the rough inside of the lintel facing outwards. Presumably, these anomalies would have been covered by the application of fresh external rendering. The altar end of the church also saw the insertion of a rather large embrasure in the south wall, possibly for a round-arched window (fig. 8.26). This is intriguing, given the tradition that the refurbishment of the church was for Catholic worship. The insertion of large windows into dimly lit medieval churches is more typically associated with the efforts of Protestant reformers who wanted to create brighter interiors more conducive to the preaching of the written word.[105] It is clear that this late medieval building saw refurbishment at some stage during the seventeenth century, though whether it was carried out by Col. Oxburgh himself remains to be proven.

A church at Kincora, otherwise known as Kilreaghan, now survives as only a slight rise in a modern graveyard. There is some evidence, however, that the

8.27 'Passion' or 'Crucifixion' plaque, originally from Kincora Church, and now at Ballylin Demesne. Various symbols of the Passion are displayed on the shield, including the Cross, the wounds of Christ, the heads of St John, the Virgin Mary and the two Roman soldiers, the dice cast by the Roman soldiers for the garments of Christ, the sword used by Peter in the garden of Gethsemane, a hammer and a number of other items. A representation of the cock perched on a pillar, which crowed on Peter's third denial, is used as the crest of the shield. The pillar itself may represent the flagellation of Christ before his Crucifixion. Stretching out from behind the shield is a pair of hands holding rosary beads, draped around the profile of the shield, terminating with the Sacred Heart.

8.28 Armorial plaque depicting the MacCoghlan coat of arms, once held in Kincora Church, and now at Ballylin Demesne.

MacCoghlans who resided in neighbouring Kilcolgan Castle patronized the refurbishment and upkeep of the church there during the reign of James II. An antiquarian account, citing Mary Ward (née King) of Ballylin House, recounts that an arch close to the path leading to the burial ground was originally embellished with a 'Passion or Crucifixion stone' on the east front and the MacCoghlan coat of arms on the west front (figs 8.27, 8.28). By 1839, the arch was reduced to a crumbling ruin and the plaques lay on the site until the Revd Henry King removed the stones around five years later to their present location in the courtyard walls of Ballylin House.[106]

The 'Passion or Crucifixion stone' is a limestone armorial plaque that carries the symbols of the Passion as well as the Sacred Heart and the Rosary. As such, it is a magnificent display of the core tenets of Counter-Reformation doctrine. A Latin inscription along the top reads: ARMA REDEMPTORIS CHRISTI JESU A 1688 (The arms of the redeemer Jesus Christ in the year 1688), while another inscription below states: AUREA RESPLENDENT SINE FRUCTU INSIGNIA REGUM ARMA REDEMPTORIS SPARSA CRUORE RUBENT (The golden banners of kings glitter unprofitably, but the arms of the Redeemer glow red bedewed with blood). The typical heraldic arrangement of shield, crowned with a helmet from which springs elaborate mantling, is employed here. The devices employed on the shield itself, however, deviate from the norm and appear to be derived from symbols of the Passion, commonly seen on Catholic memorials in this period. A representation of the cock perched on a pillar, which crowed on Peter's third denial, is used as the crest. Indeed, the pillar itself may represent the flagellation of Christ before his Crucifixion. The shield carries other emblems of the Passion, including the Cross, the wounds of Christ, the heads of St John, the Virgin Mary and the two Roman soldiers, the dice cast by the Roman soldiers for the garments of Christ, the sword used by Peter in the garden of Gethsemane, a hammer and a number of other items. Stretching out from behind the shield is a pair of hands holding rosary beads, draped around the profile of the shield, terminating with the Sacred Heart. According to local tradition, Francis Coghlan of Kilcolgan Castle commissioned the plaque.[107] This rather fine representation of the arms of Christ is without parallel in Offaly, though intriguingly another plaque was described by Mary Ward as having been placed over the hall door of Kilcolgan Castle, decorated with a cross and other emblems, bearing an inscription that also began with 'Aurea resplendent ...'[108] This suggests that the MacCoghlan family may have commissioned the production of two of these Passion plaques, one for their residence, with the other for their local church.

The overt display of Catholic symbolism in more domestic settings can be seen elsewhere: Sir John Plunkett constructed a family chapel at Dunsoghly Castle, Co. Dublin, with a plaque decorated with symbols of the Passion over the doorway.[109] In Scotland, the *Arma Christi* (before its defacement in 1651) was to be seen along with the family and royal arms above the entrance to the palace of Huntly.[110] With the Counter-Reformation, there was a greater emphasis on the devotion to Mass with its celebration of the sacrifice of Christ and a distancing from the local cults of saints.

Now people were beginning to entrust their salvation to the Passion rather than to the intercession of saints. Under this influence, symbols of the Passion were engraved onto tombs and other memorials like the plaque preserved in the courtyard of Ballylin House. Such change was also mirrored in the opening formulas of wills, in which Catholic testators no longer committed their souls to God, Mary and the saints, but now to God alone, expressing their trust in Jesus.[111]

As well as the Passion plaque and the MacCoghlan armorial plaque, other architectural fragments are preserved at Ballylin House. These pieces may have originated at the church site at Kincora, though Mary Ward did not discuss them.[112] They include the limestone surround of a round-arched doorway dressed with rough punching and linear drafting, which probably graced the main entrance to the church (fig. 8.29).[113] Another armorial plaque, this time above the doorway and too eroded for any devices to be recognized, also may have embellished the exterior of the church, given its weathered condition. As craftsmen were most likely engaged to carry out improvements to Kincora, it should come as no surprise that some of these individuals left behind some personal signature. In the same courtyard wall at Ballylin Demesne are two cut limestone blocks, one of which bears Jacobean floral work on two sides, with a third side carrying the name 'RORIE MURRY', while the second block bears the inscription 'CONOR MURRY MASON'. Such blocks may have graced an opening or a memorial in the church. It appears that a family of masons may have been contracted to carry out improvements to this church on behalf of Francis Coghlan. It is pertinent to note that while Bishop Dopping's 1682–5 visitation of Anglican churches includes Gallen and Wheery in the Ferbane district, it does not include Kincora as one of its own, suggesting that the church there was retained solely for Catholic worship at that time.[114]

While the political and cultural ethos of the authorities was largely inimical to the public display of Catholic worship, sites like Clonmacnoise and Kincora demonstrate that collective Catholic worship outside the confines of private homes was possible in early modern Offaly. Leading Protestants in seventeenth century Ireland often knew where Catholic chapels were located but, in ordinary circumstances, did not move against them, allowing for religious accommodation to be made at local level so that religious allegiances did not become the source of disruption.[115] Indeed, such a degree of tacit tolerance of religious differences existed that the practice continued of Catholic burials in hallowed grounds that were nominally held by the Church of Ireland in Co. Offaly, as well as in other planted areas such as Ulster.[116] This tolerance, however, might not necessarily have been a response to specific political and cultural conditions, as the established church was the potential provider for everyone in a given parish.[117] Any inhabitant of a parish would normally have the right of burial in the local churchyard of the established church in England, Wales and North America, as well as in Ireland.[118] The burial of Catholics in Protestant church grounds suggests that people had come to terms with the reality that Protestant services were now held in the presence of interred relatives

8.29 A round-arched doorway possibly of seventeenth-century date at Ballylin Demesne.

and friends. It also meant occasionally having to pay the Protestant minister burial fees for the privilege. It appears that evasion and accommodation were a fact of life for people living in early modern Ireland. People also chose burials at their parish church for convenience as well as out of a sense of parochial loyalty, with the church and grounds forming an important nexus in the passing of local identities and traditions from one generation to the next.

It would be misleading, however, to portray relations between the different denominations as largely unproblematic. The proprietorship of these spaces was highly contested and saw periodic tensions between Catholic and Protestant neighbours. It is not without coincidence that recorded dates for the refurbishment or embellishment of churches in Offaly for Catholic worship fall within two periods, the years following the 1641 uprising and the reign of Catholic monarch James II. At these times, it was common for Catholics to reclaim church property that had passed into the hands of the established church at the onset of the Reformation. On such occasions, furnishings used for the celebration of the Protestant liturgy were ripped out and arrangements were put in place to facilitate the holding of Masses. The church at Durrow was to suffer such a fate; in a return for the year 1694, Dopping found the church and chancel, lately in repair, much out of order by reason of 'ye troubles of Sir George Herberte', a local Catholic owner.[119] In 1689, after the surrender of Birr Castle to Jacobite forces, the local Protestant minister, the Revd Crump, deserted St Brendan's, whereupon the church revenue was seized by a receiver on behalf of King James, who then placed the glebe and tithes of the parish into the hands of the Catholic parish priest, the Revd Thomas Kennedy.[120] On these occasions, local Catholic communities sought to demean and undermine the legitimacy of Protestant claims to the church and graveyard as a repository, not only of their deceased relatives, but also of their liturgical and cultural traditions. The depth of this religious divide is amply illustrated by a number of instances during the 1641 uprising in which the remains of the 'heretic' Protestant dead were exhumed and removed from a number of parish graveyards in an act of 'cultural purification'.[121]

Death and burial in early modern Offaly

Churches and graveyards acted, in part, as stage settings; that is, as backdrops in front of which various discourses could be played out. One of the more important debates mediated upon the transience of the individual and the approach of death. The main purpose of funeral rituals was to heal the disruption suffered by the family and community on the death of one of its members. In the case of community leaders passing away, the damage to society was potentially more severe, with rituals required to address the continuity of social norms. The identity of the deceased was split between the 'private' natural body subject to death and decay, and the 'public' social body, which did not die, but whose rights and duties were passed on to the next generation.[122] Hence, the funeral was an important social institution in Ireland that not only displayed the standing of the deceased but also displayed and legitimized the passing of land and social standing on to the next generation. At these gatherings, bonds of kinship and friendship would be identified, confirmed and renewed. This was particularly important for planters who had migrated from across the water and experienced a dilution in the social networks underpinned by family and community relations back home.[123] At the same time, such familial and communal links were undergoing transformation among native circles as well. The Counter-Reformation was as much concerned with matters secular as matters religious, and it launched a concerted attack on the extended lineages of the Old English and Gaelic Irish. Funeral rites and symbolism that celebrated communal relations, such as the large wake, feasting and ritual weeping or keening, were all condemned by Counter-Reformation synods in Ireland. In the early modern period, the family moved away from extended lineages and retinues towards the humanist ideal of the small nuclear family. Education and wisdom were becoming more important hallmarks than military strength, with the process of law rather than violence being emphasized as a means to resolve disputes.[124] This is reflected in the native poetry of the early seventeenth century, with native lords now being praised for adherence to English common law, their lordships now in peace, a state of affairs surely becoming of their status.[125] With the erection of memorials, not only were the religious beliefs of the local landed elite given visible acknowledgment, but their values and principles were too. Such monuments did not merely reflect identity and status but were active material expressions of a socially acceptable identity, which was displayed in a manner to create an impression of continuity instead of disruption, a particularly important consideration given the level of social mobility in early modern Ireland.[126]

While the general upsurge in the creation of sculptured monuments in the first four decades of the seventeenth century reflects the rise in the fortunes of incoming settlers in certain cities and towns like Dublin, Limerick, Youghal and Carrickfergus, such memorials erected to the memory of newcomers before 1641 in west and south Offaly are unknown. This situation is paralleled in other planted areas of the country, such as Ulster, Longford, Leitrim, Laois and Wexford.[127] One constraint against the erection of elaborate monuments in these relatively remote areas was the scarcity of sculptors with the appropriate expertise. A monument for one of the better-known planters in Offaly, Matthew de Renzy, in the parish church of Athlone in the neighbouring Co. Westmeath, had to be ordered from as far away as the Dublin workshop of Francis Andrews.[128] Another constraint was that of expense, with estate incomes of newly established landowners in many cases falling far short of their English counterparts. Under the circumstances, it is clear that such ostentatious tombs were a financial impossibility for many settlers, including those in Offaly.[129]

Recumbent ledger slabs placed in the floors of churches or laid outside in graveyards, and mural plaques, bearing coats of arms, placed in the internal walls of churches, are the typical commemorative monuments of early modern date that have

8.30 Darby table tomb (1688) in the graveyard of Aghancon Church in Glebe. The covering limestone slab is decorated with the Darby coat of arms in bold relief, surrounded by elaborate mantling. The scroll underneath the shield is devoid of the family motto. The rest of the slab beneath the coat of arms is free of carving, except towards the bottom where there is a partially legible inscription: 'Here lieth [ ] [ ] wife of Johnathan [ ] esquire who died the [ ] February 1688'. The sides of the table tomb consist of roughly coursed sandstone rubble.

survived in west and south Offaly. The only example of a table tomb is a rather late example found in the churchyard at Glebe (Aghancon), the Darby memorial (1688), whose sides consist of roughly coursed sandstone rubble (fig. 8.30). Table tombs surmounted by full-relief effigies on flat mensae with figures of the saints placed on

8.31 There are simple headstones in the graveyard of Seir Kieran (Churchland/Clonmore), one of which bears a denuded inscription including the initials 'A.R.' and the date 1686.

side panels, commonly found in the east and southeast of Ireland in the first half of the sixteenth century, are not to be found in Offaly. Finely finished memorial slabs such as those dedicated to Sir John MacCoghlan (1576–7), Rose Coghlan (1616), Dorothy Coghlan (1630) and John O'Carroll (1681), whether presently located in the floor of the church, propped up against a wall, or lying outside in the graveyard, however, each may once have formed the mensa or top slab of a now disappeared table tomb. Only one example of a seventeenth-century headstone appears to have survived in all of west and south Offaly. This is a rather simple headstone at Seir Kieran bearing a denuded inscription, which includes the initials A.R. and the year 1686 (fig. 8.31). Headstones only begin to appear in Offaly graveyards in the early decades of the eighteenth century, with a flowering from the 1740s onwards. This trend was more specifically revealed in a study of the graveyard at Clonmacnoise by Harold Mytum, with headstones increasing in popularity decade by decade through the eighteenth century.[130]

According to Clodagh Tait, Gaelic landed families appear to have been reluctant to erect memorials, possibly preferring to use earlier family monuments.[131] As we can see from the memorial slabs cited above, however, there is evidence that some of these families in Co. Offaly embraced the use of funeral monuments. The earliest extant example is at the altar end of St Rynagh's in Banagher. This memorial, dedicated to Sir John MacCoghlan in 1576–7, is typical of late sixteenth-century ledgers, with its floriated cross carved in false relief, bearing eight arms with a rosette at the centre and a knot and knop on the shaft (fig. 8.32). This slab possibly formed the mensa of a raised tomb, of which the sides have been lost. The sides of such a tomb may have borne heraldry, personal motifs and the symbols of the Passion. A pair of long, straight bands hanging parallel to the cross shaft is an arrangement to be

8.32 Memorial slab dedicated to Sir John MacCoghlan, bearing the date 1576–7, situated at the altar of St Rynagh's, Banagher (from FitzPatrick and O'Brien, *Medieval churches of Offaly* (1998), p. 140, fig. 134). A double-line inscription in Latin runs along the head and sides of the slab. Translated, it reads '[Here lies buried] Sir John Co[ghlan] Knight, sometime chief of [his people] who caused to be made …, in the 19th year of the reign of Queen Elizabeth, the year of the termination of the exactions of Imaileac'.

8.33 Memorial slab to Rose Coghlan (1616) propped against the south wall of Temple Conor in Clonmacnoise.

found in Ireland only, and may be related to the veiling of the crucifix during Passiontide.[132] A double-line inscription in Latin runs along the head and sides of the slab. Translated, it reads:

> [Here lies buried] Sir John Co[ghlan], knight, sometime chief of [his people] who caused to be made …, in the 19th year of the reign of Queen Elizabeth, the year of the termination of the exactions of Imaileac …[133]

Paul Cockerham and Amy Louise Harris observe that the use of Roman capital letters instead of Gothic miniscule on the Coghlan slab, along with the inclusion of the regnal year of Elizabeth I, is possibly indicative of New English influence, suggesting that a degree of hybridization was taking place among the MacCoghlans in the late sixteenth century, well before the Jacobean plantations.[134] Such a supposition is given credence by another ledger of similar dimensions, this time found propped up against the internal south wall of Temple Conor in Clonmacnoise (fig. 8.33). The slab bears a cross with fleur-de-lis terminals rising from a scrolled base. Above the cross is the year 1616, while flanking the same is an incomplete inscription, not only in Roman capitals but also in English: 'HERE LYETH THE [E] [ ] VERTUS ROSE COGHL[A] ERRED'. It appears that in the years preceding the plantation of Delbhna Eathra in 1620, the landed elite there were commemorating their family members using a medium intelligible to English observers. Another slab found at Rahan in O'Molloy Country, though now missing, was recorded as also bearing the year 1616 and carrying the partial remains of an English inscription, which gave the identity of its carver as Cormack O Boghalie.[135] Continuing in the anglophone tradition is a limestone mural slab (4 feet 6 inches (1.37m) by 2 feet 6 inches (76cm)) lying by the side of a path, a short distance from Templefineen or McCarthy's Church in Clonmacnoise. It bore the following inscription:

> Pray for the soule of Cormack Mc James Coghlan and his son John They lived many years beloved of their neighbours and their corps here intered in their ancestors tomb in the year of ovr Lord God 1622.[136]

The elite in early modern society, whether native or newcomer, came to be enthralled by humanist principles, which espoused that in order to assert their pre-eminence in the world, gentlemen should be well versed in the workings of the universe. Knowledge of the sciences, literature, art, foreign languages and cultures, and an appreciation of the principles of symmetry and rationalism behind classical architecture, came to be expected. The landed classes understood the virtues of such knowledge and how it could be used to manipulate and negotiate class identities. At a time when the general population was becoming more literate, and sumptuary laws were being passed to restrain the lower orders from acquiring cheap clothes cut to the latest fashions, the patronage of buildings and memorials remained solely within the

8.34 Forth and Coffy armorial plaques mark the locations of family vaults at Lynally Glebe. The Forth monument to the left consists of an armorial plaque bearing the family coat of arms surrounded by elaborate mantling in a moulded frame. The scroll beneath the shield carries the motto *Deum Timeo Regem Honoro*. A recumbent grave slab on the floor beneath the armorial plaque marks the Forth family vault. It bears the following inscription: *HIC IACET IOHANNES FORTH DE SILVA RUBRA, MILES, VIR IUSTITIA PIETATE ET HOSPITALITATE CELEBRIS. OBIIT 22 IULII ANO. DOM, 1680 AETATIS SVAE 41.*

8.35 Armorial plaque bearing the Coffy and Hide coat of arms at Lynally Glebe. Beneath the coat of arms is a scroll carrying the motto *Non Victoria sed Providentia*. The inscription below states that 'This monument was made for Thomas Coffy Clearke and his deare wife Anne Hide and their posteritie Anno Dom 1684'. The chamfered sill of the plaque bears the denuded remains of a skull and crossbones.

8.36 Ledger close to the southeast corner of the church at Lynally Glebe, beyond the present east gable end. This slab bears a Latin inscription in incised Roman capitals: *Hic lacet corpus Domini Constantin O Molloy de Cully qui me fieri fecit Anno Domini 1683.*

capability of the elite anxious to demonstrate the virtues of gentility and polite disposition. In light of this, there was an onus on the clergy, who were members of the same elite, to provide a desirable model of civil living as an example to landlord and tenant alike.

One such cleric in Offaly was Thomas Coffy, who was a Protestant vicar and a justice of the peace for the area. A monument to the memory of Coffy and his wife Anne Hide was erected in the west wall of the church at Lynally Glebe, flanking the main entrance (figs 8.34, 8.35). The inscription reads 'This monument was made for Thomas Coffy Clearke, and his deare wife Anne Hide and their posteritie Anno Dom 1684'. Coffy's familial connections in local society are celebrated with the use of his family's coat of arms impaled with those of his wife, while his position as an agent for the religious and indeed civil agenda, as embodied in the ideals of the Renaissance, is emphasized through the use of classical architectural elements to embellish the monument. The coat of arms is flanked by a Corinthian pillar to one side, with a plinth on the other side that would have supported a similar pillar, both pillars supporting an entabulature. The chamfered sill of the plaque bears the denuded remains of a well-known mortality symbol, a skull clenching crossbones. In the Renaissance, the classical orders were imbued with a scale of moral values: the relative simplicity of the Tuscan order articulated civil virtue; the richness of the Corinthian conveyed nobility and the responsibilities of status.[137] Thomas Coffy's choice of the Corinthian order was clearly deliberate, given his spiritual and official position in the local community.

This was not Coffy's death memorial, however, as on the floor of the church directly beneath the 1684 memorial is a ledger bearing a representation of an open

Bible in bold relief (fig. 8.34). The first page bears in small, incised Roman capitals a quotation from Ecclesiastes 12:1 beginning with: 'Remember now thy Creator …', while the following page carries: 'For I know that my Redeemer liveth …', taken from Job 19:25, 26.[138] Beneath the book of scriptures is an inscription, also in incised Roman capitals:

> Here lyeth the body of Thomas Coffy Cleark Master in Arts of Trinity Colledge Dublin, Vicar of Fercall and one of his majesties Charles the II his Justices of the Peace in King's County who dyed March Ye 30 1690.

This discrepancy of six years is due to a tendency among the local gentry to commission memorials before their deaths. Such an anomaly also occurs with the 1576–7 memorial to Sir John MacCoghlan in St Rynagh's, who died in 1590, and highlights the importance of having such memorials commissioned by patrons well in advance of their passing.[139] By the manipulation of epitaphs and inscriptions, the display of heraldic devices and the demonstration of symbols of mortality, an individual's status in local society was legitimized and consolidated in the spiritual arena of the church among the local faithful.

It has come to be recognized that, by the late seventeenth century, there was a greater emphasis on the epitaph and formulaic inscriptions than on sculptural ornamentation alone.[140] Such developments can be attributed to the rise in literacy, but its spread was still very much contained by class and gender. While few tombstones in Ireland bear Irish inscriptions, both English and Latin were popular, the latter being very much the preserve of a social and intellectual elite.[141] The ledgers of John O'Carroll (1681) in Dunkerrin, Sir John Forth (1680) and Constantine O'Molloy (1683) in Lynally Glebe bear Latin inscriptions, which only a small proportion of the population could understand (fig. 8.36). The use of a classical language proclaimed an intellectual elite who were the heirs of history; a claim reinforced by armorial motifs, classical architectural styles and prominent locations within ancient churches.[142]

Armorial plaques incorporating coat of arms were an important material expression of the pre-eminence and lineage of a local landed family. The growing popularity of armorial plaques as church memorials went hand in hand with the concerns of Protestant reformers, as signs of divine power, such as saints, were replaced with signs of more earthly powers; in this case the heraldic expression of the gentry's prestige and status.[143] The heraldic funeral also became popular among elite communities, as heraldry was considered a sound indicator of social status in a society that was experiencing fluid social mobility, both upwards and downwards. The acquisition of land was a difficult and uncertain process, with gains only consolidated by the passing of these to a subsequent generation. New English settlers without ancestral or traditional links in the country needed to plant not only country estates but religious spaces as well. Appropriate graves matching their newly acquired

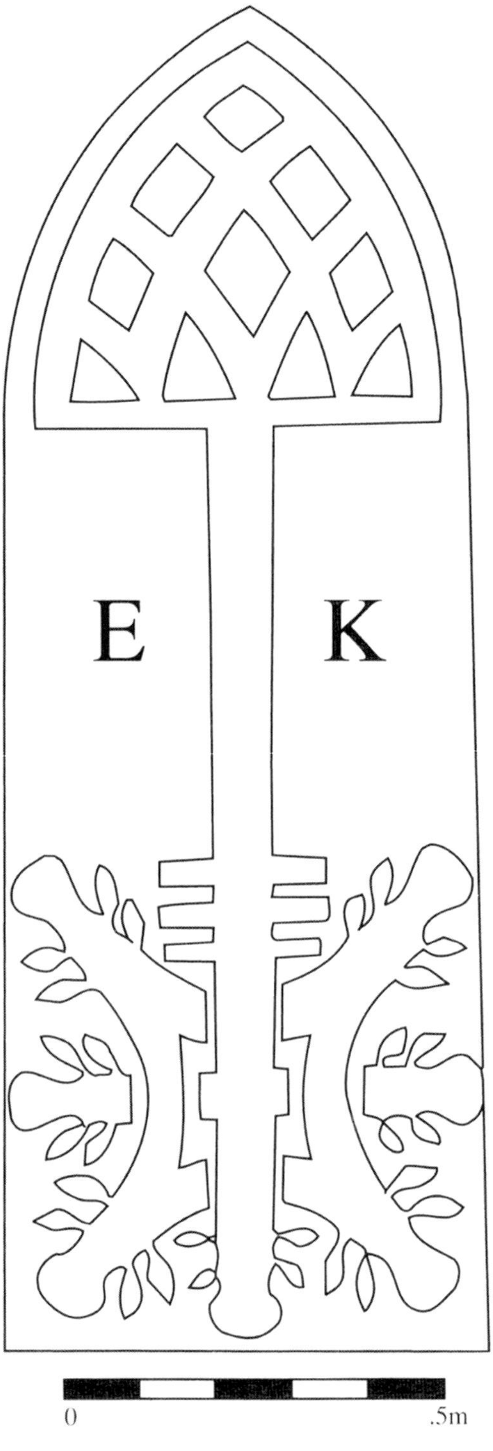

8.37 St Colman's Grave to the southwest of the church at Lynally Glebe. It consists of a ledger cut to the shape of a pointed window; its upper part is decorated with a representation of switchline tracery, while the lower part is ornamented with a debased fleur-de-lis in the form of a floriated cross. The initials E and K are placed on either side of the cross shaft (from FitzPatrick and O'Brien, *Medieval churches of Offaly* (1998), p. 144, fig. 141).

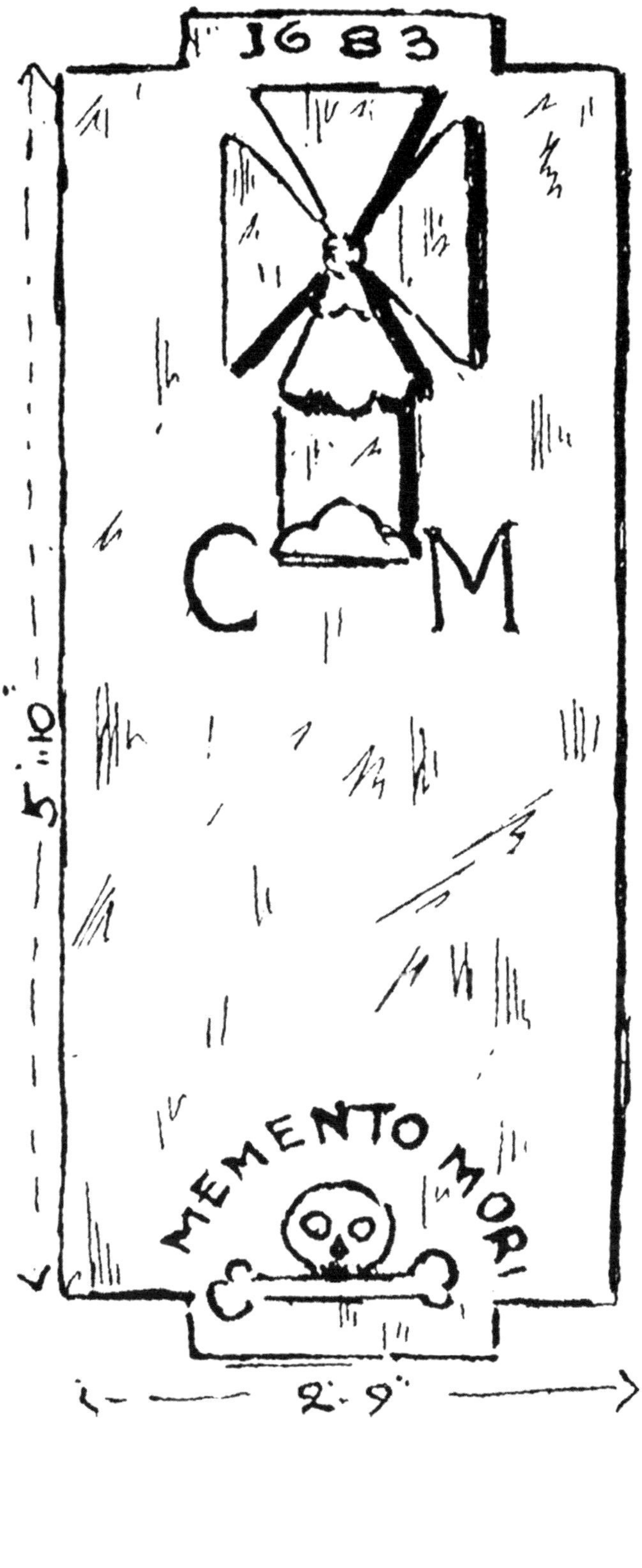

8.38 In a church at Rahan Demesne is a ledger decorated with a Maltese cross and a skull and crossbones. Inscribed on the slab are the year 1683 and the initials 'C.M.' Above the mortality symbol in Roman capitals is the phrase *Memento Mori.* Apparently, the slab was found under the floor of the church during rebuilding. It is suggested that it commemorates Charles Molloy of Cartron, who died in 1684. The discrepancy in dates may be explained by the tendency among the gentry to commission their memorials before their death (from FitzPatrick and O'Brien, *Medieval churches of Offaly* (1998), p. 146, fig. 143).

status as well as emphasizing the continuity of land holding became paramount, and heraldic devices became appropriate signifiers.[144] A study of monuments with heraldry in Co. Armagh indicates that external grave memorials appeared in the county from the 1670s, if not earlier; their use rising steadily through the eighteenth century.[145]

Armorial devices can be found on ledgers and mural plaques of late seventeenth-century date in west and south Offaly. At Durrow, there is a memorial on the threshold of the entrance to the church bearing the following inscription: 'Heare lyeth the body of Francis de Renci, who dyed in Tinicros, in the yeare of our Lord God 1665'. A coat of arms beneath is unfinished, with an unusual combination of knotwork and two stags; animals borrowed from the de Renzy coat of arms.[146] As mentioned above, there are armorial plaques at Lynally Glebe, where the Forth and Coffy coat of arms flank the main entrance in the church (fig. 8.34). The Coffy memorial, with its garlanded coat of arms on a plaque, originally framed by a pair of Corinthian pillars supporting an entabulature, is paralleled by other late seventeenth-century memorials to be found across Ireland.[147] While church memorials inspired by classical architecture first appear in Ireland in 1571 with the tomb of Sir Thomas Cusack in Trevet, Co. Meath, examples like that at Lynally Glebe demonstrate a greater command of classical proportions and style, paralleling developments in architecture at the time.[148]

There are a couple of memorials in early modern Offaly that explicitly draw upon medieval traditions of architecture and art. In the graveyard at Dunkerrin, the ledger dedicated to John O'Carroll (1681) is decorated with an incised Iona-style cross with an engrailed shaft.[149] The use of the Celtic cross as an explicit statement of ethnic affiliation can be found elsewhere: it was used as a small motif above a coat of arms on a ledger for John Magee (1617) in Co. Armagh.[150] St Colman's Grave at Lynally Glebe is a rather unusual recumbent slab, probably of fifteenth-century date, carved into the shape of a pointed window; its upper end ornamented with a representation of switchline tracery, while the lower part is decorated with a floriated cross (fig. 8.37). The ascription of a saintly origin for such a slab suggests that the memorial became an object of popular devotion at some stage. It is not clear when this devotional strategy had arisen, though it was clearly at variance with Protestant doctrine, which frowned upon devotional images and relics. The representation of more profane matters such as memorials to the dead was usually acceptable, so long as they were not abused by being worshipped. So provided an image or object was rendered 'worldly', and not of a nature amenable to worship, it was acceptable.[151] The carving of the initials 'E.K.' on St Colman's Grave, on either side of the shaft of the cross in a font typical of the seventeenth century suggests a possible attempt to render the cross slab more 'worldly' and hence more acceptable to the Protestant clergyman and his congregation who would have frequented the church at Lynally Glebe. While such a simple inscription, omitting full name, date or location, precludes a more meaningful appraisal, Sarah Tarlow suggests, using an example in St Magnus' Cathedral in Orkney, that late medieval graveslabs with floriated calvary crosses could indeed survive iconoclasm in a reformed environment by the addition of someone's initials, which diluted the overt symbolism of earlier devotional traditions.[152]

The presence of mortality symbols such as skulls clenching crossbones on the memorials at Lynally Glebe and Rahan testifies to an obsession with death. High infant mortality, a short life expectancy compared to the present, and occasional outbreaks of plague ensured that death was an ever-present reality.[153] Books on architecture, such as Hendrick de Keyser's *Architectura moderna* of 1631, depict funerary monuments engraved with the iconography of death.[154] Indeed, the Counter-Reformation encouraged the use of mortality symbols on memorials, with the skull to remind the observer not only of mortality but of piety as well.[155] Individual mortality symbols began to appear on Irish church monuments as early as the middle of the sixteenth century. The MacCragh monument displaying a skull gripping a longbone in its teeth in Lismore Cathedral, Co. Waterford, dates from 1557.[156]

The phrase 'memento mori' (remember death) found on the ledger in Rahan, inscribed also with the initials C.M. and the year 1683, is a staple of the *ars moriendi* (or art of dying) tradition, which held that people could 'learn to die a good death' (fig. 8.38). Publications and sermons on the subject of death, as well as observation of those on their deathbeds who displayed the faith, resignation and calm so necessary to the performance of a good death, played a role in a didactic discourse that mediated upon the transience and vanity of life. Such a discourse suggested that a calm, peaceful death accepted as the will of God reflected favourably upon the life of the recently deceased. Conversely, sudden, difficult or uncontrollable deaths inspired fears for the deceased.[157] The son of Sir Matthew de Renzy noted several days after his father's passing that

> It pleased the Almighty God to take to himself my dear and loving father, your lordship's faithful servant who made a religious and godly end and left all things in good order ...[158]

Phrases like *memento mori* urged the living to contemplate their own mortality and to make the best use of the time that individuals had left. Indeed, people in the early modern period are credited by historians with a much healthier attitude to death than is the case today. An acceptance of the uncertainty and transience of life, their resignation to death and the desire to persuade others to do the same, and their belief that death was not an end in itself but a necessary step into the next life are indicative of such an attitude.[159]

Conclusion

Churches and monasteries are the most visible and enduring testimony in the Irish countryside to the concerns and aspirations of late medieval and early modern society. Unlike in England, or indeed Continental Europe, where medieval churches continue to be maintained to the present day, churches in Ireland were largely abandoned in the sixteenth and seventeenth centuries due to the stresses of the Reformation and Counter-Reformation. Ireland did not follow the general European experience of *cuius regio eius religio*, where the people followed the confessional tendencies of their rulers. Official Protestantism became elitist, with Roman Catholicism maintaining a more populist appeal, a situation in direct contrast to the Reformation as experienced in England.[160] The chief problem was ambivalence on the part of the Tudor monarchs towards their Irish subjects, whether to cooperate with the Gaelic Irish and Anglo-Irish aristocracy to bring about change, or to coerce the population to conform through confiscation and colonization. Lack of resources and inconsistency in policies meant that coercive policies usually won out over more gentle persuasion.[161] As well as giving rise to periodic military and political instabilities, this ambivalence created a lack of popular support for reform, a situation exacerbated by poor finances and the scarcity of well-trained, motivated clergymen.

The church buildings and commemorative monuments discussed above provide visual testimony of people's earnest aspirations and religious beliefs. In a world where people were strongly conscious of the universe regulated by the Divine, attending masses and services, listening to the entreaties of clergy and following traditional practices and devotions, religion was part and parcel of daily life. An appraisal of sacred spaces and objects allows the archaeologist to recreate the settings through which various discourses were played out in early modern society. These discourses were multifaceted, and subject to continual change in a society characterized by fluid and unstable identities. Such discourses saw the negotiation, maintenance and subversion of identities such as ethnicity, social standing and confessional allegiance. Church architecture, furnishings and memorials, like dress and language, were all implicated in the ordering of a society that was undergoing profound transformations.

CHAPTER 9

Final thoughts: a society transformed

This book seeks to elucidate the social and cultural processes at work in west and south Offaly through the course of the sixteenth and seventeenth centuries. Traditionally, archaeology has been perceived as complementing the written sources, with the implicit suggestion that historical archaeology is 'an expensive way of telling us what we know already'.[1] Archaeologists, however, can construct alternative narratives of social organization and cultural identity free from the constraints of documentary research. This, of course, does not mean ignoring documentary sources, but involves an analysis of material remains, utilizing contemporary writings and cartographic sources as only one aspect of the evidence available, depending on its relevance to the archaeological analysis at hand. Archaeology, with its emphasis on material remains, can transcend social divides and explore and elucidate aspects of non-literate sections of early modern society. Indeed, the discipline can go beyond morphological discussions of buildings and explore the extent to which individuals influenced their own social, economic and cultural position in society. The interpretation of archaeological monuments and artefacts can clearly illustrate the creative will of an individual active in past society.

From the preceding chapters, it is obvious that human relations directly impact upon the environment, both natural and built, as people use space and form as an active agent to reproduce or transform social relations. Scattered across the landscape of west and south Offaly are the remains of tower houses, manor houses, farmsteads, churches and graveyards. Material remains such as these are not some passive reflection of a more substantial past. The creation of material forms such as artefacts, buildings or indeed landscapes allows for the communication and expression of meaning and normative behaviour. Accepting Bourdieu's notion of *habitus*, cultural norms tend to be installed and reproduced through use of materials and mundane practice, with such modes of behaviour being construed as common sense. Material culture allows for the creation of a context for discourse, defining the cultural and social mores of a particular time and space.

Following the broader trend in Ireland, archaeological research on early modern society in Offaly has been quite limited to date. This is indicative of an archaeological discourse that, up to relatively recent times, has been shy of studying early modern Irish society. The practice of archaeology is intellectually constituted in the present, with the exploration of past material culture very much informed by contemporary cultural and political norms. As a result, the past can play a critical role in the assertion and validation of modern nationalist ideology, ensuring that archaeology is commonly used in the construction of essentialist ethnic discourses.[2] The cultural and political marginalization of Irish Protestant culture meant that comparatively few archaeologists in previous decades took an active interest in the material remains of plantation-era Ireland. It could be argued that the unsettled political environment brought about by the troubles in Northern Ireland was also not conducive to the study of sites associated with the seventeenth-century plantations, a colonial legacy that was contributing to those same difficulties.

Was Ireland a colony?

Colonialism has been defined as a process that involves the intrusion into and conquest of an inhabited territory by representatives of an external power.[3] How useful though is the concept of colonialism in elucidating the nature of social relations in early modern Ireland? The dominant effect of analysing archaeology in purely colonial terms would be to deny the complex historical ambiguities of identity-formation in early modern Ireland. There has been a tendency to categorize Ireland as a post-colonial country, with the implicit notion that pre-independence Ireland functioned in a similar manner to British colonies elsewhere.[4] Unfortunately, this perception has tended to negate the complex nature of relations between Ireland and its larger neighbour. Even at the height of British imperialism in the nineteenth century, Ireland's connection to Britain was rarely described, even by nationalists, as 'colonial', with Daniel O'Connell commonly describing Ireland's status as 'provincial' instead.[5]

A more accurate appraisal of the Irish colonial experience may be gained by placing Ireland in a European context. While the Gaelic lordships of early modern Ireland witnessed the appropriation and colonization of their territories by English and Scottish settlers, such events were not unexceptional in a European context, as other peripheral regions such as Brittany, Provence and Catalonia were also assimilated by more powerful neighbours in the process of building modern nation states.[6] The word 'colony' was used by early modern writers without the imperial, political overtones it acquired in the nineteenth century; it merely meant a group of people who migrated to a new location. The notion that the kingdom of Ireland was inferior to its neighbouring kingdom impinged on the dignity of the crown, and attempts to centralize the control of Irish affairs in the English parliament 'were likely to impugn the royal prerogative'.[7]

On the other hand, aspects of Ireland's experience were not shared by other west European countries; instead, like many native societies in the New World, Ireland saw its language, legal systems, territorial organization, settlement patterns, social structures and artistic expression either replaced or radically reconfigured by an English-speaking state and culture.[8] Attitudes towards the land differed in Ireland from those in England. In an Irish context, land was easily lost or won in the seventeenth century. Uncertainty over title and repeated uprisings tempted owners to make the most of their properties by adopting short-term expedient means such as the felling of timber or the sale of parcels of land.[9] Despite claiming sovereignty over the island, English troops treated the country more as a colonial territory than as a subject jurisdiction, exercising little restraint in committing massacres, killing prisoners and engaging in scorched-earth policies in a more intensive, systematic manner than hitherto known.[10]

Still, even in periods of intense colonial activity, Ireland's sovereign status as a kingdom never disappeared from the minds of either the monarchs or their various subjects in the island. Members of the Catholic Anglo-Irish nobility like the Talbots enjoyed privileged access at court, while the Gaelic-Irish Murrough O'Brien, Lord Inchiquin, led parliamentary forces in Ireland during the 1640s.[11] The perennial issue of whether Ireland was a kingdom or a colony continued to confront English administrators. Mulling over this, William Molyneux in his work *Case of Ireland being bound by Acts of Parliament in England* published in 1698 asked:

> Does it not manifestly appear by the constitution of Ireland that it is a complete kingdom within itself? Do not the kings of England bear the style of Ireland amongst the rest of their kingdoms? Is this agreeable to the nature of a colony? Do they use the title of kings of Virginia, New England, or Maryland?[12]

Where there was a significant presence of British settlers in localities, native tenants did acquire aspects of English culture such as language. Some landlords had even managed to prevail upon their native tenants to attend Protestant church services and anglicize their names, but this was exceptional. In general, the thin spread of British settlement meant that the bulk of the population in the new plantations were of indigenous origin, resulting in acculturation going the other way, with British landowners and their agents having to learn the Irish language so as to converse with their workers. Outside of Ulster, many of the schemes like those in south and west Offaly were more plantations of gentlemen than of settlers en masse. While the economy overall was not transformed by the arrival of new settlers, with pastoral farming remaining the dominant mode of agricultural activity, there were still some innovative developments. There was the establishment of a significant timber industry, with related industries in iron smelting and glass making, while the development of fish palaces along the southern coastline also expanded the scale of sea fisheries there.

Native landowners who had lost lands and status through the years were only too willing to recoup their losses by cooperating with settlers in developing these new enterprises. Economic realities meant that mutual interdependence between the different ethnic groups was a necessity. Most British landowners were dependent on native tenants to varying degrees, while native landowners recognized the need to import skilled English tenantry if their estates were to survive in the new economic dispensation, in effect abandoning their traditional titles, tributes and exactions to become English-style landlords holding country estates under common law. This meant that there were regular face-to-face encounters between the settlers and natives across most of the country. Such encounters allowed for cultural identities and social mores to be subsumed into a process of appropriation, subversion and transformation, resulting in hybridization between the different ethnic groupings. Symptomatic of this process is Conall MacGeoghegan's translation into English of a set of Irish annals for his patron Sir Turlough MacCoghlan, the work subsequently known as the Annals of Clonmacnoise. Evidently, there were individuals among the local Gaelic nobility with an interest in the Ireland's past who preferred to read historic works in English rather than in Irish.[13]

Ireland clearly then 'resembled not so much a model colony ... but rather an unruly palimpsest, on which, though much rewritten and scored out, could be discerned in an untidy jumble "kingdom", "colony", "dependency" and faintly, "nation"'.[14] Research into the impact of colonialism should be cognisant of such ambiguities and complexities in the jurisdictional and cultural life of early modern Ireland.

The fluidity of ethnic identities in early modern Ireland

Fortified houses are typically associated with the waves of British settlers that arrived in Ireland following the demise of the Gaelic lordships. Yet, of the seventeen fortified houses across west and south Offaly, there is documentary evidence that nine were probably built by native families. Indeed, the two finest examples of plantation-era architecture in the county are to be found at the seats of two prominent native families: Kilcolgan More, which was described in 1650 as a 'faire house belonging to Terence Coghlan', and Ballymooney, constructed *c.*1622 by Donell O'Carroll.[15] These were fine buildings, the sort of residences expected of individuals who were well versed in the virtues of gentility and polite living. And yet these novel buildings were designed and occupied by families who continued to occupy tower houses, suggesting that the older buildings came to be imbued with early modern concepts of spatial ordering and social identity in native eyes as well. The fortified house at Curralanty owned by one Ony O'Carroll in 1636 advertises the new lifestyle of the landed elite and yet his own father, Mulrony, still occupied a tower house at Dungar.[16] The MacCoghlans had a particular penchant for constructing fortified houses in the shadow of earlier tower houses, as at Clonlyon Castlequarter and Garrycastle (fig. 1.3). The practice of constructing fortified houses adjacent to or in close vicinity to tower houses is well attested across the country, not only in Gaelic Irish contexts, but Old and New English as well. Thomas Raven's depiction of Sir Edward Doddington's residence at Dungiven in 1620 is a case in point, and suggests that the usage of tower houses and their successors was in no way mutually exclusive. Indeed, it can be suggested that, like the tower houses in the late medieval period, the later manor houses, with their novel forms and layout, could also be employed to obfuscate ethnic differences at a time of social and political flux. Through the architecture, we can see that material culture was in a continual process of reproduction and transformation in changing social and historical contexts. This is at variance with the essentialist perspective that places an emphasis on the one-to-one correlation between material culture and ethnicity. There is no single, unambiguous ethnic association, because no such single reality ever existed in early modern Offaly.

English colonial discourse and its contestation by native society was characterized by a level of sophistication and diversity that created situational and intricate relations between the different ethnic groups. As with the material culture, the written sources illustrate the danger that essentialist constructs of ethnicity pose in belittling the creative will of individuals or groups active in past societies. At the outbreak of rebellion in October 1641, William Parsons (son and successor of Sir Laurence) organized one hundred foot and thirty to thirty-five horse for the defence of the plantation. The one hundred foot was divided into two companies of fifty men, one of which was under the command of Captain John Carroll, cousin of another John Carroll, whose tower house at Clonlisk had previously been raided by Parsons under suspicion of sedition.[17] That a member of a native family was entrusted with the protection of the settler community in Offaly is sure testimony to the complexity of relations in early modern society. At times when social and cultural differences could arouse passions, individual relations could transcend supposedly rigid cultural and political affiliations. Indeed, the Parsons themselves maintained some semblance of good standing with their Gaelic neighbours. In March 1642, when Birr Castle was under siege from Catholic confederate forces, several letters were exchanged between William Parsons and the besiegers, including one from a Phelim Molloy, promising protection for his family including

> your good mother [Lady Ann Parsons] whom we held hitherto to be good neighbours withal assuring you that the good opinion which we conceived of you and your mother was the only cause that we behaved ourselves so mild and tender-hearted towards you ...[18]

Later in the same year, Lady Ann Parsons wrote to one of the leading rebels in the area, Col. O'Moore, to have returned her horses and carriage, which had been commandeered. He replied in most generous terms, declaring:

> I received your letter, which might easily move me to doe your ladyship any lawful service, which I have always coveted to do unto all such of your condition, virtue, and worth, and much the rather for that I find all the gentry and neighbours of these parts [the O'Kennedys, O'Carrolls, O'Molloys and MacCoghlans] do much honour esteem and love you, and in that degree that one would think you were of their blood and flesh; and they're detained against their wills and to their great grief … if I were assured no such use would be made of them [the horses], I would endeavour to get them restored, which truly I hold but a poor courtesy and nothing to what I should find myself willing to do for your ladyship.[19]

In spite of Lady Parsons belonging to the 'other', Col. O'Moore could engage in correspondence in the most familiar terms, demonstrating a pronounced degree of social interaction between native and planter families in the area. Consideration of the documentary and archaeological record illustrates that ethnic boundaries were not rigidly enforced, as contemporaries had the propensity to adopt language, social etiquette and material culture from beyond. Such boundaries could be porous, with the importance of ethnic identity varying significantly in different social contexts and between individuals.[20] Similar examples of inter-cultural interaction can be found within inns and taverns in the plantation villages of Ulster, which belie simplistic portrayals of local and planter communities continually at odds with each other.[21]

The Reformation and Counter-Reformation: its implications for local society

The church buildings and commemorative monuments discussed in this book provide visual testimony of people's earnest aspirations and religious beliefs. Intensive fieldwork across west and south Offaly has revealed that most churches do not preserve evidence for continued use in the early modern period, with most sites exhibiting a hiatus between *c.*1500 and *c.*1750. While the political, social and economic instabilities of the period conspired against the patronage and maintenance of church building, the indifference of lay impropriators who held much of the church lands and revenues was also a decisive factor. Indeed, the contribution of the latter to the pace of church reform and the fate of individual church buildings at parochial level has not been fully appreciated. One of the more committed planter families in Offaly were the Parsons of Birr, and it is not coincidental that the parish church there, St Brendan's, received more investment and continued maintenance than any other church in the county. Even though undertakers were not obliged to build or maintain places of worship, such endeavours encouraged settlement on their estates and promoted the development of villages and towns. It goes without saying that Birr did successfully develop as an urban settlement under the patronage of the

Parsons family judging from the 1634 comments of John Bramhall, a Protestant clergyman, who found that it was the only town within fifty miles 'fit to accommodate a traveller, having tradesmen in it of all kinds'.[22] Indeed, by 1641, there were at least thirty planter households within the town; enough Protestants in the community to merit the maintenance of a well-sized church there.[23]

As mentioned in the previous chapter, Ireland did not follow the general European experience of *cuius regio eius religio*, where the people followed the confessional tendencies of their rulers. Official Protestantism became elitist, with Roman Catholicism maintaining a more populist appeal, a situation in direct contrast to the Reformation in England.[24] And yet the churchyard appears to have remained an important arena in the religious lives of both Catholics and Protestants. Catholics continued to be interred in graveyards that were nominally held by the Church of Ireland. These burials suggest that local Catholics had come to terms with the reality that Protestant services were now held in the presence of interred relatives and friends. It may be the case that parochial loyalty as well as convenience prompted such compromise in the face of doctrinal differences.

The prevailing political and religious environment in the country made it necessary for Masses to be celebrated in the houses of Catholic notables where tenants could assemble, with the priest being maintained by the same landlords. Despite prohibitions of the public display of Catholic worship, however, a number of churches were re-edified by native landed families such as the MacCoghlans and the Dowlings at times when Protestant hegemony was being openly challenged, as in the 1640s with the outbreak of widespread rebellion and the 1680s under the reign of the Catholic monarch James II. The restoration of certain church buildings for the celebration of Catholic liturgy, namely Clonmacnoise Cathedral, Temple Ciarán and Temple Dowling suggests there was a conscious revival of past cultural accomplishments. Just as the native landed elite were well versed in old literary and oral traditions, such an appreciation of the past may have extended to physical monuments.

Bearing this in mind, however, it would be wrong to suggest that there was a propensity for native culture to remain inert, being solely attached to past allegiances and traditions, given the tremendous forces for change that had been ranged against Gaelic Irish society since the mid-sixteenth century. One such force was the Counter-Reformation, which sought to reform the religious and social mores of Gaelic Irish and Old English Catholics according to the dictates of the Council of Trent. The 'Passion or Crucifixion stone', now at Ballylin Demesne, but commissioned in 1688 for a church at Kincora under the patronage of the MacCoghlans, displays the symbols of the Passion as well as the Sacred Heart and the Rosary. As such, it is a magnificent display of Tridentine doctrine, suggesting a greater emphasis on the devotion to Mass, with its celebration of the sacrifice of Christ and a distancing from the local cults of saints and holy wells.

While formal Catholic worship took place within churches, serving the spiritual needs of the local communities, there was still a strong tradition of holy places in popular Catholic devotion. Michael Carroll goes so far as to assert that rather than just simply attending Mass, for most Catholics in Ireland it was participation in rituals at holy wells that underpinned their religious identity.[25] These places were associated with saints' legends in which the actions of a particular saint had sanctified a location, such locations becoming the object of pilgrimages, with some attracting specific devotions. While churches could attract specific devotions, most holy places were less specific and served as gathering places for the local Catholic population. Across Offaly, up to sixty-five holy wells, along with a number of sacred trees and rocks, have been recorded by the Archaeological Survey of Ireland. These are testimony to the strength of traditional devotion in the region. By their nature, however, it is difficult to quantify by morphological or documentary analysis alone the use of such sites in the early modern period. Many of these holy wells are no more than a small pool of water that collects around the source of a spring. In some cases, such as Lemanaghan, Letter and Clonmore (Seir Kieran), monumental structures have been placed over these wells in recent years, illustrating the continued survival of popular devotion to local saints down to modern times.

The transition from feudalism to capitalism, and the rise of the individual

> The love of [money] will sooner effect civility than any other persuasion whatsoever.
>
> Sir Oliver St John (future lord deputy), September 1614.[26]

Gaelic Irish lordships legitimized their power and authority by upholding certain values perceived as 'ancient', and embedded in land, tradition and past custom. In these territories, property rights belonged to lineage groups rather than to individuals, with the land belonging to such groups being redistributed among its members at intervals determined by custom. The liability to pay dues in money or kind to social superiors was more in the sense of mutual protection and personal fidelity than the tenurial obligation as understood under English common law.[27] In these areas, landowners relied on non-financial arrangements between themselves and their tenants, renting farmland out in return for a third or a quarter of the produce, or employing labourers who were paid in kind.[28] The presence of tower houses at the centre of such lordships provided an appropriate metaphor for the social order of a lineage-based society that still existed in the early seventeenth century. In Delbhna Eathra, Matthew de Renzy commented on the strength of lordship there in the 1610s, including the use of traditional inauguration rites, the lord's control of legal process through his own officers (brehon), the laying of charges on the population, the provision of fairs and markets solely in the hands of the lordly family, and lordly antagonism towards outsiders based on a concern with preserving authority within the lordship from any novel influences.[29] Ludolf von Münchhausen's description of a tower house in 1591 suggests that the standing of a native landed family was underpinned by public displays of lordly munificence to followers and tenants alike, often within the confines of a hall. In late medieval Ireland, hospitality occupied a more central position in legal, economic, social and political frameworks than in modern times, with literary and historical sources suggesting that a nobleman's honour and status were inextricably linked to displays of generous and liberal hospitality.

A series of profound changes in culture and architecture occurred in the early modern era. The Gaelic lordships in Offaly, and elsewhere in Ireland, could not and did not remain oblivious to such changes. The power base of these lordships was coming under threat from officials in Dublin and London, keen to regularize the status of the native lords according to the norms of civil living, common law and the market economy. Such an agenda was to be supported by the introduction of English forms of tenure, estate organization, settlement and education. With the rights and liberties of lordships being strongly encroached upon by the activities of both soldiers and lawyers, there was a need for the Gaelic landed sort to redefine and present themselves as landlords in the English tradition. Such concerns propelled native families such as the O'Carrolls and MacCoghlans to construct manor houses, the very epitome of the English country estate. This process of emulation also included the commutation of traditional dues and services to money rents that in turn encouraged the development of an early modern capitalist economy, and the consolidation of colonial commercial interests. The establishment of standardized landholding rights protected by common law stimulated a dynamic property market that opened west and south Offaly to more speculators and aspirant landowners. The change from feudal to capitalist modes of production saw efforts to increase productivity through improving animal stock, drainage and reclamation schemes. The conversion of communal open field systems into individually worked enclosed fields was symptomatic of a more capitalist-oriented economy. The foundations for the modern estate system had thus been laid and this agricultural revolution was to shape the New English reforming agenda in Ireland.[30]

With further land confiscations in the 1650s and 1690s, the decline of the native landed elite was to continue, as not one house from the second half of the seventeenth century in west and south Offaly can be attributed to native proprietors. Following the Cromwellian Reconquest and the Restoration, the parapets, the machicolation boxes, the bartizans, the double-centred doorways protected by yetts and indeed the gun opes disappear from buildings in Offaly. There was an erosion of the traditional lordship with the consequent disappearance of ancient ceremonies involving the attendance of numerous servants and retainers. There was less need for communal spaces, and more elaboration of space for the immediate household. Thus, there was a visible break with native gothic building traditions, which had been intimately linked with the display and assertion of Gaelic lordship a couple of generations beforehand. In the later decades of the seventeenth century, the form and scale of houses expressed the concerns and aspirations of a section of society that was predominantly British in origin, ranging in status from wealthy and influential gentry, to well-off farmers comparable in status to English yeomanry.

The increased popularity of household inventories from the late sixteenth century onwards illustrates the greater importance of commodities more than ever before. It is not coincidental that this process was taking place in the context of an embryonic capitalist economy that was developing on both sides of the North Atlantic. It is noteworthy that such a process is paralleled across northwest Europe, where households gradually ceased to make the products they consumed, and that neighbourly exchange declined as individuals began to acquire mass-produced goods with cash that they earned as labourers or craftsmen.[31]

The commoditization of labour, with people having to sell their labour to prospective employers, placed greater emphasis on the individual, with consequent changes in community and household relations. A few non-elite buildings are found in west and south Offaly, probably representing the homesteads of well-to-do farmers leasing land from the local landlord. While medieval homesteads were characterized by non-partitioned interiors heated by hearths, houses in the early modern period see the insertion of fireplaces served by chimney stacks, and the subdivision of living space into a number of rooms – innovations in domestic arrangements that heralded more profound social changes. The segregation of space impacted upon the nature of intra-personal relationships in the lower echelons of society as entrance arrangements were altered to provide increased control on movement and facilitate social exclusion. This emphasis on increased privacy may be related to greater changes impacting upon society in west and south Offaly as a whole, brought about largely by the transition from feudal peasantry to agrarian capitalism. The presence of segregated rooms may have reflected a trend towards the increased segmentation of workers' time, the dependency on daily wages and the segregation of people into discrete, specialized roles.[32]

The way forward: agendas for future research

The archaeological examination of a variety of buildings and monuments in the previous chapters was complemented by documentary sources and published literature on political, social, religious and architectural developments where relevant. Such a multi-disciplinary approach has allowed the archaeology of early modern Offaly to be placed against the background of a Europe that was experiencing transformation on many fronts, not least in economics, politics and religion. Until recently, archaeological discourse has tended to overlook early modern Ireland, with little appreciation of the changes taking place in the material culture of the period, and how important an appraisal of it is fundamental to understanding the development of Irish society as it exists today. In such circumstances, it is not surprising that most published literature on material culture originates from historians, historical geographers and architectural historians. However, much of their work has only gauged impressionistic trends, with little opportunity to take into account regional differences. Indeed, to date, besides Colin Breen's *The Gaelic lordship of the O'Sullivan Beare*, published in 2005, no work has looked at a specific region in total, encompassing all aspects of local society, and how the activities of different groups, whether native or newcomer, contributed to the development of the built environment and the landscape at large. Such studies on a regional level, as well as answering questions, invariably raise more, and the present research on early modern Offaly has not differed in this respect. Thematic studies looking at the achievements of particular families such as the Boyles of east Cork/west Waterford or the earls of Thomond in Co. Clare in many spheres of early modern life such as architecture, landscape, economy and religion would be fruitful, providing much contextual information at a local and regional level. This is particularly important given the nature of much historical discourse that has focused upon the 'high' politics of the period and has largely ignored the material environment of the same families whose names abound in such literature.

There has been a tendency in archaeological research to focus on the most visible aspects of the record, which are predominantly of elite status. Nevertheless, such a study of how social relations were manipulated among the lower social orders in early modern Offaly is compromised by poor levels of archaeological (and indeed historical) visibility. This is symptomatic of a trend in Irish vernacular architecture that militates against the survival of low-status early modern buildings, a situation explained by Kieran O'Conor as being due to 'their originally flimsy nature [which] makes them difficult to trace archaeologically'.[33] The earliest architectural survivals of lower-status homes in the study area are three farmsteads that are preserved to varying degrees, representing the households of well-to-do farmers established in the area during the course of the seventeenth century. Therefore, as in historical sources, there is a clear bias in survival and preservation towards sites associated with the literate elite of early modern Offaly, with the ordinary farmers, labourers and artisans relegated to the fringes of discussion. However, it is noteworthy that a few low-status houses of late medieval/early modern date have been excavated across the country, notably in west Cork and in Ulster. Two sites of similar morphology recorded by the Archaeological Survey in Co. Offaly (Balleek and Cloghatanny) may merit more detailed survey and excavation, allowing an insight into the material life of ordinary families that is not so readily apparent in upstanding castles or churches.[34]

Spanning the Atlantic, very different peoples were linked through cultural encounters, exchange and trade, political alliances, enslavement in some areas, incursions upon their territories, and the unintentional spread of disease. As a result, an Atlantic world was created, a geographical entity varied and complicated in its nature. The establishment of the plantations in Ireland was largely contemporary with the first colonial endeavours in North America, with many of the same aspirations and prejudices being brought to bear in both environments. Colonial experience in Ireland formed the only serious precedent and means of understanding the New World.[35] Concepts that colonies had to be established by military means, that native laziness justified invasion and settlement, and that natives lacked civility were important concepts developed in Ireland and reutilized on the other side of the Atlantic.[36] There was an emerging sense of geographical contiguity between Ireland and North America, with Richard Whitbourne describing Newfoundland in 1622 as lying 'near the course and half the way between Ireland and Virginia', and Fynes Moryson seeing Ireland as 'This famous island in the Virginian Sea'.[37] While archaeologists typically examine local and regional settings, given the nature of the archaeological record, a wider view of influences, social processes and connections operating upon local populations can be informative. Consequently, the concept of an Atlantic world can play an important role in the study of seventeenth-century English colonization and Gaelic-Irish responses to it, as well as other cultural processes that were transforming early modern European society, such as capitalism and religious schism. A new world had indeed been born.

Notes

Chapter 1. Introduction

1 Nicholas Canny, *Kingdom and colony: Ireland in the Atlantic world, 1560–1800* (Baltimore, MD, 1988), pp 37–8.
2 G.T. Cell, 'The Cupids Cove settlement: a case study of the problems of early colonization' in G.M. Story (ed.), *Early European settlement and exploitation in Atlantic Canada* (St John's, Newfoundland, 1982), pp 97–114 at p. 97.
3 William J. Smyth, *Map-making, landscapes and memory: a geography of colonial and early modern Ireland,* c.*1530–1750* (Cork, 2006), p. 425.
4 Ibid.
5 Audrey Horning, 'The archaeology of British expansion: Ireland and North America in the seventeenth century' in Audrey Horning, Ruairí Ó Baoill, Colm Donnelly and Paul Logue (eds), *The post-medieval archaeology of Ireland, 1550–1850* (Dublin, 2007), pp 51–70 at p. 51.
6 Idem, 'On the banks of the Bann: the riverine economy of an Ulster Plantation village', *Historical Archaeology*, 41:3 (2007), 94–114 at 97.
7 David B. Quinn, 'Why they came' in David B. Quinn (ed.), *Early Maryland in a wider world* (Detroit, IL, 1982), pp 119–48 at pp 134–5.
8 Horning, 'Ulster Plantation village', 101.
9 Ibid., 97.
10 Audrey Horning, 'English towns on the periphery: seventeenth-century development in Ulster and the Chesapeake' in Adrian Green and Roger Leech (eds), *Cities in the world, 1500–2000* (Leeds, 2006), pp 61–81 at pp 62–3.
11 David B. Quinn, *The Elizabethans and the Irish* (Ithaca, NY, 1966), p. 118.
12 Pádraig Lenihan, *Consolidating conquest: Ireland, 1603–1727* (Harlow, Essex, 2008), p. 52.
13 Ibid., p. 54.
14 Ibid.
15 Nicholas Canny, 'Migration and opportunity: Britain, Ireland and the New World', *Irish Economic and Social History*, 12 (1985), 7–32 at 30–1
16 Charles E. Orser, *A historical archaeology of the modern world* (New York, 1996), p. 22.
17 For example, N.F. Brannon, 'Excavations at Brackfield Bawn, County Londonderry', *UJA*, 53 (1990), 8–14; Colin Breen, *Dunluce Castle: history and archaeology* (Dublin, 2012); Colm J. Donnelly, 'The archaeology of the Ulster Plantation' in Horning et al. (eds), *The post-medieval archaeology of Ireland* (2007), pp 37–50; Audrey Horning, '"Dwelling houses in the old Irish barbarous manner": archaeological evidence for Gaelic architecture in an Ulster plantation village' in P.J. Duffy, David Edwards and

Elizabeth FitzPatrick (eds), *Gaelic Ireland: land, lordship and settlement, c.1250–c.1650* (Dublin, 2001), pp 375–96; idem, 'Archaeological explorations of cultural identity and rural economy in the north of Ireland: Goodland, County Antrim', *IJHA*, 8:3 (2004), 199–215; Audrey Horning and Nicholas Brannon, 'Rediscovering Goodland: Neolithic ritual site, seasonal booley settlement or lost Scottish village?', *Archaeology Ireland*, 18:3 (2004), 28–31; E.M. Jope, 'Mongavlin Castle, Co. Donegal', *UJA*, 17 (1954), 169–172; idem, 'Castlecaulfield, Co. Tyrone', *UJA*, 21 (1958), 101–7; idem, 'Portora Castle, near Fermanagh', *UJA*, 21 (1958), 107–8; idem, 'Moyry, Charlemont, Castleraw and Richhill: fortification to architecture in the north of Ireland, 1570–1700', *UJA*, 23 (1960), 97–123; Brian Lacy, 'The archaeology of the Ulster plantation' in Michael Ryan (ed.), *The illustrated archaeology of Ireland* (Dublin, 1991), pp 201–5; D.M. Waterman, 'Tullykelter Castle, Co. Fermanagh', *UJA*, 22 (1959), 127–9; idem, 'Castle Archdale, Co. Fermanagh', *UJA*, 22 (1959), 119–23; idem, 'Tully Castle, Co. Fermanagh', *UJA*, 22 (1959), 123–6; idem, 'Sir John Davies and his Ulster buildings: Castlederg and Castle Curlews, Co. Tyrone', *UJA*, 23 (1960), 89–96; idem, 'Some Irish seventeenth-century houses and their architectural ancestry' in E.M. Jope (ed.), *Studies in building history: essays in recognition of the work of B.H. St John O'Neil* (London, 1961), 251–74.

18 For example, Colin Breen, *The Gaelic lordship of the O'Sullivan Beare* (Dublin, 2005); idem, *An archaeology of southwest Ireland, 1570–1670* (Dublin, 2007); idem, 'The post-medieval coastal landscape of Bantry and Beara, 1580–1850' in Horning et al. (eds), *The post-medieval archaeology of Ireland* (2007), pp 205–19; Eric Klingelhöfer, 'Castles built with air: Spenserian architecture in Ireland' in G. de Boe and F. Verhaege (eds), *Military studies in medieval Europe* (Zellick, Belgium, 1997), pp 149–54; idem, 'Elizabethan settlements: Mogeely Castle, Curraglass and Carrigeen, Co. Cork (pt 1)', *JCHAS*, 104 (1999), 97–110; idem, 'Proto-colonial archaeology: the case of Elizabethan Ireland' in Pedro Paul A. Funari, Martin Hall and Siân Jones (eds), *Historical archaeology: back from the edge* (London, 1999), pp 164–79; idem, 'Elizabethan settlements: Mogeely Castle, Curraglass and Carrigeen, Co. Cork (pt 2)', *JCHAS*, 105 (2000), 155–74; idem, 'The architecture of empire: Elizabethan country houses in Ireland' in Susan Lawrence (ed.), *Archaeologies of the British: explorations of identity in Great Britain and its colonies, 1600–1945* (London, 2003), pp 102–15; idem, 'Edmund Spenser at Kilcolman Castle: the archaeological evidence', *Post-Medieval Archaeology*, 39:1 (2005), 133–54; idem, *Castles and colonists, an archaeology of Elizabethan Ireland* (Manchester, 2010); Denis Power, 'The archaeology of the Munster plantation' in Ryan (ed.), *The illustrated archaeology of Ireland* (1991), pp 198–201; idem, 'The archaeology of the Munster Plantation' in Horning et al. (eds), *The post-medieval archaeology of Ireland* (2007), pp 23–36.

19 Rolf Loeber, 'Civilization through plantation: the projects of Matthew de Renzi' in Harman Murtagh (ed.), *Irish midland studies: essays in commemoration of N.W. English* (Athlone, 1980), pp 121–35; idem, 'A gate to Connacht: the building of the fortified town of Jamestown, County Leitrim, in the era of plantation', *Irish Sword*, 15 (1982–3), 149–52; idem, 'The changing borders of the Ely O'Carroll lordship' in

William Nolan and Timothy P. O'Neill (eds), *Offaly, history and society: interdisciplinary essays on the history of an Irish county* (Dublin, 1998), pp 287–317; idem, 'Geographical calendar of landownership in Ely O'Carroll in the sixteenth and seventeenth centuries' (unpublished transcript, Pittsburgh, 1998); idem, 'Warfare and architecture in County Laois through seventeenth-century eyes' in Padraig G. Lane and William Nolan (eds), *Laois, history and society: interdisciplinary essays on the history of an Irish county* (Dublin, 1999), pp 377–413; idem, 'The early seventeenth-century Ulster and midland plantations, pt I: pre-plantation architecture and building regulations' in Olivia Horsfall Turner (ed.), *'The mirror of Great Britain': national identity in seventeenth-century British architecture* (Reading, 2012), pp 73–99; idem, 'The early seventeenth-century Ulster and midland plantations, pt II: the new architecture' in Turner (ed.), *'Mirror of Great Britain'* (2012), pp 101–38; Brian Mac Cuarta, 'Newcomers in the Irish midlands, 1540–1641' (MA, UCG, 1980); idem, 'Matthew de Renzy's letters on Irish affairs, 1613–1620', *Analecta Hibernica*, 34 (1987), 109–82; idem, 'A planter's interaction with Gaelic culture: Sir Matthew de Renzy (1577–1634)', *Irish Economic and Social History*, 20 (1993), 1–17; idem, 'A planter's funeral, legacies and inventory: Sir Matthew de Renzy (1577–1634)', *JRSAI*, 127 (1997), 18–33; idem, 'A settler's land disputes in a Gaelic lordship: Matthew de Renzy in Delvin MacCoghlan, 1613–18', *Studia Hibernica*, 30 (1998–9), 63–88; idem, 'The plantation of Leitrim, 1620–41', *IHS*, 32:127 (2001), 297–320; idem, '"Sword" and "word" in the 1610s: Matthew de Renzy and Irish reform' in Brian Mac Cuarta SJ (ed.), *Reshaping Ireland, 1550–1700: colonization and its consequences* (Dublin, 2011), pp 101–30.

20 Brian de Breffny and Rosemary Ffolliott, *The houses of Ireland* (London, 1975), p. 42.

21 Caimin O'Brien and P.D. Sweetman, *Archaeological inventory of County Offaly* (Dublin, 1997); John Bradley, Andrew Halpin and Heather A. King, 'County Offaly, the urban archaeology survey' (unpublished report for the OPW, Dublin, 1986).

22 Elizabeth FitzPatrick and Caimin O'Brien, *The medieval churches of County Offaly* (Dublin, 1998).

23 Paul M. Kerrigan, 'Castles and fortifications of County Offaly, *c.*1500–1815' in Nolan and O'Neill (eds), *Offaly, history and society* (1998), pp 393–437; Margaret Sheehy, 'Architecture in Offaly', *JKAS*, 14:1 (1964–65), 1–28.

24 Conleth Manning, 'Revealing a private inscription', *Archaeology Ireland*, 8:3 (1994), 24–6; Jean Farrelly and Caimin O'Brien, 'Forest glass furnaces in County Offaly', *Archaeology Ireland*, 11:4 (1997), 21–3; idem, 'Glasshouse, seventeenth-century glasshouse' in Isabel Bennett (ed.), *Excavations 1999: summary accounts of archaeological excavations in Ireland* (Bray, 2000), pp 260–1.

25 Niall Fennelly, 'An analysis of the tower houses in a County Offaly study area' (MA, UCC, 1997); Andrew Tierney, 'The gothic and the Gaelic: exploring the place of castles in Ireland's Celtic revival', *IJHA*, 8:3 (2004), 185–98.

26 Rolf Loeber, 'Documentary survey and fieldnotes concerning Offaly castles and houses' (unpublished manuscript, Pittsburgh, 1988); idem, 'Geographical calendar of landownership in Ely O'Carroll'.

27 David Austin, 'The "proper study" of medieval archaeology' in David Austin and Leslie Alcock (eds), *From the Baltic to the Black Sea: studies in medieval archaeology* (London, 1990), pp 13–14, 18.

28 Muiris O'Sullivan and Laurence Kennedy, 'The survival of archaeological monuments: trends and attitudes', *Irish Geography*, 31:2 (1998), 88–99 at 90.

29 Breen, *Dunluce Castle*; idem, *Lordship of O'Sullivan Beare*; Horning, 'Dwellings in old Irish barbarous manner'; idem, 'Goodland, County Antrim'; Horning and Brannon, 'Rediscovering Goodland'; Rolf Loeber, 'An architectural history of Gaelic castles and settlements, 1370–1600' in Duffy et al. (eds), *Gaelic Ireland* (2001), pp 271–314; Kieran D. O'Conor, *The archaeology of medieval rural settlement in Ireland* (Dublin, 1998); Klingelhöfer, 'Elizabethan settlements (pt 1)'; idem, 'Elizabethan settlements (pt 2)'; idem, *Castles and colonists: an archaeology of Elizabethan Ireland* (Manchester, 2010).

30 Tadhg O'Keeffe, 'Concepts of "castle" and the construction of identity in medieval and post-medieval Ireland', *Irish Geography*, 34:1 (2001), 69–88 at 71–2.

31 M.C. Beaudry, L.J. Cook and Steve Mrozowski, 'Artifacts and active voices: material culture as social discourse' in R.H. McGuire and Robert Paynter (eds), *The archaeology of inequality* (Oxford and Cambridge, 1991), pp 150–91 at p. 153.

32 David Austin and Julian Thomas, 'The "proper study" of medieval archaeology: a case study' in Austin and Alcock (eds), *From the Baltic to the Black Sea* (1990), pp 43–78 at p. 45; Matthew Johnson, *Behind the castle gate: from medieval to renaissance* (London, 2002), p. 69; Tadhg O'Keeffe, 'Space, place, *habitus*: geographies of practice in an Anglo-Norman landscape' in Howard B. Clarke, Jacinta Prunty and Mark Hennessy (eds), *Surveying Ireland's past: multidisciplinary essays in honour of Anngret Simms* (Dublin, 2004), pp 73–98 at pp 88–9.

33 Austin and Thomas, 'Proper study of medieval archaeology: a case study', p. 46.

34 Ibid., p. 52.

35 Ibid.

36 Matthew Johnson, *English houses, 1300–1800: vernacular architecture, social life* (Harlow, Essex, 2010), pp 15–16.

37 Gabriel Cooney, 'Theory and practice in Irish archaeology' in Peter J. Ucko (ed.), *Theory in archaeology: a world perspective* (London, 1995), pp 263–77 at p. 266; idem, 'Building the future on the past: archaeology and the construction of national identity in Ireland' in Margarita Díaz-Andreu and Timothy Champion (eds), *Nationalism and archaeology in Europe* (London, 1996), pp 146–63 at p. 146.

38 Ciaran Brady (ed.), *Interpreting Irish history: the debate on historical revisionism, 1938–1994* (Dublin, 1994); R.F. Foster, *Paddy and Mr Punch: connections in Irish and English history* (London, 1993); idem, *The Irish story: telling tales and making it up in Ireland* (London, 2001); Declan Kiberd, *Inventing Ireland* (London, 1995).

39 Bruce Trigger, 'Alternative archaeologies: nationalist, colonialist, imperialist', *Man*, 19:3 (1984), 355–70.

40 Clodagh Tait, David Edwards and Pádraig Lenihan, 'Early modern Ireland: a history of violence' in David Edwards, Pádraig Lenihan and Clodagh Tait (eds), *Age of*

atrocity: violence and political conflict in early modern Ireland (Dublin, 2010), pp 9–33 at p. 12.

41 Ibid., p. 16.

42 Ciarán J. Reilly, 'The burning of country houses in Co. Offaly during the revolutionary period, 1920–3' in Terence Dooley and Christopher Ridgway (eds), *The Irish country house: its past, present and future* (Dublin, 2011), pp 110–33 at p. 110.

43 D.G. Boyce, *Nationalism in Ireland* (Dublin, 1982).

44 Colm J. Donnelly and Audrey Horning, 'Post-medieval and industrial archaeology in Ireland: an overview', *Antiquity*, 76 (2002), 557–61 at 557.

45 Harold G. Leask, 'House at Oldbawn, Co. Dublin', *JRSAI*, 43 (1913), 314–25.

46 Klingelhöfer, 'Proto-colonial archaeology', p. 164; Orser, *Historical archaeology*, p. 21.

47 Audrey Horning, Ruairí Ó Baoill, Colm Donnelly and Paul Logue, 'Foreword: post-medieval archaeology in and of Ireland' in Horning et al. (eds), *The post-medieval archaeology of Ireland* (2007), pp xviii–xx at p. xix.

Chapter 2. The history and ideology of plantation in the Irish midlands

1 Rolf Loeber, *The geography and practice of English colonisation in Ireland from 1534 to 1609* (Athlone, 1991), p. 13.

2 Ibid., p. 14.

3 William J. Smyth, 'Ireland a colony: settlement implications of the revolution in military-administrative, urban and ecclesiastical structures, *c.*1550 to *c.*1730' in Terry Barry (ed.), *A history of settlement in Ireland* (London, 2000), pp 158–86 at p. 159.

4 Ibid., p. 158.

5 Loeber, *Geography and practice of English colonization*, p. 14.

6 Nicholas Canny, *Making Ireland British, 1580–1650* (Oxford, 2001), pp 61–2.

7 Nicholas Canny, *From Reformation to Restoration: Ireland, 1534–1660* (Dublin, 1987), p. 50; Loeber, *Geography and practice of English colonization*, pp 16–17; Avril Thomas, *The walled towns of Ireland* (2 vols, Dublin, 2006), pp 165–6, 183–4.

8 R. Dunlop, 'The plantation of Leix and Offaly', *EHR*, 6 (1891), 61–96 at 65; Loeber, *Geography and practice of English colonization*, p. 17.

9 Ibid., pp 17–18.

10 Ibid., p. 27.

11 Dunlop, 'Plantation of Leix and Offaly', 72; Loeber, *Geography and practice of English colonization*, p. 27.

12 Dunlop, 'Plantation of Leix and Offaly', 75.

13 Loeber, *Geography and practice of English colonization*, p. 28.

14 Ibid.

15 Ibid., p. 70.

16 Ibid., p. 59.

17 Dunlop, 'Plantation of Leix and Offaly', 94.

18 Mac Cuarta, 'Plantation of Leitrim', 306–7.

19 Canny, *Making Ireland British*, p. 199.

20 Canny, *Reformation to Restoration*, p. 175.

21 Mac Cuarta, 'Plantation of Leitrim', 299.
22 Canny, *Reformation to Restoration*, pp 175–6; Henry Goff, 'English conquest of an Irish barony: the changing patterns of land ownership in the barony of Scarawalsh, 1540–1640' in Kevin Whelan and William Nolan (eds), *Wexford, history and society: interdisciplinary essays on the history of an Irish county* (Dublin, 1987), pp 122–49 at pp 138, 140; Mac Cuarta, 'Plantation of Leitrim', 299, 301–2.
23 Mac Cuarta, 'Plantation of Leitrim', 302.
24 Goff, 'English conquest of an Irish barony', p. 139; Mac Cuarta, 'Plantation of Leitrim', 303–4.
25 Canny, *Making Ireland British*, p. 178; R.F. Foster, *Modern Ireland, 1600–1972* (London, 1988), pp 69–70.
26 Canny, *Making Ireland British*, p. 178.
27 Ibid., p. 179.
28 Canny, *Kingdom and colony*, p. 34.
29 Nicholas Canny, *The Elizabethan Conquest of Ireland: a pattern established, 1565–76* (Hassocks, Sussex, 1976), p. 92; P.S. Robinson, *The plantation of Ulster: British settlement in an Irish landscape, 1600–1670* (Dublin, 1984), p. 59.
30 Raymond Gillespie, *Colonial Ulster: the settlement of east Ulster, 1600–1641* (Cork, 1985), p. 208.
31 Foster, *Modern Ireland*, p. 67; Robinson, *Plantation of Ulster*, p. 59.
32 J.S. Curl, *The Londonderry Plantation, 1609–1914: the history, architecture and planning of the estates of the city of London and its livery companies in Ulster* (Chichester, 1986), p. 31.
33 Gillespie, *Colonial Ulster*, pp 39–40.
34 Canny, *Kingdom and colony*, pp 37–8.
35 Ibid., p. 37.
36 Nicholas Canny, 'Introduction: Spenser and the reform of Ireland' in Patricia Coughlan (ed.), *Spenser and Ireland: an interdisciplinary perspective* (Cork, 1989), pp 9–24 at p. 20.
37 Canny, *Kingdom and colony*, p. 34.
38 Robinson, *Plantation of Ulster*, pp 56, 58.
39 Rolf Loeber, '"Certeyn notes": biblical and foreign signposts to the Ulster Plantation' in James Lyttleton and Colin Rynne (eds), *Plantation Ireland: settlement and material culture, c.1550–c.1700* (Dublin, 2009), pp 23–42 at pp 31–2.
40 David B. Quinn, 'Renaissance influences in English colonization', *Transactions of the Royal Historical Society*, 26 (1976), 73–93 at 77.
41 Canny, *Elizabethan conquest of Ireland*, p. 85.
42 Nicholas Canny, 'The ideology of English colonisation: from Ireland to America', *William and Mary Quarterly*, 30 (1973), 576–98 at 589; idem, *Elizabethan conquest of Ireland*, p. 129.
43 Canny, *Making Ireland British*, p. 123.
44 Canny, *Elizabethan conquest of Ireland*, p. 135.
45 David B. Quinn, 'The Munster Plantation: problems and opportunities', *JCHAS*, 71 (1966), 19–40 at 22.

46 Canny, 'Ideology of English colonisation', 589; idem, *Elizabethan conquest of Ireland*, p. 129.
47 Quinn, 'Renaissance influences', 86.
48 Quinn, 'Munster Plantation', 22.
49 Canny, 'Ideology of English colonisation', 589; idem, *Elizabethan conquest of Ireland*, p. 129.
50 Quinn, 'Renaissance influences', 88.
51 Canny, 'Ideology of English colonisation', 589–90; idem, *Elizabethan conquest of Ireland*, pp 129–30.
52 Quinn, 'Renaissance influences', 90.
53 Loeber, 'Civilization through plantation', p. 125.
54 N.D. Atkinson, 'The plantation of Ely O'Carroll, 1619–1693' (MLitt, TCD, 1957), pp 50, 56.
55 Canny, *Making Ireland British*, pp 37–8.
56 Canny, *Elizabethan conquest of Ireland*, p. 121.
57 Canny, 'Ideology of English colonisation', 584; idem, *Elizabethan conquest of Ireland*, p. 123.
58 Susan Brigden, *New worlds, lost worlds: the rule of the Tudors, 1485–1603* (London, 2000), p. 254.
59 Canny, 'Ideology of English colonisation', 588; idem, *Elizabethan conquest of Ireland*, p. 128.
60 Canny, 'Ideology of English colonisation', 584; idem, *Elizabethan conquest of Ireland*, p. 124.
61 Canny, 'Ideology of English colonisation', 585; idem, *Elizabethan conquest of Ireland*, pp 124–5.
62 Canny, 'Ideology of English colonisation', 585; idem, *Elizabethan conquest of Ireland*, p. 125.
63 Foster, *Modern Ireland*, p. 29.
64 Canny, *Making Ireland British*, pp 51–2.
65 Quoted in Canny, *Making Ireland British*, p. 54.
66 Canny, 'Ideology of English colonisation', 586–7; idem, *Elizabethan conquest of Ireland*, p. 125.
67 Canny, *Elizabethan conquest of Ireland*, p. 125.
68 William J. Smyth, 'The western isle of Ireland and the eastern seaboard of America: England's first frontiers', *Irish Geography*, 11 (1978), 1–22 at 4.
69 Brigden, *New worlds, lost worlds*, p. 281; Canny, *Kingdom and colony*, p. 7; David B. Quinn, *Ireland and America: their early associations, 1500–1640* (Liverpool, 1991), p. 16.
70 Canny, 'Ideology of English colonisation', 586–7; idem, *Elizabethan conquest of Ireland*, pp 125–6.
71 Canny, 'Ideology of English colonisation', 587–8; idem, *Elizabethan conquest of Ireland*, pp 126–7.
72 Canny, *Making Ireland British*, p. 133.
73 Canny, *Elizabethan conquest of Ireland*, p. 119.

74 Matthew Johnson, *Ideas of landscape* (Oxford, 2007), p. 15.
75 Canny, *Elizabethan conquest of Ireland*, pp 66, 133; David B. Quinn, 'Ireland and sixteenth-century European expansion', *Historical Studies*, 1 (1958), 20–32 at 27.
76 Canny, 'Ideology of English colonisation', 595–6; idem, *Elizabethan conquest of Ireland*, p. 134.
77 Canny, 'Ideology of English colonisation', 593–4; idem, *Elizabethan conquest of Ireland*, p. 133.
78 Canny, 'Ideology of English colonisation', 595; idem, *Elizabethan conquest of Ireland*, p. 134.
79 Mac Cuarta, 'De Renzy and Irish reform', p. 112.
80 Canny, *Kingdom and colony*, p. 2; Quinn, *Ireland and America*, p. 17; Smyth, 'England's first frontiers', 6.
81 Smyth, 'England's first frontiers', 6.
82 Horning, 'Dwelling houses in old Irish barbarous manner', p. 392.
83 Mac Cuarta, 'De Renzy and Irish reform', p. 111.
84 Ciaran Brady, 'The road to the View: on the decline of reform thought in Tudor Ireland' in Coughlan (ed.), *Spenser and Ireland* (1989), pp 25–45 at p. 35.
85 Gillespie, *Colonial Ulster*, p. 220.
86 Brady, 'Road to the View', p. 35.
87 Canny, *Elizabethan conquest of Ireland*, p. 67.
88 Brigden, *New worlds, lost worlds*, p. 318.
89 Ibid., p. 255.
90 Smyth, 'England's first frontiers', 8.
91 Canny, *Kingdom and colony*, p. 5.

Chapter 3. English interventions in early modern Offaly

1 F.R.M. Hitchcock, *The midland septs and the Pale: an account of the early septs and later settlers of the King's County and of life in the English Pale* (Dublin, 1908), p. 52.
2 Liam Cox, 'The MacCoghlans of Delvin Eathra', *Irish Genealogist*, 4:6 (1973), 534–46 at 538.
3 Kerrigan, 'Castles and fortifications', p. 397.
4 Loeber, 'Civilization through plantation', p. 125.
5 Tim Venning, 'The O'Carrolls of Offaly: their relations with the Dublin authorities in the sixteenth century' in Nolan and O'Neill (eds), *Offaly, history and society* (1998), pp 181–205 at p. 185.
6 T.L. Cooke, *The early history of the town of Birr, or Parsonstown …* (Dublin, 1875), p. 27; Venning, 'O'Carrolls of Offaly', p. 187.
7 Venning, 'O'Carrolls of Offaly', p. 189.
8 Cooke, *History of Birr*, pp 314, 317; Liam Cox, 'The MacCoghlans of Delvin Eathra', *Irish Genealogist*, 5:1 (1974), 21–32 at 21; Venning, 'O'Carrolls of Offaly', p. 190.
9 William Carrigan, *The history and antiquities of the diocese of Ossory* (4 vols, Dublin, 1905), ii, p. 5; Hitchcock, *Midland septs*, p. 174.

10 Cooke, *History of Birr*, p. 370; Hitchcock, *Midland septs*, pp 241–2; Conleth Manning, 'Clonmacnoise Cathedral' in H.A. King (eds), *Clonmacnoise Studies*, 1 (Dublin, 1998), pp 57–86 at p. 83; idem, *Clonmacnoise, Co. Offaly* (Dublin, 1998), p. 16.
11 Cooke, *History of Birr*, p. 338; Cox, 'MacCoghlans of Delvin Eathra', 539.
12 Venning, 'O'Carrolls of Offaly', p. 192; David Edwards, 'The escalation of violence in sixteenth-century Ireland' in Edwards et al. (eds), *Age of atrocity* (2010), pp 34–78 at p. 75.
13 Kerrigan, 'Castles and fortifications', p. 393.
14 Fiona Fitzsimons, 'The lordship of O'Connor Faly, 1520–1570' in Nolan and O'Neill (eds), *Offaly, history and society* (1998), pp 207–42 at p. 215.
15 Mary O'Dowd, 'Gaelic economy and society' in Ciaran Brady and Raymond Gillespie (eds), *Natives and newcomers: the making of Irish colonial society, 1534–1641* (Dublin, 1986), pp 120–47 at p. 132.
16 Venning, 'O'Carrolls of Offaly', p. 191.
17 Ibid., p. 193.
18 Ibid., p. 195.
19 Ibid., p. 196.
20 Ibid., p. 201.
21 Cooke, *History of Birr*, pp 337–8; Cox, 'MacCoghlans of Delvin Eathra', 539; J.C. Monahan, *Records relating to the dioceses of Ardagh and Clonmacnoise* (Dublin, 1886), pp 61–2.
22 Cox, 'MacCoghlans of Delvin Eathra', 540; Walter Fitzgerald, 'Notes on Sir John MacCoghlan, knight of Cloghan, chief of Delvin-MacCoghlan, who died in 1590', *JRSAI*, 43 (1913), 223–31 at 225.
23 Cox, 'MacCoghlans of Delvin Eathra', 540; Fitzgerald, 'Notes on Sir John MacCoghlan', 226.
24 Cox, 'MacCoghlans of Delvin Eathra', 540.
25 Ibid.
26 Cox, 'MacCoghlans of Delvin Eathra', 541; Fitzgerald, 'Notes on Sir John MacCoghlan', 228.
27 Cooke, *History of Birr*, p. 317; Cox, 'MacCoghlans of Delvin Eathra', 542; James Morrin (ed.), *Calendar of patent and close rolls of chancery in Ireland, of the reign of Charles the first* (Dublin, 1863), pp 360–5; C.W. Russell and J.P. Prendergast (eds), Calendar of the state papers relating to Ireland of the reign of James I, 1608–10 (London, 1874), p. 527.
28 Fear Ceall, 'Conntae an Riogh', *JKAS*, 12:8 (1944–5), 353–74 at 372–3.
29 O'Dowd, 'Gaelic economy and society', p. 136.
30 Loeber, 'Ely O'Carroll lordship', p. 310; Venning, 'O'Carrolls of Offaly', p. 201.
31 Cooke, *History of Birr*, p. 31.
32 Loeber, 'Ely O'Carroll lordship', p. 309.
33 Venning, 'O'Carrolls of Offaly', pp 197–8.
34 Mac Cuarta, 'Newcomers in the midlands', pp 13–14.
35 Ibid., p. 24.

36 Ibid., pp 7, 11.
37 FitzPatrick and O'Brien, *Medieval churches of Offaly*, p. 81.
38 Carrigan, *History and antiquities of Ossory*, ii, pp 5–6; Venning, 'O'Carrolls of Offaly', p. 195.
39 Carrigan, *History and antiquities of Ossory*, ii, p. 5; Cooke, *History of Birr*, p. 172; FitzPatrick and O'Brien, *Medieval churches of Offaly*, p. 103.
40 Fear Ceall, 'Conntae an Riogh', *JKAS*, 13:1 (1946–7), 3–18 at 16–7; Mac Cuarta, 'Newcomers in the midlands', p. 25; O'Brien and Sweetman, *Archaeological inventory*, pp 141, 155.
41 O'Brien and Sweetman, *Archaeological inventory*, pp 141, 155–6.
42 Loeber, 'Civilization through plantation', p. 123.
43 Mac Cuarta, 'Newcomers in the midlands', p. 88.
44 Ibid., p. 89.
45 Ibid., p. 93.
46 Atkinson, 'Plantation of Ely O'Carroll', p. 47; Mac Cuarta, 'Newcomers in the midlands', pp 94–5.
47 Mac Cuarta, 'Newcomers in the midlands', p. 95.
48 Ibid., p. 137.
49 Ibid., p. 94.
50 Ibid., p. 93.
51 Atkinson, 'Plantation of Ely O'Carroll', pp 49, 103.
52 Mac Cuarta, 'Newcomers in the midlands', pp 89–90.
53 Ibid., p. 128.
54 Ibid., p. 129.
55 Ibid., p. 130.
56 Ibid., p. 132.
57 Loeber, 'Ulster and midland plantations, pt I', p. 87.
58 Mac Cuarta, 'Newcomers in the midlands', p. 141.
59 Ibid.
60 Ibid., p. 142.
61 Ibid., pp 147–8.
62 Ibid., p. 159.
63 FitzPatrick and O'Brien, *Medieval churches of Offaly*, p. 81; O'Brien and Sweetman, *Archaeological inventory*, p. 170.
64 John Feehan and Alison Rosse, *An atlas of Birr* (Dublin, 2005), p. 5.
65 Mac Cuarta, 'Newcomers in the midlands', p. 155.
66 Atkinson, 'Plantation of Ely O'Carroll', pp 80–1.
67 Ibid., p. 62.
68 Mac Cuarta, 'Newcomers in the midlands', p. 160.
69 Ibid., p. 161.
70 Ibid., p. 163.
71 Raymond Gillespie, 'The problems of plantations: material culture and social change in early modern Ireland' in Lyttleton and Rynne (eds), *Plantation Ireland* (2009), pp 43–60 at pp 49–59.

72 Peter E. Pope, *Fish into wine: the Newfoundland plantation in the seventeenth century* (London, 2004), p. 3.

Chapter 4. The human landscape of early modern Offaly

1 Kenneth Nicholls, 'Woodland cover in pre-modern Ireland' in Duffy et al. (eds), *Gaelic Ireland* (2001), pp 181–206 at p. 195.
2 Loeber, 'Civilization through plantation', p. 126.
3 R.F. Hammond and L.E. Brennan, *Soils of Co. Offaly: national soil survey of Ireland* (Dublin, 2003), p. 3.
4 Smyth, *Map-making, landscapes and memory*, pp 80–3.
5 John Feehan, *Farming in Ireland* (Dublin, 2003), p. 85.
6 Hammond and Brennan, *Soils of Co. Offaly*, p. 11; V.A. Hall, 'The documentary and pollen analytical records of the vegetational history of the Irish landscape, AD200–1650', *Peritia*, 14 (2000), 342–69 at 348.
7 Feehan, *Farming in Ireland*, p. 83; Aidan Clarke, 'The Irish economy, 1600–60' in T.W. Moody, F.X. Martin and F.J. Byrne (eds), *A new history of Ireland, iii: Early modern Ireland, 1534–1691* (Oxford, 1976), pp 168–86 at p. 172.
8 R.A. Butlin, 'Land and people, *c*.1600' in Moody et al. (eds), *Early modern Ireland* (1976), pp 142–67 at p. 152.
9 It has been argued that Spenser's *View* may have been compiled in draft form as early as 1590, though the better-known manuscripts were probably written in 1596, with one instance of the work being made available to a printer in 1598. It was eventually published by Sir James Ware in 1633 long after Spenser had passed away: see Canny, *Making Ireland British*, pp 56–8.
10 Butlin, 'Land and people', p. 152.
11 Clarke, 'The Irish economy', p. 173.
12 Ibid., pp 177–8.
13 Feehan, *Farming in Ireland*, p. 91.
14 Butlin, 'Land and people', p. 151.
15 Clarke, 'The Irish economy', p. 173.
16 Butlin, 'Land and people', p. 149; Loeber, 'Warfare and architecture in Laois', p. 384.
17 Loeber, 'Ely O'Carroll lordship', pp 292–3.
18 Butlin, 'Land and people', p. 149.
19 J.H. Andrews, 'The mapping of Ireland's cultural landscape, 1550–1630' in Duffy et al. (eds), *Gaelic Ireland* (2001), pp 153–80 at p. 173, fig. 8; Frank Mitchell and Michael Ryan, *Reading the Irish landscape* (Dublin, 1998), p. 326, illus. 173.
20 Feehan, *Farming in Ireland*, p. 84; Mac Cuarta, 'Newcomers in the midlands', pp 89–90.
21 Rory McNeary and Brian Shanahan, 'Carns townland, Co. Roscommon: excavations by the Medieval Rural Settlement Project in 2006' in Christiaan Corlett and Michael Potterton (eds), *Rural settlement in medieval Ireland in the light of recent archaeological excavations* (Dublin, 2009), pp 125–37.

22 F.H.A. Aalen and Kevin Whelan, 'Fields' in F.H.A. Aalen, Kevin Whelan and Matthew Stout (eds), *Atlas of the Irish rural landscape* (2nd ed., Cork, 2011), pp 200–11 at p. 202, fig. 5.
23 Donal Fallon, 'Continuity: the archaeological and documentary evidence for medieval to modern rural settlement and landholding in the townland of Baltrasna, Ratoath, Co. Meath' in Corlett and Potterton (eds), *Rural settlement in medieval Ireland* (2009), pp 79–90 at pp 84–7.
24 John Feehan, *The landscape of Slieve Bloom: a study of its natural and human heritage* (Dublin, 1979), p. 154.
25 Feehan, *Farming in Ireland*, p. 87.
26 Ibid., p. 90.
27 Hammond and Brennan, *Soils of Co. Offaly*, p. 11.
28 Loeber, 'Civilization through plantation', p. 123.
29 Hammond and Brennan, *Soils of Co. Offaly*, p. 134, fig. 5.2.
30 Margaret MacCurtain, *Tudor and Stuart Ireland* (Dublin, 1972), p. 39; O'Conor, *Medieval rural settlement*, p. 103.
31 Eileen McCracken, *The Irish woods since Tudor times: their distribution and exploitation* (Newton Abbot, Devon, 1971), pp 27–30.
32 Roy Tomlinson, 'Forests and woodlands' in Aalen et al. (eds), *Atlas of the Irish rural landscape* (2011), pp 186–99 at p. 187.
33 McCracken, *Irish woods*, p. 20.
34 Tomlinson, 'Forests and woodlands', p. 123.
35 Hall, 'Vegetational history of Irish landscape', 355; Nicholls, 'Woodland cover in Ireland', pp 181, 186.
36 Tomlinson, 'Forests and woodlands', p. 122.
37 Thomas Lee, *Offaly through time and its townlands* (Dublin, 2009), pp 64–5.
38 Richard Butler, *A treatice of Ireland by John Dymmok* (tracts relating to Ireland, printed for the Irish Archaeological Society, 2 (1843)), pp 5–90 at p. 43.
39 Ibid.
40 Anon., *Inquisitionum in officio rotulorum cancellarie Hiberniae assertvatarum repertorium*, 1 (Dublin, 1826), Com' Regis, 19 Car. I.
41 Hitchcock, *Midland septs*, p. 171.
42 Hall, 'Vegetational history of Irish landscape', 345, 367.
43 FitzPatrick and O'Brien, *Medieval churches of Offaly*, p. 116; C.R. Elrington (ed.), *The whole works of the most Rev. James Ussher DD* (17 vols, Dublin, 1847–64), p. lviii; Monahan, *Dioceses of Ardagh and Clonmacnoise*, p. 126; Nicholls, 'Woodland cover in Ireland', pp 182–3.
44 Hall, 'Vegetational history of Irish landscape', 367.
45 Nicholls, 'Woodland cover in Ireland', p. 196.
46 Ibid., p. 197.
47 Ibid., pp 197–8.
48 Feehan, *Landscape of Slieve Bloom*, pp 120, 247.
49 Butlin, 'Land and people', p. 162.

50 James Killen and Enda Murphy, 'Communications' in Aalen et al. (eds), *Atlas of the Irish rural landscape* (2011), pp 287–301 at p. 288.
51 Butlin, 'Land and people', p. 163.
52 Fear Ceall, 'Conntae an Riogh', 17–18.
53 J.H. Andrews and Rolf Loeber, 'An Elizabethan map of Leix and Offaly: cartography, topography and architecture' in Nolan and O'Neill (eds), *Offaly, history and society* (1998), pp 243–85 at pp 244–7.
54 Ellen O'Carroll, 'Corhill Bog, Lisdermot/Straduff: medieval gravel and wood trackway' in Isabel Bennett (eds), *Excavations 2000: summary accounts of archaeological excavations in Ireland* (Bray, 2002), p. 287.
55 National Archives, London, MPF 1/268(6).
56 Feehan and Rosse, *Atlas of Birr*, p. 13.

Chapter 5. The tower house: an old building in a new world?

1 Conleth Manning, 'Irish tower houses' in Gianni Perbellini (ed.), *Towers and smaller castles: Europa Nostra Bulletin*, 63 (2009), 19–30 at 19.
2 David Sweetman, 'The tower houses of County Louth' in Perbellini (ed.), *Towers and smaller castles* (2009), 31–4 at 31.
3 Terry Barry, 'Rural settlement in medieval Ireland' in Terry Barry (ed.), *A history of settlement in Ireland* (London, 2000), pp 110–23 at p. 119.
4 Colm J. Donnelly, 'Tower houses and late medieval secular settlement in County Limerick' in Duffy et al. (eds), *Gaelic Ireland* (2001), pp 315–28 at pp 319–21; idem, 'Decline and adaptation: the medieval Irish tower house in early modern County Limerick' in Gunilla Malm (ed.), *Archaeology and buildings*, BAR International Series, 930 (Oxford, 2001), pp 7–13 at p. 8.
5 Rolf Loeber, 'Ulster and midland plantations, pt I', pp 81–2; G.A. Hayes-McCoy (ed.), *Ulster and other Irish maps, c.1600* (Dublin, 1964).
6 Aidan O'Sullivan, *The archaeology of lake settlement in Ireland*. Discovery Programme Monograph No. 4 (Dublin, 1998); idem, 'Crannogs in late medieval Gaelic Ireland, c.1350–c.1650' in Duffy et al. (eds), *Gaelic Ireland* (2001), pp 397–417.
7 Loeber, 'Architectural history', p. 287, idem, 'Ulster and midland plantations, pt I', p. 84.
8 Loeber, 'Architectural history', pp 296, 307.
9 David Sweetman, *Medieval castles of Ireland* (Cork, 1999), p. 152; idem, 'The origin and development of the tower house in Ireland' in John Ludlow and Noel Jameson (eds), *Medieval Ireland: the Barryscourt Lectures, I–X* (Cork, 2004), pp 261–87 at p. 278.
10 James Lyttleton, *Blarney Castle: an Irish tower house* (Dublin, 2011), pp 26–8.
11 Tadhg O'Keeffe, *Medieval Ireland: an archaeology* (Stroud, 2000), p. 53.
12 Maurice Craig, *The architecture of Ireland from the earliest times to 1880* (Portrane, 1989), p. 97; Harold G. Leask, *Irish castles and castellated houses* (Dundalk, 1951), p. 79; Tom McNeill, *Castles in Ireland: feudal power in a Gaelic World* (London, 1997), p. 201; Manning, 'Irish tower houses'; O'Keeffe *Medieval Ireland*, p. 47; Sweetman, *Medieval castles*, pp 138–9.

13 Máirtín D'Alton, 'The architecture of the Leix and Offaly plantations, *c.*1540–1600' (MLitt, TCD, 2009), pp 149, 346–7.

14 O'Brien and Sweetman, *Archaeological inventory*, p. 141.

15 Peter F. Ryder, 'A survey of medieval defensible buildings in Cumbria' (unpublished manuscript held by Cumbria County Council). For details on Crofton Hall, see www.imagesofengland.org.uk: a photographic record of listed buildings maintained by English Heritage.

16 Matthew Hyde and Nikolaus Pevsner, *Cumbria, Cumberland, Westmorland and Furness: the buildings of England* (New Haven, CT, 2010), pp 177, 454.

17 Ryder, 'Medieval buildings in Cumbria'; for images of these two tower houses, see John F. Curwen, 'The castles and fortified towers of Cumberland, Westmorland and Lancashire north-of-the-Sands, together with a brief historical account of border warfare', *Cumberland and Westmorland Antiquarian and Archaeological Society Extra Series*, 13 (1913), 380–2; Denis R. Perriam and John Robinson, 'The medieval fortified buildings of Cumbria', *Cumberland and Westmorland Antiquarian and Archaeological Society Extra Series*, 29 (1998), 227, 232.

18 Ryder, 'Medieval buildings in Cumbria'.

19 R.W. Brunskill, *Traditional buildings of Cumbria, the county of the lakes* (London, 2002), pp 38–40.

20 Ryder, 'Medieval buildings in Cumbria'.

21 Anon., *Historic monuments of Northern Ireland: an introduction and guide* (6th ed., Belfast, 1983), pp 44–5.

22 Loeber, 'Architectural history', p. 272.

23 Rolf Loeber and Terence Reeves-Smyth, 'Lord Audley's grandiose building schemes in the Ulster plantation' in Mac Cuarta (ed.), *Reshaping Ireland* (2011), pp 82–100 at p. 94.

24 Loeber, 'Architectural history', p. 301.

25 Ibid., p. 301.

26 Loeber, 'Architectural history', pp 303–4; Mac Cuarta, 'De Renzy's letters', 170, 176.

27 James A. Delle, '"A good and easy speculation": spatial conflict, collusion and resistance in late sixteenth-century Munster, Ireland', *IJHA*, 3:1 (1999), 11–35 at 30; idem, 'Extending Europe's grasp: an archaeological comparison of colonial spatial processes in Ireland and Jamaica' in Geoff Egan and R.L. Michael (eds), *Old and new worlds* (Oxford, 1999), pp 106–16 at p. 114.

28 Elizabeth FitzPatrick, *Royal inauguration in Gaelic Ireland,* c.*1100–1600: a cultural landscape study* (Woodbridge, 2004), pp 24, 30; idem, 'Parley sites of Ó Néill and Ó Domhnaill in late sixteenth-century Ireland' in David Edwards (ed.), *Regions and rulers in Ireland, 1100–1650* (Dublin, 2004), pp 201–16 at p. 209.

29 Matthew Johnson, *Behind the castle gate: from medieval to Renaissance* (London, 2002), p. 122.

30 Harold G. Leask, 'Early seventeenth-century houses in Ireland' in Jope (ed.), *Studies in building history* (1961), pp 243–50 at p. 244.

31 Toby Barnard, *Making the grand figure: lives and possessions in Ireland, 1641–1770* (New Haven, CT, 2004), pp 26, 189.

32 Hanneke Ronnes, 'Continental traces at Carrick-on-Suir and contemporary Irish castles: a preliminary study of date-and-initial stones' in Thomas Herron and Michael Potterton (eds), *Ireland in the Renaissance,* c.*1540–1660* (Dublin, 2007), pp 255–73 at pp 268, 271–2.

33 Edward MacLysaght, *Irish life in the seventeenth century* (Shannon, 1969), pp 110–11.

34 Leask, *Irish castles*, pp 91–2; John O'Callaghan, 'Fortified houses of the sixteenth century in south Wexford', *Journal of the Old Wexford Society*, 8 (1980–1), 1–51; O'Keeffe, *Medieval Ireland*, p. 46.

35 Rory Sherlock, 'An introduction to the history and architecture of Bunratty Castle' in Roger Stalley (ed.), *Limerick and south-west Ireland: medieval art and architecture* (Leeds, 2011), pp 202–18 at p. 212.

36 W.D. Simpson, 'The tower houses of Scotland' in Jope (ed.), *Studies in building history* (1961), pp 229–42 at pp 235–6.

37 O'Keeffe, 'Concepts of "castle"', 73.

38 Mac Cuarta, 'Planter's interaction with Gaelic culture', 6–7; idem, 'De Renzy and Irish reform', pp 103–4, 106.

39 Jope, 'Fortification to architecture', 109.

40 Eric Klingelhöfer, 'Spenserian architecture in Ireland', p. 152; idem, 'Kilcolman Castle', 137–42; idem, *Castles and colonists*, pp 109–31; David Newman Johnson, 'Kilcolman Castle' in A.C. Hamilton (ed.), *The Spenser Encyclopedia* (Toronto, 1990), pp 416–22 at p. 422.

41 Mark Girouard, *Life in the English country house: a social and architectural history* (New Haven, CT, 1978), pp 88–118.

42 Leask, *Irish castles*, pp 91–2.

43 Manning, 'Irish tower houses', 27.

44 Loeber, 'Ely O'Carroll lordship', p. 292.

45 Johnson, *English houses*, p. 71.

46 Rory Sherlock, 'The evolution of the Irish tower house as a domestic space', *PRIA*, 111C (2010), 115–40 at 128–9.

47 Sherlock, 'Evolution of Irish tower house', 133; Jane Fenlon, 'Moving towards the formal house: room usage in early modern Ireland', *PRIA*, 111C (2010), 141–68 at 153.

48 Victor Chinnery, 'Barryscourt refurbished: the reinstatement of a late sixteenth-century Irish domestic interior' in Ludlow and Jameson (eds), *The Barryscourt Lectures* (2004), pp 177–224 at pp 200–1.

49 P.A. Faulkner, 'Castle planning in the fourteenth century', *Archaeological Journal*, 120 (1963), 216–35 at 228.

50 Charles McKean, *The Scottish Chateau: the country house of Renaissance Scotland* (Stroud, 2001), p. 8.

51 Chinnery, 'Barryscourt refurbished', p. 196.

52 Karena Morton, 'Irish medieval wall painting' in Ludlow and Jameson (eds), *The Barryscourt Lectures* (2004), pp 313–49 at p. 318.
53 Karena Morton, 'Aspects of image and meaning in Irish medieval wall paintings' in Rachel Moss, Colmán Ó Clabaigh OSB and Salvador Ryan (eds), *Art and devotion in late medieval Ireland* (Dublin, 2006), pp 51–71 at pp 58–69.
54 Chinnery, 'Barryscourt refurbished', p. 196.
55 Jane Fenlon, *Goods and chattels: a survey of early household inventories in Ireland* (Dublin, 2003).
56 De Breffny and Ffolliot, *Houses of Ireland*, p. 34.
57 Fenlon, *Goods and chattels*, p. 4.
58 Fitzgerald, 'Notes on Sir John MacCoghlan', 230.
59 Ibid., 228.
60 Chinnery, 'Barryscourt refurbished', p. 209.
61 C.M. O'Sullivan, *Hospitality in medieval Ireland, 900–1500* (Dublin, 2004), p. 65.
62 A.G. Rutherford, 'A social interpretation of the castle in Scotland' (PhD, Glasgow, 1998), p. 4; McKean, *Scottish Chateau*, p. 57.
63 Johnson, *Behind the castle gate*, p. 43.
64 McKean, *Scottish Chateau*, p. 120.
65 Mark Girouard, *Robert Smythson and the Elizabethan country house* (New Haven, CT, 1983), p. 201.
66 McNeill, *Castles in Ireland*, p. 221.
67 Loeber, 'Architectural history', p. 275; M.W. Thompson, *The decline of the castle* (Cambridge, 1987), p. 24.
68 Birr Castle A/5/19 (A) (177 in list).
69 Dave Pollock, 'The Barryscourt hall and the remains of some other medieval timber buildings' in Conleth Manning (ed.), *From ringforts to fortified houses: studies on castles and other monuments in honour of David Sweetman* (Bray, 2007), pp 261–72 at pp 261–6.
70 Dagmar Ó Riain-Raedel, 'A German visitor to Monaincha in 1591', *Tipperary Historical Journal* (1998), 223–33 at 230.
71 T.E. McNeill, 'The larger castles of later medieval Co. Limerick' in Stalley (ed.), *Limerick and south-west Ireland* (2011), pp 176–88 at pp 178, 182.
72 Leask, *Irish castles*, p. 106; for plan, see Sweetman, *Medieval castles*, p. 166, fig. 140.
73 O'Sullivan, *Hospitality*, p. 14.
74 Ibid., p. 72.
75 Katharine Simms, *From kings to warlords: the changing political structure of Gaelic Ireland in the later Middle Ages* (Woodbridge, 1987), p. 95.
76 Dave Pollock, 'The bawn exposed: recent excavations at Barryscourt' in Ludlow and Jameson (eds), *The Barryscourt Lectures* (2004), pp 145–75 at pp 167–72.
77 Klingelhöfer, 'Kilcolman Castle', 143–4.
78 Johnson, *Behind the castle gate*, pp 38, 40.
79 Ciaran Brady, 'Political women and reform in Tudor Ireland' in Margaret MacCurtain and Mary O'Dowd (eds), *Women in early modern Ireland* (Edinburgh, 1991), pp 69–90 at p. 70.

80 Elizabeth McKenna, 'Was there a political role for women in medieval Ireland?' in C.E. Meek and M.K. Simms (eds), *The fragility of her sex? Medieval Irish women in their European context* (Dublin, 1996), pp 163–74 at p. 164.
81 Vincent P. Carey, '"What's love got to do with it?": gender and Geraldine power on the Pale border' in Michael Potterton and Thomas Herron (eds), *Dublin and the Pale in the Renaissance, c.1540–1660* (Dublin, 2011), pp 93–103 at pp 98, 103.
82 Mary McAuliffe, 'The lady in the tower: the social and political role of women in tower houses' in Meek and Simms (eds), *Medieval Irish women* (1996), pp 153–62 at p. 159; K.W. Nicholls, 'Irishwomen and property in the sixteenth century' in MacCurtain and O'Dowd (eds), *Women in early modern Ireland* (1991), pp 17–31 at p. 20.
83 McAuliffe, 'The lady in the tower', p. 154; Rutherford, 'Social interpretation of the castle', p. 120.
84 Roberta Gilchrist, 'Ambivalent bodies: gender and medieval archaeology' in Jenny Moore and Eleanor Scott (eds), *Invisible people and processes, writing gender and childhood into European archaeology* (London, 1997), pp 42–58 at p. 44; O'Keeffe, 'Concepts of "castle"', 79.
85 Roberta Gilchrist, *Gender and archaeology: contesting the past* (London, 1999), p. 121; O'Keeffe, 'Concepts of "castle"', 77–8.
86 Brady, 'Political women and reform', 70.
87 Leask, *Irish castles*, pp 91–2.
88 McAuliffe, 'The lady in the tower', p. 156.
89 Ibid., p. 161.
90 Nicholls, 'Irishwomen and property', p. 19.
91 Manning, 'Revealing a private inscription', 25–6.
92 Fitzgerald, 'Notes on Sir John MacCoghlan', 225–6; Manning, 'Revealing a private inscription', 25.
93 Gilchrist, *Gender and archaeology*, p. 125.
94 Mac Cuarta, 'De Renzy's letters', p. 171.
95 There is a similar triskele stone in Trim, Co. Meath: Michael Potterton, *Medieval Trim: history and archaeology* (Dublin, 2005), p. 412.
96 Manning, 'Revealing a private inscription', 26; Ronnes, 'Study of date-and-initial stones', p. 270.
97 Johnson, *Behind the castle gate*, pp 88–9.
98 Gilchrist, *Gender and archaeology*, p. 144.
99 O'Keeffe, 'Concepts of "castle"', 77–8.
100 Donnelly, 'Tower houses in Limerick', pp 321–2, 326–8; McNeill, *Castles in Ireland*, pp 226–7.
101 Kenneth Nicholls, *Gaelic and gaelicised Ireland in the Middle Ages* (Dublin, 1972), p. 33.
102 Loeber, 'Architectural history', p. 309.
103 Ibid.
104 Johnson, *Behind the castle gate*, p. 125.
105 Edwards, 'Violence in sixteenth-century Ireland', p. 41.

106 Loeber, 'Architectural history', p. 308.
107 Kerrigan, 'Castles and fortifications', p. 412.
108 Cooke, *History of Birr*, pp 242–3.
109 Manning, 'Irish tower houses', 21.
110 Colm J. Donnelly, 'Passage or barrier? Communication between bawn and tower house in late medieval Ireland: the evidence from County Limerick', *Château Gaillard*, 21 (2004), 57–64 at 59–60, fig. 3.
111 Donnelly, 'Passage or barrier?', 60.
112 Chinnery, 'Barryscourt refurbished', p. 198.
113 Ringforts are generally considered to be the defended homesteads of the nobility and well-to-do farming classes of the second half of the first millennium AD.
114 Barry Raftery, 'The medieval settlement at Rathgall, County Wicklow' in Manning (ed.), *From ringforts to fortified houses* (2007), pp 95–106 at p. 99; T.E. McNeill, 'Excavations at Doonbought Fort, County Antrim', *UJA*, 40 (1977), 63–84.

Chapter 6. The fortified house: a colonial bastion?

1 Niall McCullough, *Palimpsest: change in the Irish building tradition* (Dublin, 1994), p. 57.
2 Girouard, *Life in the English country house*, p. 2.
3 P.M. Kerrigan, *Castles and fortifications in Ireland, 1485–1945* (Cork, 1995), p. 65; Leask, *Irish castles*, p. 129.
4 Craig, *Architecture of Ireland*, p. 133.
5 Ibid.
6 Sharon Weadick, 'How popular were fortified houses in Irish castle building history? A look at their numbers in the archaeological record and distribution patterns' in Lyttleton and Rynne (eds), *Plantation Ireland* (2009), pp 61–85 at p. 78.
7 McKean, *Scottish Chateau*, p. 16.
8 Klingelhöfer, 'Architecture of empire', p. 110; Leask, 'Early seventeenth-century houses', p. 243; Sweetman, *Medieval castles*, p. 175; Waterman, 'Some Irish seventeenth-century houses', p. 260.
9 Craig, *Architecture of Ireland*, p. 117.
10 Ibid., p. 123.
11 T.C. Barnard, 'The political, material and mental culture of the Cork settlers, *c.*1650–1700' in Patrick O'Flanagan and C.G. Buttimer (eds), *Cork, history and society: interdisciplinary essays on the history of an Irish county* (Dublin, 1993), pp 309–65 at p. 323.
12 Nicholas Cooper, *Houses of the gentry, 1480–1680* (New Haven, CT, 1999), p. 34, fig. 22; Girouard, *Robert Smythson*, pp 101, 224–7; Colin Platt, *The great rebuildings of Tudor and Stuart England: revolutions in architectural taste* (London, 1994), p. 97; Waterman, 'Some Irish seventeenth-century houses', p. 259.
13 David Newman Johnson, 'Portumna Castle: a little-known early survey and some observations' in John Bradley (ed.), *Settlement and society in medieval Ireland: studies presented to F.X. Martin OSA* (Kilkenny, 1988), pp 477–503 at p. 483; Platt, *Great rebuildings*, p. 98.

14 Waterman, 'Some Irish seventeenth-century houses', pp 262–3; Loeber and Reeves-Smyth, 'Lord Audley's building schemes', pp 94–7; Breen, *Dunluce Castle*, p. 103.
15 E.M. Jope, 'Scottish influences in the north of Ireland: castles with Scottish features, 1580–1640', *UJA*, 14 (1951), 31–47 at 33; Kerrigan, *Castles and fortifications*, p. 71.
16 Mac Cuarta, 'Newcomers in the midlands', p. 154.
17 Craig, *Architecture of Ireland*, pp 122–3.
18 Mac Cuarta, 'Newcomers in the midlands', p. 118.
19 Craig, *Architecture of Ireland*, pp 122–3; Jope, 'Scottish influences', 38.
20 Klingelhöfer, *Castles and colonists*, pp 46, 56; idem, 'Tudor overseas fortifications: a review and typology' in Eric Klingelhofer (ed.), *First forts: essays on the archaeology of proto-colonial fortifications* (Leiden, 2010), pp 65–83 at p. 73.
21 Craig, *Architecture of Ireland*, pp 147–8.
22 Craig, *Architecture of Ireland*, p. 147; J.P. Mallory and T.E. McNeill, *The archaeology of Ulster from colonization to plantation* (Belfast, 1991), p. 321.
23 Anon., *Historic monuments of Northern Ireland*, pp 59, 121–2; Donnelly, 'Archaeology of Ulster Plantation', p. 41; Waterman, 'Some Irish seventeenth-century houses', p. 262; Bill Wilsdon, *Plantation castles on the Erne* (Dublin, 2010), pp 114–15.
24 Craig, *Architecture of Ireland*, p. 148; Rolf Loeber, 'Irish country houses and castles of the late Caroline period: an unremembered past recaptured', *Quarterly Bulletin of the Irish Georgian Society*, 6:1/2 (1973), 1–69 at 4.
25 Jane Fenlon, 'Some early seventeenth-century building accounts in Ireland', *Irish Architectural and Decorative Studies*, 1 (1998), 84–99 at 90.
26 James A. Tuck and Barry Gaulton, 'Archaeology at Ferryland, 1998–2000', *Avalon Chronicles*, 6 (2001), 89–106.
27 Garry Wheeler Stone, 'St John's: archaeological questions and answers', *Maryland Historical Magazine*, 69:2 (1974), 146–68 at 155; idem, 'St Maries Citty corporate artifact', *Maryland Archaeology*, 26:1/2 (1990), 4–18 at 5.
28 Atkinson, 'Plantation of Ely O'Carroll', p. 47; Mac Cuarta, 'Newcomers in the midlands', pp 94–5.
29 Johnson, *Behind the castle gate*, p. 11.
30 O'Keeffe, 'Concepts of "castle"', 73.
31 Michael MacCarthy-Morrogh, 'The English presence in early seventeenth-century Munster' in Brady and Gillespie (eds), *Natives and newcomers* (1986), pp 171–90 at p. 182.
32 J.T. Gilbert (ed.), 'A contemporary history of affairs in Ireland, from 1641 to 1652', *Irish Archaeological and Celtic Society*, 3:2 (1880), 221.
33 Fenlon, 'Early seventeenth-century building accounts', 87; Mac Cuarta, 'Newcomers in the midlands', p. 159.
34 Birr Castle MS A/9, 16 January 1642 [*recte* 1643]; Birr Castle MS A/17, 1668; Birr Castle MS D 261 (O/2). The latter is a photostat of a map of Birr Castle and defences *c*.1691 held in the papers of George Clarke, Worcester College Oxford, MS 206.
35 TCD, MS 814, fo. 86; Gilbert, 'Contemporary history', 221; Birr Castle MS A/24, 11–12.

36 Maurice Craig, *Classic Irish houses of the middle size* (London and New York, 1976), p. 18.
37 Tadhg O'Keeffe, 'Barryscourt Castle and the Irish tower house' in Ludlow and Jameson (eds), *The Barryscourt Lectures* (2004), pp 3–31 at p. 18; D'Alton, 'Architecture of Leix and Offaly plantations', p. 282.
38 Craig, *Classic Irish houses*, p. 4.
39 Craig, *Architecture of Ireland*, p. 134.
40 Craig, *Classic Irish houses*, p. 7; Waterman, 'Some Irish seventeenth-century houses', p. 256.
41 Tadhg O'Keeffe, 'Plantation-era great houses in Munster: a note on Sir Walter Raleigh's house and its context' in Herron and Potterton (eds), *Ireland in the Renaissance* (2007), pp 274–88 at pp 277–8; Tadhg O'Keeffe and Sinéad Quirke, 'A house at the birth of modernity: Ightermurragh Castle, Co. Cork' in Lyttleton and Rynne (eds), *Plantation Ireland* (2009), pp 86–112 at pp 108–9.
42 Barnard, *Making the grand figure*, p. 84.
43 Ibid., pp 84, 96.
44 J.A. Delle, '"A good and easy speculation"', 13.
45 Henry M. Miller, 'The archaeology of colonial encounters along Chesapeake Bay: an overview', *Journal of American Archaeology*, 23 (2004/5), 231–90 at 247.
46 Miller, 'Archaeology of colonial encounters', 247–51.
47 O'Keeffe, 'Space, place, *habitus*', 76.
48 Ibid., 88.
49 O'Brien and Sweetman, *Archaeological inventory*, p. 160.
50 De Breffny and Ffolliott, *Houses of Ireland*, p. 37.
51 Chinnery, 'Barryscourt refurbished', p. 195.
52 Jean Farrelly, 'Decorative render in the late sixteenth/early seventeenth century' in Manning (ed.), *From ringforts to fortified houses* (2007), pp 237–60; Leask, 'Early seventeenth-century houses', p. 248; Loeber, 'Warfare and architecture in Laois', pp 396–7.
53 Terence Reeves-Smyth, 'Community to privacy: late Tudor and Jacobean manorial architecture in Ireland, 1560–1640' in Horning et al. (eds), *The post-medieval archaeology of Ireland* (2007), pp 289–326 at pp 296, 298.
54 O'Keeffe and Quirke, 'Ightermurragh Castle', p. 107.
55 Matthew Johnson, *An archaeology of capitalism* (Oxford, 1996), p. 170.
56 Girouard, *Life in the English country house*, p. 88; idem, *Robert Smythson*, p. 59.
57 Breffny and Ffolliott, *Houses of Ireland*, p. 44.
58 Ibid., p. 34
59 Girouard, *Life in the English country house*, p. 93; Reeves-Smyth, 'Community to privacy', p. 305.
60 Girouard, *Life in the English country house*, pp 91–3.
61 Jane Fenlon, 'Portumna: a great, many-windowed and gabled house' in Jane Fenlon (ed.), *Clanricard's Castle: Portumna House, Co. Galway* (Dublin, 2012), pp 49–82 at

pp 63–5, figs 4.15–18; idem, 'Moving towards the formal house', 156–7, fig. 3; Newman Johnson, 'Portumna Castle', pp 485–8, figs 24:2–5.

62 A.J. Fletcher, *Drama, performance and polity in pre-Cromwellian Ireland* (Toronto, 2000), p. 223.

63 Newman Johnson, 'Portumna Castle', p. 479.

64 Jane Fenlon, '"They say I build up to the sky": Thomas Wentworth, Jigginstown House and Dublin Castle' in Herron and Potterton (eds), *Dublin and the Pale in the Renaissance* (2011), pp 207–23 at p. 210.

65 Girouard, *Life in the English country house*, p. 94.

66 Ibid., p. 99.

67 Barnard, *Making the grand figure*, p. 83.

68 Mark Samuel, 'Coppinger's Court: a document in stone', *JCHAS*, 89 (1984), 58–76 at 64, fig. 3.

69 Fenlon, 'Moving towards the formal house', 156; idem, 'Portumna', p. 66.

70 Girouard, *Life in the English country house*, pp 103–4.

71 Jane Fenlon, 'The decorative plasterwork at Ormond Castle: a unique survival', *Architectural History*, 41 (1998), 67–81 at 71–2; Girouard, *Life in the English country house*, p. 104.

72 Pollock, 'Bawn exposed', pp 162–4, figs 13–15.

73 Nuala Cullen, 'Women and the preparation of food in eighteenth-century Ireland' in MacCurtain and O'Dowd (eds), *Women in early modern Ireland* (1991), pp 265–75 at p. 266; Reeves-Smyth, 'Community to privacy', p. 311.

74 Fenlon, 'Early seventeenth-century building accounts'; idem, *Goods and chattels*; Reeves-Smyth, 'Community to privacy', p. 311.

75 Maurice Craig and John O'Connell, 'Rath Reagh Church' in Harman Murtagh (ed.), *Irish midland studies: essays in commemoration of N.W. English* (Athlone, 1980), pp 136–41; Loeber, 'Ulster and midland plantations, pt II', p. 120.

76 Barnard, *Making the grand figure*, p. 87.

77 Newman Johnson, 'Portumna Castle', p. 492.

78 Barnard, *Making the grand figure*, pp 88, 152; Breffny and Ffolliott, *Houses of Ireland*, p. 34; Reeves-Smyth, 'Community to privacy', p. 311.

79 Fenlon, 'Decorative plasterwork', 78–9, n. 36.

80 Joseph Nunan, 'The fortified houses of County Cork: origin, form, fabric, function and social use of space' (MA, UCC, 2005), p. 54, fig. 15.

81 Barnard, *Making the grand figure*, pp 85–6; Girouard, *Life in the English country house*, pp 91–3.

82 Cooper, *Houses of the gentry*, p. 11.

83 Cooke, *History of Birr*, p. 179.

84 Offaly Historical and Archaeological Society, Magan Collection, vol. 4.062.

85 Robert Hedges Dunne, 'Proceedings', *Journal of the Royal Historical and Archaeological Association of Ireland*, 3 (1874–5), 161–5 at 163. The date stone was located in a shed in nearby Ferbane twenty years ago: Rolf Loeber, pers. comm.

86 Offaly Historical and Archaeological Society, Magan Collection, vol. 4.062.

87 Brannon, 'Excavations at Brackfield Bawn', 13–14; Donnelly, 'Archaeology of Ulster Plantation', pp 46–7.
88 Breffny and Ffolliott, *Houses of Ireland*, p. 51.
89 Jope, 'Fortification to architecture', 112.
90 William Roulston, 'Seventeenth-century manors in the barony of Strabane' in James Lyttleton and Tadhg O'Keeffe (eds), *The manor in medieval and early modern Ireland* (Dublin, 2005), pp 160–87 at p. 172.
91 Hugh Dixon, *An introduction to Ulster architecture* (Belfast, 1975), p. 20.
92 Breen, *Lordship of O'Sullivan Beare*, p. 154; Mallory and McNeill, *Archaeology of Ulster*, pp 312–13, fig. 8.16; Wilsdon, *Plantation castles*, p. 113.
93 Terence Reeves-Smyth, 'Irish gardens and gardening before Cromwell' in Ludlow and Jameson (eds), *The Barryscourt Lectures* (2004), pp 99–143 at p. 104.
94 Brian Shanahan, 'The manor in east County Wicklow' in Lyttleton and O'Keeffe (eds), *The manor in Ireland* (2005), pp 132–59 at pp 153–4.
95 Tom Williamson, *Polite landscapes, gardens and society in eighteenth-century England* (Baltimore, MD, 1995), p. 19.
96 Paul Everson and Tom Williamson, 'Gardens and designed landscapes' in Paul Everson and Tom Williamson (eds), *The archaeology of landscape, studies presented to Christopher Taylor* (Manchester, 1998), pp 139–65 at p. 146.
97 Johnson, *Archaeology of capitalism*, pp 140–1.
98 Rolf Loeber, 'Early Classicism in Ireland: architecture before the Georgian era', *Architectural History*, 22 (1979), 49–63 at 55.
99 Reeves-Smyth, 'Irish gardens', p. 104.
100 Ibid., p. 124.
101 Platt, *Great rebuildings*, pp 86, 166; Williamson, *Polite landscapes*, p. 31.
102 Reeves-Smyth, 'Irish gardens', p. 104.
103 Breen, *Lordship of O'Sullivan Beare*, pp 154–5.
104 R.W. Brunskill, *Traditional farm buildings of Britain* (London, 1982), pp 80–1, figs 56–7.
105 Christina Hardyment, *Behind the scenes: domestic arrangements in historic houses* (London, 1997), pp 78–83; Ross Samson, 'The rise and fall of tower-houses in post-Reformation Scotland' in Ross Samson (ed.), *The social archaeology of houses* (Edinburgh, 1990), pp 197–243 at p. 213; Williamson, *Polite landscapes*, pp 32–3.
106 Reeves-Smyth, 'Irish gardens', p. 125.
107 Ibid., pp 127–8.
108 Anon., *Historic monuments of Northern Ireland*, p. 122; Mallory and McNeill, *Archaeology of Ulster*, p. 312, fig. 8.16.
109 E.P. Shirley et al., 'Extracts from the journal of Thomas Dineley, esquire, giving some account of his visit to Ireland in the reign of Charles II', *Journal of the Kilkenny and South-East of Ireland Archaeological Society*, 6 (1867), 73–91 at 81.
110 Girouard, *Life in the English country house*, p. 86.
111 John Bradley, 'Sir Henry Sidney's bridge at Athlone, 1566–7' in Herron and Potterton (eds), *Ireland in the Renaissance* (2007), pp 173–94 at p. 180.

112 Offaly Historical and Archaeological Society, Magan Collection, vol. 4.061.
113 Reeves-Smyth, 'Community to privacy', p. 313; Loeber, 'Ulster and midland plantations, pt II', p. 118.
114 Michael J. Moore, *Archaeological inventory of County Leitrim* (Dublin, 2003), p. 213; Nunan, 'Fortified houses of County Cork', p. 75; Weadick, 'How popular were fortified houses', p. 69, table 4.3; Eamonn Cotter, 'Dún na Séad Castle: an early seventeenth-century house at Baltimore, Co. Cork', JCHAS, 115 (2010), 31–54 at 34.
115 Girouard, *Robert Smythson*, p. 2.
116 Ibid., p. 18.
117 Ibid., p. 9.
118 Margaret Murphy and Michael Potterton, *The Dublin region in the Middle Ages: settlement, land-use and economy* (Dublin, 2010), p. 250, fig. 7.52.
119 John Summerson, *Architecture in Britain, 1530 to 1830* (New Haven, CT, 1993), pp 140–1.
120 Deborah Howard, *Scottish architecture: reformation to restoration, 1560–1660* (Edinburgh, 1995), p. 2; Donnelly, 'Decline and adaptation', p. 10.
121 Johnson, *Archaeology of capitalism*, p. 163.
122 Reeves-Smyth, 'Irish gardens', pp 128, 143, n. 137.
123 Loeber, 'Early Classicism in Ireland', 55.
124 Barnard, *Making the grand figure*, p. 206.
125 Mary O'Dowd, 'Women and war in Ireland in the 1640s' in MacCurtain and O'Dowd (eds), *Women in early modern Ireland* (1991), pp 91–111 at p. 92.
126 O'Dowd, 'Women and war', pp 92–3.
127 Margaret MacCurtain, 'Women, education and learning in early modern Ireland' in MacCurtain and O'Dowd (eds), *Women in early modern Ireland* (1991), pp 160–78 at pp 167, 173.
128 Phil Kilroy, 'Women and the Reformation in seventeenth-century Ireland' in MacCurtain and O'Dowd (eds), *Women in early modern Ireland* (1991), pp 179–96 at p. 190.
129 Gilchrist, *Gender and archaeology*, pp 138–9.
130 Jope, 'Scottish influences', 38.
131 Loeber, 'Ulster and midland plantations, pt II, p. 122.
132 Charles T. Hodges, 'Private fortifications in seventeenth-century Virginia: a study of six representative works' in Theodore R. Reinhart and Dennis J. Pogue (eds), *The archaeology of seventeenth-century Virginia* (Richmond, VA, 1993), pp 183–221 at p. 183.
133 Ibid., pp 200–1, fig. 5.
134 Ibid., pp 203–5, fig. 6.
135 Jope, 'Fortification to architecture', 122.
136 Kerrigan, *Castles and fortifications*, p. 65.
137 McKean, *Scottish Chateau*, pp 50–1.

138 Rolf Loeber and Geoffrey Parker, 'The military revolution in seventeenth-century Ireland' in J.H. Ohlmeyer (ed.), *Ireland from independence to occupation, 1641–1660* (Cambridge, 1995), pp 66–88 at p. 73.

Chapter 7. Houses in early modern Offaly

1 Richard Morrice, *The buildings of Britain, Stuart and Baroque* (London, 1982), p. 34.
2 Harman Murtagh, 'Jacobite Offaly, 1689–91' in Nolan and O'Neill (eds), *Offaly, history and society* (1998), pp 319–38 at p. 319.
3 Murtagh, 'Jacobite Offaly', p. 319.
4 Loeber, 'Ulster and midland plantations, pt II', pp 114–15.
5 Ibid., p. 111; Andor Gomme and Alison Maguire, *Design and plan in the country house, from castle donjons to Palladian boxes* (New Haven, CT, 2008), pp 118–19, plan 61, fig. 152.
6 Terence Reeves-Smyth, 'Demesnes' in Aalen et al. (eds), *Atlas of the Irish rural landscape* (2011), pp 278–86 at p. 278, fig. 1; D'Alton, 'Architecture of Leix and Offaly plantations', pp 160–4, 287–9.
7 Alan Gailey, *Rural houses of the north of Ireland* (Edinburgh, 1984), p. 60; Philip Robinson, 'Vernacular housing in Ulster in the seventeenth century', *Ulster Folklife*, 25 (1979), 1–28 at 21.
8 Rory Sherlock, 'Bunratty Castle', p. 211, fig. 5.
9 Dixon, *Ulster architecture*, p. 29; William Roulston, 'Domestic architecture in Ireland, 1640–1740' in Horning et al. (eds), *The post-medieval archaeology of Ireland* (2007), pp 327–44 at p. 333.
10 Colin Rynne, pers. comm.
11 Fenlon, 'Early seventeenth-century building accounts', 89–90, 96.
12 Loeber, 'Irish country houses', 36.
13 Farrelly, 'Decorative render', pp 237–60.
14 Loeber, 'Irish country houses', 7, 28.
15 Summerson, *Architecture in Britain*, p. 144.
16 Roger Stalley (ed.), *Daniel Grose (c.1766–1838): The antiquities of Ireland, a supplement to Francis Grose* (Dublin, 1991), p. 131.
17 Loeber, 'Irish country houses', 33; Roulston, 'Domestic architecture in Ireland', pp 329–30.
18 Philip Dwyer, *The diocese of Killaloe, from the reformation to the close of the eighteenth century* (Dublin, 1878), p. 376.
19 Gailey, *Rural houses*, p. 107; Robinson, 'Vernacular housing', 22; idem, 'From thatch to slate: innovations in roof-covering materials for traditional houses in Ulster', *Ulster Folklife*, 31 (1985), 21–35 at 22–4.
20 Craig, *Architecture of Ireland*, p. 329, n. 24; Kerrigan, 'Castles and fortifications', p. 431.
21 Reeves-Smyth, 'Community to privacy', p. 298.
22 Barnard, *Making the grand figure*, p. 84.
23 Loeber, 'Irish country houses', 4; idem, 'Early Irish architectural sketches from the Perceval/Egmont collection' in Agnes Bernelle (ed.), *Decantations, a tribute to Maurice Craig* (Dublin, 1992), pp 110–20 at p. 110.

24 Barnard, *Making the grand figure*, p. 57; Jope, 'Fortification to architecture', 98; Leask, *Irish castles*, p. 150.
25 Loeber, 'Early classicism in Ireland', 49.
26 Loeber, 'Irish country houses', 25–7.
27 William J. Smyth, 'Society and settlement in seventeenth-century Ireland: the evidence of the "1659 Census"' in William J. Smyth and Kevin Whelan (eds), *Common ground: essays on the historical geography of Ireland* (Cork, 1988), pp 55–83 at pp 56 and 60.
28 Breffny and Ffolliott, *Houses of Ireland*, pp 64–5.
29 Bradley et al., 'Offaly urban archaeology', p. 26.
30 Breffny and Ffolliott, *Houses of Ireland*, p. 78.
31 O'Brien and Sweetman, *Archaeological inventory*, pp 173–4.
32 Craig, *Architecture of Ireland*, p. 329, n. 24.
33 Loeber, 'Early classicism in Ireland', 59.
34 Craig, *Architecture of Ireland*, p. 177.
35 Colin Rynne, pers. comm.
36 Craig, *Classic Irish houses*, p. 5; Rolf Loeber and Kevin Whelan, 'An early eighteenth-century house: Clonegal Rectory, County Carlow', *Journal of the Wexford Historical Society*, 13 (1990–1), 135–41.
37 Jope, 'Fortification to architecture', 119.
38 O'Brien and Sweetman, *Archaeological inventory*, p. 174.
39 Ibid., pp 172–7.
40 Colin Rynne, pers. comm.; see also John Feehan, *The landscape of Slieve Bloom: a study of its natural and human heritage* (Dublin, 1979), pp 178–9; Sheehy, 'Architecture in Offaly', 12–13, fig. 3.
41 Johnson, *Archaeology of capitalism*, pp 32, 140.
42 Cooper, *Houses of the gentry*, p. 9.
43 Johnson, *Behind the castle gate*, p. 12.
44 Summerson, *Architecture in Britain*, p. 75.
45 Craig, *Architecture of Ireland*, p. 329, n. 24.
46 Girouard, *Life in the English country house*, p. 129.
47 Ibid., pp 126, 129–30; Williamson, *Polite landscapes*, p. 27.
48 Girouard, *Life in the English country house*, p. 145.
49 Craig, *Architecture of Ireland*, pp 138–9, fig. 106; Fenlon, 'Moving towards the formal house', 157–9.
50 Fenlon, '"They say I build up to the sky"', p. 214.
51 Fenlon, 'Moving towards the formal house', 165–6
52 Craig, *Architecture of Ireland*, p. 141, fig. 108; Loeber, 'Irish architectural sketches', p. 119, pl. 6.
53 Barnard, *Making the grand figure*, p. 67, figs 15–16.
54 Loeber, 'Irish country houses', 38.
55 Morrice, *Buildings of Britain*, p. 17.
56 Barnard, 'Culture of the Cork settlers', p. 310; idem, *Making the grand figure*, p. 25.
57 Jope, 'Fortification to architecture', 104, 119.

58 Ibid., 119; Leask, 'Early seventeenth-century houses', p. 248; Roulston, 'Domestic architecture in Ireland', pp 329–30.
59 Colin Rynne, pers. comm.
60 Girouard, *Life in the English country house*, p. 123; Morrice, *Buildings of Britain*, p. 28.
61 Johnson, *Archaeology of capitalism*, p. 143; Platt, *Great rebuildings*, p. 41.
62 Barnard, *Making the grand figure*, p. 54.
63 Johnson, *Archaeology of capitalism*, pp 82–3.
64 Girouard, *Life in the English country house*, pp 136–7.
65 Ibid., p. 143.
66 Johnson, *Archaeology of capitalism*, p. 171.
67 Matthew Johnson, 'Rethinking houses, rethinking transitions: of vernacular architecture, ordinary people and everyday culture' in David Gaimster and Paul Stamper (eds), *The age of transition: the archaeology of English culture, 1400–1600* (Oxford, 1997), pp 145–55 at p. 146.
68 Loeber, 'Irish country houses', 42.
69 Barnard, 'Culture of Cork settlers', pp 323–4.
70 Barnard, *Making the grand figure*, p. 92.
71 Craig, *Architecture of Ireland*, pp 145–6; E.P. Shirley, 'Extracts from the journal of Thomas Dineley, esquire, giving some account of his visit to Ireland in the reign of Charles II', *Journal of the Kilkenny and South-East of Ireland Archaeological Society*, 5 (1864–6), 268–90 at 272, n. 3.
72 Ibid., 272.
73 Ibid.
74 Johnson, *Archaeology of capitalism*, p. 145.
75 Barnard, *Making the grand figure*, p. 197.
76 Loeber, 'Irish country houses', 47; James Lyttleton, 'Rathcline Castle: an archaeology of plantation in Co. Longford' in Martin Morris and Fergus O'Ferrall (eds), *Longford, history and society: interdisciplinary essays on the history of an Irish county* (Dublin, 2010), pp 135–59.
77 Williamson, *Polite landscapes*, pp 33–4.
78 O'Brien and Sweetman, *Archaeological inventory*, pp 165–6.
79 Loeber, 'Irish country houses', 36.
80 Richard Muir, *Approaches to landscape* (Lanham, MD, 1999), pp 156–7.
81 Barnard, *Making the grand figure*, p. 189.
82 Charles E. Orser, 'Symbolic violence and landscape pedagogy: an illustration from the Irish countryside', *Historical Archaeology*, 40:2 (2006), 28–44.
83 Everson and Williamson, 'Gardens and designed landscapes', pp 150–2; Williamson, *Polite landscapes*, p. 35.
84 Howard, *Scottish architecture*, p. 97.
85 Johnson, *English houses*, p. 61.
86 Miller, 'Archaeology of colonial encounters', 256.
87 R.M. Cleary, 'Drumlummin, Co. Tipperary' in R.M. Cleary, M.F. Hurley and E.A. Twohig (eds), *Archaeological investigations on the Cork–Dublin gas pipeline (1981–82)* (Cork, 1987), pp 116–45.

88 Breen, *Lordship of O'Sullivan Beare*, pp 167–70; Frank Coyne and Tracy Collins, *Excavation of a post-medieval settlement at Rough Point, Killybegs, County Donegal* (Limerick, 2004); Horning, 'Dwelling houses in old Irish barbarous manner'; Klingelhöfer, 'Elizabethan settlements (pt 1)'; idem, 'Elizabethan settlements (pt 2)'; idem, *Castles and colonists*, pp 24–5.
89 James Lyttleton, 'Natives and newcomers: plantation-era archaeology on Irish road schemes' in Bernice Kelly, Niall Roycroft and Michael Stanley (eds), *Encounters between peoples* (Dublin, 2012), pp 77–92 at pp 78–83.
90 Johnson, *Archaeology of capitalism*, p. 33.
91 Dixon, *Ulster architecture*, p 30.
92 Kevin Danaher, *Ireland's vernacular architecture* (2nd ed., Cork, 1978), p. 10.
93 Summerson, *Architecture in Britain*, p. 101.
94 Johnson, *English houses*, p. 12.
95 Desmond McCourt and E. Estyn Evans, 'A late seventeenth-century farmhouse at Shantallow, near Londonderry', *Ulster Folklife*, 14 (1968), 14–23 at 14.
96 Gailey, *Rural houses*, p. 230.
97 Dennis Pogue, *King's Reach and seventeenth-century plantation life* (Annapolis, MD, 1990), p. 15.
98 M.G.L. Baillie, 'A tree-ring chronology for the dating of Irish post-medieval timbers', *Ulster Folklife*, 20 (1974), 1–23.
99 Craig, *Architecture of Ireland*, p. 134.
100 Danaher, *Ireland's vernacular architecture*, p. 39; Dixon, *Ulster architecture*, p. 31; roof timbers at Berwick Hall were recently dendro-dated to *c.*1682–5: Terence Reeves-Smyth, pers. comm.
101 Robinson, 'Vernacular housing in Ulster', 17, fig. 7; idem, 'From thatch to slate', 22–4.
102 O'Brien and Sweetman, *Archaeological inventory*, p. 170.
103 Gailey, *Rural houses*, p. 186, fig. 207; Philip Robinson, '"English" houses built at Moneymore, County Londonderry, *c.*1615', *Post-medieval Archaeology*, 17 (1983), 47–63 at 52–3, fig. 3.
104 Johnson, *English houses*, pp 163–4.
105 Gailey, *Rural houses*, p. 171.
106 Ibid., pp 186–8, fig. 207; Robinson, '"English" houses built at Moneymore', 52–3, fig. 3.
107 Richard Newman, David Cranstone and Christine Howard-Davis, *The historical archaeology of Britain, c.1540–1900* (Stroud, 2001), p. 57.
108 Johnson, *Archaeology of capitalism*, pp 169–70.
109 Ibid., p. 81.

Chapter 8. Churches, glebe houses and memorials

1 Michael O'Neill, 'The medieval parish churches in County Meath', *JRSAI*, 132 (2002), 1–76; Olivia Horsfall Turner, 'Ruin and reparation: medieval parish churches in seventeenth-century and early eighteenth-century Ossory' in Roger Stalley (ed.), *Irish gothic architecture: construction, decay and reinvention* (Dublin,

2012), pp 161–99; Eamonn Cotter, 'Architectural change and the parish church in post-Reformation Cork' in Elizabeth FitzPatrick and Raymond Gillespie (eds), *The parish in medieval and early modern Ireland* (Dublin, 2006), pp 266–76.

2 Atkinson, 'Plantation of Ely O'Carroll', pp 59–60; Dwyer, *Diocese of Killaloe*, pp 96–7, 130; FitzPatrick and O'Brien, *Medieval churches of Offaly*, p. 113.

3 Clodagh Tait, *Death, burial and commemoration in Ireland, 1550–1650* (Basingstoke, 2002), pp 2–3.

4 Adrian Empey, 'The layperson in the parish: the medieval inheritance, 1169–1536' in Raymond Gillespie and W.G. Neely (eds), *The laity and the Church of Ireland, 1000–2000* (Dublin, 2002), pp 7–48 at p. 27; Felicity Heal, *Reformation in Britain and Ireland* (Oxford, 2005), pp 9–10.

5 Tait, *Death, burial and commemoration*, p. 41.

6 Rolf Loeber, 'Sculptured memorials to the dead in early seventeenth-century Ireland: a survey from *Monumenta Eblanae* and other sources', *PRIA*, 81C (1981), 267–93 at 281.

7 Raymond Gillespie, pers. comm.

8 The seventeenth-century visitations for the dioceses of Meath and Killaloe cover all the parishes in the study area, with the exception of Seir Kieran. The latter parish, although situated within Éile Uí Chearbhaill and landlocked by the diocese of Killaloe, was part of the diocese of Ossory. The Protestant diocese of Clonmacnoise, because of its poverty and alienation of its revenues, was united with the diocese of Meath during the reign of Elizabeth I.

9 Brian de Breffny and George Mott, *The churches and abbeys of Ireland* (London, 1976), p. 106; Rachel Moss, 'Reduce, reuse, recycle: Irish monastic architecture *c*.1540–1640' in Stalley (ed.), *Irish gothic architecture* (2012), pp 115–59 at pp 116–17.

10 FitzPatrick and O'Brien, *Medieval churches of Offaly*, pp 81, 99, 103, 107.

11 Mac Cuarta, 'Newcomers in the midlands', pp 9–10.

12 Carrigan, *History and antiquities of Ossory*, ii, pp 5–6; Venning, 'O'Carrolls of Offaly', p. 195.

13 FitzPatrick and O'Brien, *Medieval churches of Offaly*, p. 81.

14 Paul Cockerham and Amy Louise Harris, 'Kilkenny funeral monuments, 1500–1600: a statistical and analytical account', *PRIA*, 101C (2001), 135–88 at 143–4.

15 FitzPatrick and O'Brien, *Medieval churches of Offaly*, p. 78.

16 Ibid., pp 80–1.

17 Loeber, 'Sculptured memorials', 269; Tait, *Death, burial and commemoration*, p. 66.

18 Colm Lennon, 'The counter-reformation in Ireland, 1542–1641' in Brady and Gillespie (eds), *Natives and newcomers* (1986), pp 75–92 at p. 77; Diarmaid MacCulloch, *Reformation: Europe's house divided, 1490–1700* (London, 2003), pp 396–7.

19 Alan Ford, 'The Protestant Reformation in Ireland' in Brady and Gillespie (eds), *Natives and newcomers* (1986), pp 50–74 at pp 57–8.

20 Lennon, 'Counter-reformation in Ireland', p. 91.

21 Raymond Gillespie, *The sacred in the secular: religious change in Catholic Ireland, 1500–1700* (Colchester, VT, 1993), p. 9.
22 Gillespie, *Sacred in the secular*, p. 14.
23 Raymond Gillespie, *Devoted people: belief and religion in early modern Ireland* (Manchester, 1997), p. 87.
24 Ibid., p. 90.
25 Ibid., p. 91.
26 FitzPatrick and O'Brien, *Medieval churches of Offaly*, p. 5.
27 Gillespie, *Sacred in the secular*, p. 14.
28 Michael Corcoran, 'Challenging narratives: an early modern house at Carstown, Co. Louth' in Herron and Potterton (eds), *Dublin and the Pale in the Renaissance* (2011), pp 125–44 at p. 126, figs 6.1, 6.2.
29 Hugo Blake, Geoff Egan, John Hurst and Elizabeth New, 'From popular devotion to resistance and revival in England: the cult of the Holy Name of Jesus and the Reformation' in David Gaimster and Roberta Gilchrist (eds), *The archaeology of reformation, 1480–1580* (Leeds, 2003), pp 175–203 at pp 190–1, fig. 11; C.J. Donnelly, 'The IHS monogram as a symbol of Catholic resistance in seventeenth-century Ireland', *IJHA*, 9:1 (2005), 37–42 at 39; Newman et al., *Historical archaeology of Britain*, p. 182.
30 Victor Treadwell, *The Irish Commission of 1622: an investigation of the Irish administration, 1615–1622, and its consequences, 1623–1624* (Dublin, 2006), p. 685.
31 Blake et al., 'Holy Name of Jesus and the Reformation', pp 190–2.
32 Mac Cuarta, 'Newcomers in the midlands', p. 163.
33 Alan Ford, *The Protestant Reformation in Ireland, 1590–1641* (2nd ed., Dublin, 1997), pp 73–4.
34 Atkinson, 'Plantation of Ely O'Carroll', pp 50, 56.
35 FitzPatrick and O'Brien, *Medieval churches of Offaly*, p. 117.
36 Ford, *Protestant Reformation in Ireland*, 1590–1641, pp 76–7.
37 Ibid., p. 95.
38 Ibid., pp 117–18
39 Gillespie, *Devoted people*, p. 14.
40 Austin and Thomas, 'Proper study of medieval archaeology: a case study', p. 45; Johnson, *Behind the castle gate*, p. 69; O'Keeffe, 'Space, place, *habitus*', pp 86–9.
41 Sarah Tarlow, 'Reformation and transformation: what happened to Catholic things in a Protestant world?' in Gaimster and Gilchrist (eds), *The archaeology of reformation* (2003), pp 108–21 at p. 111.
42 Gillespie, *Devoted people*, p. 93.
43 Cooke, *History of Birr*, p. 370; Hitchcock, *Midland septs*, pp 241–2; Manning, 'Clonmacnoise Cathedral', p. 83; idem, *Clonmacnoise, Co. Offaly*, p. 16.
44 Ana Dolan, 'The large medieval churches of the dioceses of Leighlin, Ferns and Ossory: a study of adaptation and change', *Irish Architectural and Decorative Studies*, 2 (1999), 26–65 at 43.
45 Gillespie, *Devoted people*, p. 90.
46 Dolan, 'Large medieval churches', 43.

47 Cotter, 'Architectural change in Cork', p. 267; Gillespie, *Devoted people*, p. 93.
48 Dolan, 'Large medieval churches', 43.
49 Craig, *Architecture of Ireland*, pp 113, 148–9.
50 FitzPatrick and O'Brien, *Medieval churches of Offaly*, pp 113–17.
51 Morrice, *Buildings of Britain*, p. 75; Newman et al., *Historical archaeology of Britain*, p. 24.
52 William Roulston, 'The provision, building and architecture of Anglican churches in the north of Ireland, 1600–1740' (PhD, QUB, 2004), p. 238.
53 Newman et al., *Historical archaeology of Britain*, p. 25.
54 Josephine Moran, 'The shattered image: archaeological evidence for painted and stained glass in medieval Ireland' in Moss et al. (eds), *Art and devotion* (2006), pp 121–41 at pp 122–4.
55 David Parsons, *Churches and chapels: investigating places of worship* (2nd ed., York, 1998), p. 46.
56 FitzPatrick and O'Brien, *Medieval churches of Offaly*, pp 132–3, fig. 125.
57 De Breffny and Mott, *Churches and abbeys of Ireland*, pp 110–11.
58 Morton, 'Irish medieval wall painting', pp 323–7.
59 Ibid., pp 314–15.
60 Gillespie, *Devoted people*, p. 93.
61 FitzPatrick and O'Brien, *Medieval churches of Offaly*, p. 114.
62 O'Brien and Sweetman, *Archaeological inventory*, p. 97.
63 C.C. Ellison, 'Bishop Dopping's visitation book, 1682–1685', *Riocht na Midhe*, 6:1 (1975), 3–13 at 7; FitzPatrick and O'Brien, *Medieval churches of Offaly*, p. 115.
64 Dwyer, *Diocese of Killaloe*, p. 96.
65 Atkinson, 'Plantation of Ely O'Carroll', p. 82; Cooke, *History of Birr*, pp 47–8.
66 Roulston, 'Anglican churches in the north of Ireland', p. 97.
67 Ibid., p. 99.
68 Ibid., pp 213–14.
69 Murtagh, 'Jacobite Offaly', pp 331–2.
70 FitzPatrick and O'Brien, *Medieval churches of Offaly*, pp 120–1, fig. 112.
71 Fenlon, 'Early seventeenth-century building accounts', 90.
72 This gateway was reassembled in the present southern façade of Birr Castle sometime in the late eighteenth or early nineteenth century.
73 Cooke, *History of Birr*, p. 45.
74 Roulston, 'Anglican churches in the north of Ireland', pp 222–3.
75 Anon., *Historic monuments of Northern Ireland*, p. 57.
76 Bradley et al., 'Offaly urban archaeology', p. 16; FitzPatrick and O'Brien, *Medieval churches of Offaly*, p. 141, fig. 135.
77 National Archives, London, MPF 1/268(6).
78 Roulston, 'Anglican churches in the north of Ireland', p. 132.
79 Anthony N.B. Garvan, *Architecture and town planning in colonial Connecticut* (New Haven, CT, 1951), pp 38–9, 43–4.

80 John W. Reps, *Tidewater towns: city planning in colonial Virginia and Maryland* (Williamsburg, VA, 1972), p. 43.
81 Helen Bermingham, 'Priests' residences in later medieval Ireland' in FitzPatrick and Gillespie (eds), *The parish in Ireland* (2006), pp 168–85 at p. 170.
82 Bermingham, 'Priests' residences', p. 175; FitzPatrick and O'Brien, *Medieval churches of Offaly*, pp 134–6.
83 Dwyer, *Diocese of Killaloe*, p. 146.
84 Ibid., p. 147.
85 Ibid., p. 239.
86 Brian Mac Cuarta, 'Religious violence against settlers in south Ulster, 1641–2' in Edwards et al. (eds), *Age of atrocity* (2010), pp 154–75 at pp 159–60.
87 Conleth Manning, 'Some early masonry churches and the round tower at Clonmacnoise' in H.A. King (ed.), *Clonmacnoise Studies*, 2 (Dublin, 2003), pp 63–95 at p. 73, ill. 14.
88 O'Brien and Sweetman, *Archaeological inventory*, p. 93.
89 Bermingham, 'Priests' residences', p. 176; FitzPatrick and O'Brien, *Medieval churches of Offaly*, p. 117; Loeber, 'Geographical calendar of landownership in Ely O'Carroll', p. 266; O'Brien and Sweetman, *Archaeological inventory*, p. 175.
90 Craig, *Architecture of Ireland*, p. 133.
91 Barnard, *Making the grand figure*, pp 109–10.
92 Gillespie, *Devoted people*, p. 27.
93 Gillespie, *Sacred in the secular*, p. 15.
94 Gillespie, *Devoted people*, p. 89.
95 Ibid.; Rolf Loeber and Magda Stouthamer-Loeber, 'Kildare Hall, the countess of Kildare's patronage of the Jesuits, and the liturgical setting of Catholic worship in early seventeenth-century Dublin' in FitzPatrick and Gillespie (eds), *The parish in Ireland* (2006), pp 242–65 at pp 256–7.
96 Conleth Manning, 'Clonmacnoise Cathedral: the oldest church in Ireland', *Archaeology Ireland*, 9:4 (1995), 30–3; idem, 'Clonmacnoise Cathedral', p. 84.
97 Manning, 'Clonmacnoise Cathedral', p. 71, ill. 22; J.C. Monahan, *Records relating to the dioceses of Ardagh and Clonmacnoise* (Dublin, 1886), p. 61.
98 C.G. Ó Háinle and Conleth Manning, 'An unrecorded seventeenth-century Clonmacnoise chalice' in King (ed.), *Clonmacnoise Studies*, 2 (2003), pp 167–73 at pp 167, 169.
99 FitzPatrick and O'Brien, *Medieval churches of Offaly*, p. 15; Ó Háinle and Manning, 'Clonmacnoise chalice', p. 169.
100 Tait, *Death, burial and commemoration*, pp 80–1.
101 James Lyttleton, 'Seventeenth-century west Offaly: accommodating the new realities', *History Ireland*, 12:1 (2004), 14–16 at 15–16.
102 Gillespie, *Colonial Ulster*, pp 204–5.
103 Dwyer, *Diocese of Killaloe*, pp 96, 424.
104 FitzPatrick and O'Brien, *Medieval churches of Offaly*, p. 117; O'Brien and Sweetman, *Archaeological inventory*, p. 99.

105 Cotter, 'Architectural change in Cork', pp 267–8; Elizabeth FitzPatrick, 'The material world of the parish' in FitzPatrick and Gillespie (eds), *The parish in Ireland* (2006), pp 62–75 at p. 74; Roulston, 'Anglican churches in the north of Ireland', pp 230–1.
106 Dunne, 'Proceedings', 162.
107 Brendan Ryan, 'The Ferbane Arma Christi', *Offaly Heritage: Journal of the Offaly Historical and Archaeological Society*, 4 (2006), 21–34 at 26.
108 Dunne, 'Proceedings', 163.
109 Sweetman, *Medieval castles*, p. 140, fig. 114; Rachel Moss, 'Continuity and change: the material setting of public worship in the sixteenth-century Pale' in Herron and Potterton (eds), *Dublin and the Pale in the Renaissance* (2011), pp 182–206 at p. 206.
110 McKean, *Scottish chateau*, pp 217–18.
111 Raymond Gillespie, 'The image of death, 1500–1700', *Archaeology Ireland*, 6 (1992), 8–10 at 9; idem, 'Irish funeral monuments and social change, 1500–1700, perceptions of death' in Raymond Gillespie and B.P. Kennedy (eds), *Ireland: art into history* (Dublin, 1994), pp 155–68 at p. 161.
112 Dunne, 'Proceedings', 161–3.
113 FitzPatrick and O'Brien, *Medieval churches of Offaly*, p. 129.
114 Ellison, 'Bishop Dopping's visitation book', 13.
115 Gillespie, *Devoted people*, p. 4.
116 Harold Mytum, 'Archaeological perspectives on external mortuary monuments of plantation Ireland' in Lyttleton and Rynne (eds), *Plantation Ireland* (2009), pp 165–81 at p. 180.
117 Raymond Gillespie, 'Urban parishes in early seventeenth-century Ireland: the case of Dublin' in FitzPatrick and Gillespie (eds), *The parish in Ireland* (2006), pp 228–41 at p. 228.
118 Harold Mytum, *Mortuary monuments and burial grounds of the historic period* (New York, 2004), p. 144.
119 Sterling de Courcy Williams, 'The old graveyards in Durrow parish', *JRSAI*, 27 (1897), 128–49 at 136.
120 Dwyer, *Diocese of Killaloe*, p. 399.
121 Smyth, *Map-making, landscapes and memory*, p. 131.
122 Clodagh Tait, 'Colonising memory: manipulations of death, burial and commemoration in the career of Richard Boyle, first earl of Cork, 1566–1643', *PRIA*, 101 (2001), 107–34 at 127; idem, *Death, burial and commemoration*, pp 39–40; Sarah Tarlow, *Bereavement and commemoration: an archaeology of mortality* (Oxford, 1999), p. 95, citing Nigel Llewellyn, *The art of death: visual culture in the English death ritual, c.1500–c.1800* (London, 1991).
123 Raymond Gillespie, 'Funerals and society in early seventeenth-century Ireland', *JRSAI*, 115 (1985), 86–91 at 90.
124 Gillespie, 'Irish funeral monuments', pp 164–5.
125 Gillespie, *Colonial Ulster*, pp 150–1.
126 Tait, 'Colonising memory', 108; idem, *Death, burial and commemoration*, p. 105.

127 Loeber, 'Sculptured memorials', 272.
128 Ibid.
129 Gillespie, 'Funerals and society', 90.
130 Finbar McCormick, 'Reformation, privatization and the rise of the headstone' in Horning et al. (eds), *The post-medieval archaeology of Ireland* (2007), pp 355–70 at pp 356–7.
131 Tait, *Death, burial and commemoration*, p. 100.
132 Cockerham and Harris, 'Kilkenny funeral monuments', 154.
133 Bradley et al., 'Offaly urban archaeology', pp 16–17; FitzPatrick and O'Brien, *Medieval churches of Offaly*, p. 140, fig. 134.
134 Cockerham and Harris, 'Kilkenny funeral monuments', 160.
135 Walter Fitzgerald, 'Rahan Churchyard', *Journal of the Association for the Preservation of the Memorials of the Dead in Ireland*, 9 (1913–16), 105–6 at 106.
136 Walter Fitzgerald, 'Clonmacnoise burial-ground', *Journal of the Association for the Preservation of the Memorials of the Dead in Ireland*, 6 (1904), 375–82 at 379.
137 Cooper, *Houses of the gentry*, p. 25.
138 Walter Fitzgerald, 'Lynally Churchyard', *Journal of the Irish Memorials Association*, 11 (1921–5), 203.
139 FitzPatrick and O'Brien, *Medieval churches of Offaly*, p. 140.
140 Gillespie, 'Irish funeral monuments', p. 167.
141 Tait, *Death, burial and commemoration*, p. 109.
142 Tarlow, *Bereavement and commemoration*, pp 97–9.
143 Tarlow, 'Reformation and transformation', p. 111.
144 Gillespie, 'Irish funeral monuments', p. 165; Tait, *Death, burial and commemoration*, p. 71.
145 Harold Mytum, 'External mortuary monuments', p. 169.
146 de Courcy Williams, 'Graveyards in Durrow parish', 137; N.W. English, 'The Sir Matthew de Renzi memorial in Athlone', *Journal of the Old Athlone Society*, 2:5 (1978), 1–5 at 3; FitzPatrick and O'Brien, *Medieval churches of Offaly*, pp 141–2, fig. 137.
147 Homan Potterton, *Irish church monuments, 1570–1880* (Belfast, 1975), p. 19, fig. 6.
148 Gillespie, 'Irish funeral monuments', p. 163; John Hunt, *Irish medieval figure sculpture, 1200–1600: a study of Irish tombs with notes on costume and armour* (2 vols, Dublin, 1974), i, p. 112; Loeber, 'Sculptured memorials', 271; William Roulston, 'Seventeenth-century church monuments in west Ulster', *Ulster Local Studies*, 19:1 (1997), 61–79 at 61.
149 Cooke, *History of Birr*, p. 224; Dwyer, *Diocese of Killaloe*, p. 525; FitzPatrick and O'Brien, *Medieval churches of Offaly*, p. 141.
150 Mytum, 'External mortuary monuments', p. 169.
151 Tarlow, 'Reformation and transformation', p. 113.
152 Tarlow, *Bereavement and commemoration*, pp 83–5, fig. 4.3; idem, 'Reformation and transformation', p. 113, fig. 1.
153 Gillespie, 'Irish funeral monuments', p. 155.
154 Roulston, 'Church monuments in west Ulster', 74.

155 Ibid.
156 Ibid., 75.
157 Tait, *Death, burial and commemoration*, pp 7–8, 128–9.
158 Mac Cuarta, 'A planter's funeral, legacies and inventory', 18.
159 Tait, *Death, burial and commemoration*, p. 132.
160 MacCulloch, *Europe's house divided*, p. 394.
161 Ibid.

Chapter 9. Final thoughts: a society transformed

1 Anders Andrén, *Between artifacts and texts: historical archaeology in global perspective* (New York, 1998), p. 3.
2 Siân Jones, *The archaeology of ethnicity: constructing identities in the past and present* (London, 1997), p. 136.
3 Smyth, *Map-making, landscapes and memory*, p. 9.
4 Liam Kennedy, *Colonialism, religion and nationalism in Ireland* (Belfast, 1996), p. 167.
5 Sean Ryder, 'Defining colony and empire in early nineteenth-century Irish nationalism' in Terrence McDonough (ed.), *Was Ireland a colony? economics, politics and culture in nineteenth-century Ireland* (Dublin, 2005), pp 165–85 at pp 165, 178.
6 Kennedy, *Colonialism in Ireland*, p. 175.
7 Gillespie, 'Problems of plantations', p. 45.
8 Smyth, *Map-making, landscapes and memory*, p. 16.
9 Toby Barnard, *Improving Ireland? Projectors, prophets and profiteers, 1641–1786* (Dublin, 2008), pp 39–40.
10 Edwards, 'The escalation of violence in sixteenth-century Ireland', pp 61–2.
11 Lenihan, *Consolidating conquest*, p. 198.
12 Raymond Gillespie, 'Explorers, exploiters and entrepreneurs: early modern Ireland and its context, 1500–1700' in B.J. Graham and L.J. Proudfoot (eds), *An historical geography of Ireland* (London, 1993), pp 123–57 at p. 150; Lenihan, *Consolidating conquest*, p. 207.
13 Bernadette Cunningham, 'Loss and gain: attitudes towards the English language in early modern Ireland' in Mac Cuarta (ed.), *Reshaping Ireland* (2011), pp 163–86 at p. 178.
14 Stephen Howe, *Ireland and empire: colonial legacies in Irish history and culture* (Oxford, 2000), p. 23, citing Thomas Bartlett, '"This famous island set in a Virginian Sea": Ireland in the British Empire, 1690–1801' in P.J. Marshall (ed.), *The Oxford History of the British Empire, vol. 2: the eighteenth century* (Oxford, 1998), pp 253–75 at p. 254.
15 O'Brien and Sweetman, *Archaeological inventory*, pp 157, 159–60.
16 Ibid., p. 157.
17 Cooke, *History of Birr*, p. 222.
18 Ibid., pp 53–4.
19 Ibid., pp 54–5.
20 Jones, *Archaeology of ethnicity*, p. 69.

21 Audrey Horning, '"The root of all vice and bestiality": exploring the cultural role of the alehouse in the Ulster plantation' in Lyttleton and Rynne (eds), *Plantation Ireland* (2009), pp 113–31 at pp 123–4.
22 Feehan and Rosse, *Atlas of Birr*, p. 5.
23 Mac Cuarta, 'Newcomers in the midlands', p. 155.
24 MacCulloch, *Europe's house divided*, p. 394.
25 M.P. Carroll, *Irish pilgrimage, holy wells and popular Catholic devotion* (Baltimore, MD, 1999), p. 19.
26 Quoted in Clarke, 'The Irish economy', p. 174.
27 Ibid., p. 169.
28 Ibid., p. 171.
29 Mac Cuarta, 'De Renzy and Irish reform', p. 115.
30 Smyth, *Map-making, landscapes and memory*, p. 15.
31 Orser, *Historical archaeology*, p. 78.
32 Ibid.
33 O'Conor, *Medieval rural settlement*, p. 96.
34 O'Brien and Sweetman, *Archaeological inventory*, p. 20.
35 Andrew Hadfield, 'Irish colonies and the Americas' in Robert Appelbaum and John Wood Sweet (eds), *Envisioning an English empire: Jamestown and the making of the North Atlantic world* (Philadelphia, 2005), pp 172–91 at p. 174.
36 Howard Mumford Jones, 'The colonial idea in England' in John J. TePaske (ed.), *Three American empires* (New York, 1967), pp 32–55 at p. 42.
37 Quinn, *The Elizabethans and the Irish*, pp 121–2.

Bibliography

Manuscript sources

National Archives, London

MPF 1/268 (6)

Trinity College Dublin

MS 814

Birr Castle, Co. Offaly

MS A/9, 16 Jan. 1642 [*recte* 1643]
MS A/17, 1668
MS A/24, 11–12
MS D261 (O/2)

Offaly Historical and Archaeological Society

Magan Collection, vols 4.061, 4.062.

Printed sources

Aalen, F.H.A., and Kevin Whelan, 'Fields' in Aalen et al. (eds), *Atlas of the Irish rural landscape* (2011), pp 200–11.

Aalen, F.H.A., Kevin Whelan and Matthew Stout (eds), *Atlas of the Irish rural landscape* (2nd ed., Cork, 2011).

Andrén, Anders, *Between artifacts and texts: historical archaeology in global perspective* (New York, 1998).

Andrews, J.H., 'The mapping of Ireland's cultural landscape, 1550–1630' in Duffy, Edwards and FitzPatrick (eds), *Gaelic Ireland* (2001), pp 153–80.

Andrews, J.H., and Rolf Loeber, 'An Elizabethan map of Leix and Offaly: cartography, topography and architecture' in Nolan and O'Neill (eds), *Offaly, history and society* (1998), pp 243–85.

Anon., *Historic monuments of Northern Ireland: an introduction and guide* (6th ed., Belfast, 1983).

Anon., *Inquisitionum in officio rotulorum cancellariæ Hiberniæ assertvatarum repertorium*, 1 (Dublin, 1826).

Atkinson, N.D., 'The plantation of Ely O'Carroll, 1619–1693' (MLitt, TCD, 1957).

Austin, David, 'The "proper study" of medieval archaeology' in Austin and Alcock (eds), *Baltic to the Black Sea* (1990), pp 9–42.

Austin, David, and Julian Thomas, 'The "proper study" of medieval archaeology: a case study' in Austin and Alcock (eds), *Baltic to the Black Sea* (1990), pp 43–78.

Austin, David, and Leslie Alcock (eds), *From the Baltic to the Black Sea: studies in medieval archaeology* (London, 1990).

Baillie, M.G.L., 'A tree-ring chronology for the dating of Irish post-medieval timbers', *Ulster Folklife*, 20 (1974), 1–23.

Barnard, T.C., 'The political, material and mental culture of the Cork settlers, *c.*1650–1700' in Patrick O'Flanagan and C.G. Buttimer (eds), *Cork, history and society: interdisciplinary essays on the history of an Irish county* (Dublin, 1993), pp 309–65.

Barnard, Toby, *Improving Ireland? Projectors, prophets and profiteers, 1641–1786* (Dublin, 2008).

Barnard, Toby, *Making the grand figure: lives and possessions in Ireland, 1641–1770* (New Haven, CT, 2004).

Barry, Terry (ed.), *A history of settlement in Ireland* (London, 2000).

Barry, Terry, 'Rural settlement in medieval Ireland' in Barry (ed.), *Settlement in Ireland* (2000), pp 110–23.

Bartlett, Thomas, '"This famous island set in a Virginian Sea": Ireland in the British Empire, 1690–1801' in P.J. Marshall (ed.), *The Oxford history of the British Empire, 2: the eighteenth century* (Oxford, 1998), pp 253–75.

Beaudry, M.C., L.J. Cook and S.A. Mrozowski, 'Artifacts and active voices: material culture as social discourse' in R.H. McGuire and Robert Paynter (eds), *The archaeology of inequality* (Oxford, 1991), pp 150–91.

Bermingham, Helen, 'Priests' residences in later medieval Ireland' in FitzPatrick and Gillespie (eds), *The parish in Ireland* (2006), pp 168–85.

Blake, Hugo, Geoff Egan, John Hurst and Elizabeth New, 'From popular devotion to resistance and revival in England: the cult of the Holy Name of Jesus and the Reformation' in Gaimster and Gilchrist (eds), *The archaeology of Reformation* (2003), pp 175–203.

Boyce, D.G., *Nationalism in Ireland* (Dublin, 1982).

Bradley, John, 'Sir Henry Sidney's bridge at Athlone, 1566–7' in Herron and Potterton (eds), *Ireland in the Renaissance* (2007), pp 173–94.

Bradley, John, Andrew Halpin and Heather A. King, 'County Offaly: the urban archaeology survey' (unpublished report for the OPW, Dublin, 1986).

Brady, Ciaran, (ed.), *Interpreting Irish history: the debate on historical revisionism, 1938–1994* (Dublin, 1994).

Brady, Ciaran, 'Political women and reform in Tudor Ireland' in MacCurtain and O'Dowd (eds), *Women in early modern Ireland* (1991), pp 69–90.

Brady, Ciaran, 'The road to the View: on the decline of reform thought in Tudor Ireland' in Coughlan (ed.), *Spenser and Ireland* (1989), pp 25–45.

Brady, Ciaran, and Raymond Gillespie (eds), *Natives and newcomers: the making of Irish colonial society, 1534–1641* (Dublin, 1986).

Brannon, N.F., 'Excavations at Brackfield Bawn, County Londonderry', *UJA*, 53 (1990), 8–14.

Breen, Colin, 'The post-medieval coastal landscape of Bantry and Beara, 1580–1850' in Horning et al. (eds), *Post-medieval archaeology of Ireland* (2007), pp 205–19.

Breen, Colin, *An archaeology of southwest Ireland, 1570–1670* (Dublin, 2007).

Breen, Colin, *Dunluce Castle: history and archaeology* (Dublin, 2012).

Breen, Colin, *The Gaelic lordship of the O'Sullivan Beare* (Dublin, 2005).

Brigden, Susan, *New worlds, lost worlds: the rule of the Tudors, 1485–1603* (London, 2000).

Brunskill, R.W., *Traditional buildings of Cumbria, the county of the lakes* (London, 2002).

Brunskill, R.W., *Traditional farm buildings of Britain* (London, 1982).

Butler, Richard, *A treatice of Ireland by John Dymmok* (Kilkenny, 1843), pp 5–90.

Butlin, R.A., 'Land and people, *c.*1600' in T.W. Moody, F.X. Martin and F.J. Byrne (eds), *A new history of Ireland, iii: Early modern Ireland, 1534–1691* (Oxford, 1976), pp 142–67.

Canny, Nicholas, 'Introduction: Spenser and the reform of Ireland' in Coughlan (ed.), *Spenser and Ireland* (1989), pp 9–24.

Canny, Nicholas, 'Migration and opportunity: Britain, Ireland and the New World', *Irish Economic and Social History*, 12 (1985), 7–32.

Canny, Nicholas, 'The ideology of English colonization: from Ireland to America', *William and Mary Quarterly*, 30 (1973), 576–98.

Canny, Nicholas, *From Reformation to Restoration: Ireland, 1534–1660* (Dublin, 1987).

Canny, Nicholas, *Kingdom and colony: Ireland in the Atlantic world, 1560–1800* (Baltimore, MD, 1988).

Canny, Nicholas, *Making Ireland British, 1580–1650* (Oxford, 2001).

Canny, Nicholas, *The Elizabethan conquest of Ireland: a pattern established, 1565–76* (Hassocks, Sussex, 1976).

Carey, Vincent P., '"What's love got to do with it?": gender and Geraldine power on the Pale border' in Potterton and Herron (eds), *Dublin and the Pale in the Renaissance* (2011), pp 93–103.

Carrigan, William, *The history and antiquities of the diocese of Ossory* (4 vols, Dublin, 1905).

Carroll, M.P., *Irish pilgrimage, holy wells and popular Catholic devotion* (Baltimore, MD, 1999).

Cell, Gillian T., 'The Cupids Cove settlement: a case study of the problems of early colonisation' in G.M. Story (ed.), *Early European settlement and exploitation in Atlantic Canada* (St John's, Newfoundland, 1982), pp 97–114.

Chinnery, Victor, 'Barryscourt refurbished, the reinstatement of a late sixteenth-century Irish domestic interior' in Ludlow and Jameson (eds), *Barryscourt Lectures* (2004), pp 177–224.

Clarke, Aidan, 'The Irish economy, 1600–60' in T.W. Moody, F.X. Martin and F.J. Byrne (eds), *A new history of Ireland, iii: Early modern Ireland, 1534–1691* (Oxford, 1976), pp 168–86.

Cleary, R.M., 'Drumlummin, Co. Tipperary' in R.M. Cleary, M.F. Hurley and E.A. Twohig (eds), *Archaeological investigations on the Cork–Dublin gas pipeline (1981–2)* (Cork, 1987), pp 116–45.

Cockerham, Paul, and Amy Louise Harris, 'Kilkenny funeral monuments, 1500–1600: a statistical and analytical account', *PRIA*, 101C (2001), 135–88.

Cooke, T.L., *The early history of the town of Birr, or Parsonstown ...* (Dublin, 1875).

Cooney, Gabriel, 'Building the future on the past: archaeology and the construction of national identity in Ireland' in Margarita Díaz-Andreu and Timothy Champion (eds), *Nationalism and archaeology in Europe* (London, 1996), pp 146–63.

Cooney, Gabriel, 'Theory and practice in Irish archaeology' in Peter J. Ucko (ed.), *Theory in archaeology: a world perspective* (London, 1995), pp 263–77.

Cooper, Nicholas, *Houses of the gentry, 1480–1680* (New Haven, CT, 1999).

Corcoran, Michael, 'Challenging narratives: an early modern house at Carstown, Co. Louth' in Potterton and Herron (eds), *Dublin and the Pale in the Renaissance* (2011), pp 125–44.

Corlett, Christiaan, and Michael Potterton (eds), *Rural settlement in medieval Ireland in the light of recent archaeological excavations* (Dublin, 2009).

Cotter, Eamonn, 'Architectural change and the parish church in post-Reformation Cork' in FitzPatrick and Gillespie (eds), *The parish in Ireland* (2006), pp 266–76.

Cotter, Eamonn, 'Dún na Séad Castle: an early seventeenth-century house at Baltimore, Co. Cork', *JCHAS*, 115 (2010), 31–54.

Coughlan, Patricia, (ed.), *Spenser and Ireland: an interdisciplinary perspective* (Cork, 1989).

Cox, Liam, 'The MacCoghlans of Delvin Eathra', *Irish Genealogist*, 4:6 (1973), 534–46.

Cox, Liam, 'The MacCoghlans of Delvin Eathra', *Irish Genealogist*, 5:1 (1974), 21–32.

Coyne, Frank, and Tracy Collins, *Excavation of a post-medieval settlement at Rough Point, Killybegs, County Donegal* (Limerick, 2004).

Craig, Maurice, and John O'Connell, 'Rath Reagh Church' in Murtagh (ed.), *Irish midland studies* (1980), pp 136–41.

Craig, Maurice, *Classic Irish houses of the middle size* (London and New York, 1976).

Craig, Maurice, *The architecture of Ireland from the earliest times to 1880* (Dublin, 1989).

Cullen, Nuala, 'Women and the preparation of food in eighteenth-century Ireland' in MacCurtain and O'Dowd (eds), *Women in early modern Ireland* (1991), pp 265–75.

Cunningham, Bernadette, 'Loss and gain: attitudes towards the English language in early modern Ireland' in Mac Cuarta (ed.), *Reshaping Ireland* (2011), pp 163–86.

Curl, J.S., *The Londonderry Plantation, 1609–1914: the history, architecture and planning of the estates of the city of London and its livery companies in Ulster* (Chichester, 1986).

Curwen, John F., 'The castles and fortified towers of Cumberland, Westmorland and Lancashire North-of-the-Sands, together with a brief historical account of border warfare', *Cumberland and Westmorland Antiquarian and Archaeological Society Extra Series*, 13 (1913).

D'Alton, Máirtín, 'The architecture of the Leix and Offaly plantations, *c.*1540–1600' (MLitt, TCD, 2009).

Danaher, Kevin, *Ireland's vernacular architecture* (2nd ed., Cork, 1978).

De Breffny, Brian, and George Mott, *The churches and abbeys of Ireland* (London, 1976).

De Breffny, Brian, and Rosemary Ffolliott, *The houses of Ireland* (London, 1975).

De Courcy Williams, Sterling, 'The old graveyards in Durrow parish', *JRSAI*, 27 (1897), 128–49.

Delle, James A., '"A good and easy speculation": spatial conflict, collusion and resistance in late sixteenth-century Munster, Ireland', *IJHA*, 3:1 (1999), 11–35.

Delle, James A., 'Extending Europe's grasp: an archaeological comparison of colonial spatial processes in Ireland and Jamaica' in Geoff Egan and R.L. Michael (eds), *Old and new worlds* (Oxford, 1999), pp 106–16.

Dixon, Hugh, *An introduction to Ulster architecture* (Belfast, 1975).

Dolan, Ana, 'The large medieval churches of the dioceses of Leighlin, Ferns and Ossory: a study of adaptation and change', *Irish Architectural and Decorative Studies*, 2 (1999), 26–65.

Donnelly, Colm J., 'Decline and adaptation: the medieval Irish tower house in early modern County Limerick' in Gunilla Malm (ed.), *Archaeology and buildings*. BAR International Series 930 (Oxford, 2001), pp 7–13.

Donnelly, Colm J., 'Passage or barrier? Communication between bawn and tower house in late medieval Ireland: the evidence from County Limerick', *Château Gaillard*, 21 (2004), 57–64.

Donnelly, Colm J., 'The archaeology of the Ulster Plantation' in Horning et al. (eds), *Post-medieval archaeology of Ireland* (2007), pp 37–50.

Donnelly, Colm J., 'The IHS monogram as a symbol of Catholic resistance in seventeenth-century Ireland', *IJHA*, 9:1 (2005), 37–42.

Donnelly, Colm J., 'Tower houses and late medieval secular settlement in County Limerick' in Duffy et al. (eds), *Gaelic Ireland* (2001), pp 315–28.

Donnelly, Colm J., and Audrey Horning, 'Post-medieval and industrial archaeology in Ireland: an overview', *Antiquity*, 76 (2002), 557–61.

Duffy, P.J., David Edwards and Elizabeth FitzPatrick (eds), *Gaelic Ireland: land, lordship and settlement, c.1250–c.1650* (Dublin, 2001).

Dunlop, R., 'The plantation of Leix and Offaly', *EHR*, 6 (1891), 61–96.

Dunne, Robert Hedges, 'Proceedings', *Journal of the Royal Historical and Archaeological Association of Ireland*, 3 (1874–5), 161–5.

Dwyer, Philip, *The diocese of Killaloe, from the Reformation to the close of the eighteenth century* (Dublin, 1878).

Edwards, David, 'The escalation of violence in sixteenth-century Ireland' in Edwards et al. (eds), *Age of atrocity* (2010), pp 34–78.

Edwards, David, Pádraig Lenihan and Clodagh Tait (eds), *Age of atrocity: violence and political conflict in early modern Ireland* (Dublin, 2010).

Ellison, C.C., 'Bishop Dopping's visitation book, 1682–1685', *Riocht na Midhe*, 6:1 (1975), 3–13.

Elrington, C.R. (ed.), *The whole works of the most Rev. James Ussher DD* (17 vols, Dublin, 1847–64).

Empey, A., 'The layperson in the parish: the medieval inheritance, 1169–1536' in Raymond Gillespie and W.G. Neely (eds), *The laity and the Church of Ireland, 1000–2000* (Dublin, 2002), pp 7–48.

English, N.W., 'The Sir Matthew de Renzi memorial in Athlone', *Journal of the Old Athlone Society*, 2:5 (1978), 1–5.

Everson, Paul, and Tom Williamson, 'Gardens and designed landscapes' in Paul Everson and Tom Williamson (eds), *The archaeology of landscape: studies presented to Christopher Taylor* (Manchester, 1998), pp 139–65.

Fallon, Donal, 'Continuity: the archaeological and documentary evidence for medieval to modern rural settlement and landholding in the townland of Baltrasna, Ratoath, Co. Meath' in Corlett and Potterton (eds), *Rural settlement in medieval Ireland* (2009), pp 79–90.

Farrelly, Jean, 'Decorative render in the late sixteenth/early seventeenth century' in Manning (ed.), *From ringforts to fortified houses* (2007), pp 237–60.

Farrelly, Jean, and Caimin O'Brien, 'Forest glass furnaces in County Offaly', *Archaeology Ireland*, 11:4 (1997), 21–3.

Farrelly, Jean, and Caimin O'Brien, 'Glasshouse, seventeenth-century glasshouse' in Isabel Bennett (ed.), *Excavations 1999: summary accounts of archaeological excavations in Ireland* (Bray, 2000), pp 260–1.

Faulkner, P.A., 'Castle planning in the fourteenth century', *Archaeological Journal*, 120 (1963), 216–35.

Fear Ceall, 'Conntae an Riogh', *JKAS*, 12:8 (1944–5), 353–74.

Fear Ceall, 'Conntae an Riogh', *JKAS*, 13:1 (1946–7), 3–18.

Feehan, John, *Farming in Ireland* (Dublin, 2003).

Feehan, John, *The landscape of Slieve Bloom: a study of its natural and human heritage* (Dublin, 1979).

Feehan, John, and Alison Rosse, *An atlas of Birr* (Dublin, 2005).

Fenlon, Jane, *Goods and chattels: a survey of early household inventories in Ireland* (Dublin, 2003).

Fenlon, Jane, 'Moving towards the formal house: room usage in early modern Ireland', *PRIA*, 111C (2010), 141–68.

Fenlon, Jane, 'Portumna: a great, many-windowed and gabled house' in Jane Fenlon (ed.), *Clanricard's Castle: Portumna House, Co. Galway* (Dublin, 2012), pp 49–82.

Fenlon, Jane, 'Some early seventeenth-century building accounts in Ireland', *Irish Architectural and Decorative Studies*, 1 (1998), 84–99.

Fenlon, Jane, 'The decorative plasterwork at Ormond Castle: a unique survival', *Architectural History*, 41 (1998), 67–81.

Fenlon, Jane, '"They say I build up to the sky": Thomas Wentworth, Jigginstown House and Dublin Castle' in Potterton and Herron (eds), *Dublin and the Pale in the Renaissance* (2011), pp 207–23.

Fennelly, Niall, 'An analysis of the tower houses in a County Offaly study area' (MA, UCC, 1997).

Fitzgerald, Walter, 'Clonmacnoise burial-ground', *Journal of the Association for the Preservation of the Memorials of the Dead in Ireland*, 6 (1904), 375–82.

Fitzgerald, Walter, 'Lynally Churchyard', *Journal of the Irish Memorials Association*, 11 (1921–5), 203.

Fitzgerald, Walter, 'Notes on Sir John MacCoghlan, knight of Cloghan, chief of Delvin–MacCoghlan, who died in 1590', *JRSAI*, 43 (1913), 223–31.

Fitzgerald, Walter, 'Rahan Churchyard', *Journal of the Association for the Preservation of the Memorials of the Dead in Ireland*, 9 (1913–16), 105–6.

FitzPatrick, Elizabeth, 'Parley sites of Ó Néill and Ó Domhnaill in late sixteenth-century Ireland' in David Edwards (ed.), *Regions and rulers in Ireland, 1100–1650* (Dublin, 2004), pp 201–16.

FitzPatrick, Elizabeth, 'The material world of the parish' in FitzPatrick and Gillespie (eds), *The parish in Ireland* (2006), pp 62–75.

FitzPatrick, Elizabeth, *Royal inauguration in Gaelic Ireland,* c.*1100–1600: a cultural landscape study* (Woodbridge, 2004).

FitzPatrick, Elizabeth, and Caimin O'Brien, *The medieval churches of County Offaly* (Dublin, 1998).

FitzPatrick, Elizabeth, and Raymond Gillespie (eds), *The parish in medieval and early modern Ireland: community, territory and building* (Dublin, 2006).

Fitzsimons, Fiona, 'The lordship of O'Connor Faly, 1520–1570' in Nolan and O'Neill (eds), *Offaly, history and society* (1998), pp 207–42.

Fletcher, A.J., *Drama, performance and polity in pre-Cromwellian Ireland* (Toronto, 2000).

Ford, Alan, 'The Protestant Reformation in Ireland' in Brady and Gillespie (eds), *Natives and newcomers* (1986), pp 50–74.

Ford, Alan, *The Protestant Reformation in Ireland, 1590–1641* (2nd ed., Dublin, 1997).

Foster, R.F., *Modern Ireland, 1600–1972* (London, 1988).

Foster, R.F., *Paddy and Mr Punch: connections in Irish and English history* (London, 1993).

Foster, R.F., *The Irish story: telling tales and making it up in Ireland* (London, 2001).

Gailey, Alan, *Rural houses of the north of Ireland* (Edinburgh, 1984).

Gaimster, David, and Roberta Gilchrist (eds), *The archaeology of the Reformation, 1480–1580* (Leeds, 2003).

Garvan, Anthony N.B., *Architecture and town planning in colonial Connecticut* (New Haven, CT, 1951).

Gilbert, J.T. (ed.), 'A contemporary history of affairs in Ireland, from 1641 to 1652', *Irish Archaeological and Celtic Society*, 3:2 (1880).

Gilchrist, Roberta, 'Ambivalent bodies: gender and medieval archaeology' in Jenny Moore and Eleanor Scott (eds), *Invisible people and processes: writing gender and childhood into European archaeology* (London, 1997), pp 42–58.

Gilchrist, Roberta, *Gender and archaeology: contesting the past* (London, 1999).

Gillespie, Raymond, 'Explorers, exploiters and entrepreneurs: early modern Ireland and its context, 1500–1700' in B.J. Graham and L.J. Proudfoot (eds), *An historical geography of Ireland* (London, 1993), pp 123–57.

Gillespie, Raymond, 'Funerals and society in early seventeenth-century Ireland', *JRSAI*, 115 (1985), 86–91.

Gillespie, Raymond, 'Irish funeral monuments and social change, 1500–1700: perceptions of death' in Raymond Gillespie and B.P. Kennedy (eds), *Ireland, art into history* (Dublin, 1994), pp 155–68.

Gillespie, Raymond, 'The image of death, 1500–1700', *Archaeology Ireland*, 6 (1992), 8–10.

Gillespie, Raymond, 'The problems of plantations: material culture and social change in early modern Ireland' in Lyttleton and Rynne (eds), *Plantation Ireland* (2009), pp 43–60.

Gillespie, Raymond, 'Urban parishes in early seventeenth-century Ireland: the case of Dublin' in FitzPatrick and Gillespie (eds), *The parish in Ireland* (2006), pp 228–41.

Gillespie, Raymond, *Colonial Ulster: the settlement of east Ulster, 1600–1641* (Cork, 1985).
Gillespie, Raymond, *Devoted people: belief and religion in early modern Ireland* (Manchester, 1997).
Gillespie, Raymond, *The sacred in the secular: religious change in Catholic Ireland, 1500–1700* (Colchester, VT, 1993).
Girouard, Mark, *Life in the English country house: a social and architectural history* (New Haven, CT, 1978).
Girouard, Mark, *Robert Smythson and the Elizabethan country house* (New Haven, CT, 1983).
Goff, Henry, 'English conquest of an Irish barony: the changing patterns of land ownership in the barony of Scarawalsh, 1540–1640' in Whelan and Nolan (eds), *Wexford, history and society* (1987), pp 122–49.
Gomme, Andor, and Alison Maguire, *Design and plan in the country house: from castle donjons to Palladian boxes* (New Haven, CT, 2008).
Hadfield, Andrew, 'Irish colonies and the Americas' in Robert Appelbaum and John Wood Sweet (eds), *Envisioning an English empire: Jamestown and the making of the north Atlantic world* (Philadelphia, 2005), pp 172–91.
Hall, V.A., 'The documentary and pollen analytical records of the vegetational history of the Irish landscape, AD200–1650', *Peritia*, 14 (2000), 342–69.
Hammond, R.F., and L.E. Brennan, *Soils of Co. Offaly: national soil survey of Ireland* (Dublin, 2003).
Hardyment, Christina, *Behind the scenes: domestic arrangements in historic houses* (London, 1997).
Hayes-McCoy, G.A. (ed.), *Ulster and other Irish maps, c.1600* (Dublin, 1964).
Heal, Felicity, *Reformation in Britain and Ireland* (Oxford, 2005).
Herron, Thomas, and Michael Potterton (eds), *Ireland in the Renaissance, c.1540–1660* (Dublin, 2007).
Hitchcock, F.R.M., *The midland septs and the Pale: an account of the early septs and later settlers of the King's County and of life in the English Pale* (Dublin, 1908).
Hodges, Charles T., 'Private fortifications in seventeenth-century Virginia: a study of six representative works' in Theodore R. Reinhart and Dennis J. Pogue (eds), *The archaeology of seventeenth-century Virginia* (Richmond, VA, 1993), pp 183–221.
Horning, Audrey, 'Archaeological explorations of cultural identity and rural economy in the north of Ireland: Goodland, County Antrim', *IJHA*, 8:3 (2004), 199–215.
Horning, Audrey, '"Dwelling houses in the old Irish barbarous manner": archaeological evidence for Gaelic architecture in an Ulster plantation village' in Duffy et al. (eds), *Gaelic Ireland* (2001), pp 375–96.
Horning, Audrey, 'English towns on the periphery: seventeenth-century development in Ulster and the Chesapeake' in Adrian Green and Roger Leech (eds), *Cities in the world, 1500–2000* (Leeds, 2006), pp 61–81.

Horning, Audrey, 'On the banks of the Bann: the riverine economy of an Ulster plantation village', *Historical Archaeology*, 41:3 (2007), 94–114.

Horning, Audrey, 'The archaeology of British expansion: Ireland and North America in the seventeenth century' in Horning et al. (eds), *Post-medieval archaeology of Ireland* (2007), pp 51–70.

Horning, Audrey, '"The root of all vice and bestiality": exploring the cultural role of the alehouse in the Ulster plantation' in Lyttleton and Rynne (eds), *Plantation Ireland* (2009), pp 113–31.

Horning, Audrey, and Nick Brannon, 'Rediscovering Goodland: Neolithic ritual site, seasonal booley settlement or lost Scottish village?', *Archaeology Ireland*, 18:3 (2004), 28–31.

Horning, Audrey, Ruairí Ó Baoill, Colm Donnelly and Paul Logue (eds), *The post-medieval archaeology of Ireland, 1550–1850* (Dublin, 2007).

Horning, Audrey, Ruairí Ó Baoill, Colm Donnelly and Paul Logue, 'Foreword: post-medieval archaeology in and of Ireland' in Horning et al. (eds), *Post-medieval archaeology of Ireland* (Dublin, 2007), pp xviii–xx.

Horsfall Turner, Olivia, 'Ruin and reparation: medieval parish churches in seventeenth-century and early eighteenth-century Ossory' in Stalley (ed.), *Irish gothic architecture* (2012), pp 161–99.

Horsfall Turner, Olivia (ed.), *'The mirror of Great Britain': national identity in seventeenth-century British architecture* (Reading, 2012).

Howard, Deborah, *Scottish architecture: reformation to restoration, 1560–1660* (Edinburgh, 1995).

Howe, Stephen, *Ireland and empire: colonial legacies in Irish history and culture* (Oxford, 2000).

Hunt, John, *Irish medieval figure sculpture, 1200–1600: a study of Irish tombs with notes on costume and armour* (2 vols, Dublin, 1974).

Hyde, Matthew, and Nikolaus Pevsner, *Cumbria, Cumberland, Westmorland and Furness: the buildings of England* (New Haven, CT, 2010).

Johnson, Matthew, 'Rethinking houses, rethinking transitions: of vernacular architecture, ordinary people and everyday culture' in David Gaimster and Paul Stamper (eds), *The age of transition: the archaeology of English culture, 1400–1600* (Oxford, 1997), pp 145–55.

Johnson, Matthew, *An archaeology of capitalism* (Oxford, 1996).

Johnson, Matthew, *Behind the castle gate: from medieval to Renaissance* (London, 2002).

Johnson, Matthew, *English houses, 1300–1800: vernacular architecture, social life* (Harlow, Essex, 2010).

Johnson, Matthew, *Ideas of landscape* (Oxford, 2007).

Jones, Siân, *The archaeology of ethnicity: constructing identities in the past and present* (London, 1997).

Jope, E.M., 'Castlecaulfield, Co. Tyrone', *UJA*, 21 (1958), 101–7.
Jope, E.M., 'Mongavlin Castle, Co. Donegal', *UJA*, 17 (1954), 169–72.
Jope, E.M., 'Moyry, Charlemont, Castleraw and Richhill: fortification to architecture in the north of Ireland, 1570–1700', *UJA*, 23 (1960), 97–123.
Jope, E.M., 'Portora Castle, near Fermanagh', *UJA*, 21 (1958), 107–8.
Jope, E.M., 'Scottish influences in the north of Ireland: castles with Scottish features, 1580–1640', *UJA*, 14 (1951), 31–47.
Jope, E.M., 'Some Irish seventeenth-century houses and their architectural ancestry' in idem, (ed.), *Studies in building history* (1961), pp 251–74.
Jope, E.M. (ed.), *Studies in building history: essays in recognition of the work of B.H. St John O'Neil* (London, 1961).
Kennedy, Liam, *Colonialism, religion and nationalism in Ireland* (Belfast, 1996).
Kerrigan, Paul M., *Castles and fortifications in Ireland, 1495–1945* (Cork, 1995).
Kerrigan, Paul M., 'Castles and fortifications of County Offaly, *c.*1500–1815' in Nolan and O'Neill (eds), *Offaly, history and society* (1998), pp 393–437.
Kiberd, Declan, *Inventing Ireland* (London, 1995).
Killen, James, and Enda Murphy, 'Communications' in Aalen et al. (eds), *Atlas of the Irish rural landscape* (2011), pp 287–301.
Kilroy, Phil, 'Women and the Reformation in seventeenth-century Ireland' in MacCurtain and O'Dowd (eds), *Women in early modern Ireland* (1991), pp 179–96.
King, H.A. (ed.), *Clonmacnoise Studies*, 1 (Dublin, 1998).
King, H.A. (ed.), *Clonmacnoise Studies*, 2 (Dublin, 2003).
Klingelhöfer, Eric, 'Edmund Spenser at Kilcolman Castle: the archaeological evidence', *Post-Medieval Archaeology*, 39:1 (2005), 133–54.
Klingelhöfer, Eric, 'Elizabethan settlements: Mogeely Castle, Curraglass and Carrigeen, Co. Cork (pt 1)', *JCHAS*, 104 (1999), 97–110.
Klingelhöfer, Eric, 'Elizabethan settlements: Mogeely Castle, Curraglass and Carrigeen, Co. Cork (pt 2)', *JCHAS*, 105 (2000), 155–74.
Klingelhöfer, Eric, 'Proto-colonial archaeology: the case of Elizabethan Ireland' in Pedro Paulo A. Funari, Martin Hall and Siân Jones (eds), *Historical archaeology: back from the edge* (London, 1999), pp 164–79.
Klingelhöfer, Eric, 'The architecture of empire: Elizabethan country houses in Ireland' in Susan Lawrence (ed.), *Archaeologies of the British: explorations of identity in Great Britain and its colonies, 1600–1945* (London, 2003), pp 102–15.
Klingelhöfer, Eric, 'Tudor overseas fortifications: a review and typology' in Eric Klingelhofer (ed.), *First forts: essays on the archaeology of proto-colonial fortifications* (Leiden, 2010), pp 65–83.
Klingelhöfer, Eric, *Castles and colonists: an archaeology of Elizabethan Ireland* (Manchester, 2010).

Klingelhöfer, Eric, 'Castles built with air: Spenserian architecture in Ireland' in G. de Boe and F. Verhaege (eds), *Military studies in medieval Europe* (Zellick, Belgium, 1997), pp 149–54.

Lacy, Brian, 'The archaeology of the Ulster Plantation' in Ryan (ed.), *Illustrated archaeology of Ireland* (1991), pp 201–5.

Lawlor, H.C., *Ulster: its archaeology and antiquities* (Belfast, 1928).

Leask, Harold G., 'Early seventeenth-century houses in Ireland' in Jope (ed.), *Studies in building history* (1961), pp 243–50.

Leask, Harold G., 'House at Oldbawn, Co. Dublin', *JRSAI*, 43 (1913), 314–25.

Leask, Harold G., *Irish castles and castellated houses* (Dundalk, 1951).

Lee, Thomas, *Offaly through time and its townlands* (Dublin, 2009).

Lenihan, Pádraig, *Consolidating conquest: Ireland, 1603–1727* (Harlow, Essex, 2008).

Lennon, Colm, 'The counter-reformation in Ireland, 1542–1641' in Brady and Gillespie (eds), *Natives and newcomers* (1986), pp 75–92.

Llewellyn, Nigel, *The art of death: visual culture in the English death ritual,* c.*1500–c.1800* (London, 1991).

Loeber, Rolf, 'A gate to Connacht: the building of the fortified town of Jamestown, County Leitrim, in the era of plantation', *Irish Sword*, 15 (1982–3), 149–52.

Loeber, Rolf, 'An architectural history of Gaelic castles and settlements, 1370–1600' in Duffy et al. (eds), *Gaelic Ireland* (2001), pp 271–314.

Loeber, Rolf, '"Certeyn notes": biblical and foreign signposts to the Ulster Plantation' in Lyttleton and Rynne (eds), *Plantation Ireland* (2009), pp 23–42.

Loeber, Rolf, 'Civilization through plantation: the projects of Matthew de Renzi' in Murtagh (ed.), *Irish midland studies* (1980), pp 121–35.

Loeber, Rolf, 'Documentary survey and fieldnotes concerning Offaly castles and houses' (unpublished manuscript, Pittsburgh, 1988).

Loeber, Rolf, 'Early classicism in Ireland: architecture before the Georgian era', *Architectural History*, 22 (1979), 49–63.

Loeber, Rolf, 'Early Irish architectural sketches from the Perceval/Egmont collection' in Agnes Bernelle (ed.), *Decantations: a tribute to Maurice Craig* (Dublin, 1992), pp 110–20.

Loeber, Rolf, 'Geographical calender of landownership in Ely O'Carroll in the sixteenth and seventeenth centuries' (unpublished transcript, Pittsburgh, 1998).

Loeber, Rolf, 'Irish country houses and castles of the late Caroline period: an unremembered past recaptured', *Quarterly Bulletin of the Irish Georgian Society,* 6:1/2 (1973), 1–69.

Loeber, Rolf, 'Sculptured memorials to the dead in early seventeenth-century Ireland: a survey from *Monumenta Eblanae* and other sources', *PRIA*, 81C (1981), 267–93.

Loeber, Rolf, 'The changing borders of the Ely O'Carroll lordship' in Nolan and O'Neill (eds), *Offaly, history and society* (1998), pp 287–317.

Loeber, Rolf, 'The early seventeenth-century Ulster and midland plantations, pt I: pre-plantation architecture and building regulations' in Horsfall Turner (ed.), *'The mirror of Great Britain'* (2012), pp 73–99.

Loeber, Rolf, 'The early seventeenth-century Ulster and midland plantations, pt II: the new architecture' in Horsfall Turner (ed.), *'The mirror of Great Britain'* (2012), pp 101–38.

Loeber, Rolf, 'Warfare and architecture in County Laois through seventeenth-century eyes' in Padraig G. Lane and William Nolan (eds), *Laois, history and society: interdisciplinary essays on the history of an Irish county* (Dublin, 1999), pp 377–413.

Loeber, Rolf, and Geoffrey Parker, 'The military revolution in seventeenth-century Ireland' in J.H. Ohlmeyer (ed.), *Ireland from independence to occupation, 1641–1660* (Cambridge, 1995), pp 66–88.

Loeber, Rolf, and Kevin Whelan, 'An early eighteenth-century house: Clonegal Rectory, County Carlow', *Journal of the Wexford Historical Society*, 13 (1990–1), 135–41.

Loeber, Rolf, and Magda Stouthamer-Loeber, 'Kildare Hall, the countess of Kildare's patronage of the Jesuits and the liturgical setting of Catholic worship in early seventeenth-century Dublin' in FitzPatrick and Gillespie (eds), *The parish in Ireland* (2006), pp 242–65.

Loeber, Rolf, and Terence Reeves-Smyth, 'Lord Audley's grandiose building schemes in the Ulster Plantation' in Mac Cuarta (ed.), *Reshaping Ireland* (2011), pp 82–100.

Loeber, Rolf, *The geography and practice of English colonisation in Ireland from 1534 to 1609* (Athlone, 1991).

Ludlow, John, and Noel Jameson (eds), *Medieval Ireland: the Barryscourt Lectures, I–X* (Cork, 2004).

Lyttleton, James, 'Natives and newcomers: plantation-era archaeology on Irish road schemes' in Bernice Kelly, Niall Roycroft and Michael Stanley (eds), *Encounters between peoples* (Dublin, 2012), pp 77–92.

Lyttleton, James, 'Rathcline Castle: an archaeology of plantation in Co. Longford' in Martin Morris and Fergus O'Ferrall (eds), *Longford, history and society: interdisciplinary essays on the history of an Irish county* (Dublin, 2010), pp 135–59.

Lyttleton, James, 'Seventeenth-century west Offaly: accommodating the new realities', *History Ireland*, 12:1 (2004), 14–16.

Lyttleton, James, and Colin Rynne (eds), *Plantation Ireland: settlement and material culture, c.1550–c.1700* (Dublin, 2009).

Lyttleton, James, and Tadhg O'Keeffe (eds), *The manor in medieval and early modern Ireland* (Dublin, 2005).

Lyttleton, James, *Blarney Castle: an Irish tower house* (Dublin, 2011).

MacCarthy-Morrogh, Michael, 'The English presence in early seventeenth century Munster' in Brady and Gillespie (eds), *Natives and newcomers* (1986), pp 171–90.

Mac Cuarta, Brian, 'A planter's funeral, legacies and inventory: Sir Matthew de Renzy (1577–1634)', *JRSAI*, 127 (1997), 18–33.

Mac Cuarta, Brian, 'A planter's interaction with Gaelic culture: Sir Matthew de Renzy (1577–1634)', *Irish Economic and Social History*, 20 (1993), 1–17.

Mac Cuarta, Brian, 'A settler's land disputes in a Gaelic lordship: Matthew de Renzy in Delvin MacCoghlan, 1613–18', *Studia Hibernica*, 30 (1998–9), 63–88.

Mac Cuarta, Brian, 'Matthew de Renzy's letters on Irish affairs, 1613–1620', *Analecta Hibernica*, 34 (1987), 109–82.

Mac Cuarta, Brian, 'Newcomers in the Irish midlands, 1540–1641' (MA, UCG, 1980).

Mac Cuarta, Brian, 'Religious violence against settlers in south Ulster, 1641–2' in Edwards et al. (eds), *Age of atrocity* (2010), pp 154–75.

Mac Cuarta, Brian, (ed.), *Reshaping Ireland, 1550–1700: colonization and its consequences* (Dublin, 2011).

Mac Cuarta, Brian, '"Sword" and "word" in the 1610s: Matthew de Renzy and Irish reform' in Mac Cuarta (ed.), *Reshaping Ireland* (2011), pp 101–30.

Mac Cuarta, Brian, 'The plantation of Leitrim, 1620–41', *Irish Historical Studies*, 32:127 (2001), 297–320.

MacCulloch, Diarmaid, *Reformation: Europe's house divided, 1490–1700* (London, 2003).

MacCurtain, Margaret, 'Women, education and learning in early modern Ireland' in MacCurtain and O'Dowd (eds), *Women in early modern Ireland* (1991), pp 160–78.

MacCurtain, Margaret, and Mary O'Dowd (eds), *Women in early modern Ireland* (Edinburgh, 1991).

MacCurtain, Margaret, *Tudor and Stuart Ireland* (Dublin, 1972).

MacLysaght, Edward, *Irish life in the seventeenth century* (Shannon, 1969).

Mallory, J.P., and T.E. McNeill, *The archaeology of Ulster from colonisation to plantation* (Belfast, 1991).

Manning, Conleth, 'Clonmacnoise Cathedral: the oldest church in Ireland', *Archaeology Ireland*, 9:4 (1995), 30–3.

Manning, Conleth, 'Clonmacnoise Cathedral' in King (ed.), *Clonmacnoise Studies*, 1 (1998), pp 57–86.

Manning, Conleth (ed.), *From ringforts to fortified houses: studies on castles and other monuments in honour of David Sweetman* (Bray, 2007).

Manning, Conleth, 'Irish tower houses' in Perbellini (ed.), *Towers and smaller castles* (2009), 19–30.

Manning, Conleth, 'Revealing a private inscription', *Archaeology Ireland*, 8:3 (1994), 24–6.

Manning, Conleth, 'Some early masonry churches and the round tower at Clonmacnoise' in King (ed.), *Clonmacnoise Studies*, 2 (2003), pp 63–95.

Manning, Conleth, *Clonmacnoise, Co. Offaly* (Dublin, 1998).

McAuliffe, Mary, 'The lady in the tower, the social and political role of women in tower houses' in Meek and Simms (eds), *Medieval Irish women* (1996), pp 153–62.

McCormick, Finbar, 'Reformation, privatisation and the rise of the headstone' in Horning et al. (eds), *Post-medieval archaeology of Ireland* (2007), pp 355–70.

McCourt, Desmond, and E. Estyn Evans, 'A late seventeenth-century farmhouse at Shantallow, near Londonderry', *Ulster Folklife*, 14 (1968), 14–23.

McCracken, Eileen, *The Irish woods since Tudor times: their distribution and exploitation* (Newton Abbot, Devon, 1971).

McCullough, Niall, *Palimpsest: change in the Irish building tradition* (Dublin, 1994).

McKean, Charles, *The Scottish Chateau: the country house of Renaissance Scotland* (Stroud, 2001).

McKenna, Elizabeth, 'Was there a political role for women in medieval Ireland?' in Meek and Simms (eds), *Medieval Irish women* (1996), pp 163–74.

McNeary, Rory, and Brian Shanahan, 'Carns townland, Co. Roscommon: excavations by the Medieval Rural Settlement Project in 2006' in Corlett and Potterton (eds), *Rural settlement in medieval Ireland* (2009), pp 125–37.

McNeill, T.E., 'Excavations at Doonbought Fort, County Antrim', *UJA*, 40 (1977), 63–84.

McNeill, T.E., 'The larger castles of later medieval Co. Limerick' in Stalley (ed.), *Limerick and south-west Ireland* (2011), pp 176–88.

McNeill, T.E., *Castles in Ireland: feudal power in a Gaelic world* (London, 1997).

Meek, C.E., and M.K. Simms (eds), *The fragility of her sex? Medieval Irish women in their European context* (Dublin, 1996).

Miller, Henry M., 'The archaeology of colonial encounters along Chesapeake Bay: an overview', *Journal of American Archaeology*, 23 (2004–5), 231–90.

Mitchell, Frank, and Michael Ryan, *Reading the Irish landscape* (Dublin, 1998).

Monahan, J.C., *Records relating to the dioceses of Ardagh and Clonmacnoise* (Dublin, 1886).

Moore, Michael J., *Archaeological inventory of County Leitrim* (Dublin, 2003).

Moran, Josephine, 'The shattered image: archaeological evidence for painted and stained glass in medieval Ireland' in Moss et al. (eds), *Art and devotion* (2006), pp 121–41.

Morrice, Richard, *The buildings of Britain: Stuart and Baroque* (London, 1982).

Morrin, James (ed.), *Calendar of patent and close rolls of chancery in Ireland, of the reign of Charles the first* (Dublin, 1863).

Morton, Karena, 'Aspects of image and meaning in Irish medieval wall paintings' in Moss et al. (eds), *Art and devotion* (2006), pp 51–71.

Morton, Karena, 'Irish medieval wall painting' in Ludlow and Jameson (eds), *The Barryscourt Lectures* (2004), pp 313–49.

Moss, Rachel, 'Continuity and change: the material setting of public worship in the sixteenth-century Pale' in Potterton and Herron (eds), *Dublin and the Pale in the Renaissance* (2011), pp 182–206.

Moss, Rachel, 'Reduce, reuse, recycle: Irish monastic architecture, *c.*1540–1640' in Stalley (ed.), *Irish gothic architecture* (2012), pp 115–59.

Moss, Rachel, Colmán Ó Clabaigh OSB and Salvador Ryan (eds), *Art and devotion in late medieval Ireland* (Dublin, 2006).

Muir, Richard, *Approaches to landscape* (Lanham, MD, 1999).

Mumford Jones, Howard, 'The colonial idea in England' in John J. TePaske (ed.), *Three American empires* (New York, 1967), pp 32–55.

Murphy, Margaret, and Michael Potterton, *The Dublin region in the middle ages: settlement, land-use and economy* (Dublin, 2010).

Murtagh, Harman (ed.), *Irish midland studies: essays in commemoration of N.W. English* (Athlone, 1980).

Murtagh, Harman, 'Jacobite Offaly, 1689–91' in Nolan and O'Neill (eds), *Offaly, history and society* (1998), pp 319–38.

Mytum, Harold, 'Archaeological perspectives on external mortuary monuments of plantation Ireland' in Lyttleton and Rynne (eds), *Plantation Ireland* (2009), pp 165–81.

Mytum, Harold, *Mortuary monuments and burial grounds of the historic period* (New York, 2004).

Newman Johnson, David, 'Kilcolman Castle' in A.C. Hamilton (ed.), *The Spenser encyclopedia* (Toronto, 1990), pp 416–22.

Newman Johnson, David, 'Portumna Castle: a little-known early survey and some observations' in John Bradley (ed.), *Settlement and society in medieval Ireland: studies presented to F.X. Martin OSA* (Kilkenny, 1988), pp 477–503.

Newman, Richard, David Cranstone and Christine Howard-Davis, *The historical archaeology of Britain,* c.*1540–1900* (Stroud, 2001).

Nicholls, K.W., 'Irishwomen and property in the sixteenth century' in MacCurtain and O'Dowd (eds), *Women in early modern Ireland* (1991), pp 17–31.

Nicholls, Kenneth, 'Woodland cover in pre-modern Ireland' in Duffy et al. (eds), *Gaelic Ireland* (2001), pp 181–206.

Nicholls, Kenneth, *Gaelic and gaelicised Ireland in the Middle Ages* (Dublin, 1972).

Nolan, William, and Timothy P. O'Neill (eds), *Offaly, history and society: inter-disciplinary essays on the history of an Irish county* (Dublin, 1998).

Nunan, Joesph, 'The fortified houses of County Cork: origin, form, fabric, function and social use of space' (MA, UCC, 2005).

O'Brien, Caimin, and P.D. Sweetman, *Archaeological inventory of County Offaly* (Dublin, 1997).

O'Callaghan, John, 'Fortified houses of the sixteenth century in south Wexford', *Journal of the Old Wexford Society*, 8 (1980–1), 1–51.

O'Carroll, Ellen, 'Corhill Bog, Lisdermot/Straduff, medieval gravel and wood trackway' in Isabel Bennett (ed.), *Excavations 2000: summary accounts of archaeological excavations in Ireland* (Bray, 2002), p. 287.

O'Conor, Kieran D., *The archaeology of medieval rural settlement in Ireland* (Dublin, 1998).

O'Dowd, Mary, 'Gaelic economy and society' in Brady and Gillespie (eds), *Natives and newcomers* (1986), pp 120–47.

O'Dowd, Mary, 'Women and war in Ireland in the 1640s' in MacCurtain and O'Dowd (eds), *Women in early modern Ireland* (1991), pp 91–111.

Ó Háinle, C.G., and Conleth Manning, 'An unrecorded seventeenth-century Clonmacnoise chalice' in King (ed.), *Clonmacnoise Studies*, 2 (2003), pp 167–73.

O'Keeffe, Tadhg, 'Barryscourt castle and the Irish tower-house' in Ludlow and Jameson (eds), *The Barryscourt Lectures* (2004), pp 3–31.

O'Keeffe, Tadhg, 'Concepts of "castle" and the construction of identity in medieval and post-medieval Ireland', *Irish Geography*, 34:1 (2001), 69–88.

O'Keeffe, Tadhg, *Medieval Ireland: an archaeology* (Stroud, 2000).

O'Keeffe, Tadhg, 'Plantation-era great houses in Munster: a note on Sir Walter Raleigh's house and its context' in Herron and Potterton (eds), *Ireland in the Renaissance, c.1540–1660* (2007), pp 274–88.

O'Keeffe, Tadhg, 'Space, place, *habitus*: geographies of practice in an Anglo-Norman landscape' in Howard B. Clarke, Jacinta Prunty and Mark Hennessy (eds), *Surveying Ireland's past: multidisciplinary essays in honour of Anngret Simms* (Dublin, 2004), pp 73–98.

O'Keeffe, Tadhg, and Sinéad Quirke, 'A house at the birth of modernity: Ightermurragh Castle, Co. Cork' in Lyttleton and Rynne (eds), *Plantation Ireland* (2009), pp 86–112.

O'Neill, Michael, 'The medieval parish churches in County Meath', *JRSAI*, 132 (2002), 1 76.

Ó Riain-Raedel, Dagmar, 'A German visitor to Monaincha in 1591', *Tipperary Historical Journal* (1998), 223–33.

O'Sullivan, Aidan, 'Crannogs in late medieval Gaelic Ireland, *c*.1350–*c*.1650' in Duffy et al. (eds), *Gaelic Ireland* (2001), pp 397–417.

O'Sullivan, Aidan, *The archaeology of lake settlement in Ireland* (Dublin, 1998).

O'Sullivan, C.M., *Hospitality in medieval Ireland, 900–1500* (Dublin, 2004).

O'Sullivan, Muiris, and Laurence Kennedy, 'The survival of archaeological monuments: trends and attitudes', *Irish Geography*, 31:2 (1998), 88–99.

Orser, Charles E., 'Symbolic violence and landscape pedagogy: an illustration from the Irish countryside', *Historical Archaeology*, 40:2 (2006), 28–44.

Orser, Charles E., *A historical archaeology of the modern world* (New York, 1996).

Parsons, David, *Churches and chapels: investigating places of worship* (2nd ed., York, 1998).

Perbellini, Gianni (ed.), *Towers and smaller castles: Europa Nostra Bulletin*, 63 (2009).

Perriam, Denis R., and John Robinson, 'The medieval fortified buildings of Cumbria', *Cumberland and Westmorland Antiquarian and Archaeological Society Extra Series*, 29 (1998), 227, 232.

Platt, Colin, *The great rebuildings of Tudor and Stuart England: revolutions in architectural taste* (London, 1994).

Pogue, Dennis, *King's Reach and seventeenth-century plantation life* (Annapolis, MD, 1990).

Pollock, Dave, 'The Barryscourt hall and the remains of some other medieval timber buildings' in Manning (ed.), *From ringforts to fortified houses* (2007), pp 261–72.

Pollock, Dave, 'The bawn exposed: recent excavations at Barryscourt' in Ludlow and Jameson (eds), *The Barryscourt Lectures* (2004), pp 145–75.

Pope, Peter E., *Fish into wine: the Newfoundland plantation in the seventeenth century* (Chapel Hill, NC, 2004).

Potterton, Homan, *Irish church monuments, 1570–1880* (Belfast, 1975).

Potterton, Michael, *Medieval Trim: history and archaeology* (Dublin, 2005).

Power, Denis, 'The archaeology of the Munster Plantation' in Horning et al. (eds), *Post-medieval archaeology of Ireland* (2007), pp 23–36.

Power, Denis, 'The archaeology of the Munster plantation' in Ryan (ed.), *Illustrated archaeology of Ireland* (1991), pp 198–201.

Quinn, David B., 'Ireland and sixteenth-century European expansion', *Historical Studies*, 1 (1958), 20–32.

Quinn, David B., 'Renaissance influences in English colonisation', *Transactions of the Royal Historical Society*, 26 (1976), 73–93.

Quinn, David B., 'The Munster Plantation: problems and opportunities', *JCHAS*, 71 (1966), 19–40.

Quinn, David B., 'Why they came' in David B. Quinn (ed.), *Early Maryland in a wider world* (Detroit, IL, 1982), pp 119–48.

Quinn, David B., *Ireland and America: their early associations, 1500–1640* (Liverpool, 1991).

Quinn, David B., *The Elizabethans and the Irish* (Ithaca, NY, 1966).

Raftery, Barry, 'The medieval settlement at Rathgall, County Wicklow' in Manning (ed.), *From ringforts to fortified houses* (2007), pp 95–106.

Reeves-Smyth, Terence, 'Community to privacy: late Tudor and Jacobean manorial architecture in Ireland, 1560–1640' in Horning et al. (eds), *Post-medieval archaeology of Ireland* (2007), pp 289–326.

Reeves-Smyth, Terence, 'Demesnes' in Aalen et al. (eds), *Atlas of the Irish rural landscape* (2011), pp 278–86.

Reeves-Smyth, Terence, 'Irish gardens and gardening before Cromwell' in Ludlow and Jameson (eds), *The Barryscourt Lectures* (2004), pp 99–143.

Reilly, Ciarán J., 'The burning of country houses in Co. Offaly during the revolutionary period, 1920–3' in Terence Dooley and Christopher Ridgway (eds), *The Irish country house: its past, present and future* (Dublin, 2011), pp 110–33.

Reps, John W., *Tidewater towns: city planning in colonial Virginia and Maryland* (Williamsburg, 1972).

Robinson, Philip, '"English" houses built at Moneymore, County Londonderry, *c*.1615', *Post-medieval Archaeology*, 17 (1983), 47–63.

Robinson, Philip, 'From thatch to slate: innovations in roof covering materials for traditional houses in Ulster', *Ulster Folklife*, 31 (1985), 21–35.

Robinson, Philip, 'Vernacular housing in Ulster in the seventeenth century', *Ulster Folklife*, 25 (1979), 1–28.

Robinson, Philip, *The plantation of Ulster: British settlement in an Irish landscape, 1600–1670* (Dublin, 1984).

Ronnes, Hanneke, 'Continental traces at Carrick-on-Suir and contemporary Irish castles: a preliminary study of date-and-initial stones' in Herron and Potterton (eds), *Ireland in the Renaissance* (2007), pp 255–73.

Roulston, William, 'Domestic architecture in Ireland, 1640–1740' in Horning et al. (eds), *Post-medieval archaeology of Ireland* (2007), pp 327–44.

Roulston, William, 'Seventeenth-century church monuments in west Ulster', *Ulster Local Studies*, 19:1 (1997), 61–79.

Roulston, William, 'Seventeenth-century manors in the barony of Strabane' in Lyttleton and O'Keeffe (eds), *The manor in Ireland* (2005), pp 160–87.

Roulston, William, 'The provision, building and architecture of Anglican churches in the north of Ireland, 1600–1740' (PhD, QUB, 2004).

Russell, C.W., and J.P. Prendergast (eds), *Calendar of the state papers relating to Ireland of the reign of James I, 1608–10* (London, 1874).

Rutherford, A.G., 'A social interpretation of the castle in Scotland' (PhD, U. Glasgow, 1998).

Ryan, Brendan, 'The Ferbane Arma Christi', *Offaly Heritage: Journal of the Offaly Historical and Archaeological Society*, 4 (2006), 21–34.

Ryan, Michael (ed.), *The illustrated archaeology of Ireland* (Dublin, 1991).

Ryder, Peter F., 'A survey of medieval defensible buildings in Cumbria' (unpublished manuscript held by Cumbria County Council (n.p., n.d.)).

Ryder, Sean, 'Defining colony and empire in early nineteenth-century Irish nationalism' in Terrence McDonough (ed.), *Was Ireland a colony? Economics, politics and culture in nineteenth-century Ireland* (Dublin, 2005), pp 165–85.

Salter, Mike, *The castles of Leinster* (Malvern, 2004).

Samson, Ross, 'The rise and fall of tower houses in post-Reformation Scotland' in Ross Samson (ed.), *The social archaeology of houses* (Edinburgh, 1990), pp 197–243.

Samuel, Mark, 'Coppinger's Court: a document in stone', *JCHAS*, 89 (1984), 58–76.

Shanahan, Brian, 'The manor in east County Wicklow' in Lyttleton and O'Keeffe (eds), *The manor in Ireland* (2005), pp 132–59.

Sheehy, Margaret, 'Architecture in Offaly', *JKAS*, 14:1 (1964–5), 1–28.

Sherlock, Rory, 'An introduction to the history and architecture of Bunratty Castle' in Stalley (ed.), *Limerick and south-west Ireland* (2011), pp 202–18.

Sherlock, Rory, 'The evolution of the Irish tower house as a domestic space', *PRIA*, 111C (2010), 115–40.

Shirley, E.P. et al., 'Extracts from the journal of Thomas Dineley, esquire, giving some account of his visit to Ireland in the reign of Charles II', *Journal of the Kilkenny and South-East of Ireland Archaeological Society*, 6 (1867), 73–91.

Shirley, E.P., 'Extracts from the journal of Thomas Dineley, esquire, giving some account of his visit to Ireland in the reign of Charles II', *Journal of the Kilkenny and South-East of Ireland Archaeological Society*, 5 (1864–6), 268–90.

Simms, Katharine, *From kings to warlords: the changing political structure of Gaelic Ireland in the later Middle Ages* (Woodbridge, 1987).

Simpson, W.D., 'The tower houses of Scotland' in Jope (ed.), *Studies in building history* (1961), pp 229–42.

Smyth, William J., 'Ireland a colony: settlement implications of the revolution in military-administrative, urban and ecclesiastical structures, *c.*1550 to *c.*1730' in Barry (ed.), *Settlement in Ireland* (2000), pp 158–86.

Smyth, William J., 'Society and settlement in seventeenth-century Ireland: the evidence of the "1659 Census"' in William J. Smyth and Kevin Whelan (eds), *Common ground: essays on the historical geography of Ireland* (Cork, 1988), pp 55–83.

Smyth, William J., 'The western isle of Ireland and the eastern seaboard of America: England's first frontiers', *Irish Geography*, 11 (1978), 1–22.

Smyth, William J., *Map-making, landscapes and memory: a geography of colonial and early modern Ireland,* c.*1530–1750* (Cork, 2006).

Stalley, Roger (ed.), *Daniel Grose (*c.*1766–1838): the antiquities of Ireland, a supplement to Francis Grose* (Dublin, 1991).

Stalley, Roger (ed.), *Irish gothic architecture: construction, decay and reinvention* (Dublin, 2012).

Stalley, Roger (ed.), *Limerick and south-west Ireland: medieval art and architecture* (Leeds, 2011).

Summerson, John, *Architecture in Britain, 1530 to 1830* (New Haven, CT, 1993).

Sweetman, David, 'The origin and development of the tower house in Ireland' in Ludlow and Jameson (eds), *The Barryscourt Lectures* (2004), pp 261–87.

Sweetman, David, 'The tower houses of County Louth' in Perbellini (ed.), *Towers and smaller castles* (2009), pp 31–4.

Sweetman, David, *Medieval castles of Ireland* (Cork, 1999).

Tait, Clodagh, 'Colonising memory: manipulations of death, burial and commemoration in the career of Richard Boyle, first earl of Cork, 1566–1643', *PRIA*, 101 (2001), 107–34.

Tait, Clodagh, David Edwards and Pádraig Lenihan, 'Early modern Ireland: a history of violence' in Edwards et al. (eds), *Age of atrocity* (2010), pp 9–33.

Tait, Clodagh, *Death, burial and commemoration in Ireland, 1550–1650* (Basingstoke, 2002).

Tarlow, Sarah, 'Reformation and transformation: what happened to Catholic things in a Protestant world?' in Gaimster and Gilchrist (eds), *The archaeology of Reformation* (2003), pp 108–21.

Tarlow, Sarah, *Bereavement and commemoration: an archaeology of mortality* (Oxford, 1999).

Thomas, Avril, *The walled towns of Ireland* (2 vols, Dublin, 2006).

Thompson, M.W., *The decline of the castle* (Cambridge, 1987).

Tierney, Andrew, 'The gothic and the Gaelic: exploring the place of castles in Ireland's Celtic revival', *IJHA*, 8:3 (2004), 185–98.

Tomlinson, Roy, 'Forests and woodlands' in Aalen et al. (eds), *Atlas of the Irish rural landscape* (2011), pp 186–99.

Treadwell, Victor, *The Irish Commission of 1622: an investigation of the Irish administration, 1615–1622, and its consequences, 1623–1624* (Dublin, 2006).

Trigger, Bruce, 'Alternative archaeologies: nationalist, colonialist, imperialist', *Man*, 19:3 (1984), 355–70.

Tuck, James A., and Barry Gaulton, 'Archaeology at Ferryland, 1998–2000', *Avalon Chronicles*, 6 (2001), 89–106.

Venning, Tim, 'The O'Carrolls of Offaly: their relations with the Dublin authorities in the sixteenth century' in Nolan and O'Neill (eds), *Offaly, history and society* (1998), pp 181–205.

Waterman, D.M., 'Castle Archdale, Co. Fermanagh', *UJA*, 22 (1959), 119–23.

Waterman, D.M., 'Sir John Davies and his Ulster buildings: Castlederg and Castle Curlews, Co. Tyrone', *UJA*, 23 (1960), 89–96.

Waterman, D.M., 'Some Irish seventeenth-century houses and their architectural ancestry' in Jope (ed.), *Studies in building history* (1961), pp 251–74.

Waterman, D.M., 'Tully Castle, Co. Fermanagh', *UJA*, 22 (1959), 123–6.

Waterman, D.M., 'Tullykelter Castle, Co. Fermanagh', *UJA*, 22 (1959), 127–9.

Weadick, Sharon, 'How popular were fortified houses in Irish castle building history? A look at their numbers in the archaeological record and distribution patterns' in Lyttleton and Rynne (eds) *Plantation Ireland* (2009), pp 61–85.

Wheeler Stone, Garry, 'St John's: archaeological questions and answers', *Maryland Historical Magazine*, 69:2 (1974), 146–68.
Wheeler Stone, Garry, 'St Maries Citty corporate artifact', *Maryland Archaeology*, 26:1–2 (1990), 4–18.
Whelan, Kevin, and William Nolan (eds), *Wexford, history and society: interdisciplinary essays on the history of an Irish county* (Dublin, 1987).
Williamson, Tom, *Polite landscapes, gardens and society in eighteenth-century England* (Baltimore, MD, 1995).
Wilsdon, Bill, *Plantation castles on the Erne* (Dublin, 2010).

Glossary

Alure	Walkway along castle battlements
Annals	Record of historic events year by year, such as battles and obituaries of members of nobility
Ashlar	Dressed blocks of stone for building, laid in regular courses
Bartizan	Stone turret that typically projects from corner of castle. Supported by corbels. Protected castle occupants dropping stones etc. from holes between corbels onto attackers
Bawn	Walled courtyard of tower house, commonly provided with gatehouse and corner towers (word originates from Irish *bádhun* or cattle fort – an enclosure where cattle could be corralled)
Centring	Frame used to support arch under construction. In tower houses, it was common to use wicker mats to give shape to the arch. Once mortar had dried and arch had set in place, centring was removed, leaving impression of wicker mats
Chamfer	Where right-angled edge of stone has been cut away to create a third face
Crenellation	Battlements or parapets of castle punctuated with regular openings along top of wall
Demesne	Country estate of a lord
Entablature	Upper part of a classical structure supported by columns
Flanker	Towers, typically circular or rectilinear, placed at corners of bawns to cover perimeter
Garderobe	Toilet chamber in medieval building
Harling	Lime-based mortar covering used to protect external surfaces of walls
Lintel	Horizontal support (timber or stone) across top of window or doorway
Machicolation	Stone structure projecting externally from top of castle façade. Supported by corbels. Protected castle occupants dropping stones etc. from holes between arches or corbels onto attackers at base of wall
Merlon	Solid portion of crenellated parapet
Mullion	Vertical stone or timber dividing window into separate lights
Newel	Central pillar or post from which steps of spiral stairs project
Ogee	Double curve, partially concave, partially convex – commonly seen in window heads
Ope	Opening
Oriel	Bay window projecting from upper floor, supported by corbelling

Spandrel	Triangular space between outside curve of arch and surrounding rectilinear frame
Transom	Horizontal stone or timber dividing window into separate lights
Wall-walk	Walk along battlements or parapets of castle
Yett	Iron grate or grill that could be closed in front of entrance to tower house or fortified house

Index